T. E. Ruth (1875–1956)

Australian College of Theology Monograph Series

SERIES EDITOR GRAEME R. CHATFIELD

The ACT Monograph Series, generously supported by the Board of Directors of the Australian College of Theology, provides a forum for publishing quality research theses and studies by its graduates and affiliated college staff in the broad fields of Biblical Studies, Christian Thought and History, and Practical Theology with Wipf and Stock Publishers of Eugene, Oregon. The ACT selects the best of its doctoral and research masters theses as well as monographs that offer the academic community, scholars, church leaders and the wider community uniquely Australian and New Zealand perspectives on significant research topics and topics of current debate. The ACT also provides opportunity for contributors beyond its graduates and affiliated college staff to publish monographs which support the mission and values of the ACT.

Rev. Dr. Graeme Chatfield
Series Editor and Associate Dean

T. E. Ruth (1875–1956)

Preacher and Controversialist

KEN R. MANLEY

Foreword by
TIM COSTELLO

WIPF & STOCK · Eugene, Oregon

T. E. RUTH (1875–1956)
Preacher and Controversialist

Australian College of Theology Monograph Series

Copyright © 2021 Ken R. Manley. All rights reserved. Except for brief quotations in critical publications or reviews, no part of this book may be reproduced in any manner without prior written permission from the publisher. Write: Permissions, Wipf and Stock Publishers, 199 W. 8th Ave., Suite 3, Eugene, OR 97401.

Wipf & Stock
An Imprint of Wipf and Stock Publishers
199 W. 8th Ave., Suite 3
Eugene, OR 97401

www.wipfandstock.com

PAPERBACK ISBN: 978-1-7252-9960-3
HARDCOVER ISBN: 978-1-7252-9961-0
EBOOK ISBN: 978-1-7252-9962-7

07/01/21

*To my dear wife Margaret,
a wonderful support in yet another project*

Contents

List of Illustrations | viii
Foreword by Tim Costello | ix
Preface and Acknowledgements | xiii
Abbreviations | xv
Introduction | xvii

1 "A Brilliant Son of Devon" | 1
2 A Baptist Pastor in Melbourne: The Early Years (1914–15) | 30
3 Imperial Protestant | 52
4 *Wake up, Australia!* Conscription, Archbishop Mannix, and the Catholics | 67
5 Ruth and the Catholics in Tumultuous Times (1918) | 94
6 "The Commonwealth Constitutes his Congregation": Ruth in Melbourne (1918–23) | 110
7 Ruth: A Public Theologian? | 133
8 The Eschatology of T. E. Ruth | 152
9 Becoming a Sydney Identity (1923–30) | 169
10 A Political and Social Crisis (1930–32) | 195
11 "The Little Napoleon" of Pitt Street (1933–38) | 219
12 "A Good Secular Pulpit" | 244
13 Adelaide and Retirement Years (1939–56) | 274
14 Tom and Herbert: "A Religion of Loyalty" | 297

Conclusion: "Remember Me at My Best" | 321

Bibliography | 327
Index | 341

Illustrations

Figure 1: St. Andrew's Church, Aveton Gifford | 2

Figure 2: Prince's Gate Baptist Church, Liverpool | 9

Figure 3: Collins Street Baptist Church | 33

Figure 4: Tom, Mabel, and Leslie Ruth (1913) | 34

Figure 5: "The Sower of Tares" (cartoon by Low, in *Bulletin*) | 75

Figure 6: Ruth making confession to Jack Wren in *Punch*, 9 August 1917 | 89

Figure 7: Archbishop Mannix | 95

Figure 8: Pitt Street Congregational Church (1923) | 172

Figure 9: Front cover of brochure (1928) | 179

Figure 10: Cover, *Over the Garden Wall* (1928) | 190

Figure 11: J. T. Lang, Premier of NSW | 196

Figure 12: Cover, *Australia at the Crossroads* (1931) | 208

Figure 13: T. E. Ruth and friend outside Pitt Street Church (1934) | 224

Figure 14: T. E. Ruth, *Herald* (Melbourne), 5 August 1922 | 245

Figure 15: T. E. Ruth at work | 248

Figure 16: Herbert Brookes | 298

Foreword

THIS IS A RICH and eye-opening biography.

Ken Manley admits that no biographer can know the reaches and depths of another person. But when reading this work, I felt like I had been personally introduced to Tom Ruth, sat under his preaching, and been both beguiled and stirred by his vision. Simply put, I was entranced – and I believe you will be too.

Yes, this biography is rich. It is rich because Ken Manley writes with deep sympathy for this extraordinary man but remains fully aware of the historical times that shaped him and does not avoid exploring his shortcomings. Ken not only captures the larger-than-life personality that is T. E. Ruth, but explains his times, casting the "the eye of pity" on his flaws as well as commending his great strengths and making a balanced assessment.

This biography is also an eye opener. During my years in ministry at Collins Street Baptist Church (1995–2003), I stood under the name "T. E. Ruth," engraved on the Honour Board with the dates of 1914–23 beside it, each time congregants left a service. Yet apart from some muttered comments that he had taken on Catholic Archbishop Mannix at the height of the polarizing conscription debates, I knew nothing more about him. I did not know that he was the outstanding preacher in Australia during his time, nor that he was a columnist who had extraordinary public reach from his "secular pulpit." I did not know that he was such a public and political preacher and such an eloquent stirrer. Many of his themes were themes I had also engaged with from the same pulpit, such as gambling, the poor, church as the social worship of God and the social wellbeing of man, and to put your creed into deed. T. E. Ruth believed that the churches must interfere in politics and that we miss some of the most divine gifts because we do not cultivate the gift of distribution (to those in need). Was this continuity of preaching themes coincidental, or was there something in that glass of water in the Collins Street pulpit?

Of course, Ruth was preeminently a British imperialist, and the disloyalty of Archbishop Mannix and other Catholics to the British Crown, shown in their opposition to the war effort, led to Ruth's combative attacks. As a child, I had heard my maternal English grandfather speak of the perfidy of Irish Catholics and my paternal grandfather, of Irish Catholic descent, speak of the betrayal of the working man as fodder in the Great War. The split ran through my family blood. Whilst a Minister of Collins Street Church and preaching myself from T. E. Ruth's very pulpit, I ended up being elected to the 1999 Constitutional Convention as a republican opposed to Australia continuing with the Crown as our head of state. I can sense T. E. Ruth twitching in his grave at the disloyalty of one of his successors.

In his following ministry at Pitt Street Congregational Church in Sydney, this political theology that engaged the great issues of his day saw him veer into proto-fascism through his support of Eric Campbell and the New Guard. And he hated with a passion NSW Premier Jack Lang, who at the height of the Depression in 1930 was repudiating debts owed to English banks in order to protect Australian workers. Again, T. E. Ruth's rage at such disloyalty to the Crown and the undermining of empire saw him speak and lead loyalist leagues. Premier Jack Lang was later Paul Keating's influential mentor. But in the 1930s, Ruth demanded Lang not just go but that representative democracy in New South Wales be suspended and handed over to a Federal Commissioner. In his public speaking and inflammatory paper columns, Ruth appealed to the sacred image of the Anzacs and implicitly sanctioned the violence of the New Guard to overthrow democracy. But violence was not necessary, as a month after these pulpit appeals from Ruth, the Governor of New South Wales, Sir Philip Game, sacked Lang, providing the legal precedent for Governor General Kerr's sacking of Whitlam in 1975. Ruth celebrated Lang's sacking with a biblical justification, that of removing scoundrels from near the king.

And backing all this foment was the man who was Ruth's oldest and deepest friend, Herbert Brookes. Brookes was Alfred Deakin's son in law. Their beautiful letters are one of the moving insights into Ruth's deep capacity for loyalty and friendship. He was more than just Ruth's friend, but his personal benefactor and brother in arms. As founder of the Australian Paper Mills and later a founding director of the Australian Broadcasting Commission (ABC), Brookes had Ruth's back in Melbourne, supporting and funding his Protestant attacks on Mannix and the Catholics.

From a major friendship with Brookes and his wife, who was the daughter of our second Prime Minister, Alfred Deakin, to fighting Lang whose style of politics influenced our twenty-fourth Prime Minister, Paul Keating, there was inserted into the furnace of Australian politics a Baptist/Congregational preacher. Ruth was at the center of some of our stormiest political events—conscription, the lasting sectarian conflict (alive in my own family), and the dismissal of an elected Premier by the King's representative. Whether in the soaring heights of his practical preaching or in his mobilization of mass political feelings via radio addresses and paper columns, Reverend T. E. Ruth's eloquence was sure. At the same time, his range of pastoral subjects and public ability made Christian faith accessible to non-churched Australia. In this he was gifted, maybe unparalleled, in our history of churchmanship.

T. E. Ruth had every opportunity to be a prince of English Baptists. He was earmarked as Rev. John Clifford's successor but turned it down to come to Melbourne. If he had taken that pulpit, he would have avoided the narrower and more fundamentalistic climate of Australian Baptists. He would have seen greater ecumenical churchmanship and less of the Adventism and biblicism that he loathed. But he came to Australia and mastered the public space. His themes were the scandal of church division (except Catholics) and his generous openness to other religions. He was a man who believed in conversion and a Christocentric and crucicentric gospel but who entertained universalism. As a pastoral response to the First World War deaths of so many young men, he believed in the indestructibility of personality and accepted praying for the dead. As a rabid anti-Catholic, he extolled the central teachings of purgatory in the idea of the probation and purification of souls. And he argued this from Scripture, causing grief to Baptists!

This was a man with surprising contradictions and generous instincts: a British imperialist with a nativistic love of Australia, reflected in his Australian Decalogue and his exuberance for the Anzac story; a man of Scripture and preaching the gospel at every turn but with a deep love of the Romantic poets and versed in great literature. But the shadow remains. He was a man whose political vision and battles were clouded by confusing the kingdom of God with the British Empire and the Commonwealth. He remained essentially an Australian Briton.

Ruth is one of the most fascinating and influential preachers in our twentieth-century history. In this book, the enigma of T. E. Ruth is marvelously portrayed. Ken, thank you for opening my eyes to my own history. Thank you for fleshing out that worthy name on the Honour Board.

Rev. Tim Costello AO
Melbourne, Australia

Preface and Acknowledgements

THROUGH MY YEARS OF research and writing about Baptists in Australia, I have known about T. E. Ruth for some time, especially his years in Melbourne (1914–23) and his political Protestantism. I sensed, however, that there was much more to be discovered about his life and work. Other projects have delayed my pursuing this interest, but now I am grateful to be able to recount more of his story, especially his extraordinary contribution to Australian religious and political life.

Ruth was an outstanding preacher in England (1900–13) and in Australia was often described as the nation's leading preacher, not only in his Baptist denomination but across all traditions. He was also a vigorous and tenacious controversialist.

Although I have long admired the many positive achievements of Ruth, there were some aspects of his beliefs that I personally did not find attractive, notably his fervent opposition to the Roman Catholic Church, his extreme political conservatism, and some aspects of his modernist theology. Certainly, our more ecumenical age struggles to understand his extreme fanaticism against Roman Catholics. Yet I appreciate that these were important features of the religious scene in Australia during his lifetime. His diverse contributions need to be placed in this context and carefully analyzed.

While many scholars have recognized Ruth's influence, most have concentrated on condemning his sectarianism and criticizing his conservative political activities. There has been no real attempt to tell the whole story of his life. I hope that this book will bring some greater appreciation of a multitalented, if flawed, minister of the gospel.

As with any such research project, I have relied heavily on the assistance of many.

I thank the Australian College of Theology, especially Graeme Chatfield and Megan Powell du Toit, as well as all at Wipf and Stock, for their expertise in bringing the book to reality. Thanks go to editor Gina Denholm for her care in preparing the manuscript for publication.

Barbara Coe of Canberra has (once again) given me invaluable help, cheerfully tracking down Ruth's family history, photographing the extensive range of documents relating to Ruth in the Brookes Papers at the National Library of Australia and the Pitt Street Church records at the State Library of New South Wales, as well as editing the first drafts of this book and preparing the index. I am in awe of her talents and grateful for her friendship.

I also thank the many archivists and librarians who have helped me with great efficiency. In England: Ms. Emily Burgoyne, librarian at the Angus Library at Regent's Park College, Oxford and the staff in the Bodleian Library at the University; the librarian at Bristol Baptist College; staff at the Liverpool City archives for the records of Ruth's church in Liverpool; and staff at the Southampton City archives for the records of the Portland Church. In Australia, I thank the librarians at the State Library of Victoria, the State Library of New South Wales and the National Library of Australia in Canberra; Dr. John Sampson at the Victorian Baptist archives; and Collins Street Baptist Church for access to their records. Dr. Patricia Curthoys of Sydney was helpful with her knowledge of the Pitt Street Church's history.

Much of this book was written during Melbourne's extensive covid-19 lockdown in 2020, which prevented access to public libraries, but thankfully most of the research was already completed. It did release me from the possibility of other distracting activities.

I am most grateful to Rev. Tim Costello, himself a former pastor of the Collins Street Church and an influential public figure in Australia, for contributing his perceptive foreword, and I thank Professor David Bebbington, Professor John Briggs, Dr. Patricia Curthoys, and Professor Stuart Piggin for their commendations of the book. My deepest thanks, however, are offered to my wife Margaret, who has once again helped me at every stage of this project: visiting archives with me, photographing documents, and carefully reading successive drafts.

Ken R. Manley
Melbourne, 2020

Abbreviations

AB	*Australian Baptist*
ABPH	Australian Baptist Publishing House
ACW	*Australian Christian World*
ADB	*Australian Dictionary of Biography*
ALP	Australian Labor Party
BQ	*Baptist Quarterly*
BT	*Baptist Times*
BUV	Baptist Union of Victoria
CE	Christian Endeavour
CSBC	Collins Street Baptist Church, Melbourne
CW	*Christian World*
SMH	*Sydney Morning Herald*

Introduction

THOMAS ELIAS RUTH (1875–1956) was one of the most controversial Baptist ministers ever to serve in Australia. Born in a small rural village in Devon, Ruth came to personal faith in the Anglican church in Exeter. Baptized in that tradition, he seemed destined to become an Anglican minister, but characteristic independence of thought led him to Baptist beliefs about baptism and a career in Nonconformity.[1]

After ministerial education at Bristol Baptist College, Ruth became a successful pastor in Britain at three Baptist churches (1900–1913). Although widely hailed as one of the denomination's rising figures, Ruth left England to become minister of the prestigious Collins Street Baptist Church in Melbourne in 1914.

Welcomed as a brilliant preacher, Ruth soon faced sharp criticism and deep suspicion for his progressive theology and uncompromising advocacy of church unity. His own congregation, however, found him a true pastor and friend in the troubled days of war.

The ensuing political and social upheaval in Melbourne made Ruth a leading spokesman for the imperial cause and a vigorous opponent of Archbishop Daniel Mannix over conscription and, more generally, of the place of the Roman Catholic Church in Australia. Ruth endured numerous personal attacks as "a sectarian bigot" and "an imported zealot."

Leaving Melbourne, Ruth became the minister of the historic Pitt Street Congregational Church in Sydney in 1923. During the tumultuous years of J. T. Lang as Premier of New South Wales (1925–27, 1930–32) he became

---

1. See *ADB*, although this contains several errors.

a spokesperson for the right-wing New Guard movement, prompting one historian to suggest that Ruth "sought to justify Australian fascism on theological grounds."[2] Certainly he had become a leading political Protestant.

Many of Ruth's controversial sermons and speeches were published, and he contributed hundreds of whimsical and topical columns to daily papers in Sydney. Seeking to become a public theologian, Ruth advocated a form of civic religion. Able to communicate to the masses in a way few others could, Ruth was for a time one of the best-known Protestant ministers in Australia.

Ruth's all-too-often tumultuous public life raises important questions for the historian of religious life in Australia. To what extent was Ruth changed as a result of moving from England to his adopted country? Did powerful forces alter the positive and lively English Nonconformist into a "bigoted sectarian"? What was the main dynamic of his anti-Catholic efforts?

In personal and church life, Ruth proved to be a true friend and a loyal leader, and his spirituality was open and genuine. He could be charming, caring, kind, amusing, and persuasive. His spiritual impact, especially through his dynamic preaching, was striking and transformative. Ruth encouraged independent thought in theology in a denomination largely conservative and wedded to old ways and beliefs.

Was he the special man for the hour—as he was encouraged by some to believe—or was he a gifted minister so bewitched by circumstances as to lose his way in the divided Australian society of the war period and its aftermath?

T. E. Ruth remains an enigma. He was an intriguing and always interesting character whose life reveals much about Australian political and religious life in a formative period in the nation's history. Ruth's great friend Herbert Brookes addressed him extravagantly in 1924 as "Friend, Scholar-loved, God's Messenger, in Press, on Platform, and in Pulpit."[3] This provides a clue as to how he was regarded by one who knew him best.

---

2. Moore, *The Right Road?*, 96.

3. Brookes to Ruth, 30 March 1924, Brookes Papers, item 6222, Series 1, Box 7.

I

"A Brilliant Son of Devon"

THE ARRIVAL OF A new minister for the Collins Street Baptist Church in Melbourne aboard the RMS *Orama* on March 9, 1914, was what would today be called "a media event." Representatives of the church and the denomination jostled with reporters from the daily press to assure the young minister of a warm welcome. Under the heading "Rev. T. E. Ruth Arrives," the *Argus* told readers that Ruth was "a little under average height, of slight build, dark complexioned with a very quiet manner, which is roused to emphasis under the stress of ideas held with strong conviction."[1] Ruth was frequently likened in physical appearance and oratorical style to Lloyd George, the British Prime Minister, a comparison that Ruth enjoyed.[2] On a return visit to England in 1922, he was hailed as "a brilliant son of Devon."[3]

The Forming of a Baptist Preacher

Thomas Elias Ruth was born in the small Devon village of Aveton Gifford on December 17, 1875, the eldest son of George William Saunders Ruth (1852–89) and Mary Ann Elson (1856–1911), who had six children.[4]

---

1. *Argus*, March 10, 1914, 9.
2. *Herald*, June 29, 1922, 1.
3. *Western Morning News*, August 28, 1922, 7.
4. *Aveton Gifford Parish Registers*. They were married at Aveton Gifford on July 17, 1875 (so Mary was pregnant with Thomas). The other children were Charles Albert (died aged eleven months), James Seaward, Susan Saunders, Aquila Abiathar Peter (died aged two years and six months) and John Robert. See also Doughty, *Aveton Gifford*.

George was a stonemason, and members of the Ruth family had been present in the village for many generations. George Ruth died on December 26, 1889, when Tom was only fourteen.

St. Andrew's Church, Aveton Gifford

Ruth was baptized at St. Andrew's parish church on February 6, 1876: "I do not remember it, but there is documentary evidence to that effect. I did not believe in it. Indeed, I have been told that I vehemently protested. But neither for the privilege nor for the protest was I responsible." He was under twelve years old when he was confirmed in that church: "I am certain that I did not intelligently apprehend the meaning of the broken baptismal vows of my forgotten godparents," and confirmation "did not prevent my joining some other boys in raiding an orchard the next day."[5]

---

5. *AB*, June 30, 1914, 3; Ruth, *The Catholic*, 66.

Years later, as he was writing about how his understanding of faith had changed across the generations, Ruth imagined that the ghost of his grandfather (Charles Ruth) had appeared to accuse him.

> Now, my grandfather had never lived outside a lovely little village nestling in a little Devonshire valley. On Sundays he acted as "clerk" at the parish church. In the absence of a choir and a choral service, he led the responses. And he said several times at every service, "As it was in the beginning is now and ever shall be, world without end, Amen." . . . He told me he'd been a dreadful heretic in his own day, but being parish clerk, he hadn't said so, so that if he lived on the earth today he would probably believe pretty much what I believe.[6]

On several occasions he told how he came to reject the traditional evangelical belief in hell.

> Into our little Devon village when I was a boy, there came, week by week, the published sermons of one of the greatest evangelical preachers of the nineteenth century, and I vividly remember how often my soul was stirred by his powerful word-pictures of hell, how my childish imagination made of the weirdest imagery the most literal reality; sometimes making sleep a dreadful experience through fear of waking in never-dying flames; sometimes making me cry out in agony of soul, asking God to have mercy on a little boy of ten who had sinned unto death; at other times producing a period of philosophic calm when I would compare my chances with the chances of other boys with whom I had stolen apples and indulged in boyish pranks which assumed such diabolical importance in the lurid light of orthodox hell, and I would comfort myself with the reflection that if other boys could stand hell, probably I could, and then, by the mercy of God, I would forget my dreadful destiny and help raid another apple-laden orchard—but only, alas, to return to spell out the long words in some sermon on hell. . .
>
> And never as long as I live shall I forget when a playfellow of my own age was drowned—I had been minding his clothes on the bank of the river—overhearing a conversation between two men. One, a publican said, "Ah well, he is better off, anyhow," and the other a Methodist local preacher replied, "I was reading last night that there are infants a span long crawling on hell's

---

6. *Sunday Sun* (Sydney), February 26, 1933, 17.

burning floor." And that night, and many a night after, my sleep was broken by fearful visions of my boy friend's eternal torture.[7]

Many Nonconformists at this period were largely abandoning traditional ideas about eternal punishment in favor of what was called "the larger hope": hell "departed into metaphor."[8]

Ruth lived for some years at Exeter, some thirty-eight miles from his village home. Details of his spiritual awakening are sparse, but he was converted at St. Leonard's Exeter.

> When just in his teens he went to a church where the curate preached on the text, "Choose ye this day whom ye will serve." The sermon made him thoroughly disgusted with himself, and, annoyed with the curate, he went to another church. To his surprise, the same curate ascended the pulpit and preached the same sermon. At night he went to a third place of worship, where the preacher proved to be the same curate, and his text was, "Choose ye this day whom ye will serve." "It was too much for me," said Mr. Ruth. "That night I surrendered to the love that had sought me in three places."[9]

He studied for holy orders under the Rector of St. Leonard's, Exeter, which he noted was a thoroughly evangelical and evangelistic church.[10] "I felt the need for absolute personal responsibility in accepting the Christian religion, and applied for baptism by immersion in the church. Naturally it was refused. I had already been baptized in infancy." Ruth often declared, "I was made a Baptist by the present Bishop of Durham, Dr. Moule."[11] H. C. G. Moule (1841–1920) was a leading New Testament scholar and evangelical leader who became Bishop of Durham in 1901. Tom's rector had recommended that he study the teaching on the sacraments in Moule's book, *Outlines of Christian Doctrine*, where Moule advocated infant baptism and rejected the Baptist view of baptism as bodily immersion on the basis of a confessed faith as "untenable by Scripture."[12] Ruth found his arguments so unconvincing that they led him to adopt the Baptist view. His rector sensibly advised him to become a Baptist. He was accordingly baptized by

---

7. Ruth, *Progress of Personality,* 148–49.

8. Hilton, *Age of the Atonement,* 335–36.

9. Originally published in *Christian Herald* (date unknown, a clipping is in Ruth's papers at the South Australian Public library).

10. *BT,* December 20, 1901, 181.

11. *The Age,* March 10, 1914, 9.

12. Moule, *Outlines of Christian Doctrine,* 256–59.

immersion in the South Street Baptist Church in Exeter, evidently with the rector's letter still in his pocket.[13]

During 1895 Ruth was a regular preacher at evangelistic services held at the "Homely Gospel Mission" in the Pioneer Lecture Hall, Edmund Street, Exeter, and in September 1895 the South Street Baptist Church presented him with a purse of money and a watch for his "valuable services as leader of the mission" as he left Exeter for Bristol College.[14]

Bristol was the oldest Baptist College in England, and when Ruth arrived the Principal was Dr. W. J. Henderson (1843–1929).[15] He frequently acknowledged how much he owed Henderson, who had influenced him "more than any other man."[16]

Being a Baptist Pastor: Portland, Southampton

The early years of Ruth's ministry were significant for Baptists and the other Free Churches in England.[17] J. H. Shakespeare (1857–1928), secretary of the Baptist Union (1898–1924), was the leading figure in constructing much of the denomination's organization and in promoting Free Church unity.[18] More than one thousand local Free Church councils were formed all over England, and the National Council of the Evangelical Free Churches was formed in March 1896. This became both a political pressure group and an evangelistic organization.

Ruth was widely hailed as one of the denomination's rising figures. He became a successful pastor at three Baptist churches: Portland Chapel, Southampton (1901–06); Prince's Gate, Liverpool (1906–11), and Hoghton Street, Southport (1911–14).

In October 1900, Ruth was called to his first church at Portland Baptist in Southampton. He had been a visiting preacher while in college and so impressed the congregation that they called him as pastor.[19] This first pastorate was a hugely significant experience for the young pastor. Portland was the first church of the famous preacher and denominational leader Alexander Maclaren (1826–1910) who served there from 1846 until 1858.

---

13. Ruth later noted that he had been baptized by Rev. D. P. McPherson who later became an Anglican minister: *Sun* (Sydney), October 14, 1923, 13.

14. *Express and Echo*, September 12, 1895, 3.

15. Moon, *Education for Ministry*.

16. *BT*, December 20, 1901, 181.

17. See Randall, *English Baptists*, 13–112.

18. Shepherd, *Making of a Modern Denomination*.

19 *CW*, October 25, 1900, 4; 1 November, 1900, 4.

In 1902, while at Portland, Ruth married Mabel Edith Law (1870–1954), daughter of William Minter Law (a draper and deacon at West Cliff, Bournemouth) and Catherine (nee Blunt).[20] Mabel had been an "excellent" Sunday School teacher at Upper Parkstone, Dorset.[21] They had no children of their own. Leslie James Ruth, a nephew of Ruth (son of James Seaward Ruth) came with them to Australia and was often thought to be their son, although there is no evidence of formal adoption. In 1990, Miss G. M. Downing (when she was aged ninety-four) remembered hearing the story that Ruth's brother had a big family. "He was told he could choose one of his brother's ten children to bring to Australia with him. Leslie threw his boot at him, so Mr. Ruth said, 'I'll have that one!'"[22] (However, the 1911 Census shows that "nephew" Leslie, aged five, was already living with the Ruths at 4 York Avenue, Liverpool.)

Ruth was described in the Portland church's centenary souvenir as "a brilliant young student from Bristol College" who made "a speedy and complete conquest." The history continues:

> Our graph for the next four years would show a steep and continuous rise. Congregations were of the kind that most ministers see only in their dreams, while additions to the Church Roll numbered almost sixty a year. The principal business at Church Meetings seems to have been "Applications for Membership."[23]

A later report claims that 236 members were received in Ruth's time and that his church was regularly filled to capacity.[24] Ruth's ministry appealed powerfully to young people, and students from Hartley University College attended in considerable numbers. A manual for the church published in 1903 recorded a "year of increasing prosperity."[25]

Ruth pioneered another development in Portland, which many Free Churches were beginning to employ: the establishment of what were called "institutionalized churches" where a diverse range of activities sought to cater for local needs. In March 1905, he made an appeal for £8,000 in order to furnish a commodious "public home" in the heart of the town for "the social and religious reclamation of the people." The "Portland Public Home" was intended to compete with the public houses but without their drinking, and

---

20. *BT*, October 13, 1905, 718.

21. *Bournemouth Guardian*, October 22, 1910, 6.

22. Typescript record of interview between Rev. D. M. Himbury and Miss Downing on July 24, 1990 (held at Collins Street Church).

23. *Portland Baptist Centenary Souvenir 1850–1946*, 17.

24. *Western Morning News*, August 28, 1922, 7; *BT*, October 13, 1905, 718.

25. *London Daily News*, February 16, 1903, 5.

included a billiard room, "apartments" for chess, draughts, and bagatelle, and well-stocked reading rooms.[26] Ruth also conducted a "Portland tea" on Thursday afternoons where "anybody who wished a chat about anything important to them could be gratified."[27]

The main area of conflict with the State and the Anglican establishment by the Free Churches at this time was over education. The Education Act of 1902 galvanized Nonconformists into vigorous protests against having to pay rates for Church schools and led to widespread passive resistance.[28] This was the Free Church response: those accused refused to pay that part of the rates going to the maintenance of denominational schools. By November 1904, there had been 33,678 summonses, 1,392 auctions, and 54 resisters imprisoned.[29]

Ruth began his ministry in this political context, and with his church he was heavily involved. He was a speaker at the gathering of the District Free Church Council in Winchester in May 1902 when resolutions about the Education Bill were passed.[30] In March 1904, he was present at the Police Court at Southampton when he gave a "fighting speech," declaring, "We are not martyrs and we don't intend to be, but we are men who hate the Government's tyranny . . . we are prepared to become martyrs if it is necessary rather than endow Romanism."[31] Again, in April and June 1904, he was present at the third sale of resisters' goods in Southampton, condemning the government and insisting on the supremacy of individual conscience. "Let no government come between their souls and Christ!"[32]

His growing reputation as a platform speaker meant Ruth became more widely appreciated both in the denomination and in the Free Churches. After hearing him speak at a Free Church demonstration in 1905, F. B. Meyer declared, "We have heard a voice tonight which will soon be heard throughout the length and breadth of the land."[33]

Ruth gave much time to working with the other churches of the region in the Southern Baptist Association. In June 1902 at the local Evangelistic Union, he insisted that the keynote for modern evangelism was "to teach

26. *Hampshire Advertiser*, March 4, 1905, 12.
27. *BT*, October 11, 1905, 718.
28. Bebbington, *Nonconformist Conscience*, 127–52.
29. Bebbington, *Nonconformist Conscience*, 144.
30. *Hampshire Chronicle*, May 3, 1902, 4.
31. *Southern Echo*, March 17, 1904, 2.
32. *Hampshire Advertiser*, April 9, 1904, 8; *Southern Echo*, June 2, 1904, 2; *London Daily News*, June 6, 1904, 3.
33. *BT*, October 11, 1905, 718.

men to follow their reason and judgment."[34] He was a popular speaker at many young people's meetings such as that at the Baptist Annual Assembly in 1905, when he outlined "A Young Baptist's Heritage." Ruth preached at the annual meeting of Baptist churches at Southsea in June 1904 and moved a resolution against the Conservative Licensing Bill, "the vilest thing that the Government has ever done and he wished that some policy of Passive Resistance could be adopted."[35] Ruth was also well known as a Freemason, a member of the "Ancient Order of Foresters."[36]

At the diamond jubilee celebrations of Portland in 1915, the local press reported:

> The new century opened under the ministry of the Rev. T. E. Ruth, and it will be generally conceded that, for brilliance of diction and imagination, for boldness of thought and utterance, no man through all the years has excelled this gifted preacher. . . . the early removal of Mr. Ruth to Liverpool was the greatest loss the church has probably ever sustained, for he had the rare gift of attracting those who seldom cross the threshold of the doors of our places of worship.[37]

A Pastor in Liverpool and a Baptist Leader (1906–11)

In 1906, Ruth moved to Prince's Gate Baptist Church in the important port city of Liverpool where he was pastor until 1911. Following the Great Famine of 1845–49, huge numbers of Irish migrated to Liverpool, and by 1851 approximately 25 percent of the city was Irish-born. The economic strength of Liverpool had grown through trade; indeed, it was regarded as the capital of the slave trade, outdoing both Bristol and London during the eighteenth century. The impressive International Slavery Museum in Liverpool today is a moving reminder of the horrors of that infamous trade. Liverpool continued to trade along two sides of the old triangle to Africa and the Americas

---

34. *Salisbury Times*, June 6, 1902, 8.
35. *Salisbury Times*, June 17, 1904, 2; *BT*, June 24, 1904, 483.
36. *Islington Gazette*, August 3, 1904, 5.
37. *Southampton Times*, September 20, 1915. The Portland building ("a beautiful edifice of Bath brick with white stone dressings," *Southampton Annual 1899*) was destroyed in the blitz of November 1940, and the church members subsequently linked with the Carlton church on London Road (Green, "Preaching Places and Meeting Houses," 11).

and became the main importer of American and Brazilian cotton, which was the economic backbone of Liverpool and Manchester.[38]

Baptists had been present in Liverpool since the seventeenth century. The dominant Baptist figure from 1890 to 1907 was C. F. Aked (1864–1941) at Pembroke Chapel. He was a Fabian, an active worker for social justice issues who spoke out on racial inequality and for women's rights. Aked moved to New York's Fifth Avenue Baptist Church, better known as "Rockefeller's Church," in April 1907, so Ruth could only have known him in Liverpool for a short period.[39]

Ruth had been sad to leave Portland but as he wrote to the Liverpool church, "I had hoped to remain in my present church for several years to come but I am profoundly impressed by the great possibilities of Prince's Gate and an unmistakeable moral and spiritual impelling has determined my decision."[40]

Prince's Gate Baptist Church, Liverpool

The imposing Prince's Gate chapel, next to the entrance to Prince's Park and which seated one thousand, had been opened in 1877.[41] As pastor of that church, Ruth was thrust into a leading role in the vibrant city.

38. For the slave trade, see A. Tibbles, "Liverpool and the Slave Trade."

39. Smith, "Charles Frederic Aked (1864–1941)," 3–18.

40. Prince's Gate Minutes of Church Members' meetings, September 27, 1905 (at Liverpool city archives).

41. Sellers, "Baptists in Liverpool in the Seventeenth Century," 195–200, 277–81; see also Sellers, "Liverpool Nonconformity 1786–1914."

The church's membership when he began was 279, and when he left it had reached 365.[42] Several leading businessmen and other public figures were in the church; indeed, one historian has described the membership as "positively genteel."[43]

A rather patronizing report of Ruth's early days at Liverpool appeared in the *Christian World*:

> At a handsome church in Prince's-gate, not far from Sefton-park Presbyterian Church, Rev. T. E. Ruth has rapidly gained a strong grip on his congregation. He is a young man yet, an open-eyed progressive, a denominational reformer after the heart of Rev. J. H. Shakespeare. He takes Dr. Aked's interest in the social and moral reform of Liverpool, and on occasion can speak out in a way that commands public attention. Mr. Ruth loves high colors, and "apt alliteration's artful aid." These are pardonable to the exuberance of youth. When he has learned to tone down a bit, Mr. Ruth's preaching will probably commend itself more to those sober souls who start with alarm at ear-pricking sentences and dazzling "Prince of Wales's feathers" from the pulpit.[44]

Ruth soon identified completely with the great city of Liverpool, which in 1907 held an extravagant pageant celebrating what was claimed to be the 700th anniversary of the founding of the city when King John granted its charter.[45] On the Sunday before this celebration, Ruth preached on "the religious significance of the civic pageant." He lauded the achievements of Liverpool, describing it as

> the central gateway of the only purely British sea whose waters wash the shores of England, Scotland, Ireland and Wales. Indeed, it is an English, Scottish, Irish and Welsh city: there is only one city in Wales with a larger Welsh population and only two cities in Ireland with as many Irish.

Ruth pleaded: "I would beseech you to see in the parable of the pageant the need of a Christian municipality and to hear Christ's call to Christian citizenship . . . Pray for a mighty baptism into the sense of civic responsibility."[46]

Later in the year, Ruth wrote two enthusiastic articles on Liverpool for the *Baptist Times* as delegates prepared to come to the city for an Assembly:

42. Baptist Union *Handbooks*.
43. Sellers, *Our Heritage*. 54.
44. *CW*, 1907.
45. See A. Bartie et al., "Liverpool 700th Anniversary Pageant."
46. *BT*, August 10, 1907, 611.

"It is impossible to think of it without affection, or to speak of it without enthusiasm, or to write of it without the exuberance that in cold print looks like exaggeration."[47]

With its large Irish population, Liverpool was naturally a very strong Roman Catholic center and experienced considerable sectarian violence.[48] The Protestant Orange Lodge was also a powerful presence.[49] Ruth was in Liverpool on June 20, 1909, when the city experienced the worst outbreak of sectarian trouble as Catholics and Protestants clashed violently in the streets. This riot was the culmination of many years of tensions between Liverpool's Catholic and Protestant communities, especially the Orangemen.[50]

When in Australia, Ruth commented, "In some of its moods, Orangeism, as I have seen it in Liverpool, is scarcely more commendable than Roman persecution."[51] Again, raising the question of the difference between Roman and Protestant bigotry, he simply observed, "I've lived in Liverpool."[52] What is clearly evident is that the Liverpool experience weighed heavily with Ruth when he was faced with similar sectarian conflict in Melbourne.

In August 1906, the *Liverpool Post* reported that Ruth's church was a "prosperous Liverpool Church." Several baptisms had taken place: nine in June and a further thirty-one in August. Several of these people came from a successful mission at Upper Main Street.[53] Ruth preached a series of challenging evangelistic sermons with titles such as "Christianity or What?," "What Is Religion?," "What Is God?," and "What Is a Christian?" As the local paper commented,

> There is sometimes a daring in the treatment of these topics— a relentless severance of the essential from the non-essential, a resolute determination to face modern difficulties . . . The preacher's transparent sincerity and passionate earnestness always compel the closest attention.[54]

---

47. *BT*, September 13, 1907, 678; September 20, 1907, 695.

48. The most comprehensive study is Roberts, *Liverpool Sectarianism*.

49. For the Orange Lodge in Northern England, see MacRaild, *Faith, Fraternity and Fighting*.

50. Neal, *Sectarian Violence*, 224.

51. *AB*, August 4, 1914, 3.

52. *AB*, June 9, 1914, 13.

53. *Liverpool Daily Post*, August 4, 1906, 8.

54. *Liverpool Daily Post*, September 22, 1906, 10.

Large congregations responded to Ruth. Numerous reports indicate the enthusiasm with which he was received, both in local church services and at National Assembly gatherings of the Baptist Union.

Not that Ruth avoided conflict. R. J. Campbell (1867–1956) had become minister of the City Temple in London in 1903 and was the principal exponent of what was called the "New Theology" over which a major controversy erupted in 1906–7. Basically, this theology "emphasized to an unprecedented degree (as far as British theology was concerned) the *immanence* of God, that is, his active presence inside nature and human history, his indwelling within the world, as distinct from his *transcendence*, that is his difference from the world, his surpassing of the cosmos in his uniquely divine greatness."[55] In the New Theology, "the distinction between 'God' and 'world' was virtually lost."[56]

In 1907, *Christian World Pulpit* featured a series of recent sermons discussing the New Theology, including one by Ruth titled "The New Theology or the Old?" He acknowledged Campbell's powerful and magnetic spiritual power but also argued that Campbell was really teaching a Unitarian faith. In Campbell's hands, "it gets perilously near to Pantheism with its identification of God, not only with love but with hate, with wrong as well as right, with lawlessness as well as law, with sin as well as salvation." Ruth argued that what was needed was a "theology for the age" which does not ignore natural science, insists upon the application of religion to the whole round of human life and finds in history a divine revelation and purpose.[57]

Ruth was often unusual in his approach. For example, in the January 1909 issue of *Young Men* he told how during his holiday he had spent a night as a homeless tramp in a workhouse at Shep in Westmorland. Disguised, he gave his name as Thomas Elias (his first two names) and spent the night with twenty hardened casuals to learn something about a tramp's philosophy of life. One of the casuals entered into discussion with him and proceeded to denounce the New Theology. Ruth reported that not one of the casuals was prepared to give up "tramping," even if a good situation could be found with a good home and good wages.[58]

As when he was at Southampton, Ruth was in demand as a preacher for special occasions in other congregations, and when his Liverpool duties permitted he gladly obliged. In March 1907, he preached at the prestigious

---

55. Clements, *Lovers of Discord*, 20.

56. Clements, *Lovers of Discord*, 20.

57. *Christian World Pulpit*, February 6, 1907, 84–86.

58. *Islington Gazette*, January 4, 1909, 3; *BT*, January 8, 1909, 20. Ruth later gave a detailed account of this adventure in *AB*, July 14, 1914, 3 and in *Common Weal*, 28–32.

Ferme Park chapel in London, and in the following year he led a ten-day mission in that church.[59] In July 1907, he was at Christ Church Westminster shortly after F. B. Meyer's resignation "where there is much speculation as to the appointment of a successor."[60]

Keith Clements has outlined "the classic saga of the Victorian Nonconformist pulpit star," who begins in a small way in a provincial chapel where large numbers attend and then in a powerful speech at a national assembly reveals that a new "prince of the pulpit" has arrived.[61] Ruth certainly acquired a national reputation. The report of the Free Churches National Council in Leeds in March 1907 hailed Ruth as "a new and brilliant speaker":

> He carried the audience with him. It would be an injustice to him to summarise his speech. It was full of dazzling rhetorical flourishes and brilliant asides. His main theme was "the faith of the future" . . . He sat down amid a storm of cheers, after having delivered one of the best speeches of the week.[62]

A few weeks later he addressed the Baptist Union Assembly, where his assigned topic was "The Responsibility of the Church in Relation to Its Own District." Ruth suggested a common ministry, a common fund for the support of the ministry, and a common church. He attacked the Baptists as having forsaken the real meaning of brotherhood, arguing that in many places the churches had become "competitive organizations" and the pulpits "rival platforms." "I have no doubt whatever that we are in the Apostolic Succession as far as Doctrine is concerned, but I think you would ransack heaven in vain to find any Apostle willing to father our Church Polity."[63] He commented on the ministerial annuity fund insisting that they gave their veterans "a miserable pittance" for an annuity. He proposed "a kinder method":

> [Ruth] would depute every year a man of 50 to take all the men over 60 to the edge of a cliff on a glorious autumn afternoon. Pointing to the gorgeous clouds, he would say: "Within are the many mansions of the Father's House" and, bidding them take the path of golden glory, he would topple them gently over (laughter). He would then come away humming, "Part of the Host have crossed the flood and part are crossing now" or chuckling to think that his term was coming next year, knowing

---

59. *London Daily News*, March 9, 1907, 12; *Islington Gazette*, December 21, 1908, 4.
60. *Liverpool Echo*, July 3, 1907, 5.
61. Clements, *Lovers of Discord*, 26.
62. *London Daily News*, March 7, 1907, 12.
63. *Hampshire Advertiser*, April 27, 1907, 12.

that he had rendered God and his generation greater service than the annuity fund.[64]

Ruth's talk was described by the *Baptist Times* as "unconventional," "brilliant," and "audacious."[65] His speech was followed with shouts of "Encore," according to one newspaper. This led the President to comment, "You cannot encore speeches."[66] Not that all appreciated his style. "Evidently it was intended to be humorous but I would remind the reverend gentleman that only a thin line divides humour from nonsense."[67]

The cruelties being practiced in the Congo by the Belgian authorities were the subject of considerable Free Church rebuke by leaders such as Clifford, and in June 1907 a deputation had met with the Foreign Secretary.[68] Later that year the *Baptist Times* published an impassioned article by Ruth, "The Cross of the Congo Crime":

> We cannot close our ears to the bloody cruelties of the Congolese. We cannot blot out of the brain the horrible pictures of mutilated men, outraged women, and slaughtered children. We cannot forget that we are men, that we are Englishmen, that we are Christians . . . In the name of civilization, in our country's name, in the name of our country's God, we say this private speculation, this commercial exploit in the bodies and souls of men must cease . . . The time has come for England to save Belgium.[69]

The passionate speech and the appeal to imperial loyalty anticipated how Ruth would argue for the Protestant cause later in Australia.

He was also invited to address the Congregational Union when it met at Blackpool in October 1907. This speech also anticipated emphases that would dominate his Australian ministry. "Empire must not stand for mere aggrandizement and to magnify the Anglo-Saxon name, but it must stand for the Empire of God, the empire of right and love."[70]

Ruth commented on a wide range of issues. For example, in March 1908 he attacked "the modern evangelical missions" where professional

64. *Hampshire Advertiser*, April 27, 1907, 12.
65. *BT*, April 26, 1907; Shepherd, *Modern Denomination*, 87.
66. *London Daily News*, April 29, 1907, 12; *Southern Baptist*, June 11, 1907, 141. The full text of his address was in *BT*, April 26, 1907, 320–21; *Southern Baptist*, July 30, 1907, 183–84.
67. *Cornish and Devon Post*, 4 May 1907, 3.
68. Bebbington, *Nonconformist Conscience*, 111–12.
69. *BT*, November 21, 1907; *London Daily News*, November 21, 1907, 8.
70. *Lancashire Evening Post*, October 18, 1907, 4.

evangelists made "gigantic money-making machines, sometimes manipulated by the astute statesmen of great religious organizations to enrich the common coffers."[71] F. C. Spurr (1863–1942), missioner for the Baptist Union from 1890 to 1904, wrote that the young preacher's approach was

> quiet, thoughtful, psychological, persuasive . . . A new vocabulary, a fresh-exploring of the human heart and mind, the use of the new psychology, a modern application of the one Gospel— these are elements of the new missioning of which Mr. Ruth gave us an example . . . This may mean that the day of the old crowds has passed, but if it also means that we have gained in definiteness and permanent results, we shall have gained indeed.[72]

But one of the problems with being so popular and in such demand was that other churches cast envious eyes at the young minister. Ruth faced possibly his greatest dilemma during 1909 when he was invited to become assistant to John Clifford at Westbourne Park in London, with a view to becoming his successor when the time came. Clifford, probably the leading Nonconformist in Britain, had been pastor at the church since 1877.[73]

Ruth had preached at the church during the 1907 Baptist Union Assembly meetings. The sermon was described as

> original, daring, clever, and it gripped . . . It was by turns pathetic, witty, philosophical, and Evangelical, although marred occasionally by a note and gesture of scorn. The voice is clear, melodious, with a fine range . . . He has studied the orator's art, with striking results. His style is alliterative, with a danger of overdoing it.[74]

After such an exciting introduction to Westbourne Park, it was not surprising that in 1908 the church invited Ruth to become their assistant minister. The *Christian World* and the *British Weekly* kept readers informed, as did the daily press around the country. The idea was, the *Christian World* reported, that Ruth should join Clifford, who would retire when his co-pastor found himself firmly established in the pastorate. Clifford clearly supported the idea, as did J. H. Shakespeare. After a delay of some months, Ruth finally resolved to decline the invitation publicly, declaring that there were two

71. *Daily Telegraph*, March 14, 1908, 13.

72. *CW*, February 11, 1909.

73. In a curious coincidence earlier that same year, Samuel Pearce Carey, recently returned from serving as pastor of the Collins Street Church, was widely rumored to become Clifford's successor: *CW*, April 23, 1909, 11; Manley, "An Honoured Name," 113–14.

74. *London Daily News*, April 29, 1907, 12.

reasons why he had declined. The first was his own sense of inadequacy for the task; the second, the claims of Liverpool.[75]

Then came an unusual twist to the story. Ruth proposed that if he remained at the church "and entered into an honourable understanding that he would not entertain any invitation to leave the church for two or three years he should be liberated for four months of this next summer for a tour in South Africa for combined health and services."[76] The relieved deacons unanimously agreed.[77]

Ruth went to South Africa in 1909 as a representative of the Free Churches to promote Free Churches and Sunday School work. He was accompanied by his wife and Arthur Black of Liverpool, a leading figure in the World's Sunday School Association, which had been formed in 1907.[78] Ruth thought of their visit as "educational evangelism." He contributed "a fortnightly letter to young men and women" to the *Baptist Times*, and several of these long columns gave detailed reports of the South African visit.[79] Ruth and Black addressed some 220 meetings, after which Ruth and his wife had a short holiday to the Victoria Falls. Ruth later claimed that while in Johannesburg he had met Gandhi, who told him that "our only hope was to 'hug the cross.'"[80]

Ruth presented a full report to the Free Church Council meetings in Hull in March 1910.[81] He stressed that South Africans resented criticism from those who did not understand the conditions. Even so, church and Council work was "marvellously effective."[82] He optimistically suggested that there was some progress towards union among Presbyterians, Dutch Reformed, Wesleyan Methodists, Congregationalists, and Baptists.[83] Ruth stressed that all the churches were free: "They had no unjust Establishment to contend with like they had at home, making impossible national religious unity."[84] He was kept busy after his return speaking about colonial work and Sunday Schools.

---

75. *Belfast News Letter*, January 18, 1909.
76. *Times*, January 18, 1909, 5.
77. Church members' meeting, January 17 and 30, 1909.
78. See Black, *Golden Jubilee*.
79. *BT*, March 26 until October 29, 1909.
80. Ruth, *Over the Garden Wall*, 52.
81. *CW*, March 10, 1910, 5–6.
82. *CW*, March 10, 1910, 5.
83. *London Daily News*, March 9, 1910, 5
84. *Sunderland Daily Echo*, March 9, 1910, 3.

Settling back into his church and denominational work, Ruth had an even higher profile. He resumed his life in Liverpool and submitted "A Mersey Meditation" to *Sunday at Home*.[85] Political and social issues were still addressed. Ruth had long opposed the existence of the House of Lords arguing that it "stands for the denial of democratic government in this country" and especially opposed the role of bishops on the grounds of Bible teaching.[86] He insisted:

> This hereditary principle, enthroning itself above King and Constitution, is monstrously absurd. It is the apotheosis of original sin, and we are here as the heralds of the kingdom of God. The House of Lords, as at present constituted blocks the way of reform and regeneration.[87]

His commitment to church union was recognized when he gave the first speech at the Anglo-American Conference on Christian unity in London on 4 July 1910.[88]

Ruth was finding the work at Liverpool a great strain and he had "for some time been desirous of a lighter ministry than that at Prince's Gate Church, Liverpool . . . where his congregation is widely scattered and the pastoral work—even with the help of an assistant minister—is exacting."[89] (Rev. J. Landels Love had been an assistant but had left in June 1910.[90]) The *Liverpool Courier* reported that he had received an approach from Hoghton Street Baptist church in Stockport, and remarked that his loss would be keenly felt. "His environment in Liverpool colours his public utterances: belonging as he does to a sect in some things narrow and antiquated, he has become Imperial in his instincts and cosmopolitan in his religious sympathies."[91]

Becoming "Imperial in his instincts" would later clearly shape his ministry at Collins Street, but his immediate challenge was the Southport call:

> Southport appeals to me because it is a much smaller sphere, much more compact, though not less influential. I think I should be able to do more thorough pulpit and pastoral work there, without the overstrain of power and the haunting sense

---

85. *Leicester Chronicle*, May 6, 1911, 6.
86. *Liverpool Daily Post*, November 14, 1906, 9.
87. *Evening Standard*, December 17, 1909, 10.
88. *Southern Baptist*, August 11, 1910, 518.
89. *CW*, March 9, 1911, 11.
90. *Fifeshire Advertiser*, June 18, 1910, 10.
91. *Liverpool Courier* as quoted in *CW*, March 9, 1911, 3.

of having left so many things undone, of which I have been conscious here.[92]

Pastor at Southport

Southport lies on the Irish Sea coast, and among its attractions still is the Southport Pier, the second largest seaside pleasure pier in Britain. The Hoghton Street Baptist Church in Southport was indeed smaller than Prince's Gate with a membership of 193 when Ruth began in May 1911.[93]

In 1913, he reported that in the preceding year he had purchased "some very objectionable postcards" and sent them to the Chief Constable asking if something could not be done "to prevent the exposure and sale of postcards so utterly vulgar, without being funny, that they would not be offered in the shops at Blackpool or any other progressive town in the United Kingdom."[94]

Ruth and "Geoffrey Palmer"

In addition to his pastoral work and growing reputation as a preacher and platform speaker, Ruth published many sermons and articles. His first efforts were youth-oriented, such as in *Young Man* for May 1907 when he wrote on "A Young Man's Ideal and Christ's."[95] In 1908, he contributed a chapter to *Youth and Life,* a collection of talks published by the National Council of Evangelical Free Churches. His chapter was "On Getting the Perspective in Life":

> The other evening I spent a delightful hour discussing the infinite differences between tweedledee and tweedledum with some devoted—deacons! On my study table I have a verbatim report of a lengthy and heated controversy on vestments conducted by impassioned—ecclesiastics! And now the Editor of this volume, in subtle, unconscious, and delightful irony, asks me to write on "Getting the Perspective in Life."[96]

---

92. *CW,* May 18, 1911, 24.

93. I have not been able to locate any extant records for the church, which later closed. Statistics are from Baptist Union *Handbooks.*

94. *Burnley News,* April 23, 1913, 7.

95. *Young Man* (May 1907). See *London Daily News,* May 1, 1907, 4.

96. Brown, *Youth and Life,* 57–64.

In later years, he also contributed regularly to the monthly magazine *Sunday at Home*, published by the Religious Tract Society, and to a collection of essays on "The best sermon I have ever heard." Ruth concluded that the best sermon he had ever heard was the one that had led to his conversion. As the *Baptist Times* observed, "In discussing the goodness or otherwise of a sermon we are apt to forget that, after all, the real test of a sermon is that which Demosthenes said should be applied to all speaking—Does it convince."[97]

In 1910, he prepared *Four Personal Questions*, a small pamphlet that included questions often asked by Ruth in later preaching: "Why Religious? Why Christian? Why Protestant? Why Free Church?"[98]

Ernest Price (a friend of Ruth's from Bristol College days) and Ruth published essays written for a prize competition, *Our Baptist Sunday Schools* (London: Kingsgate Press, 1910). Price traced the history of the Sunday School among Baptists, while Ruth characteristically attempted a larger theme: "The Baptist Child and World Conquest." He listed five "Baptist Axioms," an approach that recalls the influential exposition of Baptist principles enunciated by the Southern Baptist theologian E. Y. Mullins (1860–1928) as *The Axioms of Religion* (1908). Ruth's axioms were related to his specific theme:

1. The Sovereignty of Christ is the soul of the Baptist faith.
2. The Sufficiency of the Scriptures is our denominational distinction.
3. The Supremacy of the Spiritual is our ecclesiastical watchword.
4. The Sanctity of life is our national plea.
5. Only the best is good enough for the Baptist in ministry and method.[99]

Ruth noted that statistically, for the period 1897 to 1907, Baptists compared most favorably with an increase of 11.6 percent in scholars, well ahead of all the other denominations. But there was no place for complacency:

> We have not properly discovered the eternal significance of the child set in the midst by our Lord Christ . . . The very words "Baptist world consciousness" will some day be seen to stand for something that is not simply denominational but Catholic, Cosmic, Christian. The essential principles of our faith are the basic principles of universal progress.[100]

97. *BT*, January 2, 1914; see also *Salisbury and Winchester Journal*, May 7, 1910, 2; *Dublin Daily Express*, December 23, 1911, 8.
98. Ruth, *Four Personal Questions*.
99. Ruth, "Baptist Child," 52.
100. Ruth, "Baptist Child," 56.

Ruth outlined reforms beginning with the infant dedication and the "Cradle Roll" but lamented that the Baptist Union *Handbook* for 1909 recorded a startling decrease of 8,816 Sunday School scholars: "There must be a great denominational forward movement for the sake of the church that is to be."

Ruth continued to publish in the *Baptist Times* and even more regularly in both the *Christian World*—possibly the most influential of the numerous religious papers that flourished at the time—and its companion publication, the *Christian World Pulpit*. For example, in 1907 he preached a sermon marking the sudden death of Charles Williams, one of his mentors, called "The Problem of Immortality":

> Charles Williams is not dead. The Coroner's jury brought in their verdict, "accidental Death." Accident! Death! It was but an incident in his life. He was never more alive than he is tonight. The mortal has put on immortality, sings the new song, drinks the new wine of eternal youth in his Father's Kingdom.[101]

Death was a theme that would fascinate Ruth all his days, and he wrote extensively on it in Australia.

He consistently demonstrated originality and unusual approaches to pastoral and evangelistic sermons. "The Social Significance of the Kingdom of God" showed how a skillful preacher and pastor proclaimed the classic liberal emphasis on the essential gospel message as being the fatherhood of God and the brotherhood of man. His sermon was based on the Lord's Prayer:

> This is the great family prayer of the domestic Christ . . . All the finest faith is there, all spiritual beauty, all social justice, all domestic bliss—in the All-Father. That is the first and the final fundamental on which is broad-based the fact of human brotherhood. Humanity springs out of that divinity, and finds its destiny in the complete hallowing of the Father's name . . . So the Lord's Prayer becomes the citizen's programme, and the Father's business the Son's ministry. The Father's will is the origin of all life. The paternal providence is the basis of all being. This simple catholicity is the soul of the Christian creed.[102]

The confident optimism of liberal preaching is demonstrated in his claim that Liverpool in 1907 was holier than Jerusalem was in the days of Jesus.[103]

---

101. *CW Pulpit*, May 1907, 249–51.
102. *CW Pulpit*, February 1908, 108.
103. *CW Pulpit*, February 1908, 108–09.

Writing anonymously as Geoffrey Palmer, Ruth had a few articles published in 1913. Some were humorous, such as "Overheard in a Devon Market" and "Holiday Fiction and Nonconformity."[104] More serious was one in which he tackled the issue of the desperate needs of the missionary societies. His principal argument was that more money was wasted in the support of superfluous churches than the missionary societies needed for world evangelism: "This is a time of crisis, not only in denominational history, but in world missions."[105]

His major literary achievement during 1910-13 was, however, three series of articles which he wrote anonymously as Geoffrey Palmer in the *Christian World*. The first series was eighteen "Letters to a Ministerial Son" by "A Man of the World" (Geoffrey Palmer), published between August 25 and December 15, 1910. This series was evidently extremely popular, as a slightly expanded version was published in hard cover in 1911.[106] A second series of sixteen "Letters to Church Folk" appeared from August 24, 1911, until March 7, 1912, while the third series was sixteen "Letters to Other Churches" from September 26, 1912, to April 3, 1913.

Taken together, these articles provide fascinating and often humorous insights into contemporary Free Church life.[107] By writing anonymously, Ruth obviously felt liberty to make criticisms about church life.

1. *Letters to a Ministerial Son*

By the literary device of being a "man of the world," Ruth cast a critical but sympathetic eye over several aspects of ministerial preparation and service such as the call to ministry, theological training, preaching "with a view," the question of "ordination" or "recognition," pastoral visiting, selecting sermon themes, pulpit politics, "church cranks," issues surrounding a minister's marriage, and "on making a national reputation."

A wide personal experience and a sharp observant style mark these papers.

> The man who wants to go into the ministry in our day is either a fool or a hero, and heroes are scarce. Many men have been misled into the ministry who would have rendered good service

---

104. *CW*, August 13, 1913, 12; September 4, 1913, 3.
105. *CW*, July 10, 1913, 11.
106. Ruth (Geoffrey Palmer), "A Man of the World" in *Letters to a Ministerial Son*.
107. For further details, see Manley, "Insider Perspectives," 88-102.

to religion if they had earned their living in some other way, and devoted their spare time to the cause![108]

Ruth, writing as "the father," showed his humor and insights. Sermon titles were regularly advertised in local newspapers, and "the father" reported some topics that he had seen advertised such as "Was Jonah's Whale a Barge?" and "A Breach of Promise Suit" (based on Rev 2:4 about "having left your first love"). "We did not know if 'Shall I smoke?' referred to a popular social custom or if it were a problem of eschatology."[109] Social, political, and literary sermons were, according to "the father," undesirable: "I question the honesty of a man who gives a political speech under the guise of a text and a sermon." (However, during his time in Australia, Ruth delivered many literary and highly political sermons such as "Are Australians Sinn Feiners?" and "Is the Papacy Anti-British?"[110])

The church should be involved with recreation and amusements: the "Man of Sorrows" was sometimes also "the Man of Laughter," as the Gospels suggest. Ruth was here defending what were called "institutional churches," such as he had introduced at Portland, which offered educational and social activities as a way of including people into the life of the church.

Parsons can become the greatest Sabbath breakers in the country when they do not properly care for their personal recreation. "Take up a hobby, and for one day in the week anyhow, live for it." Golf was commended. "You wouldn't be able to think about supralapsarianism and things of that sort, though you would probably get a good wholesome glimpse into human depravity—your own!"[111]

Commenting on the failure of the church to attract men, he suggested that the church's failure is often owing to its insistence on verbal inspiration "and insistence on the historicity of Jonah's sojourn within the hospitable whale, the conversational powers of Balaam's ass and the suicide of the Gadarene swine."[112]

A somewhat unusual letter dealt with "On Making a National Reputation"—not a common danger for many preachers, although it became a

---

108. *CW*, August 25, 1910, 9.

109. *CW*, October 6, 1910, 16.

110. See, for example, Ruth, *Wake up, Australia!*

111. *Letters to a Ministerial Son*, 172. "Supralapsarianism is the form of the Calvinistic doctrine of predestination which maintains that God decreed the election and non-election of individuals before the Fall of Adam." (Cross and Livingstone, *Oxford Dictionary,* 1560).

112. *Letters to a Ministerial Son*, 183.

personal challenge for T. E. Ruth. The dangers of a "swelled head"—one who mistakes his umbrella for his hat—were sounded.[113]

That these letters were promptly published as a book is clear evidence that they were thought to be readable, relevant, and helpful to the ministers and churches of that time.

2. *Letters to Church Folk*

The next series continued in the same vein. They offer an unusual source for understanding the inner life of local churches and denominations: the diaconate; a church secretary about to resign; the secretary of a selection committee; a candidate for the pulpit; a deacon's wife; a superintendent (of the Sunday School) who ought to resign; a Sunday School teacher; an organist; a local preacher; a missionary on furlough; a sermon taster; a church gossip; a man who rushes into print; a "general kicker"; a denominational secretary; a Free Church leader; a retired minister, and a young seeker.[114]

In his letter to an organist, Ruth suggested that church music "should make a man want to pray, not thrill his pew-imprisoned limbs with some martial improviso."[115]

Ruth sympathized with a missionary who is on deputation:

> You will rush through the country in express and other trains; you'll be driven "o'er moor and fen, o'er crag and torrent" till the furlough's o'er. You'll be disturbed by the colossal ignorance of some enlightened chairmen about "the savages in India," "the blacks in China" and "the infant widows of Africa". . . Perhaps there will be a solo entitled, "O, for the wings of a dove," and then you will give your address—one of three representing the several fields of evangelical operations. And the next night will find you giving the same performance.[116]

He showed special sympathy for retired ministers.

> It's not easy to settle down to nothing, after having been involved in so many things, is it? Poor old chap! . . . Oh, the old days, how strenuous they were, what splendid struggles they witnessed, what glorious conquests! Good old times! What men

---

113. *CW*, December 8, 1910, 31.
114. For details, see Manley, "Insider Perspectives."
115. *CW*, October 19, 1911, 15.
116. *CW*, November 2, 1911, 15.

there were, what heroes, what saints! But today! How things have changed![117]

3. Letters to Other Churches

Ruth's last series offered personal reflections on all the main denominations, as well as revealing his commitment to church unity.

The list of groups addressed is comprehensive: Roman Catholics, Anglicans, Methodists, Presbyterians, Congregationalists, Baptists, Disciples (Church of Christ), Quakers, Unitarians, Salvationists and Plymouth Brethren, as well as an "undenominationalist" and "a militant Protestant." The tone adopted is generally positive, looking for a special quality within each group. While he could often sound patronizing, his sharpest critiques were directed to those from his own tradition.

The first letter was directed to Roman Catholics.

> Dear Romanus,—I'm afraid there's not the slightest chance of my applying for admission into the "Mother Church"—yet. I'll tell you why—it isn't catholic enough. For a thousand and one things, I'd like to join you but, since you won't take me as I am, with my own freedom of faith and personal vision, I prefer to remain in the larger outside.[118]

Ruth in his Australian conflicts with Roman Catholics was commonly labelled as "sectarian," so this comment is of interest: "Militant religion—Roman or Protestant—is a very poor thing. And sectarianism—ours or yours—is a negation of Christianity."

Anglicans should acknowledge "the validity of our Churchmanship": "Our Churches already belong to the Holy Catholic Church . . . Our ministers are already properly ordained . . . We will unite with you as equal sons of the one Father of mankind—when you are ready!"[119]

Ruth observed that denominations commonly belie their names.

> Catholics—Roman and Anglo—are not catholic. The national Church isn't national . . . the Primitives scarcely stand for the primitive Methodism, nor does the United Methodist Church

---

117. *CW*, February 8, 1912, 13.
118. *CW*, September 26, 1912, 11.
119. *CW*, October 3, 1912, 13.

unite the Methodists. The outstanding thing about Methodism is its want of method.[120]

Sharpest criticism was directed towards the Congregationalists, fellow-travelers with Baptists:

> Ministerial poverty, competitive churches, wasteful sectarianism—that is the record you have to wipe out. A co-ordinated Congregationalism could provide for various ministries; could unite to evangelise the masses, secure simultaneous agitation to awaken the social, civic, and ecclesiastical conscience—and overbear evil with the solid phalanx of united good.

Turning to the Baptists, Ruth commented on the different approaches to baptism and church membership, indicating tensions between what are usually known as closed and open membership:

> Some of them think so much of baptism that they make it not one of many methods of confession of faith, but *the* confession in chief, the only ground of admission into the Christian Church, the passport to holy Communion, the one sign and seal of saintship.
>
> And others assure me that it is the essential genius of the Baptist position that it makes much less of baptism than any other community save the Friends. There is nothing magical or even mystical in the ordinance, they say, nothing sacramental at all. It is a personal thing, an individual act of faith, not related to Church membership, but to Christ.
>
> Of course, you can't both be right. And I begin to understand what *The Church Times* means by saying, "Baptists do not believe in the 'one baptism.'"[121]

On the other hand, Ruth insisted that when new chapels were being built they should make provision for "any non-Baptist practices."

> If you couldn't sprinkle the babies, somebody else could. It wouldn't do the babies any harm. And they could still be baptized afterwards—if they wanted to be . . . Baptism was never meant to be a barrier to fellowship.

Ruth was here opening up an issue that would feature in later English Baptist life. In the next century, "local ecumenical partnerships" were developed in which Baptists shared in church buildings such as Ruth had suggested and

---

120. *CW*, October 24, 1912, 13.
121. *CW*, December 5, 1912, 27.

where the emphasis was on mutual recognition of different processes of initiation into the visible membership of the local church.[122]

His comments on the smaller groups reveal even more of Ruth's confidence in his own knowledge and judgements. Special discussion was given to "A Disciple: A Member of the Church of Christ." Quakers were warmly affirmed. Regarding Unitarians, he was very positive: "Sometimes Unitarians are misrepresented by other Christian people," while some of their sanest people held "the most extraordinary opinions of our views."[123]

An "undenominationalist" was assured that by his actions he was in fact creating another "denomination."[124] The "Militant Protestant" was told that "the word reeks of controversy and division." It is not the truth of Protestantism that is the problem "but its militant temper."[125]

These are striking words in view of the extent to which T. E. Ruth was marked as a militant Protestant of the most bigoted kind when in Melbourne and Sydney.

The last two groups were distinctly British in origin: the Salvation Army and the Plymouth Brethren. The Salvationists were hailed for their energetic mission. He also knew of their holiness emphasis: "Your whole history shows how well you know the meaning of "death to sin" and "newness of life"—the inward and spiritual grace of which baptism is the outward and visible sign."[126]

Regarding the Brethren, Ruth welcomed the idea of being hailed as a "brother" but felt this was "spoilt by something symbolised in that disliked appellation 'Plymouth,' which suggests limitation and localisation."[127]

These series of letters by "Geoffrey Palmer" are of interest at several levels. They reveal an insider's knowledge of the preparation and earliest experiences of a Nonconformist minister at this period. The letters to church folk outlined aspects of a local church's life as well as developments within the denomination's life and structures. Finally, the letters to other churches revealed an awareness of the contributions of divergent denominational traditions as well as an invitation for each one—even the Brethren—to share in the unity movement in Britain. These letters, then, demonstrate the

---

122. For example, see the discussion in *Report of the International Conversations*, 44–55.

123. *CW*, January 23, 1913, 4.

124. *CW*, February 6, 1913, 9.

125. *CW*, February 27, 1913, 20.

126. *CW*, March 13, 1913, 14.

127. *CW*, April 3, 1913, 9.

extent to which this devoted Baptist was committed to the unity of the Free Churches and of the wider Christian church.

One reader thought the contributions were "racy and trenchant" but welcomed their "adventurous catholicity." Two leading ministers thought Mr. Palmer was "a sort of compound Mark Tapley and Mrs. Pankhurst."[128]

But, of course, the letters also indicate the experience and attitudes that Ruth brought to the major sectarian controversies in Australia. His literary work prepared him for the extensive series of books, pamphlets, and newspaper articles he published; the same racy and extravagant style became very popular.

Ruth does not seem ever to have publicly acknowledged these literary contributions as his work but the ideas and language confirm that he certainly was "Geoffrey Palmer." In 1914, F. C. Spurr informed Australian Baptists that Geoffrey Palmer was T. E. Ruth.[129]

The Call to Australia

In October 1913, Ruth received "an urgent invitation" to succeed F. C. Spurr in his "marvellously successful ministry" at Collins Street Baptist Church in Melbourne. He was greatly perplexed by this possibility. In many senses, Ruth did not want to accept. "I have been so happy and so well here, and my stay has been so short . . . I would not have left Southport for any place in England." He thought of reasons why he should not go, but he realized that the greatest obstacle was what he called "my own cowardly disinclination." A growing sense of duty pointed him to accept "a position so influential." Talking it over with his church officers, he was moved by their response:

> Facing all the facts, they agreed to a man that I could not be true to the Gospel I preach, of so investing life as to secure the largest returns for the kingdom of God, and decline this great opportunity of service. I have never received, and never expect to receive, a finer tribute to my ministry than their genuine sorrow swallowed up in the larger sense of the call of God.[130]

The next day he cabled his acceptance of the pastorate.

---

128. *CW*, April 24, 1913, 23. Tapley was a happy character in Charles Dickens's *Martin Chuzzlewit*, and Emmeline Pankhurst was the well-known suffragette.

129. *AB*, February 24, 1914, 4; *Australian Christian Commonwealth*, March 6, 1914, 11.

130. *CW*, October 30, 1913, 11.

The *Baptist Times*, describing Ruth as "one of the ablest ministers we have," declared that his leaving would be a great loss to Baptists in England, "but we surrender him cheerfully . . . because we are sure he will be a great force in Australia's public life, and will be a strong link uniting the mother and daughter countries together."[131]

The day after he had sent his response, Ruth was confirmed in that decision by reading "The Australian Letter" by F. C. Spurr in the *Christian World*. This suggested to Ruth that he was going to "a crisis of opportunity, when I may expect to be able to make some contribution to the great and pressing problem of Church Unity." Spurr had written about Church Union in Australia,[132] reporting on the Congress of Churches held in Melbourne in which he had been active.[133] The Baptist representatives reported that:

> Our people generally would be prepared to leave the question of baptism quite open—for each person to receive according to his conscience—and not to make it a test of church membership. . . . They would be willing . . . to cease to demand the immersion of intelligent believers as a *sine qua non* of church membership.[134]

Spurr concluded, "In a land like Australia, with its keen problems, its democratic life, its great future, and its freedom from hampering traditions, there should eagerly be established one great United Australasian Evangelical Church."

Naturally this report would have been music to the ears of Ruth and seemed to offer him a place in which his dreams of church unity could be pursued with vigor. However, Spurr was naively optimistic and out of touch with mainstream Baptist life in Australia. He misled Ruth, who was soon in trouble with some Australian Baptists for the way in which he sought to advance the cause of church unity at the imagined expense of Baptist identity.

There are several reasons why Ruth must have seemed an attractive appointment to the Melbourne church. He was still relatively young—not yet forty—and had conducted three successful ministries, including one at a busy city church in Liverpool. His preaching was uniformly appreciated as lively and original, and he could command attention on public platforms. He had served as a member of the Council of the Baptist Union, who gave him a warm commendation to Australian Baptists.[135]

---

131. *BT*, October 30, 1913 as cited by *AB*, December 9, 1913, 4.

132. *CW*, October 23, 1913, 4. The papers are also found in Spurr, *Five Years*.

133. For this Congress, see Engel, *Australian Christians in Conflict and Unity*, 187–98.

134. Spurr, *Five Years*, 254–55.

135. *BT*, February 20, 1914, 8.

His theology was known to be typical of the liberal thinking among many leading figures, as the invitation to succeed Clifford clearly attested. He was a gifted and popular writer and had not hesitated to enter into public controversy. Ruth's appeal is evident, although he would have been virtually unknown to his future congregation.

Mabel and Tom Ruth, along with Leslie, set sail aboard the *Orama* on January 30, 1914, and their great adventure began.

2

A Baptist Pastor in Melbourne: The Early Years (1914–15)

BEFORE EMBARKING ON THE long voyage to Australia, Ruth had worked at high pressure for some time, often expending eighteen hours a day, "and was very near breaking down." Once aboard the RMS *Orama*, he took to his bunk and scarcely moved from it for three days, not aware even of "a half gale" in the Bay of Biscay. On arrival in Melbourne on March 9, 1914, Ruth declared himself fit and ready for the challenges of his new ministry in a new land. More importantly, he declared that he had come "under the influence of an impelling force, a Divine guiding."[1] He had been invited "with enthusiasm and absolute unanimity."[2]

Australian press reported that he was "essentially broad in his outlook" but not an iconoclast, with "none of the zest of the demolisher." Ruth was "essentially, fundamentally, and ineradicably evangelical." He was also described as "a radical reformer of ecclesiastical grievances in his own denomination."[3] Readers of the *Australian Baptist* were told: "As a platform man he is brilliant, his thinking fresh, his phrasing piquant; his rare gifts and charming personality leading to rich flights of oratory that carry his audience with him."[4]

F. C. Spurr had written that Melbourne as a city "is a wonderfully attractive place. Its great and unmistakable feature is airiness . . . Everything is

---

1. *Argus*, March 10, 1914, 9.
2. *Leader*, November 8, 1913, 42.
3. *Argus*, November 6, 1913, 8.
4. *AB*, November 11, 1913, 2.

light, bright, airy, ample." He thought the "farther suburbs" such as Kew, Armadale, Canterbury, and Surrey Hills were "delightful residential places."[5] Ruth lived at No. 14 Monomeath Avenue in leafy Canterbury.

The new arrival presumably knew some basic details about the city's recent history. Few decades of Australian history had witnessed such dramatic changes as those between 1880 and 1914. This was especially so in Melbourne, which in the 1880s became the financial and cultural capital of the emerging nation. Extraordinary years of economic boom, which climaxed in 1888, led to the familiar description of "Marvellous Melbourne" (first used in 1885) but which, as Graeme Davison observed, has become "one of those beautiful lies, a seductive shorthand version of the city's history."[6] The 1880s were succeeded by a severe collapse, and the 1890s were years of "discord, depression, and drought."[7] Industrial strife, unemployment, and bank collapses created a climate of uncertainty that affected the churches. The city lost more people in the fifteen years after 1891 than it had gained in the period from 1860 to 1890.[8] Far from being "marvellous," Melbourne was now dubbed "miserable."[9]

However, the 1890s were in turn succeeded by a moderate recovery, marked by the jubilant formation of the Commonwealth in 1901. This was a time when loyalty to the British Empire was still stronger than loyalty to Australia, and Victoria was the most English corner of the continent. Attitudes to alcohol, gambling, and Sunday observance had been largely shaped by Nonconformists and other evangelicals. The first years of the twentieth century were the growth years of "wowserism," the pejorative term of uncertain origin used to mock those who zealously sought to reform the morals of others.[10] This was closely linked with a growing sectarian streak, strong in Melbourne, as the Irish and other Catholics had a festering resentment against what they regarded as their unequal treatment in education. They wanted their own schools to be funded by the government. Growth in the state continued until the outbreak of the Great War (later to be known as World War I) in 1914. Most Baptists had enthusiastically supported the imperial forces in the Boer War (1899–1902) and one result had been the marked growth of imperial sentiment, which rapidly developed as the Great War began.

5. Spurr, *Five Years*, 46–53.
6. Davison, *Rise and Fall*, 12, 316.
7. Macintyre, *A Concise History*, 130.
8. Blainey, *A Land half Won*, 334.
9. Davison, *Rise and Fall*, 302.
10. For "wowser," see Davison et al., *Oxford Companion*, 701–2.

As Ruth faced the challenge of serving as pastor to his church and the wider community during these divisive years, he became one of the leading protagonists of the imperial cause in the nation.

The small denomination of Baptists in Victoria reflected the fortunes of these years. During the peak boom year of 1888, Baptists in Victoria celebrated the raising of £50,000 and the establishment of the Victorian Baptist Fund that in turn led to the creation of the Baptist College of Victoria and expansion of home mission work. While many Baptists suffered huge losses in the financial collapse, a gradual recovery of confidence marked Baptist life.[11]

Baptists have always been a minority group in Australia, with the census figures showing an all-time peak of 2.37 percent of the population in 1901. Victoria was the largest Baptist community in the colonies throughout these years with some 31,244 according to the census in 1911, while the actual number of members in churches that year was 7,655.

The Collins Street Church had been formed in 1843 and had developed a large—almost institutional—life with a Gospel Hall in Little Bourke Street, an area in the city that had become something of a moral jungle and where various evangelical efforts sought to rescue the "outcasts" of society. Collins Street also ran a Sunday School in Bouverie Street, Carlton, for the poor children of the vicinity.[12] Established in 1902, this was the first free kindergarten in Australia.[13]

Collins Street was one of the city's great streets, a center of quality and style, the most exclusive clubs and the most fashionable shops. Three significant churches were a short distance from each other at the "Paris" end of the street: Scots' Presbyterian, Collins Street Independent, and Collins Street Baptist.

---

11. Manley, "From Assurance," 27–51.

12. For the Collins Street Church, see Himbury, *Theatre of the Word*. For the Gospel Hall, see Pearce, "A Humble Effort," 28–95.

13. Piggin and Linder, *Fountain of Public Prosperity*, 476.

Collins Street Baptist Church

Although always regarded as the mother church of Baptists in the state, Collins Street Church had inevitably suffered membership losses as the population drifted to the suburbs away from the city. Carey and Spurr, pastors in the first decades of the twentieth century, both brought new theology and approaches to their ministries and still attracted large numbers to special services held in either the church or the nearby Auditorium in Collins Street. While both men were warmly supported in the Collins Street Church, they encountered suspicion and opposition from more conservative Baptists around the Commonwealth.[14] However, both Carey and Spurr engaged in a vigorous mission for social justice and in that sense prepared the way for Ruth.[15]

Ruth was soon engaged in a wide-ranging and often controversial ministry in his own church, within the denomination, and in the wider community. These were undoubtedly the most demanding and fulfilling years of his life. He must often have thought longingly of that gently rocking bunk on the *Orama* and the rest it had given him.

14. See Manley, "An Honoured Name," 67–112; Manley, *From Woolloomooloo*, 132–34.

15. Manley, "'A Savonarola in Melbourne'?," 4–37.

Pastor at Collins Street Baptist (1914–23): "A Terror for his Size"

Speaking aboard ship when he first arrived, Ruth had contrasted himself with his tall predecessor F. C. Spurr: "I am come to fill the position of a big man . . . I know that, and I am only a little man, but I will do my best."[16] One Victorian minister said of him, as had been said of Lord Roberts, "He's little, but he's wise; he's a terror for his size."[17] Ruth was greeted with great enthusiasm and high expectations in what the weekly denominational paper the *Australian Baptist* (founded in 1913) called "a procession of welcomes."[18]

Tom, Mabel, and Leslie Ruth

16. *Herald*, March 9, 1914, 1.
17. *AB*, March 17, 1914, 4.
18. *AB*, March 17, 1914, 3.

The main welcome was held in the church. Peter Fleming from South Australia, who had supplied the church for the previous month, observed that their new minister needed to be like a lamp-post: "Have an iron constitution, be upright, be a bright and shining light, and have plenty of gas."[19] The city had endured seven days of humid heat as well as "ninety minutes of the close companionship in the heated building" before Ruth rose to speak. However, he soon had their total attention, and with a wealth of "apt quotation and striking illustration" welcomed the interdenominational guests with a characteristic assurance that he reveled in the thought of interchurch union. One friend wrote to Pearce Carey: "He has a lovely voice, soft as the cooing of the dove, rising to the clarion notes. I have never heard anything just like it before. It was as a violin in the hands of a master."[20]

Membership of Collins Street was 482 when Ruth arrived and grew steadily so that in 1920 it had reached 539. Attendances at Sunday services were far larger, as was common in city churches, and many of the members had joined during the war years. However, in 1920 a significant number of names (355) were removed from the roll, suggestive that many had either moved to the suburbs or drifted away from the church's active life. Thus, when Ruth left, the membership had declined to 372.[21]

Ruth was naturally called on to lead the church through a typical range of minor disputes among the members. For example, in his first year there was a major issue about the church choir. Some members had ridiculed the Baptist practice of baptism, and one of the choir members came from "one of the bitterest Roman Catholic families." After much discussion it was resolved by the deacons to request the choirmaster to resign, which he duly did. Claude Kingston (1886–1978) who had been organist since 1910, was appointed choir leader and led the choir with distinction for many years, ably assisted by his wife Ella, who was the sister-in-law of F. C. Spurr.[22]

Ruth: An Evangelical Preacher

Ruth had been widely hailed as a leading Free Church preacher in England. With a commanding presence, he always began with a striking introduction and employed common oratorical methods such as alliteration and repetition.

19. *AB*, March 17, 1914, 3.
20. *AB*, May 26, 1914, 10.
21. Statistics from the annual *Yearbooks* of BUV.
22. CSBC Deacons' Minutes, June 15, 1914; Himbury, *Theatre of the Word*, 24; for Kingston, see *ADB*.

His passion was fused with a sharp mental analysis of his theme and the judicious use of apt quotations, especially of poems or familiar hymns.

His reputation as a preacher had preceded Ruth to Australia. The *Australian Baptist*, under the editorship of J. A. Packer (1863–1941), had published a sermon by Ruth even before he arrived: "Loving God Merrily: The Soul on Holiday."[23] Packer regularly published Ruth's sermons as "The Collins Street Pulpit" during 1914. Over the following years Ruth had many of his addresses published, with the result that his influence spread far and wide within the Baptist world and beyond.

At his welcome Ruth proposed that only two questions should be asked of him, "Is it evangelical?" and "Is it catholic? (and spell the latter with a small 'c')."[24] Although he often remarked that he resented being defined by any sort of label, he was regularly described as "evangelical." David Bebbington's identification of four main features of British evangelical religion has been widely adopted. First was an emphasis on conversion, the crisis associated with turning from sin to personal faith. Second, evangelicalism was marked by activism, a commitment to leading others to conversion as well as a vigorous concern to confront evil in society and to alleviate the needs of the distressed. Third was a love for the Bible, a desire to study it personally, in family, in church and to shape all of life by its teaching and example. Fourth was a concentration in doctrine on the atoning death of Christ on the cross.[25] Conversion, activism, Bible, and cross—these leading components of evangelical religion were all evident in the early preaching of Ruth, as we shall examine shortly.

At the same time, some aspects of his preaching antagonized several far more conservative evangelicals. Perhaps he is best described, along with many of his British counterparts such as John Clifford, as a liberal or progressive evangelical. Pearce Carey was in the same tradition and had even been called "the Dr. Clifford of Australia."[26]

One of Ruth's earliest sermons in the country was on March 24, when he addressed over two thousand Christian Endeavourers (CE) in the Auditorium on "A Young Person's Religion." Arranged by cable before Ruth had left England it was a huge success: "The finest address the writer has listened to at a CE gathering in over twenty years. Witty, epigrammatic, brainy, clear and concise—it laid such emphasis on Believing, Being, Doing the Best."[27]

23. *AB*, January 13, 1914, 1.
24. *AB*, March 17, 1914, 3.
25. Bebbington, *Evangelicalism*, 3.
26. Manley, *"An Honoured Name,"* 76.
27. *AB*, 31 March 1914, 16.

Analyzing Ruth's preaching is complicated, since different sermons revealed quite distinct emphases and approaches. His first sermons were marked by a strong evangelical and evangelistic approach. As Ruth raised certain denominational challenges, he was thrust into a polemical role on issues such as church union, especially about the place of baptism in any union schemes. Again, a range of traditional liberal–conservative debates about the inspiration of the Bible and eschatology led to sharp and public differences with some influential leaders.

As war broke out, Ruth inevitably embarked on a series of "war" sermons that may be variously described as patriotic or imperialistic and, at times, jingoistic. He also preached several sermons dealing with a wide range of social problems that raise the question of whether he might be regarded as a public theologian. Then another sequence of sermons were strongly Protestant and anti-Catholic, which led to him being described as a "sectarian bigot." It is not suggested that these were successive stages in his development as a Melbourne preacher, but that at different times he emphasized different features. He also faced certain pastoral and apologetic challenges thrust up by the tragedy of the war, notably the fate of the dead.

His first year of preaching at Collins Street affords an insight into Ruth's style and the main features of his theology. No fewer than thirty-one of his sermons, mostly preached at Collins Street, appeared in the *Australian Baptist* during 1914. One other sermon, preached on September 6, was on the decidedly unusual theme of "The Passing of Pope Pius X—A Protestant Appreciation" and was later published.[28] Ruth more than once observed that "the heat and glow of the religious atmosphere" could not easily survive "the cold, death-dealing hands of the man at the linotype machine."[29] Still, the immediacy and vitality of his preaching as well as his major theological views are apparent in these printed sermons.

His first sermon at Collins Street was on March 15, when his text was "He giveth more grace" (Jas 4:6). The sermon was entitled "The Inexhaustible God." As was the custom, a brief report appeared in the *Argus* the next morning. Clearly Ruth loved to emphasize the grace of God and traced it throughout history, suggesting that Roman Catholics "made a corner" of grace but Luther had smashed this monopoly. Anglicanism offered a kind of "aristocratic exclusiveness" but also "tried to monopolise grace." Baptists sprang into being scorning all priestly pretension but "Baptists were becoming bigoted and thought to exclude all but those of Baptist belief." Ruth insisted that God

---

28. Ruth, *Wake up, Australia!*, 9–17.
29. Ruth, *Common Weal*, ii.

was still giving more grace for a new age.[30] Thus he introduced his familiar approach of comparing various denominations and also highlighted what he regarded as a Baptist problem. So, in his very first sermon he had raised some Baptist hackles, and this continued throughout the year.

His claim to be evangelical, however, was well demonstrated in these early sermons. On April 5, he preached at a communion service on "We Preach Christ Crucified" (1 Cor 1:23). This was a careful exposition of the passage and was totally Christ-centered:

> Meet Jesus anywhere. Let His personality flash across your path and you will come to His cross. All the lines of religion converge on Calvary. All the light of Revelation radiates from the cross, of Heaven and earth, of God and man, of time and eternity.
>
> Paul's religion was Christo-centric. More it was cruci-centric. And in this twentieth century it is still the centre of all our faith, all our thought, all our duty . . .

Receiving the bread and wine, Ruth confessed his personal faith:

> Here I feel that this is what my sin, allowed to run riot would do, it would kill God, crucify Christ, revile Him even in the pangs of death, stab him even after he was dead. But there is something more in my experience, for this is the birthplace of immortal hope. I can take sides with God against my own sin; I can lose my sin, and mentally, morally, spiritually, righteousness becomes available. I can get right with God and man . . . Here is the power, the reasonable, the reason-transcending power, the moral spiritual dynamic that drives out the devils of passion, of greed, of drunkenness, and every evil, here at the cross. . .
>
> Christ crucified is my only hope, your only hope, the only hope of humanity. Here the blackness of sin blushes into the crimson of the cross that towers o'er the wrecks of time.[31]

The same evangelical appeal was evident in two Easter sermons. One was on Mary Magdalene's reaction after the resurrection, when she "supposed him to be the gardener" (John 20:15). Ruth vividly recreated the famous exchange and then interpreted it as being like the parable/sermon in Matthew 25:31–46:

> We have seen Him and supposed Him to be an outcast, hungry, thirsty, sick, imprisoned and we have not ministered unto Him. . . . He comes. He is here today. You supposed it to be a

---

30. *Argus*, March 16, 1914, 7.
31. *AB*, April 21, 1914, 3.

> line of a hymn. It was the Lord. You supposed it to be a part of the prayer. It was Jesus. You supposed it to be something in the sermon. It was the living Christ.[32]

The second sermon on the same passage concentrated on the confession of Mary, "Rabboni" (John 20:16): "Mary passed in a moment from mental midnight into morning." Christ's command that she should go and tell the disciples was of great relevance for his hearers: "There are brothers of His, and of yours, all round you who do not know there is a loving Saviour."[33]

Ruth's preaching also addressed contemporary issues and challenges to faith. For example, on April 26, he spoke about "Things that are Shaken," a phrase from Hebrews 12:27, which contrasts what Ruth, in an awkward phrase, called "the periodicity of religious creeds and customs" with "the realities that remain." The Bible, "the most progressive book in the world," shows how "the partial gifts of prophecy and knowledge" are followed by the "things that remain." Ruth's appeal was to discern that which remains when the symbols are swept away.

> Eternal Reality is still at the centre and soul of things. Far back of all our science, untouched by all our criticisms, deeper than all our frenzied revolutions is this eternal reality, call it what you will, it is there, and it remains. Call it Force, call it Fate, call it Law, call it the something not ourselves that makes for righteousness, call it the Divinity that shapes our ends, call it what you will. I prefer to say, "God over all, blessed for evermore."[34]

A similar concern was expressed in his sermon, "The Ministry of the Miraculous" based on the miracle at Cana (John 2:1–11). After reflecting on some problems, he issued an impassioned personal plea:

> Will you not come to the Saviour tonight, or let Him come to you? They invited Him to the wedding. Ask Him to come to you now. He will solve your difficulties and satisfy your souls . . . I believe in a miracle-working Christ, in a miracle-working Christianity . . . He can purify your soul, illumine your mind, cleanse your conscience, invigorate your will, make the nature whole, the character complete, crown your manhood and womanhood with holiness, happiness and spiritual health. He can. I know He can.[35]

32. *AB*, April 28, 1914, 1–2.
33. *AB*, May 19, 1914, 3–4.
34. *AB*, May 5, 1914, 3.
35. *AB*, June 9, 1914, 3, 13.

Ruth sought to relate the gospel to the life of his congregation and the city. On June 7, Ruth spoke on, "Can a Man be a Christian in Business?" Despite his answer being predictably positive, his reflection was helpful: "If a man can be a Christian at all, he can be a Christian anywhere." After all, many Melbourne business leaders were still smarting from the awesome collapse of the late 1880s. Ruth argued that economic brotherhood should replace economic competition. Indeed, he pleaded for the "Christianising of commerce, of the whole system of barter and exchange."[36]

Ruth ventured into the realm of theodicy on June 14, when he preached on "The Sinking of the *Empress of Ireland*. Was It an 'Act of God'?" The RMS *Empress of Ireland* was an ocean liner that sank near the mouth of the Saint Lawrence River following a collision in thick fog with the Norwegian collier SS *Storstad* on May 29, 1914, only two years after the sinking of the *Titanic*. Over a thousand people died as the vessel foundered in only fourteen minutes. It remains the worst peacetime marine disaster in Canadian history.

In Britain, Ruth had preached and written about the *Titanic* disaster and now restated much of that argument.[37] He rejected any notion that the disaster was a Divine judgement but of course there is "a problem of pain, an awful mystery in evil, that God moves in a mysterious way." In time, when the findings were complete, Ruth suggested, the responsibility would be attached to "the ignorance or negligence of man" and nothing here should impair faith in "the infinitely wise providence of God or the revelation of His Fatherly character."[38]

Because of large numbers attending services, both S. P. Carey and F. C. Spurr had held Sunday evening meetings in the Auditorium across the road in Collins Street. This concert hall had been renovated and when reopened in May 1913 could seat 2,500 people. Ruth continued this strategy and frequently filled the theatre to overflowing.

A press report described the first of Ruth's services in the Auditorium as "religion in the abode of art." Sacred music preceded the service, as did congregational singing. The service was marked by simplicity "relieved with a little chanting, and earnestness." Ruth began: "It has been suggested that I moderate my address down to the level of a large mixed congregation. That I refuse to do. I don't mind if you go to sleep." Following a brief summary of the sermon on "What Is God?," the report concluded:

> The preacher holds his congregation by obviously careful preparation, in which every sentence has its distinctive message, and

---

36. *AB*, June 16, 1914, 1–2.
37. *BT*, May 10, 1912, 340.
38. *AB*, June 23, 1914, 1–2.

by the artistic use of a light, pleasant voice, quietly employed until at the approach of the climax it throbs and sways with passion. He used his art and his earnestness to emphasise his reasoned thoughts.[39]

The first of his Auditorium series was in July and August 1914 when he led a "Mission to the Modern Mind." This was free of the sectarian and aggressive style that would characterize some of his later Auditorium addresses. He drew on a series he had previously preached at Liverpool in England dealing with basic Christian issues: What Is Religion?; What Is God?; What Is Man?; What Is the Bible?; What Is Christ?; What Is Christianity?; What Is Sin?; What Is Salvation?; What Is a Christian?; If Not Christianity, What?; What Is Judgement?; What Is Hell?; What Is Heaven? Each sermon was published in the *Australian Baptist*. Ruth revealed his evangelical and evangelistic intentions.

In a closely argued address, Ruth began his mission with a discussion on the nature of God. He briefly considered the views of the atheist, the agnostic, and the polytheist before suggesting that pantheism is "a partial perception of a great reality." His close argument proposed a traditional Christian view of God: God is Love. "The underlying reality of all life now is, God is Love. The ultimate reality, the divine destiny of all things. God is Love."[40]

Man seems to be an infinitely small reality in a vast universe: "To you I look a very little man in this vast auditorium at this distance, as little as you look to me. But this vastness is no criterion of your value or mine." Taking Jesus's question, "How much, then, is a man better than a sheep?" (Matt 12:12), Ruth proceeded to enumerate the values of a human: he can think, he has a will and he possesses what Ruth called "a spiritual personality." Jesus is "the measure of manhood."[41]

Considerable interest was attached to Ruth's discussion about the Bible. He stressed that different views were essentially a difference between the old and the young and he imagined himself called in to mediate between the two.

> To one man the Bible is an infallible Book, its every statement is a literal fact . . . From cover to cover it is the Word of God. The other regards the Bible as a vast library of religious literature to be subjected to the same searching criticism and severe judgment as any other literature. The older man interprets life as a series of miracles—Creation, Conversion, Sanctification, these

39. *Leader* (Melbourne), July 11, 1914, 42.
40. *AB*, July 14, 1914, 3.
41. *AB*, July 21, 1914, 3, 12.

> are miracles. The younger man has frankly discarded the miraculous standpoint, regards creation as a continuing process . . .

Ruth argued that the Bible is the record of a progressive revelation. "I do not go to the Bible expecting to find there ancient writers dealing with scientific discoveries—they make no profession of scientific accuracy."[42] This modern approach to the Bible, while very common back in Britain, was to be at the heart of the fundamentalist controversies that erupted in North America, and was also a source of unrest and criticism among many Australian Baptists who by a large majority appear to have favored the position of the older man in Ruth's discussion.[43]

In tackling the question "What Is Christianity?" Ruth contrasted it with other world religions such as Buddhism, Brahmanism, Judaism, and Islam, suggesting that these religions contain "partial gleams of goodness," citing Matheson's hymn, "Each sees one colour of Thy rainbow light." He then explored the question, "What Christianity do you mean? Romanism? Protestantism in its militant or political form is no more like New Testament Christianity than Roman bigotry such as the Orangeism as I have seen it in Liverpool." The Christianity of Christ is greater than the Christianity of Rome or Protestant, Anglicans or Free, greater than the Christianity of Wesley or Spurgeon, Calvin or Paul, Peter, James, or John. Ruth concluded, "Let Christ make you Christian tonight, let Him lead you into the consciousness of this blessed and eternal relationship to God, who is your Father."[44]

The fourth address in Ruth's mission raised the question, "If Not Christianity, What?" He critiqued alternate religions, claiming that Christianity is the only religion that can live with progress. To reject "the Fatherhood and Motherhood of God" (an interesting phrase for the times) is to "deny every instinct of life and health in you."[45]

The next few addresses dealt with the more controversial eschatological doctrines of judgement, hell, and heaven. Ruth argued that personal accountability is a common feature of life and that all too often the church had failed by only referring to judgement as a future event, whereas "judgment is here and now, an evergoing-on process." Ruth then challenged the popular eschatological pastime of those who believe that they can calculate how near

---

42. *AB*, July 28, 1914, 7, 15.

43. See Marsden, *Fundamentalism*; Bebbington, *Evangelicalism*, 181–228; Piggin and Linder, *Fountain of Public Prosperity*, 489–520.

44. *AB*, August 4, 1914, 3–4.

45. *AB*, August 11, 1914, 3, 15.

is the end of all time by citing Isaac Taylor's dictum, "Scripture was not given in order that newspapers might be written in advance."[46]

The next topic was the question, "What Is Hell?" Ruth began by telling the stories of his own boyhood when he had been emotionally scarred by the zealous preachers of a literal fiery hell that awaited all sinners. Ruth came to the heart of his own belief about life after death when he insisted:

> I believe that personality persists, that the grave, as Victor Hugo said, is a thoroughfare, not a terminus . . . Hell here and hereafter is the outcome of sin but Christ is here to teach men the way of life, Christ has come to turn darkness into light, hell into heaven.[47]

The third of these sermons on the future was titled, "What Is Heaven?" and was the last in the whole mission series. Once again, he emphasized the idea of progress, despite the unfolding horrors of a war that led many liberals to question their optimism about progress in the world. The way physical life develops in a human is a divine prophecy; progress is such that "earth is already heaven compared with what it was." Intellectual power progresses and, indeed, so does religion:

> We worship an infinitely greater God than our fathers knew . . . We have somehow developed the notion that heaven is utterly unlike earth—antithetical in fact. . . . The life that is to come is not in antagonism to the life that now is. Heaven is the completion of earth, not the contradiction of it.

Ruth then cited Carlyle, who had influenced so many other Free Church thinkers and preachers: "The curtains of yesterday drop down; the curtains of tomorrow roll up, but yesterday and tomorrow both are."[48] His conclusion reflects the optimism of liberal theology: "Eternity is ever absorbing time and Heaven is swallowing up this earth."[49]

At the end of his "Mission to the Modern Mind," Ruth explained: "The whole ground of appeal has been that of the relationship of man to God as revealed and realized by Jesus Christ . . . My thought of God and man and destiny is not only Christo-centric but cruci-centric."[50]

---

46. Chapter 8 of this book considers Ruth's eschatology as shown in two of his books.
47. *AB*, August 25, 1914, 3, 14.
48. This line was from Carlyle's *Sartor Resartus* (1836).
49. *AB*, September 15, 1914, 3–4.
50. *AB*, September 15, 1914, 4. The text is 2 Cor 5:21.

These sermons of 1914 clearly reveal Ruth's fundamental theological beliefs and the demands he made on his hearers. His evangelical commitment to Christ and the gospel is transparent, as are his classically liberal emphases on the Fatherhood of God and the Brotherhood of Man. After that first year his name was widely known within his denomination as well as to the churchgoers of Melbourne. He was well placed to become something of a prophetic figure to many who struggled to comprehend the sufferings and complexities of the war as well as the tensions between Protestants and Roman Catholics during the public debates about conscription.

Ruth: Baptist Preacher and "Apostle of Reunion"[51]

In that first year in Melbourne, Ruth was inevitably in high demand by his fellow-Baptists as a speaker in their churches and denominational rallies. Victorian Baptists were especially keen to hear from their new preacher. He spoke at the Baptist Union meeting at Geelong on May 5 on "The Pattern in the Mount," based on a text in Hebrews 8:5 where Moses was instructed to build according to the pattern showed to him by God on the mountain. He challenged his hearers as to whether their local church was one that "the carpenter Christ" could be a member of in the twentieth century. Inevitably, he emphasized the "scandal" of divisions in the churches.[52]

Ruth also had a serious and public disagreement with the editor of the *Australian Baptist*, J. A. Packer (1863–1941), over the question of Home Rule in Ireland. In his occasional "English Letter" for the *Australian Baptist*, Pearce Carey had written about the recent heated debate in the House of Commons on this vexed issue: "We seemed in danger of coming under the rod of a dictatorial army" and that "a calm sagacious Prime Minister has delivered us from unspeakable peril."[53] Packer expressed his profound regret at what Carey had claimed.

> Mr. Carey has apparently been caught in the whirlpool of party politics, and for that reason it may be his vision which is limited to a few yards. Personally we stand for Liberalism in English politics, but English Nonconformists, or many of them, have made it a golden calf to be worshipped . . . The difference between ourselves and Mr. Carey on the Irish question is chiefly this: He believes in the sagacity of Mr. Asquith. We do not. There

---

51. *AB*, March 23, 1915, 13.
52. *AB*, May 12, 1914, 2, 15.
53. *AB*, May 26, 1914, 10.

is very little sagacity, to our way of thinking, in selling Ulster to make a Nationalist holiday.[54]

This editorial sparked a number of correspondents, mostly opposed to Packer's viewpoint. Ruth unwisely adopted a patronizing stance, defending Carey's perspective as an Englishman: "Mr. Carey is more likely to be right than an Australian." Ruth believed that Ulster itself favored Home Rule:

> I should be interested as a recent arrival from the land of weak-kneed Free Church men (1) If you could tell us why, if Home rule is such a dreadful thing for Ireland, you submit to it in Australia? (2) If you would point out the difference between Roman and Protestant bigotry. (This would be very interesting to me. I've lived in Liverpool . . .)[55]

Eventually Carey himself replied, noting that he had been a supporter of Irish self-government "under due Imperial restriction" for over twenty years.[56] Ruth was to become a vigorous opponent of Sinn Fein (the political arm of Irish nationalism) and its influence in Australia during his later controversy over conscription with Archbishop Mannix.

Ruth was on solid Baptist ground when he preached a sermon, "Why Baptist?" at Collins Street on June 21, 1914. He first demonstrated "the Scripturalness of our position and the validity of Believers' Baptism" and included a vivid account of his own experience as a young man. Arguing that infant baptism is "unscriptural," that the mode is immersion, and that baptism is "personal identification with the Passion and purpose of Christ," he concluded:

> The church with an open baptistery where Christ has the pre-eminence cannot wander from the central vitalising things. Baptism stands for no bloodless moralism, no spiritless ceremonialism, no mystical efficacy. The Cross is translated into symbol and the grave becomes the seed-plot of unspeakable glory.[57]

This address was published as a pamphlet.[58]

Ruth made other contributions relating to the Baptist community in 1914. He gave an address at the launch of the Baptist Men's Association in Melbourne on June 22 on "Thinking Things out Together." He introduced

---

54. *AB*, May 26, 1914, 9.
55. *AB*, June 9, 1914, 13.
56. *AB*, August 25, 1914, 14.
57. *AB*, June 30, 1914, 3, 15.
58. Advertisements in *AB* from April 1915.

ideas from J. H. Shakespeare, "the greatest ecclesiastical statesman in England," and argued that the outstanding need of the new association was "the need for corporate thinking, of fellowship in our thought, that we may think out together and make of the Baptist Church in the Commonwealth an instrument of the kingdom of God worthy the ideal of the New Testament."[59]

Invited to be the main speaker at the New South Wales (NSW) Assembly in Sydney, Ruth gave the annual sermon on "The Larger Unity": "There is to be a united Christendom, a united world, the united states of the universe. For nineteen centuries we have been moving towards this peak of vision." Diversity was also central, as no two Baptist churches or denominational bodies are the same:

> You may hold a brief for orthodoxy—indeed you may be the only orthodox man in New South Wales—even as I am in Victoria!—but you cannot claim a monopoly of grace . . . And I dare plead for a bigger brotherhood, for a fuller fraternity, for a catholic charity, for a comprehensive churchmanship, for depend upon it, our unity is the need of the kingdom.[60]

At the missionary rally during the same NSW Assembly, Ruth spoke on the individual and the great commission. He began by quoting from Alfred Russel Wallace's book *The World of Life* in which he concluded that there is "a Creative Power" which constituted matter as well as a "Directive Mind" and "an Ultimate Purpose in the very existence of the life-world."[61] From this unusual starting-point he then moved to focus on Jesus as "the touchstone of all the truth in the world of life." His vision for the gospel was comprehensive:

> If every Church member were a missionary, and every Church a missionary society and all the Churches worked together as one vast army labouring for the supremacy of the spiritual, the enthronement of truth and light and love, proclaiming far and near Christ's doctrines of the Fatherhood of God, the Brotherhood of Man, the awfulness of sin, the Saviourhood of the Cross, the sanctity of life, the dignity of labour, the stewardship of wealth, then the world-neighbourhood would speedily be changed into a world-brotherhood, wars would cease, peace be established on earth and in our home relations and foreign

---

59. *AB*, July 7, 1914, 3, 15.
60. *AB*, September 29, 1914, 5, 12.
61. Wallace, *World of Life*.

policies righteousness would reign, life would be lightened with infinite love, and truth would triumph everywhere.[62]

However, before the year was out Ruth's consuming passion for church union was to reveal a significant difference between him and many other Baptists, including Packer. Ruth spoke at the Victorian Baptist Ministers' Fraternal School of Theology on October 28 on "The Religious Ideal." His controversial talk included several bold ideas such as that Christ's prayer that "they all may be one" meant organic union. "Denominational division was a greater evil than infant baptism. We are so divided we cannot tackle any social problem successfully." He appreciated his Baptist brethren, but "to be only a Baptist meant being a bigot. To go to a Baptist heaven would possess no charm for him." He continued: "When all were united in organic union and combined effort, then he could preach baptism, and those who stood for Methodist passion, Anglican reverence, Congregational polity, could still contribute their quota to the blessing of the whole."[63]

At least two of Ruth's assertions proved to be controversial. One was the notion that Christ's prayer for unity had meant organic union. The other was the idea that to be only a Baptist meant being a bigot. Packer strongly rejected this notion: "A true Baptist cannot be a bigot; a bigot cannot be a Baptist." More basically, he disagreed with Ruth's interpretation that Christ's prayer meant organic union: "Essentially all Christians may become one, organically never."[64]

Ruth, always ready to tackle critics, chose to reply by means of a sermon at Collins Street on December 6, "Can a Loyal Baptist Advocate Church Union?" which was briefly reported in *The Age* with the observation that Ruth had "excited condemnatory correspondence." The full text was published in the *Australian Baptist*.[65] Union was not simply "a pet theme" (as Packer had called it) but "a consuming passion," and one he shared with "the greatest British Baptists of two generations": Charles Williams, Alexander Maclaren, F. B. Meyer, and J. H. Shakespeare ("the foremost British Baptist and the first Baptist statesman in the world"). Indeed, Shakespeare had said: "The plain fact is that this vast tree of denominationalism is rapidly becoming hollow; it is propped up by the iron bands of trust-deeds and funds."

Ruth insisted that he had not been reported accurately:

---

62. *AB*, October 13, 1914, 11–12.
63. *AB*, November 24, 1914, 11.
64. *AB*, December 1, 1914, 8.
65. *The Age*, December 7, 1914, 12; *AB*, December 15, 1914, 5, 13.

> The most insidious falsehood is a half-truth. I said "I belong to what I believe to be the best denomination in the world, but Baptists have no monopoly of the best. Indeed, the best thing about the denomination is the catholicity and world-consciousness into which it is merging... If I were to be shut up within Baptist barriers, having fellowship only with Baptist brethren, knowing only Baptist beatitudes, I should be a bigot and no man."[66]

The world cannot be won by a divided church: "The advocate of church union is the most effective evangelist and most practical missionary."

Packer devoted leaders in successive issues to the question of church union.[67] Ruth was unrepentant:

> As Baptists, I believe as Mr. Shakespeare believes that we are peculiarly fitted to be pioneers in this great cause of church union ... As a good Baptist, I must go on advocating Church Union, urging the return of all Churches to the catholic and comprehensive churchmanship of the new Testament.[68]

This adversarial activity concluded Ruth's first year in Australia. He had been industrious and had clearly revealed his "consuming passion" for church unity. But while this may have remained a major concern for his many friends in England, in Australia the ecumenical climate among Baptists was much cooler, even hostile. This was a paradigm that lasted for the ensuing century.[69] Back in England, *Christian World* noted that "[Ruth] had been fond of magnifying the things in which the denominations are agreed and minimizing the things in which they differ."[70]

However, while fewer of Ruth's sermons now appeared in the *Australian Baptist*, he continued to serve the Baptist community. One major address was delivered at the commencement of the Victorian Baptist College on March 9, 1915, "A Plea for the Prophet." In fact, this became an occasion for Ruth to present what was virtually an *apologia pro vita sua*. This detailed justification for his own prophetic ministry helps explain his approach during this first year and beyond. The address was published in the

---

66. *AB*, December 15, 1914, 5, 13.
67. *AB*, December 29, 1914, 8–9.
68. *AB*, January 5, 1915, 2.
69 For a survey of Baptist involvement in the ecumenical movement see Manley, *From Woolloomooloo*, 444–58. E. Roberts-Thomson lost his position as principal of the NSW Baptist College largely over this issue: see Manley, *From Woolloomooloo*, 571–74.
70. *CW*, February 5, 1915, as cited in *AB*, March 23, 1915, 13.

denominational journal over two issues and also as a separate pamphlet.[71] It ranks as one of Ruth's better sermons to his denomination.

He argued that the times were so challenging as to demand that the Church return to first principles. He told the students:

> You are called to this character-creating ministry of reconciliation at a time of social strife, of ecclesiastical sectarianism, and of the bloodiest warfare ever waged in the history of the race, the principal belligerents in which call themselves Christian.

It was no time for "a merely smug, self-complacent, tradition-bound Baptist ministry." A Baptist "priest" could find a pastorate:

> There are still communities of Plymouth Brethren who think they are Baptist Churchmen . . . But the need is not for priest, but for the prophet, the man who dares face the facts of our own time, who will not allow any tradition to throttle the truth, who deliberately disturbs the complacency of the saints . . . who breaks down the barriers of their little Bethels . . .

He added a characteristic warning:

> Do not let your study of the origins of denominational principles and prejudices dim your vision of catholic churchmanship . . . for we Baptists are apt to be much more concerned about the errors of other churches than about the errors of our own . . . It is a very much bigger thing to be a Baptist prophet than some Australian Baptists seem to think. The Baptist message was never meant to be the monopoly of scattered and segregated communities of baptised believers.

Ruth warned that after the war there would be an even greater need for prophets. "Would the end of this war lead to an end to all armaments, or would some consideration such as 'the Yellow peril' provide the excuse for the continued existence of 'swollen armaments'? The prophetic vision that burned within Ruth and directed so much of his ministry was a clear challenge to these future ministers.

In later years, Ruth spoke at Baptist assemblies in South Australia (1915) and Queensland (1918). He found a measure of "freedom" in Adelaide that appealed to him, and in retirement he would choose to live there.[72] After he moved to Sydney and a Congregational church he

---

71. *AB*, March 16, 1915, 1–2; March 23, 1914, 5.
72. *AB*, September 28, 1915, 5, 14.

naturally did not have the same prominence among Baptists such as he had received in his first two years in Australia.

Internal Criticism

The Collins Street Church remained strongly supportive of Ruth even when criticisms of his views were raised. But a deacon of the church created embarrassing problems for Ruth and his fellow deacons. In December 1914, John Downing (1854–1939), formerly a Baptist pastor, wrote a letter to the *Australian Baptist*, criticizing Ruth's view that Baptists should be willing to join in church union schemes even when their own views of baptism were not accepted:

> It probably intends to show how liberal and broadminded English Baptists are becoming, but many an Australian Baptist can, with more Scriptural reason, claim to be liberal and broadminded, without, in battling for the union of the churches, torpedo the unity of his own church.

Downing added that the "dry rot" of modern theology had destroyed other valuable doctrines. His criticism went beyond Ruth to include his two predecessors, S. P. Carey and F. C. Spurr:

> A church that has had fourteen years of this teaching, that has expended time, energy and organisation, that has maintained at great cost the highest possible state of efficiency in its public services that church has, even as a business concern, a right to look for results; and a spiritual mind also may well ask, "What is the outcome for all the prayer and service of this long time of experiment with modern theology?" There have not been ten known conversions as the direct result of all these years.[73]

This naturally created a deep concern among the Collins Street deacons, who responded to his criticism with a strong letter insisting that never before in the history of the church had "more clear and convincing sermons on baptism been preached" than those by Ruth. Moreover, since Ruth began more than three times the ten suggested were known to have been converted and that many present church members had come to faith during the pastorates of Carey and Spurr.[74]

---

73. *AB*, December 15, 1914, 13.
74. *AB*, January 5, 1915, 2.

Even more significant was that in the same issue of the journal Downing himself admitted that he had now been better advised and withdrew his letter. As he admitted to his fellow deacons on January 18, he had endured "a very bad time over the last three weeks" and expressed his appreciation of "the way the brethren had greeted him all the way through."[75] The editor of the paper felt it necessary to explain why he had published Downing's letter and expressed his regret to Ruth, Carey, and Spurr.[76]

Spurr insisted that he knew many who had been converted during Carey's time and he also knew of more than a hundred who had been converted in his time: "What is the 'dry rot' of modern theology? If preaching Christ in season and out of season is 'dry rot' then I plead guilty."[77]

Criticism was an unavoidable challenge to city preachers, especially when so many of their sermons or actions were reported in the daily secular press, but this one from within his own leadership had been unfortunate. Ruth continued to challenge the faith and intellect of his hearers. During the war years he gave his best to lead his people and the wider community of Melbourne. Sadly, his battle with Roman Catholicism would contribute to the sad history of sectarianism in Australia, a role scarcely imaginable when he first arrived in Melbourne as an "apostle of reunion."

---

75. CSBC Deacons' Minutes, January 18, 1915.
76. *AB*, 2 February 1915, 4.
77. *AB*, 23 March 1915, 2.

3

Imperial Protestant

CLEARLY THE MOST SIGNIFICANT event of Ruth's first year in Melbourne was the outbreak of the Great War in August 1914. While congregations continued to grow during what became the long war years, Ruth shared in the inevitable anxieties, challenges, and losses which came to the empire, his new country, his city, and his church.

Ruth undertook two related roles during the war years. First, he was called on to help his people and the community find some meaning in the conflict as well as bringing comfort to the families of those who lost loved ones. This raised some serious and controversial theological questions about the fate of the dead. His other role, within the wider community, was to advance an increasingly strident support for the imperial cause and harsh condemnation of all "disloyalists."

Being the minister of a Baptist church in Melbourne during the war years helped shape much of Ruth's public persona.[1] He was inevitably cast into a role that made him at once the hero of conservative forces and the hated opponent of many Catholics and radical politics. Ruth became much more than simply the pastor of a city congregation. His wider public activities made him a controversial figure—a prophet, as he understood his role—at a time of tense sectarianism in the city of Melbourne. His future ministry was shaped decisively by those war years. Much of his energy was increasingly devoted to studious analysis and criticism of traditional Catholic teachings and—even more—condemning the powerful political role that in his judgement that church played in Australia. One of the most divisive

---

1 Thwaites, "Rev. T. E. Ruth," 19–46.

tensions of Melbourne community life, that between Catholics and Protestants, hardened during those years, and Ruth must share some responsibility for his leadership in that development.

Ruth's ministry must be placed in the broad context of the role that the churches and Protestant clergy played during the war.[2] He was typical of the majority of Baptist clergy in his enthusiastic support for the British cause in the war.[3] As the horrors of the war campaign and the fearful losses among Australian troops unfolded, any criticism of Australian involvement in the war by Baptists and other evangelical groups largely faded. Stuart Piggin has remarked: "It is inconceivable that significant numbers of churchmen could have thought any other way about Empire or war."[4]

Certainly, Ruth was not alone in his conviction that the British and Australian cause was morally right. Sympathy for the "violation" of "plucky little" Belgium, such an important factor in British Baptist support for the war, resonated with Ruth.[5] It became an act of Christian virtue to support the war effort: "Rather than stemming the tide of war hysteria, clergymen contributed to it and even shaped it."[6]

An American contemporary of Ruth, Baptist preacher Harry Emerson Fosdick (1878–1969), later reflected on the way in which the war had impacted his preaching:

> What a temptation war is to a preacher! He could not be a preacher if he did not love the response of attentive audiences, the kindling answer of many hearts moved in unison. War provides a medium of deeply stirred and well-nigh unanimous emotion in which the preacher's work can become thrilling . . . I learned how to bring down the house with out-and-out-militaristic appeals.[7]

All this is also evidenced in the speaking of Ruth. But he could never have added, as Fosdick did: "I was exhilarated then but I am ashamed now."

---

2. McKernan, *Australian Churches at War*; Linder, *Long Tragedy*, and for Baptists, see Manley, *From Woolloomooloo*, 407–31, and Petras, *Australian Baptists and World War I*.

3. See Manley, *From Woolloomooloo*, 409–14.

4. Piggin, *Evangelical*, 83.

5. Clements, "Baptists and the Outbreak of the First World War," 79–92.

6. McKernan, *Australian People*, 16.

7. Fosdick, *Living of These Days*, 121–22.

"The Responsibility of Empire"

During the latter part of 1914 Ruth preached four "war sermons," which were then issued as a pamphlet at the cost of one penny.[8] The first address outlined his fundamental convictions about the empire and the role of Australia in the war. Much of his activity can best be understood in the light of this first sermon, "The Responsibility of Empire."[9]

Ruth outlined a "curious heresy" that held that a Christian was not concerned with citizenship—"to be in the world but not of it"— and that many saints were "absorbingly interested in the political events of the two tiny communities of Israel and Judah" but were strangely blind to "the political illumination of the Spirit of God in our own day":

> Why is it religious to regard God as somehow interested in the guerrilla warfare between ancient Israel and her various foes while we hesitate to address Him today as "God of Battles" . . . I ask reverently, has anything happened to God that He is less interested in men today than He was millenniums ago? . . . Or, has something happened to us that in this Christian era our religion is so soft and flabby, so lacking in blood and iron, that we are afraid to look at the facts of our own time, and the condition of our own country, and face with Christian faith the Imperial crisis thrust upon us by an arrogant and aggressive military group, as much the enemy of their own country as of the countries of the Allies?

For Ruth such an attitude "denies the religious basis of the responsibility of Empire, it bites into the very existence of imperial being and reduces our patriotism to the level of paganism."

Ruth's absolute certainty about the rightness of the war as well as his fiery eloquence were both revealed in this first "war" sermon:

> Clear and certain as the shining of the sun in the Australian sky, the call came to our nation to honour its word, to risk its sovereignty, its soldiery, its ships, its men and its money, to the last man and its last penny, to the last shred of its power, to the remotest outposts of its influence, rather than repudiate its solemn pledge to maintain the independence of smaller nations and refuse to fulfil its destiny in the higher civilisations of the race. We are fighting not for territory, but for truth, not for the aggrandisement of the British Empire, but for the defence

---

8. *AB*, December 8, 1914, 3.
9. *AB*, November 3, 1914, 3-4.

of British integrity, not for the development of our own military prowess, but for the overthrow of the most presumptuous and arrogant militarism that has ever menaced the peace of the world, and the progress of its peoples.

After all the resources of diplomacy had been exhausted, in the providence of God this enormous task had been "thrust upon our Empire":

> In fellowship with God, in humble reliance upon Him, we must realise the responsibility of Empire, and every one of us must be prepared to carry on the shoulders of citizenship and in the heart of intercession the fiery cross of this crisis. For we are all involved—King and subjects, princes and people, soldiers, sailors and civilians, in Great Britain and in Greater Britain in one common task, one great Imperial necessity laid upon us by the great God of Empires.

This assertion of a holy war motif was, of course, common to many preachers of the day both in Britain and Germany.[10]

But was "empire" the right word for citizens of a great Commonwealth? For Ruth, "imperial" meant "a brotherhood of self-governing communities."

> By Empire we mean Home . . . And our Imperial life is our family life. That is why patriotism is more than a faith with us. It is a fact woven into the fibres of our being . . . To every British colonist England is Home, and we sing "Rule Britannia," not as an idle sentiment, but as a religious song, steeped in religious faith, and aglow with religious passion . . . England is the God-given Home of our religious faith, and of our civic freedom; the loyal friend of struggling nationalities, whose flag means liberty to the slave, deliverance to the oppressed; the standard bearer among the nations for liberty of conscience, religious freedom, and constitutional government.

In all of this, Ruth clearly reflected the dominant contemporary Australian sentiment about empire. Anglican Archbishop St. Clair Donaldson (1863–1935) of Brisbane set out similar views in his *Christian Patriotism* in 1915: "I cling to my conviction that the Empire is of God."[11]

This "long distance nationalism" was the prominent feeling within the British diaspora. This ethnic identity was designed for those who were "precisely not English but rather of English descent" and allowed a

---

10. Moses, "First World War," 44–55.
11. Breward, *History of the Churches*, 264.

common identification with a homeland that had often never been seen.[12] The sentiment was well summarized in Alfred Deakin's oft-cited phrase "an independent Australian Briton" and was to remain a dominant feeling until the 1940s. Ruth's Methodist contemporary W. H. Fitchett (1841–1928) had written about *Deeds that Won an Empire* (1897) and in 1913 had published *The Romance of Australian History* in which the same imperial perception was promoted.

"Empire Day" had become an annual festival for Australians since 1905, and "loyalty to the throne meant loyalty to the empire, for this in part meant loyalty to themselves."[13] The day became "the focal point of British civil religion in Australia at the time of the First World War. It was a day which compounded civil religion and Protestantism rather than distinguishing between them."[14]

Only the radical *Bulletin* had mocked this imperial sentiment, calling the day "Vampire Day," but by 1914 this cynical description had been dropped. Campion observes that the day became "a Protestant festival," with one school inspector likening it to a sacrament, "an outward and visible sign of the inward and spiritual grace of patriotism." Catholics called May 24 "Australia Day," teaching students to embrace the sentiment that Archbishop Mannix would later define as "Australia first, and the Empire second."[15]

With memorable phrases and energy, Ruth did not hesitate to stress that this identity and loyalty fed into the call to arms for Australians.

> When a great military power, carefully choosing what looks like an opportune moment, invades neutral territory, despite its own pledged word and turns its big guns on a small and unoffending nation, there is only one course possible to the big brother of the peoples, and that is to slay the bully with its own weapons, or to perish in the righteous attempt. And such a War has the sanction of New Testament religion . . . Such civic duty is an integral part of the claim of Christ. Withdrawal from military service in defence of our country is tantamount to disloyalty to Christ, as well as to country.

Turning his fevered eye upon Europe, Ruth declared, "Thank God for the gallant little country of Belgium . . . And think of our own little country and pray that our country lanes and city streets, our churches and cathedrals

12. Young, *Idea of English Ethnicity*, 1.

13. Souter, *Lion and Kangaroo*, 138–39.

14. Piggin and Linder, *Attending to the National Soul*, 31. Discussion of Ruth's ministry as an expression of civil religion is explored more fully in chapter 7.

15. Campion, *Rockchoppers*, 83.

may not resound to the tramp of the devastating armies of the enemy." He exhorted his people not only to pray for the "men who guard the shores of old England" but also to pray for "the souls of the soldiers it is our grim but righteous necessity to slay."

Ruth was strongly criticized by the *Socialist*, which singled him out as "quite ruthless" in his comments about the Germans:

> There are men in the churches today who are willing to get up in their pulpits and incite the nation to wholesale murder on the slightest provocation . . .
> Before Mr. Ruth asks us all to fight he ought to be good enough to explain what the thousands of starving unemployed in this country have to fight for? This plutish preacher appears to think that those who work, starve and fight submissively for their materialistic master class are doing the will of Jesus.[16]

This blast against Ruth indicates that many in the working class did not support Australia's involvement, and it was the alliance between these workers with Dr. Mannix and his followers that created the major opposition to Australia's involvement in the war. *The Socialist* continued to attack "Ruthless Ruth."[17]

Ruth's subsequent "patriotic" sermons during 1914 continued to develop his imperial emphases. The second address, "Why Pray for Victory?" began with the text from 1 Samuel 10:24: "And all the people said, 'God save the King.'"[18] He continued, "We are Imperialists because we are Christian patriots. . . . If this were a war of aggression, if it were a repetition of our blunder in South Africa" it would be different.[19] Of course, Ruth admitted, the Germans pray for victory also, but "we are fighting, in the cause of humanity, for little nations, for the liberation of the race from the madness of militarism . . . fighting for the establishment of the kingdom of peace."

Ruth's third war sermon, preached on November 1, was "The Sources of Our Confidence."[20] He argued that the war was revealing "the religious meaning of Imperial Patriotism" and made the extraordinary claim that it may mean "a greater revelation of God than anything that has happened in the world since the crucifixion of Christ." Our men will not fail, he believed, and added, "There is in my soul an almost overwhelming home-sickness,

16. *Socialist*, October 30, 1914, 1.
17. *Socialist*, December 24, 1915, 2.
18. *AB*, November 17, 1914, 5, 12.
19. Ruth, like many Nonconformists, had been critical of British involvement in the Boer War.
20. *AB*, November 24, 1914, 3, 15.

chafing against the duty that keeps me here in comparative safety. I long to be at the front, to fight against the foes of home and country and Christianity." Ruth concluded: "We pray for a new vision of our imperial destiny, a new passion of reverence, a new spirit of sacrifice that we may not fail God or the race in our imperial mission."

The final sermon in the patriotic series was devoted to the theme "Church and Army," in which he also developed his familiar ideas about church unity and protested against the sectarian divisions that were "an open sore of Christendom."[21]

Ruth had no hesitation in encouraging Christian young men to enlist, to accept "the Christian duty of this imperial sacrifice":

> In the name of the King, in the name of Christ, the King of Kings, I call upon young men who are free to volunteer, to think lightly of what they at present possess, and what their future promises, and to fling themselves into this fight for national righteousness, international freedom and the Christian faith . . . Your fathers' country and yours, your fathers' God, your God, your Empire, your Church call you.

Ruth also believed, rather naively, that this terrible conflict would bring the "healing of sectarian strife and division . . . and though denominationalism dies, yet out of the ruin of the Churches, the Church catholic will rise." Rather, the war years intensified sectarian strife and division.

Ruth's support for the imperial cause was unfailing. On January 3, 1915, he spoke at Collins Street on "Wanted Men, Wanted More Men" and showed that his fervor had even increased:

> Oh, young men of the sunny south, fit and free, with enormous faith in your country, and splendid capacity for service, give yourself to save Australia's name from the slightest suspicion of underestimating the danger of Empire. Your King is calling, your country's calling, your women are calling, too: We want a hundred thousand men and the first that we want is You.[22]

The reports of the Gallipoli campaign and the courage of the Australian and New Zealand Army Corps (ANZAC) were read with both pride and tears. The day of the landing at a Turkish beach since called Anzac Cove on April 25, 1915, was to be commemorated, as it still is to this day. Ruth later wrote and preached regularly about the Anzac heroes. The extraordinary loss of life—some 8,141 were killed or died of wounds or disease,

---

21. *AB*, December 8, 1914, 3, 12.
22. *ACW*, January 15, 1915, 1–2.

and over 18,000 were wounded in that battle—was never to be forgotten by Australians and New Zealanders.

For Ruth and fellow-Baptists, there was increased prayer and support for the war. The church regularly farewelled those who enlisted. On June 10, 1915, for example, four men were solemnly commended in the lecture hall, which was decorated with striking recruiting posters. Ruth read a long list of those who had already been farewelled from the church, noting that several had already "laid down their lives for King and Empire" and that others had been wounded.

Naturally there were other local issues that concerned Ruth and his church. Sadly, Collins Street lost their "grand old man" William Hunter Selby Blake, who died in October 1917 at the age of eighty-eight. He had served as Church Secretary from 1864 for fifty-three years, and as Ruth observed, "The history of this church was written in his heart." Ruth also paid tribute to Blake as "an ideal minister's man":

> It would be impossible to exaggerate his care for the minister's comfort. He remembered the least little thing. . . . In the early summer and in autumn he would warn me against premature change of underclothing, and fearing that I might forget, would write me.[23]

The women of the church sprang into action in support of the war effort. By September 1914 the members of the Dorcas Society and the various sewing guilds had already forwarded three hundred pairs of carpet slippers to the Red Cross and the Lady Mayoress's Patriotic League for wounded soldiers.[24] After the war it was proudly recorded that the "Patriotic Sewing Circle" had produced 3,248 pairs of slippers, 143 pairs of socks, 20 sheets, 372 woolen comforts, 29 pillows and 51 cases, 50 cushions, and 27 rugs just for the Red Cross, with extra items sent to other agencies.[25]

Ruth's public activities were not restricted to the war question, although that intensified some of his other concerns. During 1915 he spoke in the Auditorium against the evils of alcohol and gambling.[26] Inevitably both these were linked with the challenges of the war. Evangelical Protestants in each state had pressed for temperance reforms including the six o'clock

---

23. CSBC *Monthly Notes*, November 1917.
24. *AB*, September 22, 1914, 10.
25. *AB*, September 9, 1919, 9.
26. *AB*, November 9, 1915, 3.

closing of hotels, citing the example of King George V who had taken a total abstinence pledge for the war's duration.[27]

Ruth also spoke about "the unholy competition and shameful tactics of the churches" which led to a public dispute with Rev. D. A. Cameron of the Presbyterian church. Ruth had proposed a joint control of home mission expansion by the denominations.[28] The *Socialist* seized upon "Ruthless" Ruth's criticisms and cheered his exposure of duplicate costs, "double the work could be done with half the money." Ruth finds, they happily noted, that Melbourne, Victoria, and Australia "chime in with the rest of the Global Gang" who are "always yelling for more money!"[29]

Doubtless this mocking was not exactly the kind of support that Ruth was seeking. He had received a more positive response from South Australian Baptists when he spoke at "an Empire demonstration" during their annual Assembly in September. He asserted, "All we have depends on the solidarity of the British Empire, every man, woman and child is personally involved in this war." He also inevitably pleaded for "denominational disarmament."[30]

Ruth still consistently campaigned for church unity. On May 28, 1915 he gave a resume of J. H. Shakespeare's book *The Free Churches at the Cross Roads* and could not help observing, "On the subject of 'Union,' I have been made to feel a voice crying in the Baptist wilderness."[31] However, the Baptist Union of Victoria during the Annual Assembly of 1916 held a conference on "What Baptists can do to facilitate Church Union," with Ruth initiating discussion.[32] He insisted that church union is not going to be achieved "by any process of elimination and the reduction of our differences to some irreducible minimum . . . it does mean the practical recognition and expression of the New Testament doctrine of unity in diversity, of diversity in unity."

He charged fellow-Baptists with having wandered from the New Testament and that their practice of baptism was not "Christocentric." He appealed to the example of John Bunyan's teaching about baptism as not being a bar to fellowship.[33]

Nor did Ruth soften his direct attacks on the liquor trade. When New South Wales Premier William Holman was in Melbourne he had

---

27. *East Gippsland Gazette* (Warragul, Vic.), May 11, 1915, 2.
28. *Argus*, December 11, 1915, 9, 11.
29. *Socialist*, December 24, 1915, 2.
30. *AB*, September 28, 1915, 8.
31. *AB*, June 13, 1916, 3. Shakespeare, *Free Churches*.
32. *AB*, October 3, 1916, 10.
33. AB, February 20, 1917, 4, 11; Bunyan, *Differences in Judgment* (1673).

commented: "I have never been able to see the connection between efficiency at the French front and the closing of a hotel in Little Bourke Street." Ruth asserted that this showed Holman was "deficient in Imperial vision, sense of solidarity, imagination, and soul."[34]

Speaking on "Christianity and the Gambling Evil" on October 31, 1915, Ruth attacked the New South Wales government for delaying its recruiting drive until after the running of the Melbourne Cup.[35] In the following year, Ruth was attacked by *Sporting Judge* for his continued opposition to the running of the Melbourne Cup.[36]

A different controversy erupted in December 1916 when Ruth criticized the popular play *Damaged Goods*, which was being performed at the Theatre Royal. Eugene Brieux's plot featured a main character wrestling with the physical and social ramifications of syphilis after an ill-chosen affair. Brieux intended the characters in *Damaged Goods* to point out social injustice—in this case, the way syphilis could be spread to innocent spouses and children—but, as Ruth argued, the only heroes in the story remain the men who also pose the greatest threat.[37]

At the same time, he continuously advocated support for the war effort. In response to a government request for a day of prayer, he asked if the government was prepared to pay the price of prayer. It was perfectly useless to pray to God unless they were prepared to do God's will. Prayer was no substitute for righteousness. He criticized the government for its lax attitude to the drink traffic and the "social evil" (prostitution).[38]

At the first celebration of Anzac Day in his church on April 23, 1916, Ruth claimed that "nothing could dim the splendid self-sacrifice of our soldiers or diminish the glory of the spirit of self-abandon that characterised the heroes of the Southern Cross."[39] He proposed that the best tribute to these Anzacs would be for thousands of men of military age and fitness to join in the fight. In following years, he regularly wrote and spoke on the Anzac theme.

---

34. *Argus*, July 10, 1916, 6.
35. *Argus*, November 1, 1915, 11.
36. *Sporting Judge*, November 11, 1916, 1.
37. *Register* (Adelaide), December 14, 1916, 4.
38. *The Age*, January 3, 1916, 8.
39. *The Age*, April 24, 1916, 10.

Baptists and the Lutherans

That the Collins Street Church was not extremely partisan in its war effort is suggested by its support for some Melbourne Lutherans. The church had welcomed a German-speaking Lutheran Church to use its lecture hall for their services since 1910, but once the war had begun anti-German sentiments in the wider community brought criticisms of the church.[40] The 1911 census revealed that nearly 33,000 residents had been born in Germany, and there were some 74,508 Lutherans in Australia, many of whom were of German descent.[41] Ruth spoke to some 2,000 people at the Auditorium in August 1915 on "Our Attitude to Germany: The Duty and Danger of Hate." His speech was described as "a thoughtful, telling, thrilling utterance."[42]

However, in 1916 *Graphic of Australia* attacked Ruth and the church with a vicious racist piece under the headline "Those Beautiful Boche Brethren who share Baptist hospitality," questioning Ruth's patriotism: "While the Baptists were worshipping the God of the Allies in the Baptist Church, the Lutherans were worshipping the god of the Huns in the Baptist Lecture Hall on the same premises ... our God is not the hun's god." [43]

Ruth vigorously rejected the charge, demonstrating in great detail just how "patriotic" he was, noting that he had two brothers fighting for the Allies. The Collins Street Church had been consistently loyal: "Before this paper existed, we had sent scores of men to the war." Ruth showed that the management of the Lutheran church had given the utmost proof of their loyalty to the Commonwealth. The incident was an unsavory demonstration of the community's anti-German hysteria at that time.

However, early in 1916 the German church had been asked to conduct their services in the English language, and special arrangements for the security of the property were made.[44]

Theological Controversy because of the War

Preaching on issues raised by the war led to more than one significant theological controversy among Baptists. Some found their convictions about Christ's second coming greatly stimulated by the war. Some twenty-five Baptist pastors in New South Wales, including leaders such as C. J. Tinsley,

---

40. See Fischer, *Enemy Aliens*; Tampke and Doxford, *Australia*, 177–97.
41. Beaumont, *Broken Nation*, 46–51.
42. *AB*, August 31, 1915, 13.
43. *Graphic of Australia*, October 6, 1916, 3.
44. CSBC Deacons' Minutes, March 20, May 15, and June 16, 1916.

W. Cleugh Black, G. H. Morling, and William Lamb, signed "A Simple Confession of Faith" since "the startling events now transpiring amongst the nations of the earth . . . have imparted a new and vivid interest to the study of prophecy." The war was "one of the fast multiplying signs of the end, and may immediately precede the great conflict."[45]

Ruth totally disagreed with this kind of teaching about the second coming as demonstrated by the provocative title of the book he published after the war, *The Advent Heresy and the Real Coming of Christ* (c. 1922).[46]

Ruth was actively involved in discussing the other pressing theological issue raised by the war: what was the eternal fate of those who died as "war heroes"? Again, was it legitimate to offer prayers for the dead? The *Australian Baptist* of September 5, 1916, posed the question directly as a headline on the front page: "Our Fallen Heroes—Where Are They?" This article really clutched at theological straws: most of those killed were young men whose character had not really been formed; some may have been secret disciples; the danger of imminent death had changed others just before they died. "We dare not doubt that these young heroes, and men of riper years, who 'dying make us rarer gifts than gold,' are now forever freed from sin and sorrow, and safe in the keeping of God their Creator."[47] It was even suggested that "perhaps they minister to those left on earth, their dear ones whose loneliness and grief live through the weary days?"[48]

That these views were not seriously challenged in the pages of the denominational paper suggests that the question was too raw and painful for discussion. Ruth, however, had a clear and consistent theology, a perspective on death that he had long articulated, which he developed in a series of sermons in 1918 and which was published after the war as *The Progress of Personality after Death.*[49]

Ruth had insisted, "I do not subscribe to the idea that death on the battlefield is a passport to heaven. I hold that death is merely an event in consciousness, that it is 'but a bend in the road of life.'"[50] In an Auditorium address on March 26, 1916, he had argued that Catholics did not have a monopoly on the idea of praying for the dead, although he refuted "the commercialised use of prayer." The spiritual experience should not be denied: "There is no principle, precept or example in the New Testament

45. *AB*, September 15, 1914, 2.
46. Ruth, *Advent Heresy*.
47. The quotation is from Rupert Brooke's poem, "The Dead" (1914).
48. *AB*, September 5, 1916, 1, 8. See Manley, *From Woolloomooloo*, 414–17.
49. Ruth, *Progress of Personality*.
50. *AB*, January 21, 1919, 1.

that precludes that experience. Everything that makes it reasonable to pray for the living makes it reasonable to pray for the so-called dead."[51] Such a prayer was a natural instinct; for example, he had continued to pray for his mother after her death.

Again, at the Auditorium on August 12, 1917, he spoke on "Purgatory and Prayers for the Dead." He argued that there was a great truth underlying the papal doctrine of purgatory and that Protestants would need to forget "the saccharine selfishness of some of your Sankey hymns and your Glory songs" if they were to know the truth.[52] Ruth provocatively argued that the basic ideas about purgatory were correct: life survives death, continuity is preserved, the communion of saints is not suspended beyond the grave, and those on earth may maintain spiritual fellowship with those who have died.

Ruth admitted that many evangelicals would want to insist that a person's spiritual destiny is fixed at death. "A man with a beautiful evangelical smile says, 'There is no repentance in the grave.' There is something wrong either with the statement or the smile—if the statement is true, he should never smile again." He recalled the text often cited in such discussions, "Shall not the judge of all the earth do right?" (Gen 18:25).

Ruth's advice was positive:

> You may pray, yes, you may pray for your friend so suddenly called into the unknown in just such fashion as you would pray if he were here. For our prayers, at best, are but wishes referred to God, and we have no right to assume that God has finished with any man when He has called him or permitted him to pass death's portal. Because personality persists, prayer is reasonable, and there is endless progress beyond the grave.[53]

Some Baptists were troubled by this positive analysis of the principles underlying the Catholic doctrine of purgatory and the practice of praying for the dead. Ruth claimed that he had been criticized by some Protestants as "a Jesuit in disguise."[54] William Lamb (1868–1944), pastor at Burton Street Baptist Church in Sydney and a devoted advocate of Second Adventism, attacked Ruth's teaching in a pamphlet *Purgatory and Prayers for the Dead. An examination of the teaching of Rev. T. E. Ruth's book Wake up, Australia!*[55] That Lamb should judge Ruth's Protestantism deficient is

---

51. Ruth, *Wake up, Australia!*, 24.
52. *Wake up, Australia!*, 150.
53. *Wake up, Australia!*, 156.
54. *Wake up, Australia!*, 46.
55. Lamb, *Purgatory and Prayers for the Dead*. For Lamb, see Ridley, *William Lamb*; Petras, "Reverend William Lamb."

an ironic twist for one whose reputation was largely to be built on being a strong critic of Roman Catholicism.

In a lengthy open letter in the *Australian Baptist*, Ruth explained that in his controversy with Roman Catholics his standard approach was first to discover what they held in common with Protestants, "to go as far as truth permits, to take pains to discover on what truth Roman error is based. It is not as easy as root and branch condemnation." Lamb's pamphlet of thirty-two pages was "a very serious libel against a brother minister" and Ruth forwarded a cheque for £25 to the editor with the request that the editor should give it to Lamb on the day that he demonstrated "any sentence or sentiment" from his book which showed Ruth's faith in the Romish doctrine of Purgatory. Otherwise, Ruth insisted, he should withdraw his publication.[56]

Ruth was probably unwise in this exchange. Yet it was especially sensitive for him, as Lamb had attacked his credibility as a Protestant. Lamb replied with an equally long open letter in which he reiterated his attack.[57] At the end of the year, *Australian Baptist* editor Packer reported that as he had never agreed to act as an arbiter, he was now returning the cheque to Ruth.[58] The whole episode was unseemly.

A year after the outbreak of war, Ruth held an "anniversary" service at the Auditorium on August 6, 1915, at which he preached on "Retribution, Restitution and Reconciliation." This combined his assertion of British Imperialism with a statement about appropriate attitudes towards Germany.

> There could be no discharge of the war until we had won on terms of peace based on international righteousness, international freedom, and international brotherhood . . . There was only one way of beating a bully who was also a thief. He must be thoroughly punished and made to restore that which he had stolen. There must be retribution and there must be restitution before there could be reconciliation.[59]

Ruth warned against hatred of Germany after full restitution had been made.

He commented that for the first fifteen months of the war he had made his pulpit "a platform for voluntary recruiting," but now he had been persuaded by "the cold logic of facts" that the voluntary system was "a grave injustice to the individual, to the home, and to the Commonwealth":

> Men physically fit and morally free, who owed the Commonwealth everything they had, who availed themselves of the advantages of compulsory education, compulsory voting and taxation,

---

56. *AB*, September 10, 1918, 4.
57. *AB*, September 24, 1918, 5, 10.
58. *AB*, December 31, 1918, 7.
59. *The Age*, August 7, 1916, 8.

> and compulsory police protection, and who compelled others who disagreed with them to join unions of various sorts under penalty of starvation, who actually lived by methods of conscription, had declined to apply to the Empire's necessity the principles of their commercial and political faith. They went on enjoying the resources and amenities of civilization secured by the shedding of blood. They had neither the courage to pay their debts to the community nor the honesty to cut themselves off from British privileges purchased by British blood—not their own.

A few weeks later, in the midst of a costly industrial dispute, Ruth urged the government to "save the country from the ruinous effects of a conflict between two forces of a common trade" in the dispute between coal miners and mine owners.

> In a crisis of this magnitude when every trade was involved in the life and death struggle of the Empire, coal was no more private property than the air or the sea. Coal must be got. If owners and men could not be conciliated, if compulsory conferences led down to a cul de sac, if arbitration was repudiated and industrial rebellion practised, the one thing that remained was coercion. But that would only be a makeshift. The final solution was neither in Socialism nor Syndicalism, nor in any scheme, schedule nor statute but in the disposition of owners and men, who ought to be above the solidarity of labour, the solidarity of capital, into the solidarity of society.[60]

Thus, by late 1916 Ruth had clearly adopted a stance allowing for the possibility of "coercion." He increasingly adopted a form of political Protestantism in the campaign for conscription and in support of conservative imperial politics. His imperialism was fused with a consistent and unceasing campaign against Roman Catholics and especially Daniel Mannix, the Archbishop of Melbourne. For much of his life, Ruth would be generally perceived as an unflagging anti-Catholic agitator and a friend of the powerful and politically conservative empire men.

"Ruthless" Ruth's shrill cry about the war, Mannix, and the Catholics, sounded from pulpit, public platforms, and in the press, is well summed up by his 1917 book, *Wake up, Australia!* That clarion call reveals much of Ruth's work during the last years of the war and in the challenges of the ensuing years.

---

60. *The Age*, November 27, 1916, 8.

4

Wake up, Australia!

Conscription, Archbishop Mannix, and the Catholics

IN BOTH MELBOURNE AND Sydney, critics increasingly castigated Ruth as a Protestant bigot, a sectarian import whose hysterical speeches were disruptive of civic harmony. Dubbed "Ruthless Ruth" by both the *Socialist* and the larrikin paper *Truth*,[1] he was, according to his Catholic critics, a Protestant imperial extremist who provoked sectarianism through unceasing attacks on their religion and their leaders, especially Archbishop Mannix. To his supporters, Ruth was a courageous hero who stood bravely for traditional British Protestant and imperial values against rabid Irish and socialist Australians—he was a religious warrior who was "not afraid of anybody."[2]

Questions suggest themselves. Did Ruth deserve the mockery and hatred of his Catholic opponents and other contemporaries? What made him such a hero to fellow Protestants? Had Ruth changed after he came to Australia? Did he remain true to those Protestant, Baptist, and evangelical beliefs that had shaped his life and ministry in England? Or was he unwittingly seduced into becoming not only a modernist in theology but also the public "puppet" of imperial and conservative political figures such as Herbert Brookes, his supporter, confidant, and—increasingly—his dearest friend?

These pivotal questions about Ruth, first raised by his years in Melbourne, remain crucial issues in any interpretation of his whole life's work.

1. *Truth*, October 27, 1917, 5.
2. Dr. Leeper of Trinity College at a farewell to Ruth as he prepared to visit Britain: *Argus*, March 9, 1920, 7.

Conscription Debates and Referenda

Early in 1916 Prime Minister W. M. "Billy" Hughes (1862–1952) was pressured to provide more troops for the European battlefield, but the supply of volunteers was inadequate. The reason for holding the conscription referendum was simply "parliamentary arithmetic." Hughes was unable to convince a majority of Labor MPs to support conscription, and as he persevered with the notion he was expelled from his party. The conscription debate was thus initiated in an atmosphere of division and angst: "War is the pasture of bigots and the solvent of principle."[3]

The lines of division about the conscription vote, as eventually drawn, were clear enough. On the one hand were Protestants, politically conservative with imperial and middle-class loyalties, who believed that "Christianity was the obverse of Empire."[4] On the other hand were Catholics, deeply Irish in composition and loyalty, working class and politically aligned with the labor movement.

Religion was certainly an important factor in political choice, as Judith Brett has emphasized:

> Australian Liberalism was built on a Protestant foundation: the virtues which underpinned Australian Liberals' claim to political power were Protestant virtues, and the vices they perceived in their political enemies were based on the vices of Protestantism's historic enemy, the Roman Catholic Church . . . British Protestantism carried a baggage of anti-Catholicism which made Catholics inevitable objects of political suspicion.[5]

The war intensified these divides. After the 1916 Easter uprising in Dublin and—even more—the vigorous suppression of the rebels by the British, Irish Catholics in Australia hardened in their opposition to all imperial concerns, even the war. However, Patrick O'Farrell has suggested that the surge of bitter resentment was not so much sympathy with the rebels or their cause but "from alarm and concern about the local implications."[6] Ken Inglis simplified the basic perceptions involved in the referendum: "To the zealous conscriptionist, the man who asked for a 'No' vote was . . . dangerously close to being a traitor. To the ardent anti-conscriptionist, the campaigner for 'Yes' could look terribly like a murderer. It was to be a bloody battle."[7]

3. Archer in Archer et al., *Conscription Conflict*, 34.
4. Inglis, "Conscription," 36.
5. Brett, *Australian Liberals and the Moral Middle Class*, 40.
6. O'Farrell, *Irish in Australia*, 263.
7. Inglis, "Conscription," 35.

The first referendum was held on October 28, 1916. After this was unsuccessful by a majority of 71,549 votes, a second on December 20, 1917, also rejected conscription with a larger negative vote (166,588). Tensions had greatly increased during campaigns for this second vote.

A referendum on this question was quite unique, without any precedent anywhere in the world, and so was a distinctively Australian experience. The conscription issue gave rise to a public debate "that has never been rivalled in Australian history for its bitterness, division and violence."[8] Many Protestants simply blamed the Catholics for the negative vote. They had seen the "Yes" campaign as a "righteous crusade against the power of the priests and the forces of Catholic disloyalty, and when it was again defeated, Protestant anti-Catholicism's belief in the sinister power of the Catholic Church seemed confirmed."[9]

Ruth is an excellent example of precisely these attitudes. Even before the referendum had been called, he had rejected voluntaryism and advocated conscription. When Hughes sought to engender a fresh enthusiasm for volunteers in June 1917, Ruth, who had campaigned for recruits as vigorously as anyone in the early days of the war, publicly declined to speak at a recruiting rally in the Town Hall. As he explained to the State Recruiting Committee:

> It is obvious that the voluntary system is cruelly unjust. The only recruits remaining to be won by the kind of appeal I should make are boys who have just reached their 18th birthday and I feel strongly that they ought not to be allowed to enlist. Fighting is a man's job . . . The best men have been sent out of the country, while shirkers are encouraged to remain. The present method of attempting to secure reinforcements is neither just to the Empire nor to the future of Australia . . . and I cannot make any more speeches in support of it. The time has come, either for the equal organisation of citizenship or for Australia to quit.[10]

Interpreting the results of the referenda is quite complex. The simple judgement, which many Protestants made, that it was the Catholics, especially after the Easter rising, who had swung the vote against conscription, is not justified. There was some major Catholic support for conscription, especially from the secondary and tertiary educated Catholics.[11] Alan Gilbert concluded that most Irish Catholics would have opposed conscription even

---

8. Beaumont, *Broken Nation*, 223.
9. Brett, *Australian Liberals*, 49.
10. *Geelong Advertiser*, June 11, 1917, 3.
11. Thompson, *Religion in Australia*, 61.

if there had been no rising in Ireland during the war. "Some voted Yes despite the rising. Commitment to labour politics, belief in the primacy of national over imperial interests, and concern about the possible conscription of Catholic teaching brothers were more important than Irish affairs in promoting many Catholics to vote No."[12] It has been noted that Catholic army recruits for the war peaked in 1916 at 19.4 percent of the total and fell by only 0.6 percent in the next year.[13]

Understanding the role of Australian Catholics in the conscription issue in the Great War is especially problematic.[14] In 1916, the Catholic Church took a neutral stand on the conscription issue and Catholic opinion leaders expressed, or were known to hold, views on both sides of the question. In the main, those views were based on considerations other than religious conviction. However, by December 1917, Catholics were concerned that leading conscriptionists regarded their religion as something to be reviled publicly without penalty, that their priests and religious brothers were to be taxed by the same politicians who were soliciting their vote, and the viability of their schools and seminaries was under threat. Members of the Catholic hierarchy and official church institutions, who had been silent during the first plebiscite, actively campaigned against conscription. Certainly most Baptists, like Ruth and J. A. Packer of the *Australian Baptist*, did blame the Catholics.[15] Ian Turner has argued that the vote of farmers, traditional conservatives concerned about finding labor in a good harvest year, was decisive.[16] Recent studies have suggested, however, that primary producers tended to be pro-conscription, and the rural vote against conscription could have been more from farm workers and other laborers.[17]

More importantly, the sectarian strife that was intensified during the conscription controversies continued unabated during the 1920s and 1930s and certainly "poisoned Protestant-Catholic relations as never before in Australian history."[18]

---

12. Gilbert, "Conscription Referenda, 1916–1917," 54.

13. Thompson, *Religion in Australia*, 66.

14. Kildea, "Australian Catholics," 298–313. See also McKernan, "Catholics, Conscription and Archbishop Mannix," 299–314.

15. *AB*, January 8, 1918, 10.

16. Turner, *Industrial Labour and Politics*, 116.

17. Thompson, *Religion in Australia*, 61; Withers, "1916–1917 Conscription Referenda," 45.

18. Piggin and Linder, *Attending to the National Soul*, 88.

Sectarianism in Australia

On the vexed question of whether Ruth was "a sectarian bigot," a crucial underlying question is the nature of sectarianism in Australia. Mark Lyons has simply observed that in Australia the term refers to the mutual antagonism between Catholics and Protestants, which was a regular feature of social and political life from the 1860s to the 1920s:

> Sectarianism was most obviously manifested in fiery speeches by sectarian champions, almost invariably clergymen, Catholic or Protestant, denouncing or ridiculing the beliefs of others and attributing to them complex conspiracies against the speaker's religion.[19]

Sectarianism is characterized by "an aggressive paranoia towards all those not of that faith," and Lyons elsewhere asserts that sectarianism has been a characteristic of Australian Catholicism since its beginning.[20] Sectarianism engendered sectarianism, and this was often manifested in political organizations of Catholics or Protestants.

Ruth's sectarianism has to be understood in this context. Kildea insists that sectarianism in Australian history derives its distinctive meaning from the fact that religious affiliation was generally identified with the three main national or ethnic groups that constituted British society: the English, the Irish, and the Scots. "In this period, sectarianism, though universally disapproved was frequently practised—always by the other, never by oneself."[21] Michael Hogan also concluded that "much of the dynamism in Australian society . . . has come from the competition for cultural ascendancy between different religious and anti-religious elites and that ethnicity has been a reinforcing factor."[22]

Similarly, in his discussion of sectarianism in Liverpool, of which Ruth had personal experience, K. D. Roberts defined sectarianism as: "the existence, within a locality, of two or more divided and actively competing communal identities, resulting in a strong sense of dualism which unremittingly transcends commonality, and is both culturally and physically manifest."[23]

So, the assertion that Ruth was a sectarian bigot needs to be seen against the general background of a community dominated by "sectarianism." An Irishman's enemy is a "bigot," but that same person is a "hero" to

---

19. Lyons, "Sectarianism" in *Oxford Companion*, 583.
20. Lyons, "Sectarian Catholics and Politics," 106–111.
21. Kildea, *Tearing the Fabric*, ii.
22. Hogan, *Sectarian Strand*, 290.
23. Roberts, *Liverpool Sectarianism*, 19.

imperial supporters. Incidentally, there can be no doubt of Mannix's social role as a hero: his popular support was extraordinary. O'Farrell links this with the Irish need for a hero after the death of the champion boxer Les Darcy in 1917, aged only twenty-one. He argues that Mannix fulfilled the role of a different kind of fighter: "It was his swinging of Irish pugnacity away from sport and into politics that made him so formidable and dangerous to the establishment."[24]

How much Ruth understood about the force and extent of sectarianism in Australian life is an important question. It is unlikely, despite his time in Liverpool, that Ruth was really prepared for the depth of sectarian antagonism in Australia into which he was thrust. To his last days, Ruth insisted that Mannix had opened his eyes to "the sinister designs of the Papacy." In that sense, then, Ruth's experience in Australia, and especially his encounters with Mannix, largely changed him into an anti-Irish, anti-Catholic imperialist.

Ruth, the Catholics, and Archbishop Mannix

Roman Catholic leaders such as Archbishop Kelly in Sydney had initially supported the war, seeing it as an opportunity to demonstrate Catholic national loyalty. Thomas Carr (1839–1917), Archbishop of Melbourne since 1886, also urged his members to "join heartily with fellow-citizens in defence of the mother country."[25] Ruth had publicly prayed for Carr and recalled that "a big, burly, and obviously militant Protestant" afterwards accosted him and said he was ashamed that prayers had been offered for a Roman Catholic Archbishop in a Protestant church. Ruth replied that he did not know the man but told him, "If you were dying I would pray even for you."[26]

After Carr's death, Ruth preached a sermon in Collins Street on May 13, 1917, "Lessons for Protestants from the Life of Dr. Carr."[27] Ruth praised Carr as a citizen who never preached disloyalty, although he entertained doubts about his successor on that score. Carr's personal qualities of "courage, courtesy, and charity" were commended to all Protestants.[28] Ruth would later cite this sermon as indicative that he was not really a sectarian.

Daniel Patrick Mannix (1864–1963), like Carr, was an Irish cleric and theologian from Maynooth College in Ireland. He was appointed coadjutor

24. O'Farrell, *Irish in Australia*, 263.
25. M McKernan, *Australian Churches at War*, 29. For Carr, see *ADB*.
26. Ruth, *Wake up, Australia!*, 55.
27. Ruth, *Wake up, Australia!*, 54–62.
28. Ruth, *Wake up, Australia!*, 62.

to Carr and arrived in Melbourne on Easter Sunday 1913, several months before Ruth. Mannix became Archbishop after Carr's death. Morag Fraser has summarized Mannix's impact: he was "for a half-century Australia's most dominant and controversial cleric, loved and reviled equally for his pungent Irish–Australian nationalism, political Catholicism and unsparing wit."[29] Campion observes that "the war placed Mannix centre-stage in Australian history,"[30] suggesting that it is "surely significant that in Australian historiography there are more books on and about Mannix than any comparable public figure, apart from Ned Kelly."[31]

Immediately upon his arrival, Mannix announced that he had not come to court popularity but to fight for what was right. As O'Farrell explains: "Confrontation, Challenge, Conflict: Daniel Mannix was this policy personified."[32] Mannix denounced the "terrible trio" of educational injustice, mixed marriages, and especially freemasonry, which he held was "a huge tumour growing upon the life and blood of the whole of the country."[33]

Mannix became the Chaplain-General of the Australian armed forces for Catholics, a situation Ruth did not hesitate to criticize, even audaciously suggesting that Mannix might well deserve the (German) Iron Cross![34] Mannix denied that the papacy favored the German cause, as some Protestants had claimed, and initially asserted Catholic support for the war. To add to the criticism by Protestants, Mannix was critical of the conduct of the war, condemning the "lust" to destroy Germans as unjust, and criticizing England as being too arrogant to deserve victory. His plea was for what he termed "a wider, nobler, better-informed patriotism here in Australia."[35]

Mannix specifically referred to the conscription issue at Clifton Hill on September 16, 1916:

> I hope and believe that peace can be secured without conscription in Australia ... I retain the conviction that Australia has done her full share—in this war. Her loyalty to the Empire has been lauded to the skies, and the bravery of her sons has won the admiration of friend and foe alike. There may be in the Commonwealth those who have not borne their full share of the common burden. But I think their number

---

29. Fraser, "Mannix, Daniel Patrick," 412–13.
30. Campion, *Australian Catholics,* 82.
31. Campion, *Australian Catholics,* 84.
32. O'Farrell, *Catholic Church,* 298.
33. O'Farrell, *Catholic Church,* 304, 318.
34. Ruth, *Wake up, Australia!,* 128.
35. O'Farrell, *Catholic Church,* 320.

> is comparatively small. It seems, therefore, truly regrettable that Australia should be plunged into the turmoil of a struggle about conscription which is certain to be bitter, and which will give joy to Australia's enemies.[36]

Conscription was the culminating point when all these suspicions, hostilities, and divisions came into sharp focus and led to "one of the bitterest political disputes in Australian history."[37] Those whom Catholics had long regarded as enemies, "the wealthy, the powerful, the militantly Protestant, the ultra-English" supported conscription. Mannix, with his flamboyant pugnacity, enraged Protestants.[38]

O'Farrell also judges that conscription created a discernible and important rift among Catholics. Those Catholics who were members of the establishment and professional classes were critical of Mannix and his supporters and "a good deal of anti-clericalism was engendered among Catholics of wealth and position."[39] Ruth highlighted this anti-Mannix attitude of some Catholics in Melbourne and Sydney by provocatively dedicating his book *The Catholic* to these men and to "all other Loyal Roman Catholics": Benjamin Hoare (1842–1932), the leader writer for *The Age*; Justice Charles Gilbert Heydon of the Arbitration Court (1845–1932); Justice Sir Frank Gaven Duffy (1852–1936); and Lord Mayor of Sydney, Sir Thomas Hughes (1863–1930).[40] Hughes and Heydon complained to the apostolic delegate Archbishop Cattaneo that Mannix was damaging the Australian Catholic Church and when nothing happened Heydon wrote to the daily papers denouncing Mannix for disloyalty to the Empire and for being untrue to the teachings of the church. Mannix duly attacked these so-called leaders of the Sydney Catholic community, declaring that they had no more followers than would comfortably "fit into a lolly shop."[41]

Mannix himself once declared that he became "a kind of lightning rod for all the abuse of the State of Victoria."[42] His capacity to enrage Protestants was unbounded. He became famous after the defeat of the first conscription referendum. Campion suggests that Hughes helped make Mannix, with his aristocratic self-image, into "a bogey to frighten wavering Protestants."[43]

36. Santamaria, *Daniel Mannix*, 79.
37. Carey in Schreuder and Ward, *Australia's Empire*, 206.
38. O'Farrell, *Catholic Church*, 328.
39. O'Farrell, *Catholic Church*, 322.
40. Ruth, *The Catholic*, ii.
41. Niall, *Mannix*, 95–96.
42. O'Farrell, *Catholic Church*, 334.
43. Campion, *Australian Catholics*, 84.

(By courtesy of the Bulletin)

THE SOWER OF TARES—(After the famous picture by Millais.)

"The Sower of Tares" (cartoon by Low, in *Bulletin*)

After the loss of the "Yes" vote in 1916 tensions increased dramatically during 1917, which Joan Beaumont has characterized as "the worst year" of the war. The tone of the conscription debates, she observes, were "more strident, irrational and hysterical."[44] When Mannix was reported (inaccurately,

44. Beaumont, *Broken Nation*, 263, 378.

it seems) in a speech at Brunswick on January 28, 1917, to have dismissed the war simply as "a sordid trade war," he evoked a hysterical response from the press, the public platforms and the pulpits of the country, not least in Victoria. Ruth was undoubtedly his most vocal critic, although many Protestant and loyal empire identities enthusiastically supported him.

Ruth thundered:

> Dr. Mannix is engaged in this country in a sordid, ecclesiastical traffic, destructive of manhood, destructive of patriotism, destructive of Christianity, and as a man, as an Englishman, as a Christian, I fling back into his teeth the offensive slander he has hurled against my country and the Empire that gives him protection. It is he who is engaged in a sordid trade war, a sordid trade war with the souls of men, with the free institutions of a free country, with the doctrines and principles of a free Gospel. He is fighting to reduce mental and moral manhood to terms of ecclesiastical machinery, patriotic politics to the level of sordid bargaining and Christian truth to a commercialised paganism . . . But there is one thing that this ecclesiastical commander-in-chief of a sordid trade war forgets—Australia is not Ireland. The average Australian is not priest-ridden. The Australian patriot is a British patriot.[45]

Ruth had begun the year with a spirited address on "The Commonwealth and Britain: A Plea for Christian Imperialism." He justified his intrusion into the political realm by insisting that the divorce between religion and politics was "as bad for religion as for politics and was neither scriptural nor sensible."[46]

Ruth took every opportunity to speak on public platforms to excited and enthusiastic crowds. No one could doubt the depth and sincerity of his emotional, religious, and intellectual response to Mannix and Catholics. During 1917–18 two books of his sermons as preached in the Auditorium appeared, both largely concerned with the Archbishop and his church: *Wake up, Australia!* (1917) and *The Catholic* (1918).

These were exciting days. Ruth claimed to have been threatened with violence and to have received hate mail during these years.[47] Claude Kingston, organist and choir leader at the Collins Street Church and later a successful theatrical entrepreneur, claimed that police, members of the choir and church officials had to provide an escort for Ruth on Sunday

---

45. Ruth, *Dr. Mannix as Political Commander in Chief.*
46. *Argus,* January 29, 1917, 9.
47. Ruth, *Wake up, Australia!,* 173–74.

evenings as he crossed Collins Street from the church to the Auditorium where he gave these lectures/sermons. With less probability, he believed that Ruth would occasionally leave those Sunday evening meetings and take supper with Dr. Mannix.[48]

Of course, Ruth also maintained a preaching ministry in which a wide range of topics were addressed. A weekly column called "Church and Organ" in *Punch* listed numerous church services in the city and suburbs, often adding witty or sarcastic comments. For example, in March 1916 Ruth spoke on "Is Ecclesiasticism Dead?" These perceptive comments were made:

> He is only talking about denominationalism . . . Really, the clergy seem to be mainly engaged in letting dogmatic Christianity down gently . . . The preachers fish for what will take—the topical. More political than theological. If the people don't want to hear about sin, it is kept in the background . . . Meanwhile, Mr. Ruth's hottest foes are in his own household—the Baptist.[49]

The columnist commented on Ruth's address on what Catholics and Protestants have in common (included in *Wake up, Australia!*), and *Punch* also reported that Ruth preached a series of thirteen Sundays on "Thy Kingdom Come: Christian Socialism":

> Doubtless this does not fit in with the ideas of a number of Baptists. Mr. Ruth has foes within the fold. The old-time idea was that the morning sermon should be expository, for the benefit of the faithful, but the evening one should be an appeal for the conversion of sinners. The Church seems to be going largely out of that line . . . Really, some preachers appear to say, "Only believe in the War."[50]

In 1916, he gave a series that included an address on "Capital and Labour," leading the *Punch* columnist to report:

> It is not difficult to imagine the opposition within his own fold . . . Mr. Ruth makes one think of Kingsley. What an outcry there was against him for his "Yeast" and "Alton Locke," and preaching which proceeded somewhat to Chartism. Very strict Baptists will say that Mr. Ruth does not instruct his own flock as he should. However, here he is, striking out after a fearless and

---

48. Kingston, *It Don't Seem a Day*, 46–47.
49. *Punch*, March 23, 1916, 2.
50. *Punch*, June 15, 1916, 2.

original style. Yet take our opinion that his absolute fair play will satisfy neither Capital nor Labour."[51]

When Ruth went on holiday early in 1917, *Punch* commented: "Much Baptist dispute over his preaching. Old School declare it is not Gospel. However, the majority is with him."[52]

On Being Anti-Catholic

Ruth was most emphatically a Protestant Anti-Catholic. To be anti-Catholic could, however, mean many things. John Woolfe has developed a helpful clarification of four different varieties of anti-Catholicism, "all of which have rich and complex and in some respects distinct, histories of their own."[53] Boundaries between these categories were fluid but they offer a helpful basis for analyzing the phenomenon. He proposed four categories: first, constitutional-national; second, theological; third, socio-cultural, and fourth, popular. Each one is relevant for the Australian scene, and at different times Ruth illustrated all four.

The first form was a perception of the Catholic Church as an extra-territorial power, aiming to achieve political supremacy sometimes thought to be by the papacy and at other times through the Jesuits. While this has a long historical sweep, it undoubtedly flourished in Australia during Ruth's time, especially after his initial clash with Daniel Mannix. Indeed, Woolf cites Ruth from his Adelaide days in 1944 as an Australian illustration of this category of anti-Catholicism even after constitutional-national anti-Catholicism had largely moved from the political mainstream. Preaching at Flinders Street Baptist Church, Ruth attacked the papacy as "an excluding caste, an ecclesiastical clique, a clerical combine, an aggressive monopoly, concentrating its resources on the conquest of the British Empire—and succeeding passing well in Australia."[54]

Focus on the perceived doctrinal errors of Catholicism extends back to the Reformation era and was of course the genesis of Protestantism. Ruth devoted considerable thought and energy to understanding and refuting many aspects of Roman dogma and practice. His books *Wake up, Australia!* and *The Catholic* are both excellent examples of this.

51. *Punch*, July 6, 1916, 2.
52. *Punch*, February 15, 1917, 2.
53. Woolfe, "Comparative Historical Categorisation," 182–202.
54. Woolfe, "Comparative Historical Categorisation," 188; Ruth, *Is the Papacy Anti-British?*.

From the later nineteenth century onwards, theological anti-Catholicism was increasingly secularized, and "tended to retreat into sectarian and fundamentalist *milieux*."[55] Once again, Ruth illustrated this tendency towards sectarianism (but not towards fundamentalism).

Socio-cultural anti-Catholicism focused on core perceptions such as the charges that Catholicism fostered immorality, especially in sexual matters. Criticism of priestly celibacy as unrealistic and unhealthy, linked with imagined sexual liaisons with nuns, represented this form of anti-Catholicism. Criticism of the confessional was one form of this attack. While Ruth did not condone the more salacious forms of this criticism, he certainly did focus on the role of the priest in the confessional and deplored a few tales of sexual and moral failures among Catholic clergy.

Popular anti-Catholicism covered a great variety of approaches, often oral and not printed. These could become entangled with ethnic antagonisms, and in Australia this was above all with the Irish. In Ruth's case, the alleged control by Sinn Fein was a recurrent and obsessive theme, especially during the war years and the conscription referenda. As Mark Doyle commented about Belfast, "Sectarianism was not a nebulous force that simply lay dormant until some evangelical minister came along to activate it; it was a way of thinking and acting that was rooted in each group's social relationships and shaped by the city itself."[56] This was as true for Melbourne as Belfast where in both places the Orange Lodge was active.

Ruth seems to have developed his strong anti-Catholic sentiments in Australia. That he illustrates all four categories proposed by Woolfe confirms that in the Australian context he became an extreme example of a Protestant and imperial anti-Catholic. This inescapable conclusion must color any interpretation of his total ministry in Australia.

An analysis of Ruth's anti-Catholic sermons and writings clarifies his approach and convictions.

Wake up, Australia!

Ruth's book, with the title drawn from the text "While men slept the enemy sowed tares among the wheat" (Matt 13:25), was a rallying cry against what the subtitle listed as "Sectarianism, Sinn Feinism, Sedition and I.W.W.ism."[57]

---

55. Woolfe, "Comparative Historical Categorisation," 192.

56. Doyle, *Fighting Like the Devil*, 80.

57. Ruth, *Wake up, Australia!*, title page. "IWWism" refers to the International Workers of the World, or "The Wobblies" as they were commonly called, a militant socialist international movement.

The publisher was "Modern Printing" of which Alfred Dunn (d. 1927) was the sole proprietor and who added an unambiguous "Publisher's Note":

> Singularly free from sectarian prejudice, broad in outlook, intensely patriotic, utterly fair to opponents, master of the psychology of the crowd, Mr. Ruth appeals to churchmen of every sect and loyalists of every political creed.
>
> These seventeen Sunday Evening addresses were delivered in the Melbourne Auditorium, seating 2,500 people. The place was crowded, and many hundreds of people on every occasion were unable to obtain admission.
>
> No more sensational book has been published in the Commonwealth. In the conflict in which we are engaged nothing is so sensational as actual facts.
>
> "Wake up, Australia!" is not published for pecuniary profit, but for patriotic propaganda, for purposes of enlightenment, information and inspiration.

Ruth dedicated his book to Dr. Mannix "whose 'Defaming of the Empire' opened the author's eyes to the sinister designs of the Papacy." His foreword noted that the addresses were printed "precisely as preached and bear the peculiar marks of the written word—a direct style, a personal appeal, and some unashamed repetition." But he still hoped that his printed sermons would "win the criticism of conscience; expose the danger of an uncatholic Catholicism; demonstrate the need of a really catholic citizenship; and inspire Protestants to set their house in order."[58]

His sermons reveal wide reading, a preacher's command of rhetoric and detailed study of Catholic teaching. He read several expositions of Catholic beliefs and attended Catholic public lectures such as those given by the Jesuit Father W. J. Lockington (1871–1948), friend of Mannix and an outstanding communicator and educationist.[59] Ruth's addresses were not really sermons in the traditional sense but public Protestant lectures. Ruth repeatedly condemned sectarianism, quite convinced to his own satisfaction that he was not guilty of this abhorrent charge. Undoubtedly, he protested too much, but at least he was aware of the inevitable criticisms that would be made about him.

Most of the seventeen sermons were preached during 1917, but a couple of earlier sermons were included. One was "a Protestant Appreciation" of Pope Pius X, preached in September 1914, shortly after the outbreak of

---

58. Ruth, *Wake up, Australia!*, 5.
59. For Lockington, see *ADB*.

war.[50] Ruth concluded by hoping that those who had been divided would now stand side by side to defend the empire. Ruth also included his 1917 sermon in appreciation of Archbishop Carr.[61]

Another typical address was his analysis of what Protestants have in common with Roman Catholics (preached in the Auditorium on March 26, 1916).[62] He began by insisting that Protestantism is something more than an organized criticism of Roman Catholics: "I am suspicious of people who think themselves good Christians mainly because they hate the Catholics." He described the Protestant disease, in a phrase he often used, as "the dissidence of dissent" and that the only cure was to be found in "a common and catholic churchmanship," precisely the argument that his earlier writings in England had proposed.

Pleading for "a sort of league of mutual understanding between the various sects," he recalled a friendship with a Roman Catholic priest in Liverpool who remarked that when churches forget their differences they made up "the church of jolly good fellows."[63] No such church appeared in Melbourne in Ruth's time.

He admitted that much Catholic literature enriched Protestants and that they enthusiastically sang some of their hymns. What he asked for was "the same charity and catholicity" to be extended to Protestants. "No church can monopolise God and Christ and the Holy Spirit. No church can establish an exclusive claim to mental illumination, moral grace and spiritual power."[64]

Ruth tried to identify what was common. Catholics taught baptismal regeneration but "baptism stands for spiritual regeneration" and he questioned if regeneration could be conditioned by any rite or was the monopoly of any church. Regarding "the Blessed Sacrament," Ruth claimed that Protestants "do not confuse the symbol with what is symbolised." Confession was a common spiritual experience: "I would willingly confess my faults to a Roman Catholic priest if he would confess his faults to me." With regard to prayers for the dead, Ruth repudiated "the commercialised use of prayer" but insisted that the spiritual experience ought not be denied to any soul.[65]

60. Ruth, *Wake up, Australia!*, 9–17.
61. Ruth, *Wake up, Australia!*, 54–62.
62. Ruth, *Wake up, Australia!*, 18–26.
63. Ruth, *Wake up, Australia!*, 19.
64. Ruth, *Wake up, Australia!*. 22.
65. Ruth, *Wake up, Australia!*, 23–24.

Sensitive again to the charge of bigotry, he commented, "I am not going to meet bigotry with bigotry."[66] This proved to be as forlorn a hope as Ruth ever expressed, but he concluded this sermon with a typical rhetorical flourish:

> Christ's catholics come from the East and the West, North and South, and sit down in the kingdom of the all-Father. Francis of Assisi and Elizabeth Fry, Newman and Kingsley, Basil and Booth, Augustine and Spurgeon; and in the comprehensiveness of history, in the light of eternal love, in the catholicity of the Kingdom of God, they laugh to scorn all ecclesiastical exclusiveness.[67]

A more personal sermon was preached almost a year later on March 11, 1917, when the conscription issue and the influence of Mannix had become apparent: "An Englishman's Impressions of Religion in Australia."[68] To describe himself in this way may not have been wise when he was seeking to win Australians to his perspective, but he showed good humor and a great affection for the land of his adoption even if he could never forget that he was English:

> Every Australian believes in the greatness of Australia and every Englishman, resident here, agrees with him. Indeed, he is bound to agree with him, if he wants to live here—the Australian's faith in Australia is apt to be aggressive. He may never have crossed the Equator; he may be deficient in standards of comparison; but there is nothing lacking in his local loyalty.[69]

Ruth praised the beauty of "the only continent over which the flag of a single people flies." Here is a fitting home for spaciousness of soul and solidarity of life. But, he lamented, we have "party strife in an Imperial crisis when no man should be for part but all should be for the State."[70]

As for religion, here too was confusion. About his own denomination he contrasted his experiences as a Baptist minister in England and in Australia.

> I was taught to believe that the Baptist faith was eclectic and catholic and never heard that claim questioned until I exchanged the geographical confines of the Old Country for

---

66. Ruth, *Wake up, Australia!*, 24.
67. Ruth, *Wake up, Australia!*, 25.
68. Ruth, *Wake up, Australia!*, 26–34.
69. Ruth, *Wake up, Australia!*, 26.
70. Ruth, *Wake up, Australia!*, 28.

the almost limitless land of the Australian Continent, and the British breadth and charity of theological thought for the tradition-bound obscurantism of much of the Commonwealth denominationalism. And during these three years I have never ceased to marvel at the largeness of its natural life and the littleness of its religious outlook.[71]

He repeated his familiar criticism about the divisions and competitive spirit among Protestants.

> Here is a country claiming to be free from the prejudices of the Old Land actually enslaved by a system of English village sectarianism, obsolete in England, deplored by all English Churchmen, repudiated by the most conservative of our fellow denominationalists in the Mother Country . . . that here, ecclesiastically and theologically, I must needs think myself back into a century, a century before Australian history began, means a greater somersault than I can turn. Your ecclesiastical obscurantism is so out of harmony with the advance of which you boast in other directions—that is the outstanding impression . . .
>
> Australian Protestantism is weak, anaemic, divided, negative and therefore, in practical affairs, sometimes negligible.[72]

He insisted that a "merely political Protestantism is playing into the hands of the enemy." Dr. Mannix is "the finest Protestant asset we have" but Protestantism lacks the religious character to use this. Protestantism in fact "often practises as virtues what it denounces as vices in Rome. It can be as mean and as little, as censorious and exclusive, as bigoted and as blind as the other party—and often is."[73]

Again, he lamented the fact that Catholics exerted political influence and they know what they want. Protestants dissipate their power in "the dissidence of dissent . . . Occasionally we know what we want and we get it . . . We wanted Six O'clock Closing of liquor bars, and Roman Catholics notwithstanding, we got it. And we could get anything we wanted if we wanted it badly enough to get together to get it."[74]

Ruth was surely inconsistent here. To suggest that if only Protestants would unite and give up establishing their competitive churches, if only they could emulate Catholics with their "concentration of energy and proper distribution of forces" they could have a greater impact is surely

---

71. Ruth, *Wake up, Australia!*, 30.
72. Ruth, *Wake up, Australia!*, 31.
73. Ruth, *Wake up, Australia!*, 32.
74. Ruth, *Wake up, Australia!*, 33.

articulating a vision of "a merely political Protestantism," precisely what he had condemned in Australia.

The Auditorium could not contain all who wished to hear Ruth's address on "'A Sordid Trade War.' Ecclesiastical Traffic and Australian Home Rule."[75] His attack was duly reported as far away as Belfast.[76] Ruth began in as provocative and direct a way as ever:

> Dr. Mannix is the kind of Roman Catholic that some militant Protestants think all Roman Catholics to be—which is unfortunate for Romanism, equally unfortunate for our common Christianity. The truth is that really religious Roman Catholics repudiate the political machinations adopted by Dr. Mannix ... Dr. Mannix brings discredit upon Roman Catholic religion by his persistent preaching, for political purposes, of what Mr. Benjamin Hoare, himself a Roman Catholic, calls "an offensive slander, as far removed from accuracy as it is from loyalty."[77]

The "sordid trade war" reference was simply a silly lie: "I regard it as the wild utterance of a wild Irishman in whom Hibernian hate of England is so ingrained that he couldn't tell a pleasing truth about England even by an Irish accident." Ruth pressed his attack by turning the "sordid" quotation back on Mannix: "What is his business in Australia? ... What is his political mission? Is he not the commander-in chief of a sordid ecclesiastical war?" With great relish he quoted Benjamin Hoare's claim that Mannix had "defamed the Empire." Mannix was not only anti-English, thundered Ruth, he was "bitterly anti-British; as well as anti-Australian, pro-Irish, pro-Sinn Fein, pro-Fenian, pro-Roman but in everything social, political and ecclesiastical, anti-catholic, anti-democratic, anti-Christian ... He is most malignantly militant."[78]

Encouraged by the enthusiastic cheering of his hearers, Ruth proceeded to claim that Mannix was not deterred in his lying description of the war as "a sordid trading war ... by the martyrdom of Australia's bravest sons, the bereavement of Australian homes and the anxiety of Australian hearts." His despair mounted:

> What is it that in this democratic country permits an Irish Roman Catholic Archbishop to repeat with impunity sentiments more utterly base and ingrate, and a hundred times more

---

75. *The Age*, March 26, 1917, 6.
76. *Belfast News*, May 28, 1917, 4.
77. Ruth, *Wake up, Australia!*, 35.
78. Ruth, *Wake up, Australia!*, 37.

influential in their anti-British, anti-recruiting effect than the statements of other men who have very properly been punished? ... As a man, as an Englishman, as a Christian, I fling back into his teeth the offensive slander he has hurled against my country and the Empire that gives him protection.[79]

He was not yet finished with Mannix: "As a Britisher, resident in this British Commonwealth, I protest against the importation of Irish hate in Australian politics ... Everywhere the priest is the enemy of Christianity."[80]

His sermon was so powerful that the journalist and publisher Frank Critchley Parker (1862–1944), a fervent pro-conscriptionist, published it as number eighteen in his series of "Patriotic Pamphlets."[81]

A second pamphlet in this series of pamphlets called "Mannixisms" was in fact Ruth's sermon of April 29, 1917, included in *Wake up, Australia!*: "America's Reply to Dr. Mannix, and Australia's Opportunity."[82] Ruth here took up the distinction that Mannix had once made that he was speaking as a private citizen and not as a cleric. Ruth retorted, "I do not keep my religion and my politics in separate watertight compartments" and as patriots, not as Protestants, he was defending British integrity against this "defamer of Empire": "Our patriotism is not a party political pastime, but a religious passion."

The reference to America was that they had been so convinced that the war was not a trade war as to form the Anglo–American alliance. The sermon included a detailed personal attack on Mannix:

> He eats British bread. He owes his life, his liberty, his learning, his living, to British institutions. He claims as his Alma Mater Maynooth College in Rome-ruled Ireland—and personally I believe Home Rule would cure Rome Rule. Maynooth College, in Rome-ruled Ireland, after having received a huge sum towards its building receives from £20,000 to £30,000 a year of British Government money for the training of Roman Catholic priests. Yet this ingrate brings into this free country his anti-British sentiments.

His conclusion was typical of Ruth in emotion and sounds all the notes of the Imperial call so that even "reformed Russia" could be included:

---

79. Ruth, *Wake up, Australia!*, 39.
80. Ruth, *Wake up, Australia!*, 43.
81. For Parker, see *ADB*.
82. Ruth, *Wake up, Australia!*, 45–53.

> We are called, called by the Anzacs who have fallen, called by the Anzacs who are maimed, called by the mothers of our men—that their sacrifice be not in vain—called by bleeding Belgium, called by crucified Servia, called by the martyred Armenians, called by fair France, called by reformed Russia, called by our own beloved Britain, called by all religious, political and commercial conditions of the Commonwealth, called by everything that makes us men, that makes us British, that makes us Christian, called to win the war.[83]

Yet a third sermon was published as a pamphlet, "Rome Rule in Australia." This was preached on May 27, 1917, as "The Archbishop's Bid for Political Leadership and the Pope's Temporal Sovereignty." The bulk of his address was to detail papal claims to temporal power and he cited several Roman Catholics in order to refute these claims.

Ruth also addressed the Roman statement *Ne temere*, which was the basis of opposition to "mixed marriages."[84] Again, Ruth made an emphatic appeal: "Australian citizens, it is high time to awake out of sleep. The temporal power of Rome is gaining ground in the Commonwealth."

For the fourth winter in succession, Ruth conducted a series of ten Sunday evening addresses. In 1917, it was called a "Mission to Citizens" but was in fact a systematic and critical review of Catholic teaching. Ruth insisted that his inclinations were "eclectic not iconoclastic," but the attacks made upon our "common freedom and common faith" impelled him to speak. In essence, he continued to question how Mannix could act in the way that he had: "On what doctrine of Divinity is disloyalty based?"[85]

The first topic discussed was "The supremacy of Peter, the sovereignty of the Pope and the rights of the people" in which he made the familiar argument that "neither Roman Catholics nor Protestants have a monopoly of spiritual privileges."[86] Ruth quoted Catholic claims that the Pope was "One Supreme and Infallible Ruler" and that "Peter still lives in the person of the Pope."[87] He replied that "The papacy is not Christian in its origin, in its history, or in its ideals."

Inevitably, Catholic apologists replied to Ruth. The Melbourne Catholic paper the *Advocate* identified the question of authority as a key difference

---

83. Ruth, *Wake up, Australia!*, 53.

84. *Ne temere* (literally, "lest rashly") was a decree issued in 1907 regulating the canon law of the church regarding marriage for practicing Catholics and concerned the validity of all marriages involving Catholics.

85. Ruth, *Wake up, Australia!*, 75.

86. Ruth, *Wake up, Australia!*, 74–83.

87. Vaughan, *Purpose of the Papacy*.

between the two traditions. Picking up on Ruth's oft-made critique of disunion among Protestants, the paper argued that this was due to "the revolt from the one Church that was competent to deal with all heresies . . . in the absence of authority, how can he hope to settle the differences which are the cause of the disunity he deplores?"[88]

In an address titled "The Authority of the Church and the Conscience of the Citizen," Ruth replied that the New Testament knows nothing of "the exclusive claim of the Roman or the Protestant Church." He insisted that notwithstanding the "lamentable and melancholy" divisions within Protestantism he still believed in the right of private judgement: "without the aid of priest or parson, the ordinary man may find the Word a lamp unto his feet."[89]

Ruth next spoke about "The priest in politics and democratic government," yet again lamenting "the schism of sectarianism," which he regarded as "the poisonous snake of political life." He then rehearsed several Catholic texts that claimed that only a Catholic state could expect total loyalty from Catholics: "From the point of view of civil law, of common citizenship, of democratic government, the Papacy stands condemned by its own claims."[90]

On July 15, 1917, Ruth turned his attention to the place of the priest in the church, contrasting this with the Protestant teaching on the priesthood of all believers:

> Who, with the New Testament in his hand, can find room for the official priest? . . . The Official Priesthood, by its celibacy casting a slur upon matrimony, by its confessional invading the region of sacred morality, by its presumptuous prerogatives exercising a dire despotism over everything divine in human nature, the official priesthood is a preposterous imposition, a corruption of New Testament Christianity, and the enemy of real religion.[91]

In the ensuing talks, Ruth tackled a familiar set of distinctive Catholic teachings, beginning with "The Blessed Virgin and the Emancipation of Women."[92] Lockington had claimed that his Church strove for the emancipation of women and gave as a model, "Our Blessed lady, Mary the Mother of God." Ruth replied that belief in the Virgin birth "is not declared anywhere in the New Testament to be a condition of salvation." He personally

88. As cited by Ruth, *Wake up, Australia!*, 84.
89. Ruth, *Wake up, Australia!*, 90–93.
90. Ruth, *Wake up, Australia!*, 97.
91. Ruth, *Wake up, Australia!*, 115.
92. Ruth, *Wake up, Australia!*, 117–28.

believed in the Virgin birth but did not regard it as an integral part of the gospel. By way of contrast, he quoted Pope Leo XIII, as Lockington had done: "As no one goeth to the Father but by the Son, so scarce any man goeth to Christ but by His Mother."

Ruth's basic response was to insist that every Christian respects and reverences the Mother of Jesus, "but the way to show it is to respect and reverence every other woman." He insisted that Christ taught equality of human beings and there is no such thing as "a woman's view of classics, mathematics, science or art . . . Women have equal capacities of thought, and in the imperial struggle in which we are engaged, they have been doing men's work, and have converted the strongest opponent of woman's suffrage." Ruth briefly expounded what he regarded as the role of women:

> While woman's kingdom is pre-eminently in the home, and her highest office that of wifehood and motherhood, while her chief glory is the governing of family . . . there can be no doubt that woman's emancipation is of the most far-reaching social importance . . .
> I call you women of Australia, women of Greater Britain, to labour for the establishment of a really catholic church that finds in all doers of Christ's will His brothers and sisters and mother.[93]

The next Catholic practice discussed by Ruth was confession, which he suggested was a common practice in the Bible and was part of turning to Christ. But the main thrust for Christians was, in the words of James, "Confess your sins to one another" (Jas 5:16); "it is a mutual obligation and a mutual benediction."[94] "I would not have the slightest hesitation in confessing my sins to Dr. Mannix—if he would confess his sins to me."[95] After this unimaginable possibility, Ruth concluded: "My friend, you need not set any priest or any parson between your soul and God. God is as accessible as the air."[96]

The next three sermons dealt successively with penitence and penance, purgatory and prayers for the dead, and "the blessed sacrament." The same combination of folksy exaggerations and detailed quotations from Roman sources was maintained. Penance, he asserted, was "a superfluous sacrament," and he summarized and rejected the classification of sins into original, venial,

---

93. Ruth, *Wake up, Australia!*, 127.
94. Ruth, *Wake up, Australia!*, 131.
95. Ruth, *Wake up, Australia!*, 134.
96. Ruth, *Wake up, Australia!*, 138.

and mortal as well as the doctrine of priestly absolution. "By his own conscience, not by the Confessional, a man stands or falls."[97]

Regarding the blessed sacrament or "the Holy Sacrifice of the Mass," Ruth sounded familiar Protestant objections, drawing on Martin Luther as well as others. He had an unusual personal story about how he understood the words of Jesus, "This is my body." He was traveling in a train carriage when he heard someone say—not to him—"So this is Mr. Ruth." He was not looking at Ruth but at a cartoon in *Punch*. Ruth continued his story.[98] He replied,

> You are quite right. But I am Mr. Ruth. And we both laughed at the cartoonist's clever cartoon and fell to discussing the advantages of mutual confession. I did not deny what he had said, not of me but of a two inch cartoon, 'So this is Mr. Ruth.' And I know what Jesus means when he says "I am the Vine" or "I am the Door"; and also when he says, "This is my body."

Ruth making confession to Jack Wren in *Punch*, 9 August 1917

97. Ruth, *Wake up, Australia!*, 149.

98. Ruth, *Wake up, Australia!*, 168; *Punch*, August 9, 1917, 8. The cartoon depicted Ruth and John Wren, the notorious confidante of Mannix, hearing each other's confessions, picking up on Ruth's comment that prominent people should confess their sins to each other. Another cartoon showed Mannix and Dr. Rentoul confessing to each other.

While this personal story may not have been the most apposite illustration, Ruth's main argument was against the "professional priesthood" which he insisted was contrary to Christ's teaching: "The whole Church was a royal priesthood for the offering of spiritual sacrifice" (1 Pet 2:5).

Ruth positively admitted that Christ's "Real Presence" was in the mass, "as it is everywhere." He confessed his own experiences, unusual for a Baptist pastor:

> More than once, I have watched the ritual of the Mass, and, forgetful of the foreign impositions of the priest, I have found myself worshipping with the people, just as once in a Mohammedan mosque in Port Elizabeth, all sense of the grotesque prostrations passed away and I was well-nigh overwhelmed by the feeling of the presence of God.[99]

Ruth also admired the way in which the Roman service extolled the crucified Christ but insists that "the theory of transubstantiation is made untenable by almost every truth there is."[100] He quoted Martin Luther: "There is no other baptism than that which any Christian may confer; there is no other memorial of the Lord's Supper than that which any Christian may make in obedience to Christ's command."[101]

The 1917 Auditorium series concluded with what sounded at first like a more positive challenge, "The Duty before Protestant Citizens." He admitted that the series had been a "duty, difficult and distasteful" and insisted that if in any way he had "violated the Christian law of equity and of brotherhood" he would unreservedly apologize.[102] He rejected any other way of dealing with an opponent, citing the threats made against him as an example of what he had endured in delivering these addresses.

Ruth then proceeded to list several Catholic statements, including one by Mannix as reported in the *Argus*, asserting the Roman Church's right to use such means as she deemed necessary for her purposes. This made Ruth launch into a critique of "the easy-going, tolerant trustful British Australian to sleep while the enemy sows tares among the wheat." He confessed to having been sound asleep himself until Dr. Mannix had wakened him by "the noisy manner in which he attempted to use British machinery to sow in British fields the Papal seeds of sedition."[103]

---

99. Ruth, *Wake up, Australia!*, 162.
100. Ruth, *Wake up, Australia!*, 165.
101. Ruth, *Wake up, Australia!*, 172.
102. Ruth, *Wake up, Australia!*, 173.
103. Ruth, *Wake up, Australia!*, 178.

Now he was sounding the bugle, "Wake up, Australia!" Wake up if you want to save Australia from becoming another Ireland. Wake up, Labour men and Liberals to a church that will sell themselves to the highest bidder. "Politicians, even Protestant politicians, can laugh at the scattered forces of Protestantism, but almost without exception, they fear the solid vote of the Irish Catholics."[104] Here lay the seeds for the formation of the Victorian Protestant Federation in 1918.

Ruth offered several steps that Protestants should take in the face of the Roman challenge. The first was a "revival of personal religion": A New Reformation, "overwhelmingly individualistic," was needed. "Our hope is not in a merely militant or politically protesting Protestantism, but in a positive eclectic catholic Christianity, in which we are personally sure of the Saviourhood and Sovereignty of Christ, of His Priesthood and Reign."[105]

The second insistence was ecclesiastical. "We must close up our ranks. The apostle of Church Union is the real Protestant, the real evangelist, the real missionary advocate. We are enfeebled by division, by spiritual declension, and our sectarianisms have alienated vast sections of the community."[106]

The third challenge was "corporate action for civic purposes. We want liberty for all, Roman Catholics included." He demanded that Australia enact a law to apply to all clergy alike, a law which provides for punishment for all damage done to the nation and its free institutions. He continued to articulate his vision and appeal:

> The care of the Commonwealth should be the concern of all our Churches. We want free men in a free Church in a free state, a fair field for all, and political favours for none . . . Let us fight with clean hands, with spiritual weapons, with swords bathed in heaven, all the foes of the common faith, the common hope, the common love of the redeemed sons of men.
>
> Let every Protestant citizen say—
>
> "I will not cease from mental strife,
> Nor let the sword sleep in my hand,
> Till we have built Jerusalem
> In Austral's fair and sunny land."[107]

This last stanza, adapted from Blake's famous poem "Jerusalem" and often sung as a hymn to Hubert Parry's rousing setting, shows how the British

---

104. Ruth, *Wake up, Australia!*, 181.
105. Ruth, *Wake up, Australia!*, 182.
106. Ruth, *Wake up, Australia!*, 182–83.
107. Ruth, *Wake up, Australia!*, 184.

Imperialist wanted to retain his truly Anglo sentiment even as he transferred his dreams to "Austral's fair and sunny land."

The cumulative effect of Ruth's sermons in this series was significant. His rhetorical skills were undoubtedly powerful alongside what *Punch* called his "characteristic sarcasm."[108] Protestant leaders enlisted him for their public rallies. For his part, Ruth's long enthusiasm and commitment to church union must have made him feel that this was his hour in Australia. Constantly reiterating his dread of sectarianism, his desire to be fair to his opponents by taking great care to quote from official Catholic texts, often at great length, and personally listening to their official spokesmen in Melbourne, Ruth still maintained a vigorous and unrelenting criticism of Mannix and his Irish Catholicism. Inevitably, he frequently descended into personal attacks and could not avoid the charge of promoting Protestant sectarianism. Ruth demonstrated that at heart he still retained his evangelical beliefs but whether any Catholic hearers or readers were persuaded to adopt these beliefs seems very unlikely, especially as tensions escalated dramatically during 1918, the last year of the war.

Naturally, not all were appreciative of Ruth's book. *The Truth* attacked him under the banner headline "Ruthless Ruth. Bellowings of a Baptist Boanerges" and accused him of "scandalous attacks on Archbishop Mannix" and "stirring up sectarian strife." The article began:

> There is a Baptistical Bible-banging Boanerges of a prating, pragmatic pulpiteer in Melbourne whose name is Ruth. This somewhat Hebrew-sounding cognomen does not prevent him from bawling forth to all and sundry from his pulpit that he is "British to the backbone," which, of course, he may well be. The British people are a very mixed people; and from days when the Romans first invaded Britain, and civilized the inhabitants, have been compounded of all nations.[109]

The "review" correctly noted that despite the promise of the book's subtitle there was nothing about Sinn Feinism or the IWW but "plenty of sectarianism . . . The blatant bellowings of this Baptist Boanerges suggest that he is making a bid for the position of 'Protestant Pope.'" The use of alliteration was clearly not restricted to Ruth.

The campaign in the latter part of 1917 leading up to the referendum on December 20 had become even more hysterical. This is well illustrated by "The Anti's Creed," which was distributed by the Reinforcement Referendum

---

108. *Punch*, March 29, 1917, 2.

109. *Truth*, October 27, 1917, 5. *Truth* was established in 1902 in Melbourne as a subsidiary of Sydney's *Truth*.

Council. A parody of the historic Christian creeds, it demonstrates the fears and hysteria of loyalists like Ruth. Significantly, Ruth was later to issue a positive creed for Australia, prompting the question of whether his hand was also shown in this Anti Creed:

> I believe the men at the Front should be sacrificed.
>
> I believe we should turn dog on them.
>
> I believe that our women should betray the men who are fighting for them.
>
> I believe in the sanctity of my own life.
>
> I believe in taking all the benefit and none of the risks.
>
> I believe it was right to sink the *Lusitania*. . . .
>
> I believe in the I.W.W.
>
> I believe in Sinn Fein.
>
> I believe that Britain should be crushed and humiliated. . . .
>
> I believe that treachery is a virtue.
>
> I believe that disloyalty is true citizenship. . . .
>
> I believe in handing Australia over to Germany.
>
> I believe I'm worm enough to vote NO.[110]

Ruth continued in the struggle against his Catholic opponents and all who sought to diminish imperial loyalty. Even more challenging days lay ahead.

---

110. Beaumont, *Broken Nation*, 386

5

Ruth and the Catholics in Tumultuous Times (1918)

RUTH WAS IN A somewhat despondent mood as he spoke in the Auditorium on the last Sunday night of March in 1918. The building was crowded as usual, but the war still had not ended. The Roman Catholic forces, led by Mannix, were even more aggressive in what Ruth truly believed to be disloyal attacks on British Imperialism and Protestantism. Even more depressing for Ruth was that no matter how often he pleaded for all denominations to unite in order to fight their common foes, nothing seemed to happen. He confessed, "One is like a broody hen sitting on a china egg."[1]

But as he detailed his vision and articulated his criticism of Roman teachings, Ruth's mood recovered, and he became more like a crowing rooster in his fervent response to Catholic teaching and influence. Certainly, they were tumultuous times in Australia. Ruth's book *The Catholic* (1918) containing his Auditorium addresses immediately received widespread support.

The sectarian atmosphere had intensified during 1918. During the St. Patrick's Day procession, Mannix doffed his biretta for a banner inscribed, "To the Martyrs of Easter Week" but failed to do so for the National Anthem. British loyalists were enraged and details of Mannix's action were repeated at numerous Protestant meetings. Mannix was also reported as having declared at a St. Patrick's Day breakfast: "Let Ireland

1. Ruth, *The Catholic*, 17.

bide her time; let Ireland watch her opportunity, let Ireland take it," after which the gathering sang, "God Save Ireland."[2]

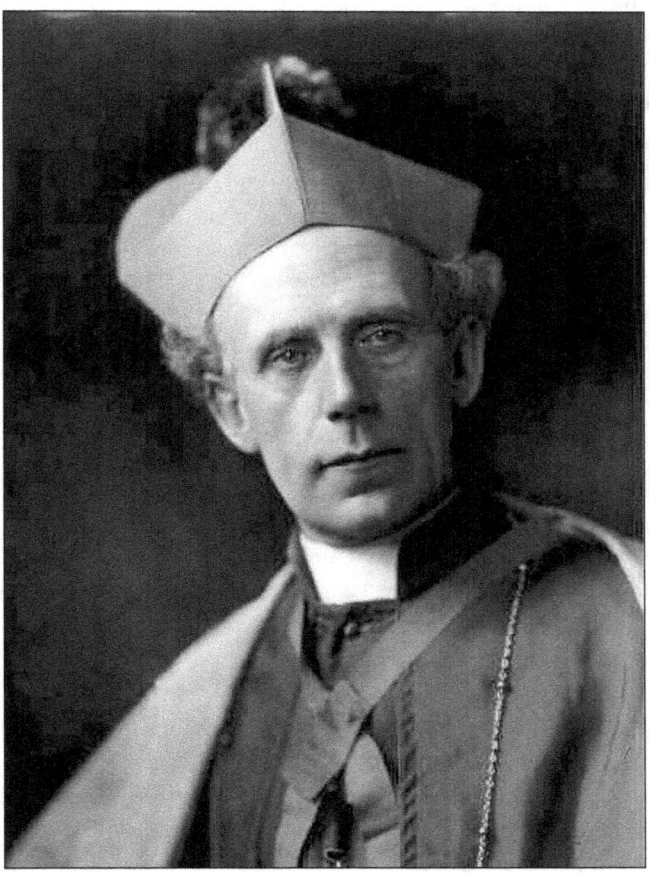

Archbishop Mannix

Dr. Alexander Leeper (1848–1934), Protestant Irish and Warden of Trinity College, University of Melbourne, was furious and wrote to the *Argus*, "How long are loyal members of the community expected to endure the insults which every few days are heaped upon them and the Mother Country by Dr. Mannix who shamelessly abuses the liberty he enjoys under the British flag?"[3] He joined with prominent industrialist Herbert Brookes (1867–1963) to convene a meeting in the Town Hall on March 21 to form

2. Rivett, *Australian Citizen*, 62.
3. As cited by Rivett, *Australian Citizen*, 65.

a Citizens' Loyalist Committee. It was a tumultuous meeting. Brookes arranged for Prime Minister Hughes to receive a deputation urging him to proclaim Sinn Fein as a disloyal organization and asked Benjamin Hoare, a leading lay Catholic, to move the motion of condemnation. Even so, Brookes felt that none of the speakers had stimulated the crowd sufficiently and somewhat out of character was so deeply moved that he made an inspired speech. He later recalled his fifteen-minute "oration":

> I use the words "oration" deliberately, since I seemed to be lifted up by some Unseen Power and became for the time being the living voice of that united and passionate demonstration . . . For the time being, and the only time in my life, I felt the thrill of the orator who was able to sway the crowd because he was giving appropriate utterance to their long pent-up feelings of protest against an ugly traitor in our midst. It was a glorious experience to feel yourself not yourself, but an instrument in the hands of that Power that works for righteousness.[4]

Brookes announced that he was leading a deputation to the Prime Minister at the federal offices and a couple of thousand supporters processed up Collins Street, Brookes carrying both the Union Jack and the Australian flag. Hughes agreed to meet the crowd and spoke from the roof of a motorcar outside the Treasury building after Brookes had asked him to proscribe Sinn Fein as an illegal organization. Brookes concluded his account, "I went home in the car with my wife and the flags and had a well-earned rest."[5]

Brookes subsequently became a strong supporter of Ruth, often providing him with materials to assist in the cause. Ruth was able to sway crowds regularly, just as Brookes had on that one exciting occasion. Brookes was not a member of any church, but his mystical religion was expressed in his reference to "some Unseen Power." He was, more importantly, fiercely imperialist.

Following these events, John Wren (1871–1953), well-known and controversial Catholic supporter of Mannix, arranged for a meeting at his Richmond racecourse when 30,000 demonstrated in support of the Archbishop. Ruth attended this rally: "I was there, and, incidentally prior to the speeches, heard myself discussed, and helped discuss myself."[6] He added that the crowd, including "many muscular men of military age," sang over and over again, "Glory, glory, hallelujah, Billy Hughes wants a phenyle bath."[7]

4. Rivett, *Australian Citizen*, 65–66.
5. Rivett, *Australian Citizen*, 67.
6. Ruth, *The Catholic*, 25.
7. Ruth, *The Catholic*, 13.

In response, Protestant citizens organized a large meeting on April 9 at the Royal Exhibition Building to declare their loyalty to the King. An estimated 40,000 empire loyalists attended, and many more could not gain admission. Some 239 policemen were stationed at different parts of the building, but there was only one small disturbance when several men were hustled out. Five platforms were erected throughout the building with special speakers at each one. *The Age* declared it was "the most remarkable gathering which has ever been held in that huge structure." Frequent outbursts of cheering "literally shook the building" and the enthusiasm was "simply tremendous." Almost everyone present held a Union Jack "and the scene when they stood and waved their flags was most inspiring." Rousing singing of the National Anthem was followed by "Rule Britannia," "The Red, White and Blue," and "Australia Will Be There." The Prime Minister in his absence was given three cheers and a round of "For He's a Jolly Good Fellow." Most of the speakers vigorously denounced Dr. Mannix and the Sinn Fein movement as well as calling for renewed loyalty to the imperial cause. The fiery Dr. Rentoul scorned the suggestion that the loyal movement of that night was sectarian: "It is a malign, dark, and disloyal falsehood," as the meeting was composed of "persons of all classes and creeds."[8] The charge of promoting sectarianism was clearly a sensitive issue. Brookes also spoke, as did several politicians, ministers, community leaders and politicians.[9]

Ruth had been delayed by "church duties" and could only get to the meeting late in proceedings but was impressed by what he did see.[10] His following Sunday evenings at the Auditorium were clearly focused and his powerful sermons when published seemed to give valuable ammunition to fellow Protestants in the struggle to which they were unceasingly called during 1918.

The Catholic

The Catholic, Ruth's collection of sermons and addresses, was timely and relevant. His method of attacking Catholicism was not of the sensationalist kind that rehearsed lurid tales (such as imprisoned nuns escaping from convents) but rather of the precise but at times tedious refutation of specific statements from Catholic sources. This was, perhaps, his way of trying to

---

8. *Argus*, April 10, 1918, 9. J. L. Rentoul (1846–1926), an Irish-born Presbyterian, was Principal of the theological hall at Ormond College, University of Melbourne, and a fiery controversialist. See *ADB*.

9. *The Age*, April 10, 1918, 9.

10. Ruth, *The Catholic*, 23.

avoid charges of sectarianism. The topicality of his work, especially the exhaustive references to Mannix, has inevitably limited its relevance as Protestant apologetic for later generations.

Ruth added five other talks to the fourteen given in the "Mission to Catholics" series. The first was the topical "Are Australians Sinn Feiners?" delivered on November 25, 1917.[11] Insisting that Sinn Fein simply means "ourselves alone," Ruth rebuked the Melbourne Catholic paper the *Advocate* for pretending that "Sinn Fein" is "scarcely more than a synonym for Home Rule," and that "the whitewash is very weak." Naturally, Ruth's main target was Mannix, who "quite openly avowed and advocated Sinn Feinism." Quoting from the *Advocate*, he showed that for Mannix the Irish policy was "to shake the dust of the British Parliament off their feet" and to declare, "You here in Australia are Sinn Feiners, though you do not call yourselves by that name."[12]

Ruth insisted that he was by conviction a constitutional Home Ruler, "but the men who have prevented Home Rule in Ireland are the men who are responsible for the Rome Rule that is the actual and potential enemy of the Irish race."[13] Sinn Fein is "sheer selfishness, utterly unethical and anti-Christian... utterly anti-democratic and utterly anti-social... anti-national and anti-humanitarian."[14] A characteristic appeal concluded his passionate address: "I appeal to the people of Australia to rise and tell the traitor, who calls them Sinn Feiners, that the truth is not in him, that Australians are not Sinn Feiners, they are Britishers, they are men, they are not fools and blind. They stand for God and King and Empire."[15]

On March 31, 1918, Easter Sunday evening, Ruth again took up the cudgels against Mannix in his Auditorium address, "The Enemy within Our Gates."[16] This was the strongest and most sustained attack that Ruth had yet made. He began by quoting a Sydney Roman Catholic paper, the *Freeman's Journal*, which claimed that Freemasonry was "the enemy within our gates" and suggested that the Labor Party should make membership of the Masons a reason for disqualification from the Party. While defending Freemasonry, Ruth observed that in a sense he hoped the Catholics were right: "The enemies of Roman Catholic control are the friends of all free men." Rejecting the jibe that he had "a Mannix microbe on the brain,"

11. Ruth, *The Catholic*, 1–12.
12. Ruth, *The Catholic*, 4.
13. Ruth, *The Catholic*, 8.
14. Ruth, *The Catholic*, 10–12.
15. Ruth, *The Catholic*, 12.
16. Ruth, *The Catholic*, 13–22.

Ruth tellingly quoted Justice Duffy, the Roman Catholic judge in Sydney, who had said Mannix "cannot complain if his fellow citizens regard him as an enemy within the gates."[17]

Turning his attention to the scandal surrounding Mannix at the St. Patrick's Day march, Ruth commented:

> I wish Irish and Scottish, Welsh and English would unite to honour St. Patrick and St. Andrew, St. David and St. George, in a sort of All Saints' Day, just as I wish Roman Catholics and Protestants would unite in the name of the common Christ to fight the foes of our common faith, and let brotherly love take the place of sectarian strife.[18]

Ruth pressed the authorities to act lest the politicians "fall into line" with Papal policy. He described the situation as he understood it:

> They let the Papal sword flash over the Commonwealth and State Governments. They let the Papal party run some of the departments of civil service in some of which "No Protestants need apply"—Holy Mother Church must be considered. They permit Roman Catholics to parade the public streets in their sectarian regalia, and prevent the same privilege being granted to the Loyal Orange Institution.[19]

Ruth became even more overtly political when he insisted:

> British Parliamentary positions should not be open to anti-Britishers, British public service is for British public servants. We want union, comprehension, brotherhood, common struggle. If they want Sinn Feinism, let them pay its proper price, and clear out of British employment, public and private.[20]

Twenty thousand copies of this address were distributed at the Loyalist Demonstration at the Exhibition Building.[21]

Ruth's sermon on April 28, 1918, was delivered after the exciting rival meetings held by the Catholics and then the loyalists at the Exhibition Building. His question continued the political emphasis by asking "Is the Papacy Anti-British?"[22]

---

17. Ruth, *The Catholic*, 14.
18. Ruth, *The Catholic*, 17.
19. Ruth, *The Catholic*, 20.
20. Ruth, *The Catholic*, 21.
21. *AB*, May 14, 1918, 9.
22. Ruth, *The Catholic*, 23–33.

Ruth also had to answer the criticism that his comments about public service positions being open only to British supporters amounted to a Catholic boycott. Ruth's response was that he had not proposed a Catholic boycott but one only for those who were anti-British and, of course, as he admitted, many Catholics were loyal. "On the one hand," he insisted, "no man must be penalised for his religion," but no man has any right "to make his religion a cloak for political treason." He clarified his demands: "I would insist on every man entering any branch of the Public Service, taking an oath of allegiance to King George and make double allegiance impossible."[23]

A somewhat different atmosphere was found in another inclusion in *The Catholic*, an address he had given in the Hawthorn Town Hall for the Baptist Union on "Protestantism—Its modern application."[24] Protestantism was "rooted in Patriotism," and, he asserted, "We say 'No' to Rome because we have said 'Yes' to Christ." The Protestant ideal was a free man in a free state and a free church.

By this stage of his thinking, despite his "protestations," Ruth had undoubtedly embraced a political Protestantism and did not hesitate to detail what the modern application of Protestantism might look like in Australia.

> If it is right to allow Roman Catholics in their sectarian regalia to parade the streets, it is wrong to prevent the procession of the Loyal Orange Lodge.
>
> If it is right to insist on the inspection of factories and workshops, it is wrong to prevent the public inspection of sectarian trading institutions.
>
> If it is right to make tradesmen pay rates, it is wrong to grant sectarian tradesmen rate concessions.
>
> If it is right for society to elect its own legislators to make the laws for the community, it is wrong for any section of the community to declare the marriage law null and void.
>
> If it is right for the State to devise and manage its own system of education, it is wrong for any sect to keep the Bible out of the schools and declare these schools to be "secular, Godless and pagan."
>
> If it is right for a man to receive his education in a British-endowed institution, it is wrong of that man to conduct an anti-British campaign in a British community.

---

23. Ruth, *The Catholic*, 33.
24. Ruth, *The Catholic*, 34–42.

> If it is right for men to declare that their policy is "to shake the dust of the British parliament off their feet," it is wrong for such men to keep their feet on British soil.
>
> If it is right to imprison the agitators of the Independent Workers of the World, it is wrong to grant license to the impudent wreckers of the empire.
>
> If it is right to prevent the display of Sinn Fein emblems or the wearing of a Sinn Fein button, it is wrong to allow men publicly to declare they are "Sinn Fein to the backbone" and advocate the policy of sedition.
>
> If it is right to insist that King George V is King of the British Empire, it is wrong to allow Benedict XV to take precedence over the King.
>
> If it is right to say Australian civil service is British civil service, then it is wrong to admit to our civil service men who acknowledge the Sovereignty of a foreign potentate.[25]

The last of the extra sermons that Ruth added to his Catholic series was titled, "The Real Issue—Pope or King?"[26] The answer to this rhetorical question, like many another preacher's, was entirely predictable. Full of extensive quotations from a wide range of sources, which included British politician Gladstone, historian W. E. H. Lecky, Thomas Aquinas, Pope Leo XIII, and (inevitably) Mannix to answer his own question, "If this is a British country, let the British king reign!"[27]

What was unusual about the Auditorium series in the winter of 1918 was that Ruth conducted it in conjunction with the Roman Catholic series of "Talks to Non-Catholics" at the Cathedral Hall. He had been invited to attend each session and responded with his own series, "A Mission to Catholics (with a Small 'c')." This title, he explained, was because he hoped to appeal to "the common citizens, the cosmopolitan crowd, the interdenominational adherents" of his Auditorium crowd such as the lady who told him, "Every day I pray the Blessed Mother of God to sustain you in your service."[28]

Thus his first address asked, "Who Are the Non-Catholics?" After listening to Mannix explain the purpose of the Cathedral talks, Ruth argued that Roman Catholics stand in urgent need of a series of simple talks concerning Protestantism. He concluded in characteristic fashion:

25. Ruth, *The Catholic*, 40–41.
26. Ruth, *The Catholic*, 43–53.
27. Ruth, *The Catholic*, 53.
28. Ruth, *The Catholic*, 55.

> O, churchmen of many sects, churchmen with catholic creed, churchmen with a catholic gospel, churchmen who worship a catholic Christ, pray unceasingly and labour with both hands earnestly to build up in this country a genuine catholic Church worthy of the catholic Christ, worthy the Commonwealth and worthy this twentieth century of grace.[29]

Succeeding weeks saw a familiar range of topics covered. Simply to list the remaining titles gives an accurate depiction of their tone and content.

2. The Catholic Christ and the Un-Catholic Church
3. Is Romanism Rational?
4. Roman Pewter and Catholic Gold
5. Jesuitical Camouflage
6. Roman Cisterns and the Open Sea
7. Confession and the Confessional
8. Where is the One Holy Catholic Church?
9. The Nearest Priest and Peter
10. England as "Mary's Dowry"
11. The Mass: Religiously, Commercially, Politically
12. Saints, Relics and Indulgences
13. Has Rome the Right of Censorship over the English Bible?
14. Australia's Need of a New Reformation

Ruth linked his comments with reports of what the Catholic missioners had claimed, observations from fellow-attendees, or accounts in the press. On one occasion Ruth proposed a parody of the famous 1 Corinthians 13:

> Though I speak with the tongues of men and of angels, and I am not a Roman Catholic, I am become as sounding brass or a tinkling cymbal.
> And though I have the gift of prophecy, and understand all mysteries and all knowledge; and though I have all faith, so that I could remove mountains, and am not a Roman Catholic, I am nothing . . .
> Roman Catholicism never faileth . . .[30]

---

29. Ruth, *The Catholic*, 63.
30. Ruth, *The Catholic*, 68.

Ruth claimed that he had heard two young ladies discussing his mission. The conversation went something like this, Ruth reported. "'Have you heard him?' 'No, Have you?' 'Yes . . . Nothing much to look at. Nothing much to talk to. But when he once gets going—my word!'"[31]

In his attack on "Jesuitical Camouflage," Ruth defended the Anglican Archbishop of Melbourne, who had used the term "Jesuitical" as meaning "that the end justified the means" in a reference to Catholic defense of gambling. The Jesuit Father Lockington had attacked him for this, and Ruth in turn defended the term "Jesuitical" at first by quoting literary figures, such as Milton and Carlyle, who had used it.[32]

In some of these addresses, Ruth inevitably repeated subjects he had raised in *Wake up, Australia!* However, the direct reporting of the Catholic lectures and Ruth's often sarcastic responses must have made the issues much livelier and more topical for his hearers.

Ruth had no problem in identifying remarkable claims made by the Catholic lecturers such as Father Dwyer who asserted what Ruth described as "utterly naked and unashamed paganism":

> Angels must weep when, day by day, thousands of baby souls fly in clouds to the gates of God's city, and are turned away because, through the crime of their murderers, they are not able to get the robe of baptism, without which there is no entrance into heaven.[33]

Again, he quoted from the Catholic paper the *Advocate*, which told about a newborn baby, in danger of dying, so that two Catholic nurses baptized it and named it "Daniel Mannix." A non-Catholic nurse later again baptized the infant declaring, "You are all right now!" However, it emerged that the baby was a girl!

How could anyone think, Ruth thundered, that God was "the slave of a sacramental system"?[34] Ruth did not hesitate to insist again and again that the Catholics—and, he added, the Anglo–Catholics and the Mormons—claimed to be the one true church. Rome's method of achieving church union, he suggested, was "union by anathema."[35]

---

31. Ruth, *The Catholic*, 73.
32. Ruth, *The Catholic*, 100.
33. Ruth, *The Catholic*, 131.
34. Ruth, *The Catholic*, 135.
35. Ruth, *The Catholic*, 139.

To emphasize this theology, Ruth quoted a long poem, drawn from the imagery of Revelation 21, which proclaimed a universalism that appealed to him:

> Are there not twelve gates to heaven,
> > North and south and east and west?
> May not they of every doctrine,
> > Enter that eternal rest?
> Every kindred, clime and colour,
> > Every creed and tenet too—
> Shall they not be represented
> > With the dogma taught by you?

The poem continues to include various denominations as well as other religions:

> Amethyst of Wesleyan beauty,
> > Pearl of Presbyterian hue,
> Topaz washed in Baptist waters,
> > Emerald of the Pagan, too.[36]

Ruth greatly appreciated what Phillips Brooks had called "the fantastic absurdity of Apostolic Succession" and the claim that there was an unbroken succession of 274 Popes to Peter. Ruth launched into a typical barrage of questions:

> Did Peter preach that innocent babies must wear the robe of baptism or be forever turned away in clouds from God's city? Did Peter ever administer the sacrament of infant baptism? ... Did Peter ever preach the ecclesiastical celibacy of the clergy? If so, what did Peter's wife's mother say?[37]

The presentation about Mary by Father Boylan, another Catholic lecturer, Ruth thought was as devout as any, and he resolved not to criticize the religious reality that he had experienced. His response rather was to state that he did not believe that God has a mother, "but I do believe God is a Mother ... I reverence the Mother of Jesus who teaches us to reverence all the mothers of the race."[38]

---

36. Ruth, *The Catholic*, 142.
37. Ruth, *The Catholic*, 153.
38. Ruth, *The Catholic*, 157.

What angered Ruth was a claim that Mary had been presented with England as her "Dowry," a claim that he found stated in a Catholic text (he had been careful to quote Roman Catholics for all his "authoritative statements"). Roman Catholics were praying for the recovery of "Mary's Dower," a concept which was interpreted as the intended papal conquest of Britain. He despaired of what had been described as "The Anglophobia of the Vatican."[39]

Ruth was on more familiar grounds when he rejected the Catholic understanding of the Mass. He suggested that Protestants are not as ignorant of Roman Catholicism as Roman Catholics are of Protestantism. Ruth claimed that between three hundred and five hundred Catholics attended his services in the Auditorium.[40] He then proceeded to reject Roman dogma about transubstantiation and other aspects of that sacrament as they understood it. He took special delight in rejecting the "sordid" idea that one of the purposes of the Mass was to help souls in Purgatory.[41]

He rejected the veneration of saints, relics, and especially the practice of indulgences, the commercialization of which was the spark that began the Reformation. In a style reminiscent of Erasmus, Ruth told the story about a mouse in France that had eaten the holy wafer and has since been venerated as the "Holy Mouse."[42]

After thirteen weeks in succession, Ruth finally came to the last of the Catholic lectures. "I thought I had lost my very power of surprise," Ruth commented, but Father Merner's talk on "The Church and the Bible" was "the most arrogant of the series."[43] Merner claimed that "the Roman Catholic Church wrote the Bible, has exclusive authority to interpret it and has the Divine Copyright." The Bible was in the hands of the priests and once again Ruth found any number of Catholic authorities to support that claim. Ruth insisted that the real witness to God is not an infallible book nor an infallible Church but "something within, the actual experience of the soul."[44]

A New Reformation for Australia?

After the conclusion of the rival Roman Catholic addresses Ruth preached his last response on September 1, 1918, with "Australia's Need of a New

39. Ruth, *The Catholic*, 164.
40. Ruth, *The Catholic*, 168.
41. Ruth, *The Catholic*, 172.
42. Ruth, *The Catholic*, 181.
43. Ruth, *The Catholic*, 193.
44. Ruth, *The Catholic*, 198.

Reformation."⁴⁵ In this, he attacked Mannix's ridicule of the "Strength of Empire" movement.⁴⁶

What especially offended Ruth and other Protestants was the accusation by Lockington that there were people in the community "who wanted to teach children in arms the secrets of the brothel." Ruth retorted,

> If people want to teach the secrets of the brothel, they might borrow from some celibate Father Confessor his Liguori's "Moral Theology," only that it is kept in Latin because it is so licentious that it could not be published in the common tongue even by the gutter press of the Commonwealth.⁴⁷

Ruth's main argument for a "New Reformation" was that the influence of the papacy seemed to be everywhere. This reformation was not so much theological as political—although, as Luther found, the two cannot easily be separated.

> The red flag no longer flies over the Trades Hall, but, as a matter of fact, unseen but nevertheless real, the Papal flag is flying there, and practically over every British institution in this Southern land. The Pope takes precedence to the King; the Papal flag to the Union Jack; and "God save Ireland" to "God save the King."⁴⁸

The papal flag flies over Australian homes because of its marriage laws. It flies over Australian schools "because Mannix claims the right to dictate to the State Schools as to their reading books." It flies over the Australian newspaper offices where "Rome has enormous influence." Australian libraries and Australian Houses of Parliaments are all under this foreign influence.⁴⁹

Ruth articulated his plans to tear down this obnoxious flag.

> If any priest dares to say that any man or woman married according to Australian laws is living in adultery, let that priest be severely punished by Australian law.
>
> If Catholic schools will not cease making their arrogant demands, I believe the time has come to prevent more private schools being built. Democracy demands education, education is compulsory. Good citizenship ought to prevent any Sinn

---

45. Ruth, *The Catholic*, 203–25.
46. Ruth, *The Catholic*, 205.
47. Ruth, *The Catholic*, 204.
48. Ruth, *The Catholic*, 209.
49. Ruth, *The Catholic*, 209–11.

Fein policy in the education of children. Education ought to be catholic with a small "c" and not be sectarian at all.⁵⁰

He repeated his earlier proposals:

> Every person entering the Australian Public Service in any capacity whatever, in municipal affairs, in trading concerns, in the teaching or any other profession, should take an oath of allegiance to the Throne and Empire, and absolutely repudiate any double allegiance, and all institutions of every kind, charitable and religious, must be open to inspection for the sake of democracy.⁵¹

How Ruth imagined this would all be achieved is not stated, but clearly it was a political agenda, clothed in imperial and religious language. His rhetorical conclusion was typical in its emotional appeal:

> O men of England—for Australians are men of England—in the name of your Motherland, I call you, I call you, in the name of the Commonwealth, I call you, for the sake of a free manhood, a free Church, and a free State, I call you, I call you to a new Reformation, to make Australia free, free from poisonous hate, free from sectarian strife . . . The dynamic of the New Reformation is love of Christ, and glory in His Cross. There is no hope for the Commonwealth save as its government is upon the shoulder of Christ, save as its religion is Christocentric and Crucicentric.⁵²

This concluding appeal, as was the whole book, was well received by Protestants. Publisher J. A. Packer described it as "one of the most remarkable books ever issued from the printing press in this country":

> We would go further and say that the addresses place the whole Protestant community under obligation to Mr. Ruth, and it should be the duty of every Protestant and every Protestant organisation to see that the widest possible circulation is secured for this book. Its value, at the present time, in combating the spurious, specious and subtle claims of the Papacy in Australia cannot be exaggerated.⁵³

---

50. Ruth, *The Catholic*, 213.
51. Ruth, *The Catholic*, 213.
52. Ruth, *The Catholic*, 214–15.
53. *AB*, November 26, 1918, 6–7.

The *Presbyterian Messenger* gave a similar welcome, insisting that "every Protestant in the Commonwealth should read this book."[54] The *Victorian Independent* also offered a warm response to this "racy and bracing kind of book" in which Ruth cast his "dialectical rapier" through Roman claims.[55] In Sydney, the *Watchman* (a Protestant paper that J. A. Packer had once edited) suggested that Ruth's book "ought to be in every lodge library and on every Protestant's shelf."[56]

A Victorian layman arranged for copies of this book and Ruth's *The Common Weal* (also published late in 1918) to be sent to every Baptist minister and Home Missionary in the Commonwealth.[57] Extracts from letters sent by those who had gratefully received these books appeared in the *Australian Baptist* in the following weeks. T. J. Malyon (1844–1921), Principal of the Queensland Baptist College, claimed that these books were "just what the times require," while A. W. Bean, appointed Ruth's associate pastor later that year, simply asserted that "Baptists should prize him."[58] Packer sent copies to the Prime Minister and the Premier of New South Wales, while another donor arranged for copies of *The Catholic* to be sent to every member of the New South Wales Parliament.[59]

Malyon thought that Ruth was "evidently a man raised up for the times." A similar response is to be noted. W. S. Rollings (1871–1944), who had served as a Baptist minister in both Australia and New Zealand, after reading Ruth's book wrote a personal but open appeal to him. This was published on the front page of the *Australian Baptist* on February 25, 1919. Headed "God's Australia. An Appeal to Mr. Ruth," he confessed that he had been greatly impressed with Ruth's writing and in particular his address, "The Strength of Empire," which was mainly about the issue of prohibition.[60] Rollings suggested that Ruth was just the man who was needed at this time:

> In Australia Goliath is swaggering and threatening on the battle plain, and fooling himself into the belief that his right of way cannot be challenged. But God is on the field; only He wants a man; and He wants behind His man the forces of His Israel, before the issue can be joined.

54. As cited in *AB*, December 24, 1918, 7.
55. As cited in *AB*, January 7, 1919, 5.
56. *Watchman*, January 23, 1919, 1.
57. *AB*, December 31, 1918, 3.
58 *AB*, January 21, 1919, 7; February 18, 1919, 10.
59. *AB*, January 28, 1919, 9; February 4, 1919, 10.
60. *AB*, January 28, 1919, 4, 8.

Will Mr. Ruth be the man?[61]

Rollings concluded by stating that his prayer was that "Mr. Ruth may be Christ's man to lead in this war."

What Ruth thought about this is unknown. But perhaps the thought did occur to him that if there was a need for a new reformation, as he envisioned it, then perhaps there was a need for a new reformer or at least a leader who would be free to lead the charge. What is known is that a few years later, encouraged by Brookes, Ruth did envisage some form of a new Commonwealth-wide ministry. He resigned from the Collins Street Church with this intention still undefined.

But in the few years before that confusing decision, Ruth still had much to do in Melbourne. An expanded and challenging role opened before him, one that would lead him into even more public controversy and more charges of sectarian bigotry. Was he the man that Australia needed? Or, at least, could he be part of a movement that Australia needed?

61. *AB*, February 25, 1919, 1.

6

"The Commonwealth Constitutes His Congregation"

Ruth in Melbourne (1918–23)

Less than a year after the 1917 conscription referendum, the Great War was finally over. The *Australian Baptist* on November 12, 1918, the day after the Armistice was signed, enthused: "This has been the greatest week in history."[1] Jubilant demonstrations throughout the nation and the world celebrated peace, but the terrible human toll of those long years was still to be calculated. The bare statistics convey something of the cost: "More than 58,000 Australian soldiers, sailors, and airmen died or were killed during the war years: around one in ten of all men aged 18 to 45. Another 156,000 were wounded, gassed, or taken prisoner. Perhaps 2,000 spent the rest of their lives in hospital."[2]

For T. E. Ruth, preacher, platform orator, and controversialist, there were many battles still to be faced. He became even more of an enigma during these last years in Melbourne (1918–23). He condemned sectarianism but was criticized by *The Age* as "an imported zealot." Highly critical of "political" Protestantism, he seemed to be advocating precisely that movement. An apostle of church reunion, he managed to drive wedges between himself and some other denominations. He was a Baptist but regularly antagonized his fellow-religionists with extravagant and seemingly unorthodox ideas. After savage attacks on Archbishop Mannix and Roman Catholic teaching, Ruth

1. *AB*, November 12, 1918, 6.

2. Wilcox, "World War I," in *Oxford Companion*, 699. For detailed statistics, see McKernan, "War," in Vamplew, *Australian Statistics*, 410–14.

then took it upon himself to advocate a form of public theology that was devoted to democracy, peace, and harmony in society. He was a preacher in Melbourne but, as the *Australian Baptist* declared in 1920, "the Commonwealth constitutes his congregation."[3]

Ruth's contributions to church, city, and nation sometimes conflicted him. The welcome interlude of a visit back to England and to America for several months in 1920 gave him some respite and new energy for his pastorate, but almost immediately he continued to dream of some wider Commonwealth-wide ministry. These were exciting if demanding challenges for the proud "Son of Devon."

Pastor and Preacher

Ruth continued to lead and support his Collins Street people. Many tributes to his personal and intensely spiritual ministry need to be placed against his more public and controversial persona in the city. There was evident pride in the popularity of the Auditorium services and their minister's regular public notice. Ruth took a personal interest in the Sunday School. Baptisms were conducted frequently. Weddings were regularly conducted, though not all were as fashionable as that between church organist Claude Kingston and Mabel Ella Thompson on May 13, 1916. The sick and dying needed to be visited. Funerals were planned and conducted, in some cases with large numbers present, such as that for the church's "Grand Old Man," former church secretary William Blake, in November 1917.

The war years also saw several sad notes about those members or friends who had been killed or wounded while on active service. In October 1916, the church unveiled a temporary roll of honor with more than a hundred names of members and others associated with families of Collins Street. The roll had been designed and made by architect William Lucas, who himself suffered a tragic loss. Norman Carey Lucas MA, BSc (Edinburgh), son of William and Mrs. Lucas, was killed in Macedonia in 1916. After a brilliant academic career, Norman had enlisted just after completing his second degree.[4] His distraught father prepared and self-published a commemorative book about his son, who had served with the Royal Irish Rifles.[5] This loss was, of course, a major reason why William Lucas became deeply devoted

---

3. *AB*, December 21, 1920, 4.

4. *Monthly Notes*, December 1916.

5. *Life and Letters of Norman Carey*. For William Lucas, see Richardson, *Creating Remembrance*, 46–53.

to the design and planning of war memorials. After the war he explained precisely what the design of the memorial conveyed.[6]

In a tribute to Norman in the Collins Street *Monthly Notes* for December 1916, Ruth wrote:

> So many fathers and mothers in like case sympathise with Mr. and Mrs. Lucas. On every hand they have been assured of the ministry of intercession. To the comfort of the Father–Mother God we commend them, and to the comradeship of the Christ who still leads on, and Who will not fail to bring all His friends into the light and love and laughter of the Home of God, which is the home of men.

Ruth seems to have brought comfort to the Lucas family. He insisted:

> It is impossible to think of a man of his gifts as dead . . . Goodness cannot die. It would be intellectually absurd and morally monstrous to imagine that death destroys character and annihilates qualities carefully nurtured and developed. Surely something more than the religious instinct survives the experience of death and is carried into the life revealed, not as a church but as a city, and amid the manifold activities of the City of God the gifts and graces won out of sacrifice will be utilised.[7]

William Lucas preserved a moving personal note from Ruth in which he pointed to Christ "who is our Comrade as well as Saviour."[8]

After the war, special services of thanksgiving were held. Ruth conducted a major service in the Auditorium with a printed liturgy and order of service. The Victorian Returned Sailors' and Soldiers' League Band provided the musical accompaniment, which included playing Chopin's "Funeral March." The National Anthem began the service, and hymns included the familiar "Lead, Kindly Light," "Rock of Ages," and "The Recessional," as well as T. Craven Browne's "God bless our land":

> God save Australia's sunny land,
>
> Our home of wealth and scenes so grand;
>
> Thy love bestow on every hand,
>
> God bless our land! . . .

---

6. *Monthly Notes*, December 1919.

7. *Monthly Notes*, December 1916.

8. Ruth to Mr. and Mrs. Lucas, November 13, 1916 (Lucas Papers at Victorian Baptist archives).

> We ask Thee, Lord, to bless each State,
>
> And portion of the Empire great;
>
> Watch every shore and harbour gate,
>
> And guard our land.

Ruth spoke on "Australia's Duty to her Dead."[9]

Then on August 21, 1919, Collins Street held a "welcome home" social for all the returning men: "Never has the Lecture Hall been more beautifully decorated." Wattle was everywhere and the ladies provided refreshments. Ruth began by solemnly affirming, "Our first debt is to the dead," and then recited some lines adapted from Edith Wharton's poem, "Munsey's."

> Every one of you won the war,
>
> You, and you, and you.
>
> Each one knowing what it was for,
>
> And what was his work to do.
>
> Every one of you won the war,
>
> Obedient, unwearied, unknown.
>
> Dung in the trenches, drift on the shore,
>
> Dust to the world's end blown . . .
>
> Every one of you won the war,
>
> But you, most of all, you Dead![10]

Attending the weekly prayer and Bible Study meeting was a priority for many members. Ruth was as busy as any minister caring for his people's needs and the church's demanding programs. The church still had oversight of the Bouverie Street Sunday School in Carlton and the Mission Hall in Little Bourke Street. Various Christian bodies sought use of the church building for their gatherings. The property had to be maintained, and the deacons supervised finances with regular reports brought to the members' meeting. The Auditorium services had a loss of about three guineas each service. Ruth's salary had been raised to £800 in 1917. When Ruth was about to leave for six months' leave, which the deacons had strongly recommended

---

9. "Order of Service" in Lucas papers.

10. *Monthly Notes*, September 1919. Edith Wharton (1862–1937) was an American novelist and poet. *Munsey's Magazine* was an American periodical.

to the church meeting, they recorded their gratitude for "the harmonious way in which we have worked together."[11]

But, of course, Ruth's most significant role within his church was as a preacher. A few examples of his preaching across these last years in Melbourne demonstrate his versatility. The first shows him taking a biblical theme and linking it with the challenges facing society because of the war. Hope and confidence were needed. In May 1918, while the war was still waging, he preached on "The Lamb at War with the Beast," utilizing the imagery of the book of Revelation which, as Ruth observed, had been "a happy hunting ground for exegetical ingenuity." Eschewing such fascinating possibilities, Ruth focused on the image of the Lamb as Christ, showing the powerful relevance of this in troubling times. The Lamb is making war with the Beast and this, Ruth insisted, is "the actual meaning of all history—the history of all nations and of each man." The Lamb is the only answer to the problems of international, governmental, and social life as well as of domestic life. [12]

A second example found him dealing with a personal living issue: "The Waste of Worry." Drawing on the Sermon on the Mount, he also noted his own failures:

> I can recall many sleepless nights and consequent days of impaired ministry because I have attached too much importance to the censoriousness of a crank or the malice of a malcontent associated with the outer business of the House of God. I have worried because some mischief-maker has magnified the molehill of a ministerial mistake into a mountain of error.[13]

This combination of biblical exposition and confessional preaching dealing with the realities of life for most people was a very effective method for Ruth.

For the new year of 1919 Ruth preached on "The Soul's Power of Prestige," basing this on the old biblical story of David and Goliath. He suggested that this story might be regarded as "an epitome of history, of the conflict of the past few years and of all the conflicts of time." This is a picture of the warfare between good and evil, between right and might:

> The gigantic Goliath was slain by the daring David. The German became afraid of the "contemptible little army." And in

---

11. Details in CSBC Deacons' Minutes.
12. *AB*, May 21, 1918, 4.
13. *AB*. June 4, 1918, 7.

the vaster conflict, the most colossal evil will be conquered by Christian courage. Right shall be might.[14]

In February 1919, the deadly Spanish Flu pandemic came to Melbourne. Quarantine stations were established at state borders. All public life was controlled and many churches were closed as was Collins Street for several weeks. Some churches held services in the open air and encouraged attendees to wear masks. One Methodist minister objected to nuns being used as nurses in the Exhibition Building because they were "a sacerdotally trained band of anti-Protestants" but the retort was made that there had been no distinction of sects on the battlefields. Still, some saw this move as "the pushfulness of Dr. Mannix" at work.[15] A vaccine was developed and eventually given to 819,000 Australians. Ruth did preach on "Our Unseen Environment" on March 16, a sermon based on 2 Kings 6:17, but this did not evidently address the pandemic as such.[16] (Gradually life returned to normal, but a century later Collins Street was once again closed for public services because of the covid-19 pandemic.)

Another example of Ruth preaching to the life needs of his people came in October 1919 when he preached on "God and Reconstruction," likening the present Australian situation with that of Israel after Jerusalem had been sacked. Echoing Masonic language, Ruth insisted that "Reconstructionists must be acquainted with the plans of the Great Architect of the Universe and must cooperate with God." A great proportion of returned men had not returned to their normal life: "Many a man had been broken on the wheel and needed not scientific skill so much as a sympathetic soul." Churches should work with missions, hospitals and institutions, schools and governments, since "what men wanted most of all was comradeship and brotherhood."[17]

A quite unusual sermon for a Baptist congregation—although Ruth's people were accustomed to the unexpected—had been preached earlier in 1919, "The God of the Great Out-of-Doors." This is a striking example of the continuing influence of Romanticism, which had impacted many evangelicals in the nineteenth century through poets like Coleridge, Keats, and Browning. By "Romanticism" is here meant, as Bebbington distinguished, not so much the literary generation that had faded early in the nineteenth century, but the movement of taste that stressed "the place of feeling and intuition in human perception, the importance of nature and

14. *AB*, January 21, 1919, 1, 2.
15. Beaumont, *Broken Nation*, 524.
16. *Argus*, March 17, 1919, 8.
17. *Argus*, October 13, 1919, 7.

history for human experience." The quintessence was what has been called "natural supernaturalism," the ability to discern spiritual significance in the everyday world.[18]

This is an unambiguous example of these ideas in Ruth's preaching. He explained the genesis of this address in strongly Romantic fashion:

> The subject was first suggested to me by the reading of a poem, by the side of an open-air altar from which the incense of the good brown earth was ascending, and what time the winds made music with leaves and flowers, and the great Southern Ocean sounded out its angry mystic message of healing and of health.
> "I will preach about it, some day," I said to myself.[19]

This was undoubtedly a reference to an event at "Arilpa," the holiday home of Herbert Brookes at Point Lonsdale in Victoria, where Ruth and his wife often stayed. Brookes built an open-air "altar" of stones only a few yards into the scrub from the wide sweeping wooden verandah that ran around his house.

The poem "God of the Open Air" by Henry Van Dyke (1852–1933) acted virtually as a text for this sermon.

> Thou who hast made thy dwelling fair
>
> With flowers beneath, above with starry lights,
>
> And set thine altars everywhere—
>
> On mountain heights,
>
> In woodlands with many a dream,
>
> In valleys bright with springs,
>
> And on the curving capes of every stream:
>
> Thou who hast taken to thyself with wings
>
> Of morning, to abide
>
> Upon the secret places of the sea,
>
> And on far islands, where the tide
>
> Visits the beauty of untrodden shores,
>
> Waiting for worshippers to come to thee
>
> In thy great out-of-doors!

18. Bebbington, *Evangelicalism in Modern Britain*, 80–81.
19. *AB*, April 1, 1919, 1, 8.

> To thee I turn, to thee I make my prayer
>
> God of the open air.

Ruth's main point was that "Christ is the Messiah of the mountain side, the Preacher of the sea-shore . . . His cross was in the open-air, and when they put Him in the tomb, angels rolled away the stone and again He stepped into the open universe, and when He disappeared it was into the sky!"[20]

Ruth the Protestant Agitator

Ruth's demanding ministry in his own church did not distract him from his ongoing commitment to the Protestant imperial campaign for which he was regularly attacked by *Punch* and *Truth* as well as Catholic papers. Possibly with a not-too-subtle reflection on Ruth's alliterative style, *Truth* headed one report "Magging at Mannix. Ravings of Ruthless Ruth. Pluto's Pulpiteers Pepper a Popular Prelate."[21]

Ruth's influence spread far beyond his own state into Tasmania[22] and in Queensland where he was greeted as "a fearless exponent of righteousness" while he concentrated on the familiar theme of the need for a genuine catholicity.[23]

In June 1919, the Loyalist League issued a 3d. pamphlet titled *The Menace of Mannix and Co.*, which contained three of Ruth's addresses.[24] When T. J. Ryan, the Roman Catholic Labor Premier of Queensland, was invited to enter the Federal Parliament, Protestants were convinced that there was a papal plot, linking Labor and Rome. The Loyalist League issued a booklet containing Ruth's address on *The Challenge of Papal Politics*. His theme was unambiguous:

> For some years the Papal party has been looking for one strong man outside the priesthood to champion its cause in the Commonwealth, and it has been looking longingly towards Queensland, the only state with a Papal Premier . . . They have wanted to find a powerful man, strong, honest and obedient and the Roman papers tell me they have found him.[25]

---

20. *AB*, April 1, 1919, 1.
21. *Truth*, April 6, 1918, 5.
22. *AB*, April 2, 1918, 8.
23. *Daily Mail* (Brisbane), September 18, 1918, 4; *AB*, September 24, 1918, 6–7.
24. *AB*, June 17, 1919, 8.
25. Quoted in Murphy, *T. J. Ryan*, 466.

The Victorian Protestant Federation was established in 1918 with Baptist minister Rev. J. C. Farquhar as its pioneer President. Brookes and Congregationalist minister Rev. Walter Albiston (1889–1965), together with Ruth, Leeper, and Rentoul, were the driving forces. The Federation's monthly paper the *Vigilant* featured "For God, King, Empire" on its masthead and defended the empire against all "Bolshevist attacks" as well as maintaining a relentless campaign against such issues as government funding of religious hospitals and schools.

Murray Goot observes that "there was no Protestant equivalent to Mannix."[26] Ruth, encouraged by Brookes and other friends, may well have imagined himself to be that Protestant equivalent, but he lacked the church structures and status as well as the presence of Mannix. Ruth was no match for the suave and charismatic Daniel Mannix.

A Welcome Holiday

In June 1919, Ruth asked his deacons to grant him a leave of absence. He felt the need for rest and a change as he feared staleness. The deacons agreed and took it to the church meeting which gladly granted him eight months to visit England and the USA, after which he would resume his work at Collins Street. When this latter commitment was announced at an Auditorium meeting, the crowded congregation burst into "loud and prolonged applause."[27]

The church then invited as associate minister the experienced pastor Rev. A. W. Bean, born in 1876 so almost the same age as Ruth, a Scottish graduate of Spurgeon's College who had served in pastorates in Tasmania and South Australia as well as with the YMCA during the war. Bean was inducted at Collins Street on December 7, 1919, thus ensuring that in Ruth's absence overseas the work would be well maintained. Ruth reported to the congregation that he had longed for such a partner as Mr. Bean, "a man with a man's message; a man among men; a man of God. Some things I have had no time to do; some things I have no qualification for doing, he will now do, and in the diversities of our gifts and duties, there will be the same Divine Spirit." During the induction, Ruth took Bean by the hand and said, "God give you Mr. Bean, a tender heart, a quick conscience, and a thick skin. God give you clear vision, the grace of initiative, the strength of courage."[28]

26. Groot, *Conscription Conflict*, 136.
27. CSBC Deacons' Minutes, June 16, 1919; *AB*, 22 July 1919, 3.
28. *Monthly Notes*, January 1920.

The church organized a social farewell for Ruth on Tuesday March 2 at which Bean remarked that "the back seats of Collins Street Church were in the remote places of the Commonwealth."[29] His last services on Sunday March 7 were crowded and emotional. Among many other thanks, Ruth mentioned the testimony of "one who had known great sorrow and who said, 'You have made Jesus real and human to me.'"[30]

The Loyalist League organized what became a magnificent farewell for Ruth in the Melbourne Town Hall on Monday March 8, 1920. Brookes organized a collection from friends and supporters "unassociated with his church" for Ruth, whom he described as "a man who has done so much to expose disloyalty in our midst and to awaken all our citizens to the dangers that menace our liberty." This gift would free Ruth from financial care and enable him to make "close investigation both in Great Britain and in America into the methods and practices of the one common enemy to Anglo–Saxon civilisation." Over £200 was collected, which Brookes raised to £300.[31]

The *Argus* and *The Age* both reported that many could not gain admission to the crowds wishing to farewell Ruth.[32] Dr. Leeper was in the Chair, and the Federal Treasurer Watt presented the cheque. Flags waved; enthusiasm and emotion were high. Leeper noted that "Ruth was a man who could not be well spared": how few there were to take on disloyalty and sectarianism. Ruth was "not afraid of anybody," and they "ought to thank God that they had a man such as Ruth among them (applause)."

After having been greeted with prolonged cheers and the singing of "For he's a jolly good fellow," Ruth replied, giving special thanks to Brookes as well as the Freemasons (Ruth was Senior Warden of the Austral Lodge).[33] He gave a typically rousing speech. "Six years before he had come to Australia, a Britisher from Britain, and he would return to Great Britain still a Britisher. (Cheers) In eight months' time he would come back to Australia to continue his Australian ministry. (Applause)."[34]

Through the generosity of Brookes, their adopted son Leslie was able to accompany his parents on the trip, "thereby multiplying the pleasures a

---

29. *AB*, March 9, 1920, 4.

30. *AB*, March 16, 1920, 3.

31. Typed circular letter from Brookes, 25 February 1920, Brookes Papers, NLA 1924/48/13, with written notation about the sum collected. The Brookes Papers (143 boxes) is one of the larger collections at the National Library of Australia. There are seven folders related to Ruth.

32. *Argus,* March 9, 1920, 7; *The Age* March 9, 1920, 7.

33. *BT*, February 23, 1922, 70.

34. *The Age*, March 9, 1920, 7.

thousandfold for his mother and me."³⁵ They traveled aboard the RMS *Mantua* via Fremantle where representatives of the local Baptists gathered to hear Ruth give "an all-too brief recital of recent Melbourne experiences and some brilliant and humorous comments on the present religious outlook."³⁶

Settled in England at Leicester, Ruth was scathing in his comments about the daily newspapers and some of the English preachers. Dr. W. Orchard, for example, "in some respects the ablest preacher in London, enormously influential in some quarters" is a pacifist "and drags pacifism in by the skin of its teeth whenever possible." But he is "a brilliant if irrelevant preacher."³⁷ He met Sir Arthur Conan Doyle and several other people for whom Brookes had given him letters of introduction.

The *Baptist Times* and the *Christian World*, for both of which Ruth had often written before going to Australia, welcomed him "home." The Baptist journal published an extended "chat" with him, titled "Heretic and Loyalist." Ruth thanked S. P. Carey and Spurr for giving him "the freest pulpit and the finest people to be found anywhere." He enjoyed meeting with Pearce Carey; "what a great little man he is."³⁸ The interviewer suggested that Ruth must be regarded as a heretic by the majority of religious Australians. His challenges to the Roman Catholics were summarized, as well as the controversy over his views on purgatory. He reported some progress on church union, at least in South Australia, but was not at all optimistic about Baptists participating in such movements.³⁹

The *Christian World* reported that it was the "psychic quality" of Ruth's preaching that determined his influence as he "ministers to the long-starved instinct for immediacy, vision, transcendence" as well as demonstrating "a robust practicality, an impassioned insistence upon the social implications of the gospel."⁴⁰

Ruth preached at several places, including the historic Congregational Church at Carrs Lane in Birmingham in June and just before leaving England he was at Westbourne Park, the pulpit that he might have shared with John Clifford.⁴¹ He naturally visited Liverpool where he

---

35. Ruth to Brookes, RMS *Mantua*, at sea, 10 March 1920, Brookes Papers, NLA 1924/48/25.

36. *AB*, March 23, 1920, 3.

37. Ruth to Brookes, 5 July 1920, Brookes Papers, NLA 1924/48/28. W. E. Orchard (1877–1955) was then minister at King's Weigh Congregational Church in London, but in 1932 he converted to Roman Catholicism.

38. Ruth to Brookes, 16 October 1920, Brookes Papers, NLA 1924/48/31.

39. *BT*, May 28, 1929, 361.

40. As cited in *AB*, September 28, 1920, 4. October 19, 1920, 4.

41. *Birmingham Daily Gazette*, June 19, 1920; *AB*, October 26, 1920, 4.

denounced Archbishop Mannix who had been denied entry to England, and Southampton where he doubtless caught up with many friends and relatives.[42] Ruth also represented Australian Baptists at a Baptist World Alliance Conference in London.[43]

In the USA, he gave particular attention to the prohibition issue as well as visiting New York, Niagara Falls, Washington, and Chicago before joining the Santa Fe railroad for their journey to Los Angeles.

He commented to Brookes about the reception given to Mannix in the USA where, Ruth suggested, "He did the devil's own work."[44] Mannix had left Australia after a triumphant St. Patrick's Day march in Melbourne for which Wren had organized fourteen winners of the Victoria Cross, each mounted on a white horse, to make a guard of honor for Mannix's open limousine. But St. Patrick's Day was only the beginning. When Mannix announced that he was leaving in May to pay his obligatory visit to the Pope, a grand farewell was organized and some 30,000 came to the Exhibition Building.[45] Mannix arranged to tour the USA with Eamon de Valera (1882–1975), one of the most powerful men in Ireland. The tour was wholly political, asserting the claims of an independent Ireland. The British Government would not allow Mannix to land in Ireland, and he was forced to stay in England. He returned to Melbourne on August 11, 1921. As Ruth observed to Brookes, "Our city will go green for a week."[46]

The Ruth family returned to Melbourne by train from Sydney on December 8 and was welcomed at Spencer Street station by a large contingent of Baptists and friends. He told the waiting press that the USA was "teeming with prosperity," which he attributed to prohibition, while the majority of the people were determined in their opposition to Sinn Fein. He assured his hearers that he had come out nearly seven years ago as "a missionary of the Empire" and as such he had returned.[47]

On his first Sunday back Ruth preached on "The place whereon you stand is holy ground," "the Holy Land of Australia."[48] He insisted that the outstanding necessity in the social life of England and Australia was not

42. *Liverpool Echo*, August 6, 1920, 8.
43. *AB*, September 21, 1920, 4.
44. Ruth to Brookes, 16 October 1920, Brookes Papers, NLA 1924/48/31.
45. Niall, *Mannix*, 146–48.
46. Ruth to Brookes, 11 August 1921, Brookes Papers, NLA 1924/48/51.
47. *Argus*, December 9, 1920, 6; *The Age*, December 8, 1920, 10.
48. *AB*, December 21, 1920, 4.

liberty "but discipline to prevent liberty already achieved from degenerating into license."[49]

Final Challenges in Melbourne 1921–23

Ruth was immediately back into the demands of church and community. While he had been away the deacons had acted to remove the names of some 141 people who were now non-attenders at services. A "Back to Collins Street" was held on the evening of December 4 in an attempt to renew interest and support.[50]

Meanwhile, sectarian feelings were still running high in the city. The immediate spark had been a Sinn Fein resolution passed by the Australian Railways Union. On March 17, 1921, a "Great Loyalist Demonstration" was held in the Melbourne Town Hall. Welcomed by cheering that lasted several minutes, Ruth moved a resolution which declared that the formation in Melbourne of the "Self-determination for Ireland League" constituted a "deliberate challenge and insult to the loyal citizens of the Commonwealth." He insisted that this League was "an enemy organisation."[51]

Protestants were again incensed by the St. Patrick's Day march when they claimed that offence was given to the Union Jack when a flag was burnt. Ruth spoke to a crowded Auditorium and demanded that the City Council heeded their warning not to permit any further "seditious processions" or else they would themselves seek to hold a loyalist march next St. Patrick's Day. Ruth spoke at great length on "Seditious Priests and Loyal People" in which he thundered about such priests: "They are anti-English and they are essentially anti-Australian . . . It is time for the Government to prevent these seditious priests from sheltering behind their sacred office."[52]

His agitation continued throughout that year. In May, he asked the Auditorium crowd, "How long will Australia remain British?" He warned against listening to "the siren song of separation and sedition"; else they would "find themselves on the Sinn Fein rocks." After the address the congregation stood and recited the special "Australian Creed," which Ruth had composed.[53] He also claimed that the British had shown how to deal with

---

49. *Argus*, December 13, 1920, 9.
50. CSBC Deacons' Minutes, July 19, 1920, August 16, 1920.
51. *Vigilant*, March 17, 1921, 4–6.
52. *Vigilant*, April 14, 1921, 1–5.
53. *Argus*, May 30, 1921, 7. For this creed, see chapter 7.

Mannix: they had not interfered with his spiritual liberty but "reduced him to political impotence as a seditionist."[54]

Ruth resumed his role as pastor and agitator. He enjoyed visiting South Australia in August where he preached at the diamond jubilee services for the Flinders Street Baptist Church on "The World's Debt to Dreamers."[55] Later that month he resumed his political emphases when he protested against Patrick O'Leary's cable to de Valera in Ireland, asserting that Australia would support the Irish in their opposition to Britain. He also asked the question, "Does Archbishop Mannix misrepresent Australian democracy?" Familiar notes were sounded: "Australian citizens should stand by Australian independence, Australian institutions, Australian freedom of thought, freedom of faith, freedom of legislation, and Australian loyalty to God, King, and Empire."[56] *The Age* reported that his address had been frequently interrupted by "enthusiastic cheering."[57]

Severe tonsillitis kept Ruth out of action for seven weeks late in 1921.[58] He also had an operation for "slight nasal trouble" in the following year.[59] Moreover, A. W. Bean resigned as associate pastor in April 1922 in order to become Superintendent of the Melbourne City Mission.[60] This clearly was a challenging time for Ruth.

Ruth tackled quite a different type of topic on March 19, 1922, when he spoke—as a practicing Mason—about "The Open Secrets of Freemasonry," which was later published as a booklet by the Loyalist League of Victoria, indicative of the links between the two groups. His talk was not critical of Masonry in any way, and the pro-Grand Master F. T. Hickford (1862–1929), a prominent lawyer, shared in the service. Ruth ridiculed as absurd the idea that a Christian in Freemasonry "must hide his light under a bushel."[61] His basic claim was that the craft was "on so catholic and comprehensive a basis that it offered a common meeting place for free men of every clime and colour, caste and creed." He admitted that in the public mind it was associated with "mysteries, with secret signs and symbols"; in fact, it was "in some sort of spiritual succession in the ancient mysteries of Egypt, Asia Minor, Greece and Rome."

---

54. *The Age*, May 30, 1921, 6.
55. *Advertiser*, August 8, 1921, 10.
56. *Argus*, August 29, 1921, 6.
57. *The Age*, August 29, 1921, 7.
58. *Propagandist*, October 5, 1921; December 5, 1921, 12.
59. *Herald*, June 29, 1922, 1.
60. CSBC Deacons' Minutes, April 11, 1922,
61. Ruth, *Open Secrets of Freemasonry*, 1.

"There was no magic in Masonry, only simple morality."[62] Ruth claimed that there were four secrets of Freemasonry which he listed as freedom, fraternity, faith, and loyalty. This was undoubtedly not quite what the expectant crowd had hoped to hear about the secrets of the "Craft."

Precisely why Ruth elected to address this topic is uncertain, although he knew that Mannix had called Masonry "the most insidious enemy of God and country ... a huge tumour growing upon the life and blood of the whole of the country."[63] What Ruth's talk did reveal was how important Orange and Masonic lodges were for the Protestant and imperial cause. Between 1920 and 1954, when the Australian population grew by two-thirds, the number of Masonic lodges almost trebled, peaking at 330,000 members.[64] Graeme Davison has commented, "Masons were pro-British, anti-Catholic, respectable and loyal to their brethren in the craft. In business and politics, the Masonic handshake opened doors and discreetly shut them too. About half the first federal parliament and most non-Labor leaders from Barton to McMahon were 'grippers.'"[65]

Another political talk was given at the Auditorium on March 26 when Ruth deplored Australian parochialism, suggesting that the Federal Capital offered "a powerful parable, both of the possibilities and the parochialisms of this southern continent." The plan posited a population of a hundred million, but given the White Australia policy this was absurd. He then attacked this same policy as "condemned by the revelation of God and the reason of man." Canberra should be thought of as "a parable of promise—a time when Australians would rise out of the parochialisms and prejudices which were the peril of personal and public life into wholeness which would be public health."[66]

What promised to be a conciliatory address was given by Ruth in April 1922 and published as a pamphlet, *The Terms of Sectarian Peace*. Ruth asked, "On what equal conditions can Protestants and Patriots take 'The Hand of Friendship' held out by Dr. Mannix?" Ruth had read that Mannix had offered this "hand of friendship to all who will take it" and this was his response. Agreeing that in the interests of churchmanship and citizenship sectarianism should cease, Ruth proposed principles that should be common ground. (1) Both Protestants and Roman Catholics are Churchmen

62. *Argus*, March 20, 1922, 6.

63. *The Age*, February 15, 1916, 8. See Franklin, "Catholics Versus Masons."

64. Harland-Jacobs, *Builders of Empire*, 244.

65. Davison, "Religion," in Bashford and Macintyre, *Cambridge History of Australia* vol. 2, 226.

66. *Argus*, March 27, 1922, 6. See also *Queensland Times* (Ipswich, Qld), April 4, 1922, 2. The full text is in the (Melbourne) *Herald*, July 8, 1922, 13.

with a common creed and a common Christian cause. (2) Both Roman Catholics and Protestants are citizens "with a common civic heritage and a common civic duty."[67]

But the real reason why sectarianism was so rife was precisely because both of these grounds had been denied, said Ruth. Ruth was prepared to take the hand of Mannix on equal conditions of churchmanship and citizenship. Even as Mannix asks for old sores to be healed, "he pours scorn on the policy of civic authorities and publicly ridicules the very prayers of a Protestant Archbishop." Ruth was here commenting on Mannix's attitude towards the Melbourne Anglican Bishop Dr. Harrington Lees (1870–1929).[68] The Catholic paper had ridiculed the consecration of the Archbishop in St. Paul's Cathedral London, writing that "if such a service conveyed any special grace or blessing it would be because the Cathedral had been in full communion with Rome for nearly a thousand years before the schismatic and defective 'Edwardine Ordinal' of episcopal consecration was drawn up."[69]

Ruth continued by cataloguing several speeches by Mannix condemning Protestantism and his frequent ridicule of civic leaders. "If we are to have sectarian peace we must cease to have sectarian politics." Both Mannix and Ruth had appealed for sectarian peace but no one, certainly not those two warriors, could have doubted that such a possibility was in a far distant time. Indeed, the Second Vatican Council (1962–65), well after the active time of both Ruth and Mannix, profoundly influenced interchurch relations and initiated a genuine decline in sectarianism between Catholics and Protestants.

However, a tragic murder in London triggered another round of bitter sectarianism. Field Marshal Sir Henry Hughes Wilson (1864–1922) was assassinated by two IRA gunmen in London on June 22, 1922. Wilson was a distinguished military man, an Irish Unionist and security advisor to the Northern Ireland government. Ruth was incensed and organized a special service at the Auditorium on July 2 in association with the Loyalist League. He printed a "Common Prayer" with a liturgical response and his address, "Anathema and Assassination," was published by the League.

This address sounded many familiar notes, but the emotion of the occasion was intense. Ruth intoned:

> We have met tonight as citizens of this British Commonwealth to pay our tribute to the memory of a man beloved of his King; respected by the kingly men of the whole civilised world;

67. Ruth, *Terms of Sectarian Peace*, 5.
68. For Lees (1870–1929), see *ADB*.
69. *Advocate*, January 12, 1922; as quoted by Ruth, *Terms*, 8.

revered by every decent citizen of the British Empire; and feared by the foes of freedom and fair play—a man magnificently endowed, and whose magnificent powers were magnificently disciplined and dedicated without reserve and in utter selflessness to the cause of his country, and whose body was riddled with bullets because it was the instrument of a soul utterly loyal to God and King and Empire.[70]

Linking this murder with the Sinn Fein movement, Ruth suggested that the influential ideas behind this act were "political Anglophobia and religious anathema." He characteristically proceeded to name several Catholics who had admitted the ferocity of "Irish political priests" who were the real source of the murder. The Melbourne *Tribune* claimed that Wilson's death was "brought about by his own brutality." This was almost too much for Ruth to contemplate as he rehearsed the anathemas issued by the Roman church. In conclusion, he invited the congregation to bid farewell to a brave soldier and "to pray for Lady Wilson and those who mourn with her." The congregation stood as Ruth prayed that God would comfort the widow "by communicating to her the strength of vision that could see through the iron gates that are pearly on the other side."[71]

Doubtless this had been an emotional service for Ruth to conduct, and he was upset when *The Age* criticized the presentation of his address:

Throughout the address, which was of a particularly bitter character, Mr. Ruth used his emotional powers to the utmost, and finally, with tears in his eyes and sobs in his voice, he requested the large congregation to stand and thus give him permission to write to Lady Wilson expressing sympathy with her in her bereavement.[72]

Two Collins Street deacons promptly wrote a letter to *The Age* disputing this account, insisting that they had been seated near Ruth and saw no tears nor heard sobs in his voice, but their letter was not published. On the following Sunday Ruth stated that the report was "a caricature" and with his anger quite transparent, added, "There is no fair play about such a report, no hard-hitting argument about it—it is just a low-down German or Prussian game." *The Age* suggested that Ruth's equilibrium had been upset, but rejected the

---

70. Ruth, *Anathema and Assassination*, 5.
71. Ruth, *Anathema and Assassination*, 16.
72. *The Age*, July 3, 1922, 7.

criticism.⁷³ The Catholic paper the *Advocate* supported *The Age*'s account.⁷⁴ This in turn prompted Ruth, unwisely it would seem, to write to the paper that published his letter, adding extended editorial comment on several of the quotations he had included in his address. The *Advocate* seized the opportunity to comment on Ruth's "bitterness," which meant he must be regarded "as beyond the pale of reasonable controversy."⁷⁵

In fact, Ruth had confronted *The Age* earlier in the year after he had been named as an "imported zealot." Always sensitive to criticisms, Ruth gave a long and blistering reply which was published in the *Vigilant* as "'The Age' and Imported Zealots."⁷⁶ Acknowledging that there was a ministry of the press as well as a ministry of the pulpit, Ruth added that there were times when the press needed to attack the pulpit and times when the pulpit should attack the press. Both were necessary: "Pressmen and preachers are not foes but friends and fellow-workers." Ruth then made an intensely personal confession, adopting apostolic language and stance:

> Today I am beginning the ninth year of my ministry in this church. I have never had an easy time. I do not expect an easy time. I have had to choose between mere popular preaching and a prophetic ministry. I have offended a good many people. I shall probably offend a good many more, here or elsewhere... I have had to do things my friends have not liked. I have had to do things I have not liked myself. I have not liked any of the Auditorium missions since the first three in 1914, 1915 and 1916. But necessity was laid upon me, and I conferred not with flesh and blood, though I know how dear flesh and blood may be.⁷⁷

Ruth cheerfully admitted that he was an "import"; indeed, the editor of *The Age* was himself an import. Many of the preachers in Melbourne were imports. He then denounced the paper for its support of the St. Patrick's Day procession, which was "not even remotely in honour" of the saint. He rehearsed how he had not been alert to the dangers of Roman Catholicism in Australia until the arrival of Dr. Mannix and that the street parades were in fact to promote "undiluted treason," as one of the lay Catholic leaders had claimed. For his part, he stood by "the authority of Australian law, to prevent Sinn Feiners from destroying Australian Self-determination."⁷⁸

73. *The Age*, August 7, 1922, 8.
74. *Advocate*, August 10, 1922, 27.
75. *Advocate*, August 17, 1922, 26.
76. *Vigilant*, March 16, 1922, 1–4.
77. *Vigilant*, March 16, 1922, 2.
78. *Vigilant*, March 16, 1922, 4.

Leaving Melbourne

After all these pressures and a sense of some larger calling, it was perhaps no real surprise when Ruth announced in June his resignation from Collins Street, to be effective at the end of the year. He had raised this with the deacons on May 15 and formally resigned from the church on June 27, 1922. Ruth told the church that he had felt "the finger post of facts, within and without the Church." He was willing to conclude before the end of the year if "a likely man happens along." As his decision was the result of many months' quiet thinking and prayerful consideration, he trusted the church would understand that his resignation "must be regarded as final."

A special minute was recorded assuring Ruth of their "full recognition of his great service so devotedly rendered to the Church and city." They especially recalled his "courageous and able leadership on questions of commanding National importance during the War period," which won him "a congregation which extended beyond all denominational limits, a position which he most ably retains in relation to both Church and National life."[79]

The *Herald* gave full coverage to the news. Ruth declared, "My attitude at present may be likened to that of Abraham, when he received a message to 'get out.' Abraham went, he knew not whither." He felt that he had resigned "with Divine approval" and had "some half-formed intentions, but as I do not know with any certainty what I shall do, my lips are sealed for the time being." Ruth added that he was not giving up preaching but did intend to leave Melbourne, although he also reflected on several rumors that had followed his resignation, including that he was about to marry a rich widow with four children or that he was about to enter politics. Ruth acknowledged that the Collins Street Church was "the freest pulpit in the world" and that the most cordial relations existed between the pastor, the officers and the congregation.[80] Ruth told *The Age* that he might perchance be heard from a soapbox on the Yarra Bank or the Sydney Domain.[81]

Some weeks later Ruth preached at the 89th anniversary of the Pitt Street Congregational Church in Sydney. At one point in his sermon Ruth, ever the dramatist, paused and remarked, "I am tempted to say something about myself." As the *Australian Baptist* reported:

> With the knowledge of his pending retirement from the Collins Street pulpit, the large congregation was immediately on the qui vive. Was the question which has been so often asked

---

79. CSBC Church Minutes, June 27, 1922.
80. *Herald*, June 29, 1922, 1.
81. *The Age*, June 28, 1922, 11.

as to his plans for the future to be answered? Mr. Ruth did not, however, yield to the temptation. All he did say of a personal character was that "whatever may happen, I shall never turn my back on my Baptist principles." But later on in his sermon he declared that the greatest need in Australia today is a "mission of conscience," and there were those in his congregation who thought that in that sentence they could read Mr. Ruth's objective in the near future.[82]

Ruth agreed to preach for another Sunday at Pitt Street, and the *Australian Baptist* reported that there was a large congregation, "nearly half of whom were Baptists, glad to have the opportunity of hearing Mr. Ruth, and not a little proud to think that there is room in the denomination for a man with Mr. Ruth's message." [83]

Precisely what Ruth hoped to do was never made public but it is clear that he and Brookes had discussed possibilities as early as December 1921. Ruth wrote that after Brookes had floated the idea in a late evening conversation at "Winwick," the Brookeses' home in South Yarra, he had been reflecting on what might be done. They had clearly envisaged some Commonwealth-wide ministry. Ruth noted that his Australian Creed and the Decalogue (as outlined elsewhere) should cover "the religious, political and industrial field in which seed would be sown and the kind of seed I should scatter." The program would cover all the capital cities and principal towns "in an educational and coordinating itinerancy." The work would be linked with the Protestant Federation, and rallies would be held in association with Ruth's visits. Other loyalist groups would be regarded as auxiliaries, while the Anglican Church and the Masons would be important allies. A small committee would be established with Brookes, Leeper, and the Masonic leader Hickford as key figures. Seeing that he would be stressing industrial democracy, some representatives from the Chambers of Commerce and "some loyal man on the Labor side" could be added. Ruth told Brookes, "I put this crying infant in your arms and ask you to pace the floor with it. It is the price to be paid for paternity."[84]

Ruth often met with Brookes to discuss the possibilities. In July 1922, Ruth wrote that he hoped to make the *Herald* "a good secular pulpit for a while" and asked Brookes to pray "that I may properly invest my life—so many things turn on the next move."[85] In the new year, he spoke of "the

---

82. *AB*, August 29, 1922, 4.
83. *AB*, September 5, 1922, 4.
84. Ruth to Brookes, 21 December 1921, Brookes Papers, NLA 1924/48/64.
85. Ruth to Brookes, 10 July 1922, Brookes Papers, NLA 1924/48/71.

long-dreamt-of Crusade... is now of necessity in something of a cul-de-sac. The fire still burns in my bones."[86]

Ruth was still kept busy in Melbourne. On August 6, he spoke on "The Religious Heritage of Protestantism" at Collins Street in the morning and then in the evening at the Auditorium on "The Political Heritage of Protestantism" to mark the annual convention of the Victorian Protestant Federation.[87] He responded to criticisms in the *Tribune* which had called him "This circus clown, who combines smug Christian platitudes of the pious order with the most un-Christian mendacity. For this Ruth is nothing more than a shabby hypocritical bigot and a bare-faced liar."[88] Ruth addressed his topic by arguing that the heritage of Protestantism was "an unsectarian God, a constitutional King and a comprehensive Empire." This was of course reflected in the Federation's motto, "For God and King and Empire." On the following Tuesday at the Federation's dinner in the Town Hall, Ruth resumed his attack on *The Age* after they had further insulted him by describing him as "suffering from emotionalism and silly obsessions."[89]

In the same month, Ruth preached "The Congress Sermon" at the 1922 Australasian Baptist Congress in Melbourne, choosing to speak on "The Cosmic Christ." In this eloquent and inspiring sermon on the place of Christ and the Cross in history and modern life, Ruth did not raise the controversial questions that had occupied so much of his time but led the congregation to the Communion table. This sermon was truly "Christocentric and cruci-centric" as in the evangelical tradition that Ruth had claimed when he first arrived in Australia.[90]

At the "Back to Collins Street" service on December 6, Ruth announced that he had accepted an invitation from the Pitt Street Church to preach on Sunday evenings for three months from April 1923. As Collins Street was still without a pastor, Ruth had offered to serve Collins Street until the end of March.[91] Ruth added that he was beginning "a great experiment":

> I am withdrawing from the Australian Baptist ministry to become the servant of all the churches for the preaching of the theology, the philosophy, the domestic economy of loyalty, loyalty to ourselves and to one another, loyalty to God and King and Empire, in any church of any denomination in any of

---

86. Ruth to Brookes, 1 January 1923, Brookes Papers, NLA 1924/48/73.
87. *Vigilant*, August 17, 1922, 3–7.
88. *Vigilant*, August 17, 1922, 3.
89. *The Age*, August 7, 1922, 8; *Vigilant*, August 17, 1922, 6.
90. *AB*, September 5, 1922, 1–2.
91. *AB*, December 12, 1922, 4.

the capital cities of the Commonwealth with sufficient courage to invite me.[92]

Similarly, the *Herald* reported Ruth as claiming, "The best way to describe my move is that I am becoming a roaming Catholic."[93]

Finally, a farewell by the church was held for Ruth and the family on March 29, 1923, when Ruth was given a new preaching robe, a gift from the ladies of the church. He claimed that during his time at Collins Street "not more than five percent of his sermons had been concerned with controversial subjects, and he had tried to make even the controversy an evangel."[94]

An extraordinary "New Year's Wish" for Ruth was published in the church's January–February *Monthly Note*. Virtually a hymn of praise to Ruth, this anonymous poem marks a suitable epitaph for his time in Melbourne and reveals the deep affection and respect in which his people held him.

To T. E. R.
A New Year's Wish. January 1, 1923.

Strong son of Empire,

Soldier of Jesus Christ,

Thy flashing zeal has purified

The atmosphere of city and of State;

For thou did'st make us see the enemy—

The heartless enemy within our midst—

Emissary of the invisible fiend,

Masquerading in a garb divine.

Clear on thine ear did'st sound the clarion call—

The peremptory call—

Blown from the battlements of the Invisible.

With thy dauntless courage,

With thy breast-plate of faith,

And with thy sword of the Spirit

Thou shalt still lay siege to this citadel of evil

---

92. *AB*, February 6, 1923, 4.
93. *Herald*, March 24, 1923, 4,
94. *Argus*, March 26, 1923, 7.

T. E. RUTH (1875–1956)

Throughout this Commonwealth

In the New Year and after.

Lead thou us on to lawfully contend,

And fight a conflict noble,

And live to see God's victory assured,

Though still far off.

Good British Australian!

Good Christian Imperialist!

With thy help we shall yet plant our flag

Upon the ramparts of free souls.

7

Ruth: A Public Theologian?

ALTHOUGH RUTH'S YEARS IN Melbourne (1914–23) were demanding and varied in their responsibilities, he spent the longer part of his Australian days in Sydney (1923–38) and in Adelaide (1939–56). In these places, he was still a pastor and a Protestant defender of the empire but also played a significant role as writer of several popular books, mostly drawn from his regular columns in the local press. Through this medium, "a good secular pulpit" as he called it, he enjoyed a widespread influence which, if not unique, was unusual for a Protestant minister. During these years he became possibly the best-known Protestant leader in the country. This raises the question of whether Ruth was a public theologian in that he had ready access to the general populace and regularly introduced moral and religious themes. While this approach began in his Melbourne days it came to fuller expression in Sydney.

Both "public" and "political" theology are terms that are not always used consistently, although both may be linked with the notion of "civil religion." Political theology deliberately seeks to use the disciplines of theology to show the relation between politics and religion. Ruth was not really this kind of theologian. Public theology, however, insists that Christian theology has indispensable resources for forming, ordering, and morally guiding institutions of religion and civil society.[1] Both political and public theology are concerned with social justice, share similar concerns and

---

1. Stackhouse, "Civil Religion," 275–93.

seek to build the common good.² Ruth, it may be argued, was a public theologian of considerable influence.

Not that he was unique in this role. His Baptist contemporary F. W. Boreham (1871–1959) was much better known and valued through his sermons and books of essays which sold in prolific numbers, as well as his newspaper editorials written from 1912 in Dunedin, Hobart and in Melbourne's *The Age*.³ A careful analysis of some 2,500 editorials led Dr. Geoff Pound to conclude that in the interplay between faith and life, shown in these editorials, Boreham fulfilled the role of a public theologian.⁴ A similar claim may be made for Ruth.

Civil religion is a form of patriotic self-celebration, a kind of religion of the state when "widely held beliefs or religio–political traits are tied with the nation's history and destiny."⁵ This is most commonly linked with the United States.⁶ Many scholars have agreed that a clear example of civil religion in Australia is the meaning given to Anzac Day.⁷ It combines the national, the sacred, and the military into what Graeme Davison has called "the binding rituals of the nation."⁸ Anzac Day marks "a shift from a British to some sort of Australian civil religion."⁹ Religious symbolism is inherent in the memorials and in the services on the actual day.

Ruth, who often spoke and wrote about Anzac Day, thought of it as "a community sacrament":

> It is associated with national sacrifice. It is significant of a common sanctity. It is a call to public consecration. It is an occasion for which only a sacramental vocabulary is adequate . . . Anzac Day is an Australasian sacrament.¹⁰

For Anzac Day in 1921 Ruth proposed "An Australian Creed," cast in the form of the historic Christian creeds:¹¹

---

2. Lee, "Public Theology," in Hovey and Phillips, *Cambridge Companion*, 53.
3. Manley, "Boreham, Frank William," in Larsen, *Biographical Dictionary*, 66–68.
4. Pound, "F. W. Boreham the Public Theologian."
5. Pierard, "Anzac Day Phenomenon," 245.
6. For example, Pierard and Linder, *Civil Religion and the Presidency*.
7. Pierard, "Anzac Day Phenomenon," 239–54; Inglis, *Sacred Places*, 458–71.
8. Davison, *Narrating the Nation in Australia*, as cited in Hudson, *Australian Religious Thought*, 67.
9. Piggin and Linder, *Attending to the National Soul*, 88.
10. Ruth, *Playing the Game*, 290.
11. *Argus*, April 27, 1921, 8.

> I believe in the Commonwealth of Australia as a Federation of sovereign States into a Sovereign Nation, under the Sovereign Head of the British Empire.
>
> I believe in its free, equal and democratic Constitution, providing protection for life, liberty and labour, adapted and adaptable to the needs of a growing people, for which the great men of our race laboured exceedingly and the Anzacs laid down their lives.
>
> I believe in Australia's fealty to the British throne, in its loyalty to the British flag, and its ability to work out its own industrial and political salvation without the interference of alien agitators.
>
> I believe it to be my duty to love my country, to obey its laws, to labour to keep its Constitution inviolate, its faith free, its imperial loyalty aflame, and its national patriotism a burning passion; to defend it at all costs against its enemies, and to see that Australia plays a worthy part in the contribution of the British Empire to the civilization of the world.[12]

Ruth seems to have been carried away by this sentiment and a week later also proposed, as "a companion statement," an "Australian Decalogue," a political parallel to the Ten Commandments and which was widely published in the local press as far away as Port Pirie. This shows both an awareness of Australian life and Ruth's gift for striking originality.

> I. Thou shalt not acknowledge any allegiance to any alien power.
>
> II. Thou shalt not apply the name of Democracy to a mere section of society, but preserve for every man, the prerogatives of a free man.
>
> III. Thou shalt love the land which the Lord thy God hath given thee.
>
> IV. Remember that thou keep holy the day of elections—that the city may be clean, the State pure and the Commonwealth prosperous.
>
> V. Honour thy Mother Country, that, in loyalty to the British Throne, thy days may be long in the land which the lord thy God hath given thee.
>
> VI. Thou shalt not kill the sense of civic responsibility by indifference or neglect.

---

12. Ruth, *Playing the Game*, 256.

VII. Thou shalt maintain the fidelities of common life, the sanctity of the home, the dignity of labour, the stewardship of wealth, and the integrity of politics.

VIII. Thou shalt not deprive any man of the fruits of his industry, nor make any man fearful for the security of his possessions, for the common rights of property are woven into the social fabric of the State.

IX. Thou shalt not bear false witness, nor suffer false witness against any of the country's public men.

X. Thou shalt not covet any position for which thou art not fit, nor any office for which thou art not worthy, nor any wealth for which thou wilt not work, but shall dedicate and devote thy life and thy labour to the well being of the whole community, doing unto others as ye would that others would do to you, that love may be the fulfilling of the law.[13]

Similarly, when in Sydney, Ruth composed a parody of the famous "faith" chapter in Hebrews 11, insisting that "Australians should believe in Australia as they believe in God." This affirmation of Australian faith is quite long with some twenty verses and reveals an imperial understanding of Commonwealth history:

Now, faith is the substance of things hoped for, the evidence of things not seen.

For by it, the older Australians obtained a good report.

By faith we understand that the Australian nation was founded in the fear of God, that it might make a distinct contribution to British democracy and to the civilization of the world.

By faith Captain Cook showed greater courage than the armchair geographers of his time, and set sail for the only continent entirely in the southern hemisphere . . .

By faith Flinders surveyed the coast, and his charts remain to this day . . .

By faith Wentworth incorporated the Sydney University and fathered the Federal movement . . .

By faith Deakin sensed the significance to Australia of a Christian Imperialism, and invested his genius in it . . .[14]

---

13. *Recorder* (Port Pirie), July 6, 1921, 3.
14. Ruth, *Playing the Game*, 268–69.

Ruth was convinced that "the background of faith is essential, that the religious setting of our national life is rational, that the supreme need of our times is spiritual vision."[15] A notable omission is any awareness of the rights of Indigenous Australians, although he did elsewhere discuss their situation. None of these creative attempts to bring the nation into an awareness of its spiritual destiny seems to have been widely adopted.

Pro-war sentiment among the churches was fueled by a civil religion then integral to the ethos of the British Empire: "It was a religion which sacralised blood, understood in terms of race and sacrifice."[16] "Culture Protestantism" or "Civic Protestantism" are alternate terms for civic religion.[17] However defined, Ruth is an excellent example of the phenomenon.

In a recent history of Australian religious thought, public theology in Australia was focused on significant Anglican figures like E. Burgmann (1885–1967), Bishop of Goulburn, and A. P. Elkin (1891–1979) of the University of Sydney.[18] Both were influential academics and widely published authors. Although Ruth produced relatively ephemeral publications, these may certainly be defined as public theology, which Wayne Hudson terms "an attempt to address issues in public life from a theological perspective in terms that could be understood by a wide public."[19]

Indeed, two series of Ruth's sermons from the Auditorium quite specifically attempted to address these kinds of issues in a popular style for a wide public.

The Common Weal

Ruth delivered fifteen of these addresses from June 1918 and added another three in his book *The Common Weal*, published by the Australian Baptist Publishing House in December 1918. Ruth indicated that his studies were "really notes of simple and red-hot addresses delivered on Sunday evenings" and that he had made no attempt to camouflage the "heat and glow of the religious atmosphere."[20]

---

15. Ruth, *Playing the Game*, 270.

16. Piggin and Linder, *Attending to the National Soul*, 33.

17. Breward, *History of the Churches in Australasia*, 248; Ely, "Forgotten Nationalism," 59–67.

18. Hudson, *Australian Religious Thought*, 81–90.

19. Hudson, *Australian Religious Thought*, 81.

20. For a useful summary of this work, see Benson, "T. E. Ruth and *The Common Weal*."

More significantly, Ruth listed several publications to which he was indebted. This reads like a short bibliography of classic Christian Socialist works.[21] He also had read "a score of other books, and many Australian and English newspapers." The social gospel movement in Australia has been described as "the product of a recovery of the message of the prophets of the Old Testament combined with a discovery of the insights of sociology and socialism, especially Fabian socialism."[22]

Included was a foreword by Professor Meredith Atkinson (1883–1929) of the University of Melbourne, who had been active in the Workers' Educational Association and declared "a patriot" by Ruth, presumably because of his advocacy of conscription.[23] Meredith, who had no church connections, thought that these studies "breathe the spirit of Christianity as our age peculiarly needs it." He commented that "a long experience of the working-class has shown me that they despise and distrust the Churches," so Ruth's essays were welcomed.[24]

The first address was the basis of all that followed. "The Social Significance of the Kingdom" was introduced by reference to the Lord's Prayer with the idea of the Fatherhood of God and his Kingdom.[25] This is "our creed and the citizen's programme." In Ruth's distinctive emphasis, "Thy will be done on earth" becomes "the prayer of an Imperialist and the prayer of a reformer." He argued that "we are living in the age of the social question" and that "this is the supreme characteristic of the twentieth century." This is demonstrated not only in the clash of arms in Europe but in "a strike mania" in Australia. Social enthusiasts complained that the churches had left the preaching of social revolution to "Red Revolutionaries," but what was needed now was authentic social reconstruction. Ruth quoted from Edwin Hatch's major study of the early church: "The unaccomplished mission of Christianity is to reconstruct society on the basis of brotherhood."[26] He concluded by inviting his hearers to express their faith "in some practical good Samaritanism."[27]

---

21. Ruth, *Common Weal*, iii; Peabody, *Jesus Christ and the Social Question*; Keeble, *Industrial Day-Dreams*; Abbott, *Christianity and Social Problems*; Gladden, *Social Salvation*.

22. Piggin and Linder, *Fountain of Public Prosperity*, 475.

23. For Atkinson, see *ADB*; Ruth, *The Catholic*, 49.

24. Ruth, *Common Weal*, iv–v.

25. Ruth, *Common Weal*, 1–8.

26. Ruth, *Common Weal*, 7; Hatch, *Organisation*.

27. Ruth, *Common Weal*, 8.

Ruth next turned directly to a most pressing issue in Australia, "The reconciliation of Capital and Labour."[28] He noted that in the war between capital and labor a third party was involved—the general community. While there were no specific instructions in the gospels about "economic machinery," the real question was that of "horizon," of setting daily duty in its relation to wholeness and by refusing to subordinate "profits to personality." The solution to the admittedly great problem of conflict between labor and capital is, quite simply, the Golden Rule.[29]

In "Industrial Prussianism," Ruth extended his analysis of industrial relations, suggesting that in the current coal strike "Prussianism" (a ruthless and despotic attitude similar to the Prussian generals and the Kaiser in the war) was dominating the industrial scene.[30] Capital Prussianism led to "a calculated capitalistic contrivance that crushes independence, that makes a workman nothing but a machine for grinding out wealth." "Labour Prussianism" had attained an unprecedented perfection of organization and can order rank and file unionists to "down tools" as though they were military conscripts. Ruth did note, however, that Trade Unions were necessary for the protection of labor interests, and that he also believed in the agitator, "though not in too many of them and not at all in Prussianism." It ought to be impossible for an agitator to declare a strike without a secret ballot and that married men should have at least three times the influence of single men. Once again, the Golden Rule was invoked as the way to industrial peace.

Turning to a similar theme, "Workers and Non-Workers," Ruth began with an extended rehearsal of his adventures when he posed as a tramp in Westmoreland (as described in chapter 2). This led him to suggest that "nothing can be done for a vast section of humanity until laziness is recognised as a crime."[31] He was, however, sensitive to the tragedy of prolonged unemployment and gave a thoughtful and informed summary of how this came about in Australia. He blamed class warfare between labor and capital, but also appealed to the individual: "There is no real collectivism that is not based on personal character."[32]

Ruth then commented on a major social issue, "Houses and Homes." After witty comments about real estate salesmen's exaggerated descriptions of properties, he insisted on the familiar distinction between a house and a home. He noted the common tragedy of slums:

28. Ruth, *Common Weal*, 9–16.
29. Ruth, *Common Weal*, 16.
30. Ruth, *Common Weal*, 17–27.
31. Ruth, *Common Weal*, 32.
32. Ruth, *Common Weal*, 34.

> It is really amazing that in a new country, having a new city to make and a clean map on which to place it, and with ample land to spare, and with the horrible examples of the old country before them, that the authorities should have permitted such places as slums to disgrace this land of sunshine and vast spreading spaces . . . A slum is not merely a blot on the beauty of a place, and not merely a menace to physical health, and a centre of moral filth—a slum is the negation of civilization, the negation of Christianity.[33]

Responsibility for the slum, of course, lay not with the victims but with the slum-owners. He praised the Garden City movement in England as an example of what might be done in town planning, but the most important challenge was with the families who lived in houses. The family was the fundamental social organization: "Marriage is not a human contrivance, a civil contract, a common enterprise—it is a divine order."[34] Ruth concluded:

> The nearest image earth holds of hell is the loveless, joyless home, where God is not known, where contempt has supplanted reverence, where hate has cast out love. And the nearest image earth holds of heaven is the home where God is known and worshipped, where father, mother, children know God well enough to laugh in His presence, where perfect love casts out fear, the place of light and love, holiness and humour, mirth and music, song and sacrifice.[35]

For his sixth talk Ruth spoke on "Literature and Life and the Devil in Ink." Inevitably he recalled visiting Germany where he saw the reputed ink-stains on the wall of the room in the Wartburg castle where Luther was said to have thrown ink at the devil. True or not, "it is certain that the devil has been flinging ink ever since."[36] Fine literature and depraved filth are both produced by the printing process. One danger was sensationalism, but Ruth was particularly concerned to attack "the positively indecent" in newspapers and in the immoral magazine or the sex novel.[37]

Probably the most difficult address, because of "the extreme delicacy of the subject," was "Problems of Sex." Not that he was unaware of the ideal which is "altogether a beautiful and divine thing," but he felt he did need to

---

33. Ruth, *Common Weal*, 39.
34. Ruth, *Common Weal*, 43.
35. Ruth, *Common Weal*, 44.
36. Ruth, *Common Weal*, 47.
37. Ruth, *Common Weal*, 49.

tackle "certain problems."[38] He began by a reference to "the Hebrew poem of the beginning of things" (Genesis 1) where "all sex is seen to be of divine origin." The genesis of the father–mother idea is in God. Indeed, the physical union of man and woman in the Hebrew prophets becomes "the symbol of the union of God and the soul."

Yet there was the fearful problem of sexual immorality, of letting lust take the place of love:

> We can transgress the ordinance of God and men, and the penalty is written in bodies blighted by loathsome disease, that spreads its poisons of putrefaction, not only among the sensualists of society, but among innocent men and women and children, bequeathing even to children unborn a heritage of foul blood and depraved instincts.[39]

Statistics regarding syphilis in Australia were alarming. Ruth claimed that children's deaths in Australia attributed to a syphilitic cause amounted to 3,326.[40] Prohibition, segregation, and regulation had all failed. Christ's method was fundamentally different. He did not regard any woman as "an abandoned woman . . . She is not shut out from the congregations or from His personal conversation."[41] Christ didn't condone in man what is condemned in woman. Ruth also insisted:

> There are illegitimate parents but there are no illegitimate children. There never have been, there never can be any illegitimate children. The children born of illegitimate parents ought never be penalised by the community. In any case the child is the best asset of the community, and the community ought to care much more for the child.[42]

Ruth supported sex education but was dubious about this being taught in State schools by ordinary teachers; rather, this should be done by "an expert, preferably a medical man or woman."[43]

The next five lectures were all devoted to the problems of alcohol in the Australian community. In "A Case against the Drink Traffic," Ruth rehearsed familiar arguments in favor of total abstinence. Alcohol caused physical deterioration, mental deterioration, affected the moral nature and

38. Ruth, *Common Weal*, 52.
39. Ruth, *Common Weal*, 55.
40. Ruth, *Common Weal*, 55.
41. Ruth, *Common Weal*, 57.
42. Ruth, *Common Weal*, 58.
43. Ruth, *Common Weal*, 59.

so inevitably had "the gravest social significance." Ruth asked all his hearers to "personally abstain."[44]

In the ninth chapter, Ruth defended the church's role in temperance reform. The church "had been founded by Christ for the salvation of the world" but also had the duty of the salvation of society: "The mission of the Church is not only to the individual, but to the social conscience."[45] His concluding appeal was both direct and personal:

> How slight a thing it is you are asked to do—not to drink that which causes another to fall. Besides, total abstinence is not simply a temporary expedient for a critical condition of society. It is one of the conditions of the highest physical, mental, and moral efficiency. Pledge yourself to Christ. Pledge yourself to the State.[46]

The temperance theme was continued in the next chapter, "The Drink Traffic and Public Life" in which he examined the social and political ramifications of the liquor industry from the perspective of "a citizen and a British Imperialist."[47]

An unusual feature of his next address, "'Vested Interests' versus 'Victory,'" was his text, two volumes of *Hansard*, the record of Parliamentary Debates Numbers 20 and 21. The point of these extensive quotations from *Hansard*, doubtless read with great dramatic flair, was to show that the prohibition of the "Strength of Britain" movement, which advocated temperance, had been motivated by vested interests of the liquor industry.[48]

This all flowed into his twelfth chapter, "Why Not Censor the Drink Traffic?" His basic argument here was that since a form of literature censorship was adopted in Australia for war purposes, the drink traffic ought also to be censored. He called for a great citizens' movement:

> The people are ready. And the leaders are ready. Arrangements are under way . . . And this is real church service—service for the good name of God, service for His glory and our fellows' good . . . Our immediate duty is to secure a proclamation of prohibition against the misuse of the alcohol God has made, during

---

44. Ruth, *Common Weal*, 60–66.
45. Ruth, *Common Weal*, 68.
46. Ruth, *Common Weal*, 75.
47. Ruth, *Common Weal*, 82.
48. Ruth, *Common Weal*, 94.

wartime, and the time of demobilisation. That is our immediate duty. And may God help us.[49]

For the next three addresses Ruth turned to that other familiar target of many Protestants: gambling, which he characterized as "Australia's Pet Vice." Ruth declared it to be theft, even when linked with some charitable purpose.

Ruth asked in his next address, "What's Wrong with a Bet?" He offered a concise definition of Christianity: "Christianity is Christ's revelation of the Fatherhood of God, the brotherhood of man, the sanctity of life, the dignity of labor and the stewardship of wealth. And gambling is the practical denial of every one of these."[50] Ruth insisted that for the Christian man "there is never any justification for a gamble," any gains are "tainted money, a sort of Judas treasure, stained with blood."[51]

And there was more! "After the Referendum, the Cup!" picked up Ruth's deep agitation over the conscription referendum and the insistence by many that notwithstanding all the tensions and divisions in society the Melbourne Cup, already an Australian institution, must be run and with, at least in Melbourne, a public holiday. This was too much for Ruth, who recalled that no holiday was given for the conduct of the referendum: "Everything is completely surrendered to the Cup."[52]

His sixteenth chapter dealt with Sunday and the question of whether it could be "saved as a democratic institution." Observance of Sunday or "the Sabbath" had long been a controversial issue for many church people, certainly among Baptists.[53] Ruth claimed that Sunday was "a great democratic gift from God," by which he meant that it came "laden with spiritual opportunities of eternal value." The pleasures of Sunday were usually "purchased with somebody's pain . . . Sunday amusements mean Sunday employment."[54] He hoped politicians would see the benefits of Sunday rest but must proceed on "purely political grounds and not in the interests of religion."[55]

Another challenge was taken up by Ruth in "Christianity and Amusements." Rejecting the notion that Christianity had no connection whatever with amusements, he suggested that "Christianity is connected with every real interest of life and with amusements and recreation no less than with our daily

---

49. Ruth, *Common Weal*, 104.
50. Ruth, *Common Weal*, 113.
51. Ruth, *Common Weal*, 116.
52. Ruth, *Common Weal*, 124.
53. See Manley, *From Woolloomooloo*, 363–67.
54. Ruth, *Common Weal*, 128.
55. Ruth, *Common Weal*, 131.

work."[56] Ruth suggested three guidelines. We must avoid unnecessary association with evil. We must guard against excess even of legitimate pleasure. We must make amusements our ministers, not our masters.[57]

The final lecture in the series had the intriguing title, "Why Can't We Cast Out Devils?" This was based on Matthew 17, which records three disciples going up the Mount of Transfiguration with Jesus and then, after their descent, Jesus healed an epileptic boy. The disciples who had not been able to help the boy asked Jesus, "Why could we not cast it out?" Jesus replied, "Because of your little faith." Ruth suggested that life is "a constant alternation between mountain glory and valley gloom."[58] The devils of modern times had been named as selfism, sensualism, skepticism, and superstition.[59] Christ constituted the Church as "the moral Exorcist," but too often it fails. The problem was the same one that the disciples found: a lack of faith.[60]

Although Ruth had tackled some familiar Protestant issues (gambling, alcohol, sexual immorality, and Sunday observance) his approach was lively, and he was remarkably well read. *The Common Weal* suggests that Ruth did speak to his community and acted as a public theologian.

Mission to Democracy

This sixth series of nine talks from July 1919 proved to be the last that Ruth preached in the Auditorium, and they appeared weekly in the *Australian Baptist*. This is the clearest revelation of Ruth bringing a theological perspective to some of the key problems of his community's life.

The first in this series was "The Democratic Ideal," defined as "Every man a Christian in the Church, every man a Saviour in the State."[61] Many of Ruth's familiar emphases were reaffirmed. The New Testament is "the most democratic document in the world" because it reveals the Fatherhood of God, and when this is affirmed as "our Father" it becomes the basis of brotherhood on which society is to be reconstructed. The first affirmation in his introduction was slightly changed to read "Every man a priest in the Church," and again he stressed the priesthood of all believers:

---

56. Ruth, *Common Weal*, 133.
57. Ruth, *Common Weal*, 137.
58. Ruth, *Common Weal*, 142.
59. Ruth, *Common Weal*, 143.
60. Ruth, *Common Weal*, 149.
61. *AB*, July 29, 1919, 1.

"Every man a priest in the Church, in touch with God, offering spiritual sacrifices, living in benediction."[62]

To this ideal was linked the ideal in society: "Every man a saviour in the State"; "Every son of man is sent into the world to save." In the New Testament, this phrase was used of the unique mission of Jesus as the Son of Man (Mark 10:45), so Ruth was daring in this application of the phrase.

The year 1919 was a record year for strikes in Australia. There were 460 industrial disputes involving 157,591 workers. All up, 6.3 million working days were lost. The most prominent dispute of 1919 was the three-month seamen's strike.[63] Ruth argued that precisely as the church had allowed priesthood to become a caste and not applied to every believer, so "we have delegated social saviourhood to committee, clique and caucus," hence "a disastrous strike, delegating responsibility to men whose profession it is to create strife, and who refuse to listen to reason and the demands of democracy."[64] Ruth's appeal was "overwhelmingly individualistic": "Don't sell your conscience to any combine, capital or labour."[65]

His concluding affirmation about what he thought Christ would do in contemporary Australia should be carefully noted: "I do not think He would hesitate to use force to secure the safety of the State, the sanctity of the home, the right to work, and the securing of daily bread."[66] But how would Christ "use force"? Ruth here foreshadowed the stance that he adopted in Sydney in days of civil unrest when he advocated support for the New Guard movement and raised the possibility of using force in the state.

The second address in the series was titled, "The Priest, the Profiteer, and the Average Citizen." This address was replete with familiar attacks on Mannix and the Catholic Church, but it was not only the priest but also the profiteer and the professional strike-promoter who engaged in exploiting the people. He drew on Matthew 18:15–17 to suggest that there were three stages in the resolution of any conflict: personal interview, a deputation, and then a compulsory conference. But if none of these achieves resolution then a third party, "the community, the Government should step in and take strong action to defend the homes of the people, the sanctity of the State, the right to work, the right to earn daily bread."[67]

62. *AB*, July 29, 1919, 2.
63. Macintyre, "Strikes and Lockouts," in *Oxford Companion*, 620–21.
64. *AB*, July 29, 1919, 4.
65. *AB*, July 29, 1919, 4.
66. *AB*, July 29, 1919, 4.
67. *AB*, August 12, 1919, 1.

He then digressed to argue that just as Mannix and Sinn Feiners had worked to disrupt the war effort, so the Irish controlled the workers' movements: "Australia is being run by Messrs Walsh, Kelly, Denley, Burke, O'Neil and O'Neill . . . The Walsheviks have followed in the wake of the Papacy in their methods of controversy."[68] Of course there were profiteers as well, so Ruth confessed: "and for a moment I do not wonder at the socialist threat of revolution." Ruth pleaded for "a saner sense of relationship, a spirit not of revenge but of justice, a spirit not of mutual recrimination but of mutual recognition, a spirit of personal and social righteousness—the entire issue comes back there."[69]

The third talk had the somewhat provocative title, "A Plea for One Big Union. Really Big Enough." The "One Big Union" was an idea in the late nineteenth and early twentieth centuries among trade unionists to unite the interests of workers and offer solutions to all labor problems. It was linked with the International Workers of the World (the "Wobblies"). Ruth admitted that when he had planned the series:

> No one anticipated that the entire social atmosphere would be vitiated, that industrial reason would be dethroned . . . that the seamen's strike would be used to point the moral of every reference to capital and labour and that the subject would therefore be so inflammatory . . . We cannot ignore the seamen's strike and discuss social problems in an academic fashion and close our eyes to the actual conditions that obtain in our city.[70]

Ruth believed that the claims of the seamen were "just and reasonable" while the shipping companies had made millions of pounds during the war. But the problem was with the union which was more concerned with inflicting injury upon the community "for the sake of a particular method of social rebellion which would not only plunge the city of Melbourne into darkness but involve democracy in defeat and disgrace."[71] He defended the place of arbitration in the dispute. He argued that there was "One Big Union" that was more important: the Union of the Commonwealth of Australia and the government as its executive.

Ruth likened the problem with the unions to that with the churches: "In religion we call it sectarianism. In Labor we call it class-consciousness. Class-consciousness is really industrial sectarianism."[72] If we needed

68. *AB*, August 12, 1919, 2.
69. *AB*, August 12, 1919, 3.
70. *AB*, August 26, 1919, 1.
71. *AB*, August 26, 1919, 2.
72. *AB*, August 26, 1919, 2.

inter-denominationalism, we also needed "One Big Union," which is the dream of certain industrial revolutionaries. But this vision is not big enough, and the cure is a "Commonwealth-consciousness," an actual partnership which includes profit-sharing. He believed in this as a possibility because he believed in the possibilities of public righteousness, in the establishment upon earth of the kingdom of God. One example of what might be done was what he had read about in the USA where the labor organization of Mississippi had appointed "labor-chaplains."[73] After all, his dream was of "the One Big Union" that was really big enough, that takes in God and Christ and Eternity.

The fourth talk was devoted to a similar theme, "Work, Wages, Wealth. The Common Right to Riches." His hope was certainly ambitious, to relate the world of labor to the world of God's work in the world.

> What is wrong with Walshevism or Bolshevism is its avowed class-consciousness, its industrial sectarianism, its substitution of a section of society for the whole . . . And that is what is often wrong with the so-called capitalistic class—class consciousness, the exclusive combine spirit, want of balance, proportion, sympathy and sense of relation.[74]

He rankled at the suggestion that if only he was a worker he would understand the problems:

> I don't plough a paddock, carry a hod, lay bricks, stoke engines or secretary a seaman's union. I do not ply tools with my hands or bear burdens on my back, or earn my bread in sweat of brow—though I earn it. I am trying to do my bit in the making of manhood, in the ministry of reconciliation, involving expenditure of nerve force and brain fag, and I am not a working man forsooth![75]

He admired the achievements of Australia as "the social laboratory of the world": the eight hour day, the factory acts, the public health acts, the wages boards and arbitration courts. More is needed—something more than price fixing, something like profit-fixing—in order to prevent profiteering.

His next talk was even more directly related to the present challenges in the industrial area: "Industrial Sectarianism versus Industrial Democracy." He argued that the war "had precipitated another world-wide conflict, a conflict not between labor and capital, but between anarchy and order, between

---

73. Pearce Carey had also advocated an active link between labor and the churches: see Manley, *"An Honoured Name,"* 102–3.

74. *AB*, September 9, 1919, 1.

75. *AB*, September 9, 1919, 1.

industrial sectarianism and industrial democracy, between industrial Sinn Feinism and the sovereignty of the people."[76] His emphasis on what he termed "industrial sectarianism" enabled him to declare that he would ship all the Sinn Feiners back to Ireland, the Bolsheviks to "the Bolshevik Soviet system" and as for the suffragettes—he would not send them back to England but keep them in political restraint as a species of super-spinsters who "didn't raise her boy to be a soldier"![77]

Ruth regularly studied the workers' papers and quoted extensively from the *Australian Worker* with its sharp criticism of a recent State Labor Conference, which was "a spectacle to make the angels weep." He proposed "industrial democracy," which would mean "not simply a civilised wage, it will mean participation in profits. It will mean the principle of joint control. The workers will have a share in the wealth and a voice in the management."[78]

Study number seven was "Men as Money-Making Machines or as Men." This covered familiar themes, drawing on the life of US millionaire Andrew Carnegie (1835–1919). His sources ranged through John Stuart Mill to the *Australian Worker* to demonstrate that man was more than a money-making machine. He enthused about Australian firms which were applying "principles of co-partnership," including most especially the Australian Paper Mills, of which his close friend Brookes was Chairman of Directors and which Ruth had personally visited to talk with employees.[79] He concluded, "The word is get together as employees and employers. Meet as men and women, not as parts of a money-making machine."[80]

The eighth talk was titled, "Revolution or Evolution." His basic argument was clear:

> Christ and the Apostles did not acquiesce in slavery, though they instituted no social or political rebellion against it. They did not set the entire social fabric in flames. They were not destructive revolutionaries. They were progressive evolutionists. They initiated certain evolutionary ideas that ultimately abolished slavery.[81]

With the optimism of a true liberal he asserted, "And now at last the day of democracy has dawned." He then attacked the "evil trinity": "Russian Bolshevism is own brother to Irish Sinn Feinism and they are both brothers to

---

76. *AB*, October 7, 1919, 1.
77. *AB*, October 7, 1919, 1.
78. *AB*, October 7, 1919, 3.
79 *AB* October 28, 1919, 2; Rivett, *Australian Citizen*, 52–53.
80. *AB*, October 28, 1919, 3.
81. *AB*, December 2, 1919, 2.

German Prussianism." What we need, asserted Ruth, was not foreign revolution but rather "Australian evolution":

> A progressive educational programme, a progressive social and industrial programme and a progressive political programme, and we must have men of executive power who will fulfil their platform promises and give practical expression to democratic ideals in the schools and universities; in municipal councils and in conditions of labor; in State and Federal Houses of Parliament.[82]

The churches, which he believed held the key to the whole situation, must stand by the people. Newspapers must become "reason sheets of life and labor." He thundered his conclusion:

> We must see light not through the key-hole and the chinks of the door of a class-consciousness dungeon. We must fling open the doors and windows of our minds and hearts in the Divine Democracy of the Christ, the Son of Righteousness risen with healing in his wings and labor for the dawn of the divine day.[83]

Ruth concluded his "Mission to Democracy" with "Both Sides of the Counter" in which he insisted that Christianity must prevail over all transactions in life. Christ is more than "a Sunday Christ, King only in a Church-Kindergarten sense." More than half Christ's parables concern business life and yet some still try to make some distinction between sacred and secular callings. "The meaning of Christianity and the meaning of business is brotherhood," which Ruth interpreted as demonstrating truth, honesty and chivalry.

The one law for all social and business life was the Golden Rule: "Whatsoever ye would that men should do unto you, do ye even so to them":

> Practise incarnation. See the other man's point of view. Put yourself in his place. The incarnation will lead on to the cross—you will help bear the other's burden. But the cross leads to the coronation of character and the linking of earth to heaven ... Men who do business under the shadow of the Cross will have commerce with the skies. And men who have commerce with the skies are the men who will save Australia, establish a Divine Commonwealth, a Kingdom of God on earth—Theocracy through Democracy.[84]

---

82. *AB*, December 2, 1912, 11.
83. *AB*, December 2, 1919, 11.
84. *AB*, December 16, 1919, 3.

So ended Ruth's mission series for 1919 but in 1922 he contributed nine articles for the Melbourne *Herald*, a further demonstration of his desire to speak to the Melbourne public and an anticipation of his numerous contributions to the daily papers in Sydney. The first article was "The Canberra Compromise,"[85] and over the next four weeks a further four talks from his democracy series were published.[86]

Then in October and November 1922, the *Herald* published four more contributions by Ruth in a series of "Domestic Articles, Specially Written for the Herald." One was a remarkable essay on "Woman. A Natural Archpriestess in Religion and a Queen in Her Own Realm," while another on "Sex and the Race" provoked a positive endorsement from Lawrence Adamson (1860–1932), the Principal of Wesley College, regarding the provision of sex education within schools.[87]

Ruth's essay on "Woman" expresses views well in advance of his time among Australian Baptists.[88] A brief overview of the traditional place of woman in religion noted that leadership had always been male and listed comments by some Church Fathers on women, such as Tertullian's infamous phrase, that women were "the gate of hell."[89] Ruth concluded that women had every right to mock man who has paid the price for exclusivity, as his ecclesiastical policy has split the church, and his theology has made religion hateful to multitudes. Noting a recent controversy over whether the word "obey" should be used in the marriage service, Ruth commented that in twenty-one years in the ministry he had only once inserted this word, and that was in Australia at the request of the bride. He regarded marriage as "a mutual obligation": "In the domestic sphere a woman is rather more than a man's equal, unless he happens to be a chef." Each great age can claim "some great-souled women." As the feminine influence in religion is traced, the masculine blunder in seeking to repress it is revealed. Once the place of woman is recognized, "Domesticity will take the place of dogma ... It is the woman soul that gets behind the elaborate structures of ecclesiastical theory and theological dogma into the sovereign simplicity of life ... In

---

85. *Herald*, July 8, 1922, 13.

86. These were "What can we do for Australia?" (July 15); "Work, Wages and Wealth" (July 22); "One Big Union" (July 29); "A plea for Industrial Democracy" (August 5).

87. *Herald*, November 9, 1922, 11. The articles were "Woman" (October 28); "Sex and the Race" (November 4); "Houses and Homes" (November 11); and "The Devil in Ink" (November 18).

88. *Herald*, October 28, 1922, 13.

89. On the Apparel of Women, Book I, Ch. I.

Australia the Christian law of spiritual equality finds complete expression in the political equality of the sexes."

Ruth claimed even more. Woman is more than a story of emancipation:

> The crimson years of war brought the most amazing revelation of women's physical endurance, powers of industrial management and practical capacity for public affairs. And life can never be the same again! The old dominations have been tremendously weakened if not destroyed—the domination of militarism; the domination of money; the domination of caste and clique; and the domination of sex. The word Woman stands for a distinct revelation of God. The exigencies of language mislead us into thinking of God as masculine. But God is Mother as well as Father. When He made man "in His own image," "male and female created He them."

Ruth insisted, "Woman as a revelation of God stands richly related to every part of life, and brings to man light and love and the kind of laughter in which angels join."

This was a fascinating exposition by Ruth in a secular paper and represented a progressive perspective on the place of women in the church. Sadly, it was to be decades before the place of women in leadership was further developed among Australian Baptists.[90]

Ruth's desire to be a public theologian, relating the principles of the gospel to both personal and community life, were clearly expressed in Melbourne. His days in Sydney gave him even wider opportunities to fulfil his prophetic calling.

---

90. See Manley, *From Woolloomooloo*, 730–36.

8

The Eschatology of T. E. Ruth

RUTH WAS A POPULAR preacher and writer, but not a systematic theologian. However, two of his major books dealt with eschatology, "the doctrine of last things." Both undoubtedly arose from his public ministry in Melbourne. Both, as was the case with so much of Ruth's preaching, were controversial to the minds of traditional and conservative evangelicals.

These books are essentially sermons rather than theological tomes. Ruth's rhetorical skills such as repetition, alliteration, cumulative phrasing, and a robust, confronting style are on display. His arguments are not presented with any academic pretension but with that raciness of style, passion, and dogmatism that marked most of his preaching. There are no footnotes or careful documenting of sources although he does clearly name all those writers whom he quotes extensively. Poets and philosophers as well as theologians and preachers are cited. The two books are linked by two eschatological themes: the meaning of death in Christian thought and the Second Advent of Christ. The second was a long-time obsession of Ruth's as he was deeply offended by many millenarians who flourished in the heated atmosphere of war days.

Both these books have been cited as examples of liberal teaching among Baptists in New South Wales, although both were written in Melbourne.[1]

---

1. Hansen, "Churches and Society," 58–59, 62–63.

The Progress of Personality after Death[2]

This book clearly arose from the pastoral responsibilities of comforting the bereaved during the war, although he had shown the same belief in England when speaking about the death of the noted preacher Charles Williams.[3] Many faced the challenge of finding hope and meaning in the loss of loved ones, but especially those whom he frequently identified as "martyr soldiers" or "soldier sons." He welcomed the opportunity to preach a coherent and comforting doctrine for all people whatever their circumstances. Ruth believed that this hope was at the very heart of the gospel that he felt called to deliver.

Naturally, Ruth often preached on this theme during the war years, as did so many. He shows wide reading not only of his beloved Romantic poets and theologians but also of the more significant works by contemporary preachers and theologians who tackled this theme. His book demonstrates how one thoughtful and original preacher in Australia faced these real challenges to faith and Christian living. Published in hardcover in 1919, the book of 192 pages was dedicated "To My Wife and Comrade."

Ruth always enjoyed antagonizing "comfortable" evangelicals. He had already faced a controversy with fellow-Baptist William Lamb over his statements about purgatory, and he recounts this.[4] The broad theological position adopted by Ruth is what is commonly defined as universalism. Although this has a variety of forms, it basically insists that eventually all human beings without exception will attain salvation.[5] Various English theologians had extended debates on the subject with many rejecting the idea of hell and everlasting punishment. The hope of a continued spiritual growth even after death has direct links with the evolutionism of the Romantic Movement, which as we have seen was influential on much of Ruth's theology.[6] Many evangelicals were drawn to this theological position for it offered hope that world-wide suffering and the deaths of innocents, such as the war produced in distressing numbers, was not the final word to humanity. No one will be eternally damned and ultimately all will "go home" to God.

Inevitably, those who argued for the absolute authority of the Bible believed that universalism undermined the relevance and necessity of saving

---

2. Ruth, *Progress of Personality*.

3. *CW Pulpit*, May 1907, 249–51.

4. Ruth, *Progress*, 68–71.

5. See "Universalism," in Ferguson and Wright, *New Dictionary of Theology*, 701–3.

6. For the background of Romanticism, see Reardon, *Religion in the Age of Romanticism*.

faith without which no one could be saved. Ruth dismissed this kind of formulaic argument as simply an "evangelical shibboleth."[7] Universalism was also held to deny the necessity or at least the urgency of evangelism, since no one will be lost in any case. Conservatives also suggested that universalism rejects the assertion that Christianity is the only true faith since generally for the universalist there are many roads to God. This of course raises the question of the relationship between Christianity and other world religions.

The interpretation of several complex biblical texts and ideas was fiercely contested. These affected the perception of God, as well as the nature and extent of his love. Many felt passionately about this theology as Ruth's book clearly demonstrates. His is an excellent example of how a dogmatic and passionate exposition of universalism (though the word is rarely used by Ruth) could make this view so appealing and relevant for grieving and hopeless people.

Several other books from this period attempted to bring similar guidance and hope. A few of these are cited by Ruth and demonstrate just how urgent this question became during the war. For example, Arthur Chambers (c. 1853–1918), an Anglican vicar, published two books quoted by Ruth. *Our Life after Death or The Teaching of the Bible concerning the Unseen World* (1894) went through several editions in his lifetime (and no less than seventy-seven by 2015) while what he called "that illuminating book," *Man and the Spiritual World* (1900) was also extremely popular.[8] Ruth followed Chambers's basic approach in style and content.

Another significant recent volume utilized by Ruth was "the great book," *Immortality: An Essay in Discovery. Co-ordinating Scientific, Psychical, and Biblical Research*. This scholarly and ambitious book included two biblical chapters by the distinguished British New Testament scholar B. H. Streeter (1874–1937).

A more devotional study was the small book of sixty-four pages by the leading English Baptist evangelical F. B. Meyer (1847–1929), *Our Sister Death* (1915). Meyer told the story of how a leading minister every day asked God to "pass on the message of his dear love to his daughter" who had died some time before. Meyer commented—and this appealed to Ruth—"We trust our prayers to Christ: may we not also entrust our love messages?"[9] In another book, *Where Are Our Dead?* (1918), Meyer had suggested that seekers after truth might be able "to pursue their own light after death."[10]

---

7. Ruth, *Progress*, 128.
8. Ruth, *Progress*, 124. Chambers, *Our Life after Death; Our Self after Death*.
9. Ruth, *Progress*, 143. Meyer, *Our Sister Death*.
10. Meyer, *Where are our Dead?*, Randall, *Spirituality and Social Change*, 56.

Another writer whom Ruth also quoted extensively was the Welsh Congregational minister of Bournemouth, John Daniel Jones (1865–1942), who had visited Australia in 1914. Ruth quoted from his books *The Great Hereafter. Questions Raised by the Great War Concerning the Destiny of our Dead* (1915) and *If a Man Die* (1917).[11]

Welsh theologian Ebenezer Griffith-Jones (1860–1942) wrote "a great book," *Faith and Immortality: A Study of the Christian Doctrine of the Life to Come* (1917).[12] Harold Begbie (1871–1929), the English author and journalist and J. Rendle Harris (1852–1941), biblical scholar and curator of biblical manuscripts, were also authors cited by Ruth.[13]

All these writers contributed to Ruth's thinking although his originality must not be minimized. He ranged widely in his search for helpful quotations or allusions. Public figures noted were as varied as Herbert Spencer, Arthur Balfour, Ralph Emerson, Socrates, Oliver Lodge, Oliver Wendell Holmes, Samuel Johnson, John Bunyan, Jonathan Edwards, and C. H. Spurgeon. He also regularly included snatches, or in some cases long extracts, from famous poems and hymns. Ruth drew on a rich variety of literary and theological sources as well as biblical texts. Poets most frequently used were (supremely) Alfred Tennyson, Rudyard Kipling, Charles Kingsley, James Russell Lowell, Robert Browning, Francis Thompson, John Greenleaf Whittier, and Arthur Russell Wallace.

One key puzzle lies in the title of the book. What exactly did Ruth mean by the "personality" that progresses beyond death? He seems to use "personality" as an equivalent of "soul" as in the doctrine commonly called "the immortality of the soul." Asserting that "personality persists beyond death," Ruth used the story of Dives and Lazarus (Luke 16:19–31) to argue that the life beyond death is "personal, full, vivid, conscious."[14] Personality is "this consciousness that becomes self-conscious, into the self-consciousness, with its sub-consciousness and its super-consciousness, its creative thought and action and its survival of the shock of death."[15]

> I am a living soul, touched by the deathless spirit—that is I myself, the mental, moral, invisible, persistent being, clothing itself for a while in a physical body, but being of such enormous value that our Lord sets it in the balance against the whole physical

---

11. Ruth, *Progress*, 77–78, 105, 126–27, 135.
12. Ruth, *Progress*, 73.
13. Ruth, *Progress*, 105, 146.
14. Ruth, *Progress*, 33.
15. Ruth, *Progress*, 49.

universe and asks, What shall it profit a man if he gains the whole world and lose his own self.[16]

Chapter one asked the question, "Is Death a Terminus or a Thoroughfare?" He quoted from J. M. Barrie's *Peter Pan* with the cheery refrain, "To die will be an awfully big adventure."[17] Death is inevitable, and physical death is "such a privative power." Various answers have been given as to what happens then. The "mere credalist" brings little more comfort than the atheist. "When any dogmatist declares that any of our dead heroes . . . have been condemned to suffer endless torment in some eternal hell, I do not want, I will not have that dogmatist's God."[18]

Indeed, humans at death enter upon a kind of impersonal immortality here on earth: "Abel being dead, yet speaketh." So, "many masters of science and art and literature" have continuing relevance. In another sense, the desire for immortality is "profound and persistent." Life's inequalities and injustices seem to demand some possibility in the future life. "If there is a God, if God made the world, if God is good, if God is just, there must be some other world to save the present world from the contempt of honest men."[19] Ruth quoted an old Scottish epitaph:

Here lie I, Martin Elginbrod,

Hae mercy on my soul, Lord God,

As I would do if I were God

And ye were Martin Elginbrod.

So, the world's injustices and inequalities demand "a world beyond, a world of compensation, larger, infinitely larger than the world of our old evangelical conception . . . And the judge of all the earth is not the slave of any sect."[20]

Here the gospel message proclaims that "Christ hath abolished death, broken down its barriers and brought life and immortality to light" (2 Tim 1:10), a text which Ruth repeated regularly throughout his book. He then quoted the little boy's voice in Maeterlinck's famous play, *Blue Bird*, which always "thrills the theatre": "There are no dead."[21] A quotation from John

---

16. Ruth, *Progress*, 49–52.
17. Ruth, *Progress*. 11.
18. Ruth, *Progress*, 16.
19. Ruth, *Progress*, 23.
20. Ruth, *Progress*, 24.
21. Ruth, *Progress*, 27.

McCreary's poem, "There is no Death," with the same affirmation completed Ruth's first chapter:

> And ever near us, though unseen,
>
> The dear immortal spirits tread,
>
> For all the boundless universe
>
> Is life. There are no dead.[22]

The second chapter was "Responsibility Carried Forward." Ruth suggested that never before in history had there been "such crowds of unfinished lives sacrificed to untimely death" and "the premature fall of the curtain on the incomplete act" constituted a tragedy.[23] While the New Testament is "reserved and reticent" in its revelations of what is beyond, there are broad guidelines, principally that personality persists and that responsibility is carried forward. Humans are accountable in this life: "the divine jurisdiction is involved in the very structure of the soul," and we will remain responsible beings after death; it is "an eternal thing."[24]

Many "utterly grotesque and un-Godlike" poems and pictures have depicted the judgement, but the Bible "dresses its mightiest moral realities in mystic garb."[25] We shall be judged by Christ, Ruth insists, and he is the same on the throne as he was on the cross: he judges that he may save. "No prison can keep out the Saviour of souls," Ruth claimed. "He will burn the evil out of us"; judgement is "but an examination with a view to higher education."[26]

In his third chapter, "Progressive Memory," Ruth argues that, in Browning's phrase, "Life is probation."[27] We are free to exercise choice, and death is only "an event in consciousness."[28] Life on earth is an apprenticeship and is not forgotten.

> You may certainly say of your soldier husband, soldier son, soldier brother, soldier lover—no matter at what stage of spiritual development he had arrived—you may certainly say of him, "He still lives. He still loves. He still serves." And you may be perfectly certain that wherever he is in God's vast world, he

22. Ruth, *Progress*, 28. John Lucky McCreary (1835–1906), "There is no death."
23. Ruth, *Progress*, 29–30.
24. Ruth, *Progress*, 32–37.
25. Ruth, *Progress*, 40.
26. Ruth, *Progress*, 43–44.
27. Ruth, *Progress*, 47.
28. Ruth, *Progress*, 48.

remembers you, that his memory is not destroyed by death, that his individual consciousness continues, that he is the same identical person, person as you are person, spirit as you are spirit—remembered, recognisable, and to be reunited.

For all this there is abundant Scripture—but even if there were no Scripture, it would still be true. There were revelations before there was any record, and revelations will not cease so long as God lives and man is a receptive soul.[29]

Ruth argued for this belief from the post-resurrection appearances of Jesus to Mary, the disciples on the road to Emmaus, Thomas, and Peter, concluding that "We shall carry with us when we die the faculty of memory."[30]

Returning to a familiar theme, he next addressed the topic, "The Truth behind Purgatory."[31] Quotations from Protestant writers Arthur Chambers, Principal Griffith-Jones, and Dr. J. D. Jones all confirmed Ruth's judgement that while Roman Catholic doctrine and practice of purgatory was an error, there were three truths behind purgatory that should be accepted. The first was the idea of a probation after death. The second was that purification continues after death, and the third truth was the idea of progress after death.

Chapter five addressed the biblical question, "With What Body?" (1 Cor 15:35). Ruth summarized his belief that the gospel taught the immortality of the soul as well as "a spiritual resurrection of the body—the redemption of the whole man." "The other side is not a land of ghostly existences, of disembodied spooks, of inane occupations. It is as real, as solid, as substantial as anything here."[32] Following the Apostle Paul's discussion in 1 Corinthians 15, he argued that resurrection of the body did not mean a literal resurrection of the physical body and turned to the poets to express his hopes, such as Tennyson's poem, "By an Evolutionist":

> The Lord let the house of a brute to the soul of a man.
>
> And the man said, "Am I your debtor?"
>
> And the Lord—"Not yet, but make it as clean as you can,
>
> And then I will let you a better."[33]

---

29. Ruth, *Progress*, 61.
30. Ruth, *Progress*, 66.
31. Ruth, *Progress*, 68–85.
32. Ruth, *Progress*, 87.
33. Ruth, *Progress*, 92.

"In death and through death and after death, we shall be clothed, be embodied. There will be resurrection, advancement, progress."[34] He thought that there was evidence for this "psychic" reality in the gospels with the stories of Christ on the Mount of Transfiguration and the resurrection appearances of Christ.

Ruth attached great importance to the idea of the spiritual body as an instrument of self-identity: "It is part and parcel of the persistence of personality . . . I do not learn from the Gospel that I shall ever be a disembodied ghost. God prepares us a body . . . We shall need the spiritual body as a medium of recognition."[35] Ruth then quoted a passage from the Hindu Sanskrit scripture the Bhagavad-Gita:

> As one who layeth
>
> His worn-out robes away
>
> And taketh new ones, sayeth
>
> "These will I wear today."
>
> So putteth by the spirit
>
> Lightly the garb of flesh,
>
> And passeth to inherit
>
> A fairer garb afresh.[36]

In a more conventional selection, he turned to Tennyson's words from his long poem, "In memoriam AHH":

> Eternal form will still divide
>
> The Eternal soul from all beside,
>
> And I shall know him when we meet.[37]

The spiritual body promises recognition, friendship, and fellowship. "There is no isolated individualism in which personality is lost, but society, free, joyous, happy; no cloistered cells, no sectarian-split souls, no exclusive Church; but a city, a commonwealth, a kingdom."[38]

The dangers of sentimentality could not be avoided when Ruth discussed "The Possibilities of Communion" in his sixth chapter. For this

---

34. Ruth, *Progress*, 94.
35. Ruth, *Progress*, 100.
36. Ruth, *Progress*, 100.
37. Ruth, *Progress*, 101.
38. Ruth, *Progress*, 103.

theme he reflected on Hebrews 11 where the author identifies the great heroes of the faith, who make up "so great a cloud of witnesses" (Heb 12:1) to those living the faith today. The doctrine of the communion of saints is a traditional truth that many Protestants have not always appreciated. He rejected the idea that when someone dies we drop them from our prayers and fear that "somebody will hiss 'Spiritualists' at us, as though anyone can hiss spiritual realities out of existence."[39] More positively, Ruth asserted that "our living dead" were not in some vague and distant heaven. They had been very real to the first Christians. "Without us they are not made perfect," as Hebrews 11:40 suggests. His immediate pastoral challenges were revealed as he wrote: "Your soldier son, your soldier husband, your soldier lover, thinks of you, loves you, ministers to you."[40] Francis Thompson's powerful poem "In No Strange Land" concluded this key chapter as Ruth quoted all six stanzas. Beginning with "O world invisible, we view thee" it concludes with the oft-quoted lines:

> And lo, Christ walking on the water,
>
> Not of Gennesareth, but Thames![41]

An intriguing question, then, was the next chapter, "What may we pray for our living dead?" He defended prayers for the dead citing two recent scholars, Arthur Chambers and J. D. Jones, who both argued that in attacking the Roman practices associated with the notion of purgatory, Protestants had rejected the idea of prayers for the dead. He insisted:

> The idea that at death a man's destiny is determined for evermore, even if it be eminently orthodox and evangelical, is so irrational and un-Christian as the Romish doctrine of Purgatory. In one case, God is controlled by creed, which is more or less incidental; in the other He is controlled by cash, which is also more or less incidental.[42]

It is interesting how easily Ruth seems to discard any identification with the evangelicalism that had been such a prominent assertion when he had first arrived in Australia. Still, he was able to quote British evangelical F. B. Meyer, who had accepted the idea of eternal progress: "We may not arrive at the perfect appreciation of Christ for untold millenniums."[43] Ruth

39. Ruth, *Progress*, 109.
40. Ruth, *Progress*, 120.
41. Ruth, *Progress*, 122–23.
42. Ruth, *Progress*, 128.
43. Ruth, *Progress*, 129.

also claimed that John Wesley had believed in praying for the dead as had Richard Baxter, Bishop Heber, John Keble, Charles Kingsley, "and many other men of irreproachable loyalty to the Gospel of Christ."[44]

But what may be prayed for "the living dead"? Ruth's basic answer was simple: "Love dictates."[45] Many mothers had been praying for their soldier sons even though, unknown to them, they had long been slain. He declared, "Death did not take your beloved further away from God than when he was in Australia or in Gallipoli or in France. His personality persists, and with personality probation. And you may pray for him now what you prayed for him then."[46] As a guideline he quoted the long prayer that Arthur Chambers prayed at the graveside of his mother, including this petition: "We pray that uplifting influences from her expanding spirit may reach and help us as we pass along the highway of the Temporal to the Eternal."[47]

Hymns and poems helped clarify what Ruth felt. He cited Julia Dorr (1825–1913):

> How can I cease to pray for thee?
>
> Somewhere
>
> In God's universe thou art today,
>
> Can He not reach thee with His tender care?
>
> Can he not hear me when for thee I pray?[48]

Tennyson's famous sentence, "More things are wrought by prayer than this world dreams of,"[49] together with lines from "In Memoriam," were also included:

> How pure in heart and sound in head,
>
> With what Divine affections bold
>
> Should be the man whose thought would hold
>
> An hour's communion with the dead.[50]

For his next chapter Ruth selected the paradoxical title, "The Mercy of Hell." He recounted at length his own childish memories of being terrified by

---

44. Ruth, *Progress*, 131.
45. Ruth, *Progress*, 133.
46. Ruth, *Progress*, 134.
47. Ruth, *Progress*, 139.
48. Ruth, *Progress*, 140.
49. Ruth, *Progress*, 145. The line is from Tennyson's "Idylls of the King."
50. Ruth, *Progress*, 141.

teaching on hell, and with these he linked passages from Roman Catholic guides for confessionals, which also included similarly frightening pictures of torment. His point here was that such dreadful caricatures "made men much more careless in regard to eternal realities than any unconditional universalism or the utmost latitudinarianism could have done."[51]

Ruth noted, however, that the idea of retribution is universal and found in every religion, and the Bible certainly affirms the reality of retribution. He argued that retribution is in fact "the natural reaction of sin upon the sinner"; it is "a self-determined destiny." Death, in his understanding, is not a barrier between here and hereafter: "death is only a bend in the road," and hell is simply "a most obvious reality" as the experiences of a gambler or a drunkard demonstrate.[52] Retribution is known here and now and is "the rebound of violated law"; "hell is simply sin further on." He insists, "There is no idea of an everlasting hell in the New Testament." Rather, "the doctrine of eternal damnation . . . is based on a few mistranslated and misapplied texts."[53] The awfulness of sin can only be measured by the Cross of Christ. "He tasted death. He went into the outer darkness. He "descended into hell." To such an extent did He love us." Ruth concludes, "the greatest joy of heaven is emptying hell."[54]

Having argued so positively, the last chapter asks a question to which the answer is already known, "All Home at Last?" The question needs to be addressed to God. Ruth summarizes his conclusion that personality persists:

> We believe that on the other side there will be intellectual activities and ethical advancement—that memory will be progressive; that there will be progressive purity and increasing vision; that the spirit will be clothed in a body that will preserve self-identity, ensure recognition and be perfectly adapted to service . . . that the communion of saints is not only an article of faith but a fact of actual experience . . . We have insisted that "lost" means "not found yet," that to be "unsaved" does not mean to be "unsavable" . . . that the God of the everlasting hell of eternal damnation does not exist, that He is simply an ecclesiastical bogey: that the Great Architect of the Universe will not waste any soul-stuff.[55]

The optimism of Ruth's faith is what he believes the gospel proclaims:

---

51. Ruth, *Progress*, 155.
52. Ruth, *Progress*, 159–63.
53. Ruth, *Progress*, 164.
54. Ruth, *Progress*, 169–70.
55. Ruth, *Progress*, 173–75.

Every man must realise his relationship. Every man must repent and set out for his proper destiny, and ultimately every man must arrive, must be forgiven, must come home, even if the Father has to say of him, "This My son was dead and is alive again," must, must, because of the nature of God that is in him, must because his home-coming is necessary to the happiness of God.[56]

He concludes, "Yes. All home at last! We can leave out the mark of interrogation. It becomes an affirmation of a certain faith . . . God cannot be denied His own for ever."[57] He devotes several pages to various biblical texts that justify his conclusions.[58] His conclusion is: "We shall all come home at last."[59]

American poet John Greenleaf Whittier's epic poem "The Grave by the Lake" concluded Ruth's argument:

> Through all the depths of sin and loss
>
> Drops the plummet of Thy cross!
>
> Never yet abyss was found
>
> Deeper than that cross could sound.[60]

Ruth added a sentence that echoed his faith avowal when he had first arrived in Melbourne: "Life here and hereafter is Christo-centric and crucicentric." Then in capital letters came the triumphant confession: CHRISTUS CONSUMMATOR.[61]

One full and thoughtful review appeared in the South Australian Methodist paper, *Australian Christian Commonwealth*.[62] It was called an "Easter book," making a strong appeal to Christian thought although perceptively observing that "in his impatience with orthodoxy [Ruth] is not always fair." His final chapter was "universalism pure and simple," which results from his recoil from harsher eschatology. Suggesting that the book was "a live wire," the anonymous reviewer concluded, "read with discrimination it is worth reading."

The *West Gippsland Gazette* republished an extensive and positive review from the *Harbinger of Light*, the leading Spiritualist magazine published

---

56. Ruth, *Progress*, 179.
57. Ruth, *Progress*, 181–82.
58. Ruth, *Progress*, 182–89.
59. Ruth, *Progress*, 190.
60. Ruth, *Progress*, 192.
61. Ruth, *Progress*, 192, "Christ the fulfiller."
62 *ACW*, April 11, 1919, 11.

in Melbourne with the support of the Theosophical Society.[63] "It is a long time since we read a book, from the pen of a clergyman that afforded us so much delight," and the writer compared it with Arthur Chambers whose books, as we have noted, Ruth quoted extensively. The review suggested that Chambers's mantle had fallen on Ruth. The views in Ruth's book "are as far removed from 'orthodoxy' teachings as the poles are asunder." This comment was scarcely calculated to encourage evangelical readers should they have wandered into the pages of the Spiritualist paper.

One inevitable result was that Ruth came under suspicion as having become a Spiritualist. The possibility of life after death fascinated Ruth.[64] On September 28, 1919, Ruth preached on "A Plea for Christian Spiritualism" at Collins Street during which he declared that "the whole scheme of things was shot through with spiritualistic phenomena." However, he warned that "Spiritualism, with its wonderful possibilities of fellowship with the Risen Man, might easily descend to the level of the witchcraft of Endor." There was a need for a Christian spiritualism.[65]

This report caused sufficient unrest that the *Collins Street Monthly* published a full statement from Ruth about what he had actually said and that had not been reported in the press.

> My plea is not for the use of a planchette or a so-called psychic pencil. I am not pleading for mediums and materialisations. Table tilting and spiritualistic séances make no appeal to me. I know nothing about any of them. I have never attended a spiritualistic meeting of any kind . . .
>
> There is as much difference between Spiritism and Spiritualism as there is between Astrology and Astronomy, between Superstition and Science, or between Paganism and Christianity . . .
>
> The need in our day is for a Christian Spiritualism—the need is for the recognition of the Christian revelation of the nature of God, the Christian revelation of the nature of man, the Christian revelation of the method of communication between God and man . . . And the Mediator between God and man, who reveals the spirituality of God, the spirituality of man and the spirituality of the universe . . . is Jesus Christ.[66]

When Sir Arthur Conan Doyle (1859-1930), the well-known author and spiritualist, visited Sydney in 1920, he noted that there were in Australia

---

63. *West Gippsland Gazette*, June 3, 1919, 3. For theosophy, see Roe, *Beyond Belief*.
64. *ACW*, April 9, 1915, 1.
65. *Argus*, September 29, 1919, 8.
66. *Monthly Notes*, October 1919, 3.

only a few clergymen not wholly opposed to Spiritualism and named four ministers, including Ruth.[67]

The Advent Heresy and the Real Coming of Christ[68]

Unsettling times had produced an extraordinary burst of Adventism during and after the war. Jill Roe observed, "Historically, movements proclaiming the imminent return of Christ to this world have flourished in periods of cultural unease and transition; and at no time in modern history was a literal reading of the biblical book of *Revelation* more plausible."[69]

This prompted another unusual but revealing book by Ruth. This study was a smaller work of ninety-five pages, including an appendix of seven pages with extended quotations from authoritative writers on "Chiliasm" or millennial theories.[70] Naturally these all supported his position, which was strongly opposed to all theories of millennialism.[71]

Ruth gave a patient if devastating mockery of current Advent theories. In his introductory "preliminary pen chat," he noted with sorrow—doubtless reflecting his own experience—that many conservative evangelicals immediately regarded anyone who disagreed with these popular Adventist views with suspicion. He enjoyed showing that many who passionately proclaimed a belief in the imminent return of Christ in fact lived as though this were not true. They invested and planned for long-term results. Ruth mocked these inconsistencies and insisted that there were "practical, personal, pastoral and political problems for which neither pre-millennialism nor post-millennialism offers any solution." Post-millennialism, the view held only by a minority among conservatives, argued that Christ would return after the millennium. Pre-millennialism was associated with fundamentalism, a growing movement in the USA and also in Australia at this time although Adventist millennial sects had established a presence in Victoria from its earliest days.[72]

In his second chapter, "Armageddon in 1934?," Ruth began by quoting at length the extraordinary speech made in the Federal Parliament on November 3, 1921, by New South Wales National Party member Walter

67. *AB*, November 30, 1920, 4.
68. Ruth, *Advent Heresy*.
69. Roe, *Beyond belief*, 259.
70. Ruth, *Advent History*, 89–95.
71. For a brief overview of Baptists' changing views on the second coming, see Featherstone, "Millennial Voice."
72. Featherstone, "Millennial Voice," 233–63.

Marks (1875–1951).[73] Marks caused a sensation as he predicted that Armageddon would be fought in 1934 when the British navy would collect the Jewish people to form a great nation in Palestine. The millennium would come after Armageddon. The British Empire must be prepared for the second coming of Christ. Marks insisted that everything is to be found in the Bible if we look for it.[74]

Ruth had little difficulty in demonstrating the absurdity of Marks's theories but also ventured the comment that Australia seems to be "peculiarly a breeding-ground for a distinctly irrational and thoroughly obscurantist Adventism, with a very grave tendency to malign ministers who disagreed and to make these views a kind of theological test for certain pulpit and teaching positions."[75] Perhaps he had in mind the experience of Alexander Gordon, who was obliged to resign in 1921 from the Principalship of the New South Wales Baptist College in part because of Adventists who attacked him.[76]

Ruth then detailed various millennial crises across the centuries and suggested that still today some neurotic people were "kept in a state of nervous tension" by these wild date-fixing teachers.[77] The problem was a failure to understand the distinctive nature of apocalyptic literature which was designed to speak to their own generations not to secrete away clues about the date of Christ's return and other mysteries of the future.[78]

Chapter three explored the question, "Is Millennialism Scriptural?" Ruth showed that the basic concept, of course, was derived from Revelation: "a single and amazingly symbolic passage in the most amazingly symbolic document of all the sixty-six publications that make up the divine library we call the Bible." Ruth followed most commentators in insisting that "John is concerned with the sorrows of his own day, with the persecution he and his fellows have to face . . . you need not think he was thinking of your particular problems twenty centuries later."[79] He concluded, "Millennialism, material, political millennialism, 'pre' or 'post' must be written down as unscriptural."[80] Illustrating some of the absurdities he had discovered in millennial literature—signs of The End in Melbourne and Wangaratta and elsewhere—Ruth asserted,

73. Ruth, *Advent History*, 19–20. For Marks, see *ADB*.
74. *Parliamentary Debates* (Commonwealth), 1921, 12406.
75. Ruth, *Advent History*, 22.
76. See Manley, *From Woolloomooloo*, 483–88.
77. Ruth, *Advent History*, 27.
78. Ruth, *Advent History*, 33.
79. Ruth, *Advent History*, 43.
80. Ruth, *Advent History*, 46.

> I am driven to the conclusion that millennialism with its mischievous method of quoting miscellaneous texts without reference to context, time or circumstance is as unscriptural as it is unscrupulous in the matter of the almanac and the guessing of dates.[81]

Chapter four continued this attack, "Adventism at the Bar of History." He first lamented that biblical prophecy "had become identified in the popular mind with predictions of coming events—postponed for several millenniums."[82] Adventists base all their arguments on a literal interpretation of symbolic passages while ignoring the most obvious meaning to the first hearers. Moreover, they add to this literalism a belief in "the weirdest things written in the sky and in the signs of the times." Their assumptions are "unscriptural, historically untenable, logically irrational and psychologically inexplicable."[83] He concluded, "At the bar of history, which is God's Calendar, Adventism stands condemned by the very passing of time."[84]

His final chapter was an attempt to offer a positive demonstration of interpreting the last book of the Bible, "The Core of Revelation." His exposition concentrated on the image of Christ as the Lamb of God. His final exclamation was, as in his previous book, CHRISTUS CONSUMMATOR.

That such a book was needed is evident, and Ruth offered a scholarly and relevant alternative. How many evangelicals were persuaded to his viewpoint is uncertain; certainly, a large number of Australian Baptists treasured their millennial beliefs and preached their message of "the blessed hope."

Sydney city draper and ardent Adventist William Buckingham (1854–1928) wrote a long criticism of Ruth's book.[85] A savage criticism also followed from the former Primitive Methodist Rev. Samuel Harrison (1860–1936), of the Harris Street Baptist Church in Sydney:

> Of all the ministerial tragedies of our time, i.e., praying for the dead, playing with spiritism, pooling the Churches, no matter what they do or say, passing nice ladies into church membership because they are seeking protection, and regale the preacher with photos usually dressed up in tights—of all these tragedies,

---

81. Ruth, *Advent History*, 49.
82. Ruth, *Advent History*, 53.
83. Ruth, *Advent History*, 62.
84. Ruth, *Advent History*, 68. A helpful attempt to define the various forms of dispensationalism is Sweetnam, "Defining Dispensationalism."
85. *AB*, August 29, 1922, 10.

none is more terrible than the one now so lovingly cherished, viz. to destroy the Scriptures in order to save the Church.[86]

William Lamb's book *Dark Days and the Signs of the Times* had been remarkably successful, with some 17,000 having been sold by April 1917.[87]

Ruth's book was an entertaining, thoughtful, and educated response to a prevailing theology that he judged to be dangerous and foolish.

These two books show Ruth expounding an eschatology that was typically liberal in scope and style. They may be placed alongside his more sectarian writings to reveal a thoughtful and passionate preacher–theologian.

Ruth revealed inner tensions. He was intensely pastoral and felt the pain of others, especially of those who had lost loved ones in the war. At the same time, he delighted in being unconventional in his beliefs, dismissing traditional orthodoxies with gusto. He loved literature and life and was never happier than when he could startle hearers with his ideas. His energy was remarkable and his friendships enduring. An advocate of dignified worship in ways not common among Australian Baptists he could yet preach the most unusual sermons with a relaxed confidence. Although he constantly sought to address urgent social issues among Australian people, he was also an enigma among Australian Baptists, at once their champion against traditional foes such as Roman Catholics and the alcohol and gambling industries and yet a provocateur in issues such as church union and in his opposition to millennial Adventism.

---

86. *AB*, October 17, 1922, 11.
87. *AB*, April 3, 1918. For Lamb's eschatology see Petras, "Life and Times," 4–8.

9

Becoming a Sydney Identity
(1923–30)

MOVING TO SYDNEY COULD not have been easy for Ruth and his family. Having often visited the beautiful harbor city, he knew it to be a very different world from Mannix-dominated Melbourne. With "a pen tipped with emotion," he told his Melbourne *Herald* readers of his deep affection for the city and its people during the "eventful years of my Melbourne ministry."[1] Still questing to discover precisely what his haunting vision of an imperial role in the Commonwealth might actually be, Ruth took one giant step forward into the unknown by leaving Collins Street, his Auditorium platform, and an enthusiastic army of loyalist colleagues to settle in Sydney. Initially, he had only agreed to preach at evening services for three months at the Pitt Street Congregational Church, but in fact Pitt Street proved to be his last and longest pastorate. He not only moved from Melbourne but also from his Baptist identity. This seems to have freed him theologically to adopt an even more overtly liberal position.

Ruth had suggested that "the best way to describe my move is that I am becoming a roaming Catholic," but many must have been confused about what this meant. Why move to Sydney? Was it simply, as he himself asserted, a response to a divine—even if uncertain—"impelling"? Could his message be less adversarial and more pacific away from sectarian Melbourne? In the event, he actually achieved even greater notoriety in the alarming political life of New South Wales when led by the Premier whom Ruth later called

---

1. *Herald*, March 24, 1923, 4.

"that political maniac Lang."[2] In Sydney, Ruth was not such "a sectarian bigot" but did develop into a controversial political figure.

An Unspeakable Loss

The family's first year in Sydney was marred by an unspeakably sad tragedy. Leslie Ruth had grown into a young man with considerable promise. He began to work for Burns Philp, a major Australian shipping line and merchant, and was baptized by Ruth in the Bathurst Street Baptist Church on May 16, 1923.[3] However, as Ruth told Brookes, Leslie "managed to get Typhoid (probably through a milk shake at a Dago shop)" and was admitted to St. Ives Private Hospital.[4] As Leslie's condition worsened, Ruth stayed night and day at the hospital, sleeping in a room adjacent to his son's.[5] Sadly, Leslie died on October 18 and was buried the next day at the Northern Suburbs Cemetery.[6]

Ruth had long comforted the bereaved and preached and written about death and grief. Now he and Mabel themselves experienced the sharp pain of this separation. Many from all over the country expressed their sympathy, not least their numerous friends from the Collins Street Baptist Church.

Tom and Mabel had a simple reply card printed.[7] The front had the text, "We were in trouble and you comforted us." On the other side of the card was the following account of the death of their adopted son:

> Leslie was taken ill with typhoid on his 18th birthday, Thursday September 6th and was removed to St. Ives Private Hospital on the following Tuesday.
>
> Assisted by the best medical science available and the most skilful nursing, for nearly six weeks, he put up a very plucky fight, and indeed his spirit never succumbed, but his dear body, worn by high fever, failed him; and on October 17th, uncomplaining and unafraid, having won, and richly deserved, a reputation among the sisters and nurses as "A Gallant Little Gentleman," he passed into the Eternal Kingdom, bearing his youth as a banner.

---

2. Ruth to Brookes, 3 March 1931, Brookes Papers, NLA 1924/48/130. J. T. Lang (1876–1975) was the controversial Premier of New South Wales (1925–27, 1930–32).
3. *AB*, May 6, 1923, 4; May 29, 1923, 3.
4. Ruth to Brookes, 18 September 1923, Brookes Papers, NLA 1924/48/73.
5. *AB*, October 16, 1923, 4.
6. *SMH*, October 22, 1923, 10.
7. A copy is in the Lucas papers at the BUV archives.

> There was so wonderful a spiritual development, such unfailing chivalry and cheerfulness, such thoughtfulness for others, that it was almost uncanny and wholly unearthly.
>
> The manner of his passing makes us strangely proud and high-spirited.
>
> For us the road will be lonely for many a day to come, but death has simply liberated him from a physical frame, which it now appears, had very serious limitations.
>
> At times we wish we knew just what he is doing. That is hidden from us. Perhaps the glory of it would smite us with blindness. But we know he will "follow the Lamb whithersoever He goeth." And he will love doing it.
>
> Every day we "greet the unseen with a cheer."

The experience perhaps mellowed Ruth in his sectarian attitudes. In 1925, he wrote about a reader "who does not live in my theological world at all" and recalled:

> But as long as I live I shall associate a beautiful and Christ-like thing with his faith. One morning a great bereavement befell me, and in the afternoon of my sorrow, he spoke to me with the sort of sympathy that communicates strength, and with the tenderest diffidence said he knew how unprepared such happenings sometimes found us, and if I was in any way financially straitened would I draw on him to any amount, and no one would ever be the wiser. Even if I had need of such help, the sympathy would have been of much more worth than the actual assistance. And that night, and without apology, I paraphrased certain words of the Apostle Paul, and the Scripture read, "Neither is Roman Catholicism anything, nor Protestantism, but the spirit of Christ."[8]

Pitt Street Congregational Church

Known as Pitt Street Uniting Church since 1977 but honored as the "mother church" of Congregationalism in Australia, the Pitt Street Church had been founded in 1833.[9] The building on the present site in Pitt Street was opened in 1846 and was extended twice in the nineteenth century. In 1877,

---

8. Ruth, *Playing the Game*, 123–24.

9. Lockley, *Congregationalism in Australia*, 107–14. For the history of the church, see Emilsen et al., *Pride of Place*. The chapter dealing with Ruth's term is by Patricia Curthoys.

the church built a school hall to the north of the chapel comprising a hall, an infants' section, a library, and ten large classrooms. The church later established the Sussex Street Mission to provide welfare for needy residents of the city. This work was relocated to Devonshire Street in Surry Hills after the residential population of the city declined. When Ruth arrived the church maintained a significant ministry although numbers had declined and the building was in a poor state of repair.

Pitt Street Congregational Church (1923)

Although Ruth eventually became the church's minister from 1925 until 1939, he first came for a short term as the evening preacher in 1923. He had been invited to come to Pitt Street on the initiative of the minister Rev. N. J. Cocks (1867–1925), a much-loved philosopher and poet who had served the church since 1907.[10] Anxious about falling attendances, Cocks asked the deacons to invite Ruth for three months as the evening preacher with the obvious hope that his aggressive and popular style would attract many more hearers. This was an opportune invitation for which he received £10 per Sunday.[11]

---

10. For Cocks, see *ADB*.
11. Pitt Street Deacons' Minutes, November 13 and 20, 1922.

Ruth's first sermon was devoted to the theme of the necessity of having "big and wide visions."[12] His reputation had preceded him and significant numbers attended his services. The *Congregationalist*, monthly paper of the New South Wales Union, warmly greeted Ruth:

> Here is welcome Mr. Ruth! Speak strongly, speak fearlessly to the pagans, and as you well can, say some things, with a good deal of forked lightning mixed in, to the Christians . . . We wish you every success but one, and that is that you should not entice the saints from their little Bethels in the suburbs![13]

This last word of caution stresses the problem that a strong city pulpit could present for smaller suburban churches. In September 1923, Ruth told Brookes that between twelve and fourteen hundred were attending his services at Pitt Street.[14]

At a memorable "Back to Pitt Street" service on July 22, 1923, Ruth outlined his vision for his adopted city:

> Here is this Sydney of yours, where everything that God has made is so surpassingly beautiful, where the surrounding beauty is a sort of Divine challenge to men to make the city commensurate with the imperishable ideal. Here is a climatic paradise, with people pretending to be pagan but at heart wistfully and eagerly seeking something big and whole.
>
> What an opportunity the city offers, not only for wide streets and open spaces, and great schools and temples of trade, and palaces of pleasure, but for the development of great hearts and broad minds, of golden thoughts and the kind of pleasure that makes the New Jerusalem good enough and glad enough for God![15]

Ruth also began writing regular articles for the Sunday *Sun*. Selected columns were revised and included in some of his books.[16]

In his preaching, Ruth was soon discussing controversial religious themes such as his "Plea for a Catholic Liberty" at a "community service" in August 1923. This was a response to New South Wales parliamentary discussions regarding the *Ne temere* decree about marriage.[17] In September 1923,

---

12. *SMH*, April 2, 1923, 6.
13. *Congregationalist*, April 10, 1923, 1.
14. Ruth to Brookes, 18 September 1923, Brookes Papers, NLA 1924/48/73.
15. *Telegraph*, July 23, 1923, 4.
16. Ruth, *Playing the Game* (1925); *Australia at the Crossroads* (1931).
17. *Telegraph*, August 13, 1923, 5.

he gave a series of "sermon-lectures" on "Progressive Protestant Principles," which reprised his Melbourne addresses; however, this kind of sermon did not come to characterize his ministry in Sydney.

Ruth and his wife were guests at afternoon tea with the Royal Colonial Institute hosted by Sir Hugh Denison (1865–1940) where Ruth (described as "a well-known writer and speaker on all matters pertaining to Australia") gave an "inspiring" address on "Australia Today as Treasure held in Trust."[18] Denison later gave £100 to the Pitt Street appeal.[19] In October, Ruth spoke at the Millions Club of New South Wales, which had been founded in 1912 with the aim of making Sydney the first Australian city to reach a population of one million. Ruth, who became a member of the prestigious club, suggested that what was wrong with Australia was "its sectionalism, its sectarianism, its class consciousness and its stupid little jealousies."[20]

Ruth agreed to extend his commitment to Pitt Street, initially to the end of 1923. Average weekly offerings at these services were more than three times what they had been in 1922. Later, he agreed to continue as evening speaker for another year at the salary of £520 per year. Ruth was, however, still agonizing over his long-term future, as he had asked Brookes: "Pray that I may purposely invest my life—so many things turn on the next move."[21] Cocks had resolved to retire after more than seventeen years at Pitt Street but sadly died in January 1925 before the church had been able to hold a farewell for him.

Becoming a Church's Minister Again: "Only a Fool or Hero"

The church turned to Ruth, but he hesitated to commit himself. As he wrote to Brookes on March 12, 1925: "I have told the deacons that the church (apart from the evening congregation) is so nearly derelict that only a fool or a hero would saddle himself with it. And I'm neither. They apparently hold another view."[22] Eventually, on Sunday May 3, 1925, he publicly accepted the invitation.

---

18. *Sun*, August 29, 1923, 8. Denison was the son of Baptist figure Robert Dixson but had changed his name by deed poll in 1907. Denison founded the *Sun* newspaper, was chairman of Australian Paper Manufacturers, and a friend of Brookes.

19. Ruth to Brookes, 6 August 1925, Brookes Papers, NLA 1924/48/89.

20. *SMH*, October 3, 1923, 12.

21. Ruth to Brookes, 10 July 1922, Brookes Papers, NLA 1924/48/71.

22. Ruth to Brookes, 12 March 1925, Brookes Papers, NLA 1924/48/83.

I shrink from the difficulties of the task. I am fearful of my own inadequacy. But my duty is clear. I am convinced by the Providential happenings associated with my relations to the church that it is God's will that I should accept what I can only regard as a Divine call.[23]

Neither Ruth nor his new church seemed to be troubled by his Baptist identity. The claim that Ruth had "renounced his denominational allegiance" is not how he regarded it.[24] A full statement of Ruth's position had been made to the church on April 5, 1925. "Baptists are Congregationalists," he had told the church, and they seemed comfortable with that claim. Indeed, Ruth observed that Pitt Street was "more like my English churches than any church I know in New South Wales." He held that if he was to be their minister he was free, "as Congregational ministers all over the world are free, to baptize believers on confession of faith." He had always held that admission to church membership should be on a profession of faith, irrespective of baptism. He commented, "Often in Baptist churches I have made much more of the dedication of infants than seems to be customary here, actually receiving them as 'wards of the church and congregation.'"[25]

In 1921, the two denominations had similar numbers of church members in New South Wales: 5,918 Baptists and 5,250 Congregationalists.[26] Both Ruth and his wife had been received as members of Pitt Street at the February 1925 church meeting, and they had moved to their own home at View Point, Clifford Avenue, Manly, during 1924.

At Ruth's public welcome, leading Methodist preacher Rev. S. J. Hoban declared, "I do not hesitate to say that he is easily the first preacher in Australia."[27] As he told the church in his April 1925 statement, Ruth had given much thought to this "great civic center." The evening congregation proved "that the community does respond to effort and appeal. I have been much moved by requests which have come to me from men who are sometimes assumed to be indifferent to religion and to Churches." He invited the church to consider a "bold and aggressive policy" along three lines. The first related to the present membership of the church and a "deepening of its spiritual quality . . . the saving of the membership from a cold and casual churchmanship." The second issue was to provide "adequate pastoral care" for which he admitted that he was not personally

---

23. *Pitt Street Church News* June 1925, as cited by Curthoys, *Pride of Place*, 200.
24. Hansen, "Churches and Society," 75.
25. Statement by Ruth with Church Minutes, April 22, 1925.
26. Vamplew, *Australian Historical Statistics*, 428.
27. *Mail* (Adelaide), December 12, 1925, 17.

"fitted by nature nor grace . . . having neither strength nor genius" for such work. The hope was that the church would be "an ever open Sanctuary . . . a Community Cathedral." Third was a concern for "the complete renovation and modernising of Church premises."

Ruth already had in mind an associate minister who could undertake pastoral care. Rev. W. T. Kench was a gifted minister with an established identity in the denomination, and he agreed to come as part-time assistant minister for a salary of £300 per year. He would serve as ministerial secretary for the Congregational Union as well as serving Pitt Street for two afternoons each week and preaching on alternate Sunday mornings. This proved to be an admirable arrangement with regular visitation and a growth in youth work until Kench resigned in August 1928.

Meanwhile Ruth pursued his other aims as proposed to the church. He proved to be as energetic and driven as ever. Ruth conducted Tuesday midday services which attracted good numbers.[28] The church had a capable and supportive group of deacons, an admired choir, and an extremely gifted organist, Lillian Frost (1870–1953), who by 1925 had been church organist for thirty years. Ruth gave special encouragement to Frost and has been described as "one of Frost's most enthusiastic fans." He frequently reflected on the value of her genius to the experience of worship at Pitt Street and in later years shared in special events of poems and music with her.[29]

Undoubtedly the largest challenge faced by Ruth and the church was the deplorable condition of the property. A detailed inspection in 1925 revealed that "the roof leaked, the walls were crumbling, parts of the ceiling were falling, the window woodwork was rotten, there were holes in the floor caused by dry rot, and white ants and borer had been found."[30] Ruth led a campaign for "straight-out" giving by church members and friends in the city. The *Sun* carried a personal appeal from Ruth, a reproduction in his handwriting:

A Personal Appeal.

> I have lately become minister at the largest non-Episcopal Church in NSW, a Church which lends itself to the kind of community service Sydney needs, offering a platform to Churchmen of any school.
> But I have to fight against Dry Rot, White Ant and Borer. We want to raise 4,000 guineas without a Bazaar or Fete.

---

28. *Congregationalist*, October 10, 1924, 1.
29. Hunt, "Cultivating the Arts," 296–300.
30. Curthoys, *Pride of Place*, 208.

> Simply to preserve this fine old city church <u>we must have £1600 immediately.</u>
>
> I am told people will not respond to an appeal for straightforward giving. I don't believe it.
>
> On Wednesday (up to 9.30) I shall be in my Church office to receive gifts.
>
> If during the last 2½ years my articles have inspired you, or even if they have irritated you, will you help me? If I could be sure <u>you</u> would send me something, I should be sure of success.[31]

On the following Sunday the paper reported that £3,078 had been given, and "many had acknowledged that their response was due entirely to his personal appeal in last Sunday's *Sun*."[32] By early 1926 the fund totaled £3,633.2.9.[33] Extensive renovations were completed by March 1926.[34] The congregation had met in the nearby Criterion Theatre for evening services during this period.[35]

Ruth preached on Easter evening about the symbols included in the renovation:

> In a non-sacramentarian Church, so situated as to be a sort of Community Cathedral, designed to be a House of Prayer and Praise for all people, there must needs be some strong, simple symbolism. When the symbol stands for something vital, something instinct with reality, when through the symbol reality can be easily reached, when the symbol is so suggestive that the spiritual significance can scarcely be missed, then the symbol is the servant of the soul.[36]

Over the central door was an empty cross that was illuminated at night, "the symbol of our common faith, sends its divine message into the night, the only distinctly Christian witness in Sydney's Great White Way."[37] In the vestibule was a painting, a copy of the masterpiece by Norwegian Axel Wender (1853-1929), *The Morning of the Resurrection*, done by Sydney artist Herbert Beecroft (1864-1951). Ruth preached about the painting, which depicted three women at the empty tomb being greeted by an angel,

---

31. *Sun,* August 23, 1925, 17.
32. *Sun,* August 30, 1925, 5.
33. Curthoys, *Pride of Place,* 209.
34. Details in Curthoys, *Pride of Place,* 209-10.
35. *Congregationalist,* February 10, 1926, 3.
36. Ruth, *Picture,* 5.
37. Ruth, *Picture,* 5.

stressing that worshippers were in the presence of the "Living Christ." Ruth concluded:

> The cross is shining. The tomb is empty. The Christ is risen. This is the Church of the Cross. This is the Church of the Empty Tomb. This is the Church of the Risen Lord.
>
> This is the Church, this is the Commonwealth, this is the century of the Living Christ. And He is alive for evermore. In His hands not merely the print of the nails, but the problems of our time. In His heart not the problems of past Palestine, but the affairs of the whole world. Go ye into all the world and preach the Gospel to every creature. He is risen. And all life rises with Him.[38]

But there were still more challenges. Later in 1926 Ruth led the church to consider the remodeling of the school hall with a three-story building at an estimated cost of £12,000. This would provide some income from rentals for the church. In the end, an even more ambitious scheme for a six-story building was adopted. This project inevitably involved numerous meetings and further fund raising, an intensely strenuous program for Ruth and his people. Finally, with secure lettings, including for the Congregational Union, the building was opened in 1928. Ruth had again led a successful straight-out giving appeal as the church now had a total mortgage of £45,000. Once again both the *Sun* and the *SMH* supported the project with Ruth arguing that businessmen in the city "owed the Church a great deal" even if they did not share in services: "The power which, above all other powers, kept down the restless flood of Communism and revolution was Christianity, and only because of Christianity was business possible."[39]

---

38. Ruth, *Picture*, 10.
39. *SMH*, October 26, 1928, 14.

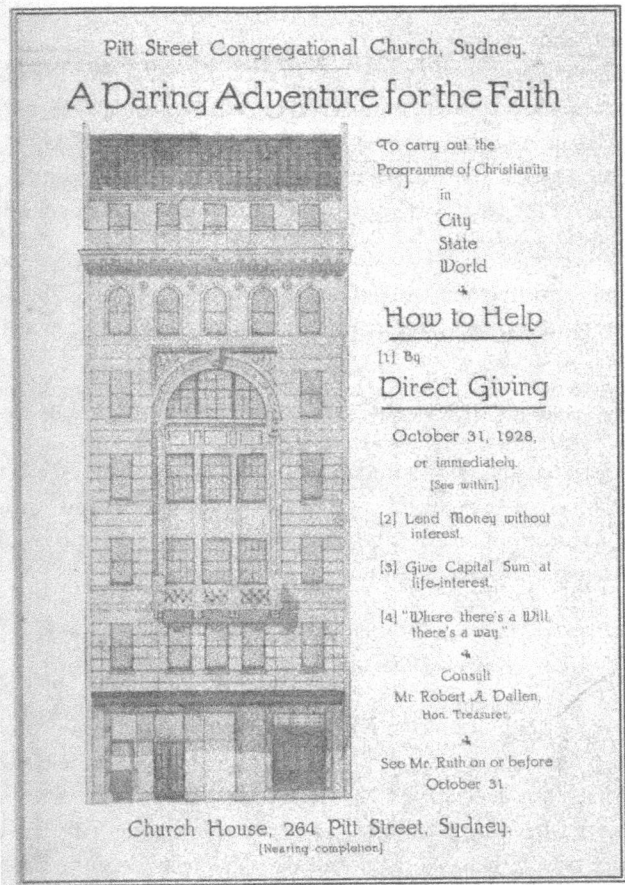

Front cover of brochure (1928)

Again, the *Sun* reported an extended interview with Ruth, headed "Asking for it and expecting it," in which he rehearsed the contributions of his church to the city and mission work. The *Sun* also reproduced another handwritten appeal from Ruth in which he asked his readers to "send some bricks, I mean, money to buy bricks (There are 380,000 at £1 for 100.)"[40]

After the day's waiting in his office, Ruth reported to a thanksgiving service that he "believed in human nature" and that almost £6,000 had been given as well as a fur coat (by a lady who had no money to give), which he was prepared to sell "at a profit." He suggested that many Sydney

40. *Sun*, October 28, 1928, 25.

citizens had been praying, "O God, let me not see Ruth today; or if I see him, don't let him see me."[41]

This appeal process suggests how significant Ruth's profile had become in the city. His sermons were regularly reported, often at great length, in the daily press; many evening services were broadcast while thousands read his weekly newspaper columns and his books. Ruth's achievement in helping raise the money for what was known as "Church House" was acknowledged in the denomination's paper:

> What the effort must have cost him it would be impossible to say, but the success of it means that for all time £360 a year is already secured towards the objects which are to be helped ... city charities, Congregational Mission and Church work and the London Missionary Society.[42]

This report noted that since Ruth had become "definitely associated with Congregationalism three years ago he has personally raised no less than eleven thousand pounds, or £3700 a year for property purposes alone ... His enthusiasm must be contagious."

Playing the Game

In March 1925, Ruth published *Playing the Game* which was a collection of fifty-five articles he had written for the *Sun*. He dedicated the book, a hard cover of three hundred pages, to "the great company of correspondents whose letters I have been unable to answer." He wrote: "My one concern is to inspire people with courage and with gaiety to face the problems of living, and to play the game. Playing the game is the British way of saluting the universe."[43] Ruth divided the book into six sections: Playing the game in personal character; at home; in religion; in the churches; industrially; and in the Commonwealth.[44]

Reviews were extremely positive, especially in the regional tabloid papers. The *Launceston Examiner* claimed that "there is no more brilliant preacher in Australia; and that his pen can be just as effective." This was "a very fine book, rich in epigram and humour, and with a very strong appeal

---

41. *Telegraph*, November 1, 1928, 4.
42. *Congregationalist*, November 10, 1928, 9.
43. Ruth, *Playing the Game*, "Preface."
44. The contents of this book are discussed in chapter 12 in the review of all his newspaper articles.

for Australians."[45] The *Barrier Miner* in distant Broken Hill noted that Ruth "tries to rescue Christianity from the 'churchianity' which deters many of those who could like to go to church from doing so."[46] Ruth and the *Bunbury Herald and Blackwood Express* in Western Australia agreed that his book would be published in weekly chapters.[47]

Minister in "this Americo–British City"

Ruth's ministry continued in what he called "this Americo–British city."[48] In 1929, the church increased his stipend to £1,000 per annum. He was pleased when Sir Joseph Cook (1860–1947), the former Prime Minister (1913–14), attended a morning service in 1927, and many other notables, whenever in the city, came to Pitt Street.[49] He conducted monthly "Book services" and maintained his high profile through his writing and preaching.

Inevitably, some of his preaching was controversial. On September 14, 1924, his address on "The Artists' Ball and the Artistic Temperament" was widely reported, even drawing favorable comment from the labor press.[50] Headlines in the *SMH* read "Art and Animalism. The Orgy at the Town Hall. A Trenchant Sermon." Ruth began with an obscure reference in Exodus (31:2) to Bezaleel, "an artist by Divine appointment," in order to suggest that art was of divine origin and had a mystic quality: "Worthy art was an offering of worship." But the fancy dress ball of these artists in the Sydney Town Hall had become "an occasion for mere animal beastliness."[51]

Ruth's public profile sometimes led him into strange places. Late in 1926 he was quoted extensively in support of a campaign that *Truth* ran against "Sex Saturated Press" (even though it had itself regularly published salacious material). It purported to be running a campaign against the journalism which exploited "the beauty of young Australian girls for its own commercial ends," accompanying its report with titillating photos of what was being condemned. On November 28 it claimed that "the heads of the church" had officially commended *Truth* for the article. The "heads" were selected by the

---

45. *Examiner*, April 4, 1925, 20.

46. *Barrier Miner*, May 30, 1925, 1.

47. *Bunbury Herald and Blackwood Express*, December 4, 1925, 2. These ran from December 1925 until June 1926.

48. Ruth to Brookes, 1 April 1929, Brookes Papers, NLA 1924/48/114.

49. Ruth to Brookes, 10 October 1927, Brookes Papers, NLA 1924/48/102.

50. *Labor Daily*, September 15, 1924, 5; *Mudgee Guardian*, September 18, 1924, 15.

51. *SMH*, September 15, 1924, 8.

paper and included the Roman Catholic Archbishop Kelly of Sydney, Baptist pastor Rev. J. Rogers, Rev. R. J. Williams ("a broadminded Methodist"), and Ruth, who was the only one to have his photo included. Ruth deplored the "insidious aspirations of Beauty competitions . . . No prize money in the world can repay woman for the loss of her modesty."[52]

More of Ruth's traditional themes emerged. On May 22, 1927, like most other Australian preachers, he delivered an Empire Day sermon: "Canberra, Commonwealth, and Empire—Can Australia remain British?"[53]

In June, he preached on "What To Do With Dreamers," based on the story of Joseph, claiming that in many professions dreamers were slain by slander. Perhaps there was a personal memory in his comment that even in clerical circles it was not unknown: "Let a clergyman strike out a new line of thought and action, and his brethren in the ministry will say, "Come now, let us slay him . . . and see what will become of his dreams! And they will see what will become of his dreams! There will be a harvest of them. There always is . . ."[54]

During 1927 the *Sunday Times* gave a brief outline each week of what Ruth would preach on that day. His topics which ranged through "On Being Secular," "As If God Were Dead," "Jonah without the Whale," and "The Weather," which he called "a word of God." A full report was published of his address on "Sydney as the New Jerusalem" in which he responded to the chapter about Sydney in Francis Jackson's book *Byways of Romance*.[55] Jackson had claimed that "all the evils and malediction of Western civilization are here, in this Vanity Fair of the Antipodes." He also criticized public schools as well as two groups that Ruth had addressed, the Millions Club and the Royal Colonial Institute, which latter had as its main function "the unswerving rectitude of Imperial policy, the dangers of Bolshevism and to teach Britishers the National Anthem of self-satisfaction." Ruth admired Jackson's style and wit but insisted that there was an even more inspiring vision for Sydney:

> There is something beyond beauty of form. There is beauty of soul. And Sydney should in no wise substitute Athens for the New Jerusalem. In Sydney, beauty haunts us on every hand, in all the highways and byways, God has thrust so much loveliness into our lives that we ought not to be blind to the infinite Beyond!

52. *Truth*, November 28, 1926, 1.
53. *Sunday Times*, May 22, 1927, 20.
54. *Sunday Times*, June 19, 1927, 22.
55. F. Jackson, *Byways of Romance*.

Ruth had a vision: "Sydney beautiful for situation, would become the city of God, the city of liberty, fraternity, equality, righteousness, peace, and joy."[56]

Jackson, who was the Master of Foreign Languages at Sydney Grammar School, basically agreed with Ruth, arguing controversially that the GPS Head of the River regatta should be abandoned and schools should concentrate on a renewed system of education that included "reverence for sacred things."[57]

Ruth did not hesitate to preach after a disaster on November 3, 1927, when a steamer and a ferry collided on Sydney Harbour, leaving thirty-seven dead. Ruth insisted that the disaster was "a disappointment to God": "Premature death is not His will, but accidents happen to Him as well as to men." It was not God's special occupation to prevent men from getting hurt. This was all too subtle for some readers. J. McPhee, a fifteen-year-old, read Ruth's comments and wrote to the *Workers' Weekly*.

> Now, in one sentence, he calls God the Almighty, and in the same breath states he is not. This just goes to prove that these so-called saviours of mankind cannot say thirty words without lying, and as the bible is their syllabus it must tell lies and teach them to tell lies also.[58]

Early in the new year of 1928, Ruth continued his style of startling sermons with an address on "Sinners in Sydney." He insisted that there were as many sinners inside the church as outside.[59] This was music to the ears of church critics, with Brisbane *Truth* wholeheartedly agreeing with Ruth about all the hypocritical sinners in the church. After all, they observed, "the Solomon Islander who has a taste for missionary stew" knows no better, but these hypocrites also have an unchristian attitude.[60]

Roman Catholics in Sydney had long anticipated the International Eucharistic Congress to be held in their city in 1928. Archbishop Kelly had assured his people that this would be a grand demonstration of Catholic piety while Father William Lockington declared that "the Congress will mark the first occasion under the Southern Cross that Christ has come into His own" and anticipated a wonderful procession that would stop the streets of Sydney.[61] When the impressive Catholic procession came to Sydney, Ruth

---

56. *Sunday Times*, July 24, 1927, 3.
57. *Sunday Times*, July 31, 1927, 5.
58. *Workers' Weekly*, December 2, 1927, 3.
59. *SMH*, January 16, 1928, 10.
60. *Truth*, Brisbane, January 16, 1928, 10.
61. *AB*, March 2, 1926, 1.

completely disassociated himself from "the un-Protestant and unpatriotic suggestion that a procession, permitted by the Government, should be prevented by any sort of militant Protestant mobilisation at some strategic centre."[62] However, in the *Vigilant* Ruth emphasized that Protestants should accept the challenge that the procession implied. They should let Roman Catholics know that they regarded it as "ceremonial paganism."[63]

In August 1928, although Dame Nellie Melba denied having advised Clara Butt, "Sing 'em Muck; it is the only thing they understand," Ruth lamented that it was only too true that "muck" was what most men wanted: "Look at your theatres. Even case-hardened newspaper critics declare that some of our best-acted plays portray morality on a lower level than that of the fowlyard."[64]

Another example of his preaching was when he declared that "Christ had a Money Bag in which he kept his savings" and urged his hearers, "Be rich! Use your money well, and get more of it!" . . . Your ledger is as important to God as your Bible. Business is but the practical side of prayer."[65] Adjacent to this report in the paper was a breathless account of how shots had been fired by strikers as "free laborers" had attempted to break the picket line at Port Melbourne. Dangerous times were brewing, and Ruth not only encouraged the honest making of money but could not remain silent about the unfolding political and industrial crisis in the nation.

A comprehensive interview with Ruth was published by the *Evening News* as part of a series on "Pulpits and Personalities." Ruth was number ten in the series after people and congregations like John Complin of Bathurst Street Baptist, Hugh Paton of St. Stephen's Presbyterian, Archbishop Kelly of St. Mary's Cathedral, and also the Chief Rabbi of the Great Synagogue. Ruth trotted out his oft-repeated self-identity as "Anglopresmethbapgationist" and claimed again that Pitt Street was like a "community cathedral" while he was said to stand for "progressive churchmanship" and his theology was "modernist." There was no mention of "evangelical" in this interview, as when he had arrived in Melbourne in 1914. "The modernist," Ruth explained, "does not deny that God did inspire men. He only insists that while God is alive, and while man is spiritually responsive, the process of revelation and the experience of inspiration cannot cease."

On a more personal level Ruth admitted that he occasionally saw a "good wholesome" play, enjoyed a good cigar "of choice bouquet," and

62. *Daily Telegraph*, May 7, 1928, 4.
63. *Vigilant*, June 14, 1928, 15.
64. *SMH*, August 13, 1928, 10.
65. *Daily Telegraph*, September 24, 1928, 3.

played golf, not very well.⁶⁶ He also enjoyed swimming at Manly. On a later occasion a "Gossip of the Town" column described how Ruth found sunbathing reinvigorated his nervous system. "His garden at Manly is as secluded as a Turkish harem. Dressed in nothing but a pair of shorts Mr. Ruth has made this sequestered spot his study, with no fear of intrusive eyes, except from an aeroplane."⁶⁷

Ruth was thus clearly identified as minister of a progressive church, a modernist in theology (with a love of sunbathing). Above all, he also remained intensely loyal to the empire as was demonstrated in 1929 when the King was seriously ill and prayers were offered for his recovery around the world. "Loyalty was not merely a civic policy, a political principle, not a question of trade necessity or national security. It was a question of blood and bones. Loyalty was life, loyalty was love. England was home."⁶⁸ On this occasion, the King survived.

Australian Congregationalists

Ruth's place in his new denomination was demonstrated by his sharing in several events around the nation. He was a prominent figure in the NSW Union but was also welcomed interstate. In April 1929, he asked the NSW Union why there was a dearth of candidates for the ministry. A young minister often found himself as "a sort of errand boy to an audience, the collector of his own meagre salary, a manager of bazaars, a sort of bush lawyer." Ruth insisted:

> They want to be preachers but that is the last thing they are expected to be . . . The preacher who has to fight poverty has no energy left to fight the devil . . . If the churches want men who will say only the things expected of them, in stereotyped fashion, they may as well use dictaphones.

The Congregational Union of Australia and New Zealand had been formed in 1888 and held regular national assemblies.⁶⁹ Ruth participated fully in the meetings of the Eleventh Congregational Union meetings in Brisbane in May 1929,⁷⁰ substituting for Rev. Lionel Fletcher at a large demonstration in His Majesty's Theatre on the Sunday afternoon. He preached

66. *Evening News*, June 22, 1929, 3.
67. *Daily Pictorial*, May 11, 1930, 7.
68. *SMH*, July 8, 1929, 12.
69. Lockley, *Congregationalism*, 341.
70. *AB*, June 4, 1929, 8.

on Christ as the only source of genuine brotherhood.[71] Ruth was also the preacher at a public rally in the City Congregational Church on May 23 when he stressed that every minister, "no matter how far back or lonely his parish," should understand himself as "a minister of the Commonwealth." There was opportunity to build "a free church in a free State," and, typically, he urged his hearers to make a commitment to church unity. Ruth's message was as plain to his new denomination as he had made it to his old.

While in Brisbane Ruth had addressed the Constitutional Club on "Constitutionalism and Communism" during which he stirred his listeners to applause or to laughter at his "witty sallies." He suggested that communism was working for the downfall of England. "The relationship of Communism to the Commonwealth is precisely the relationship of a rat to cheese or to a sack of wheat."[72]

In the same year, Ruth went to Adelaide to deliver the Bevan lectures to the theological students at Parkin College.[73] He also preached at the annual conference of the South Australian Congregational Union in Stow Memorial church where he spoke on "The Revelation of the Atom in a Drop of Water." This science emphasis was also the focus in his lectures, an unusual theme for this kind of theological series, and was reminiscent of the approach taken by Henry Drummond (1851–97) in his famous books *Natural Law in the Spiritual World* (1883) and *The Ascent of Man* (1894). Drummond had sought to interpret the Darwinian theory of evolution in the light of his evangelical faith, and "although his synthesis was criticised by both theologians and scientists he was a pioneer in serious evangelical engagement with modern science."[74] Ruth constantly argued that both religion and science were revelations of God. Titles for the Bevan lectures were "Mother Earth and the Starry Scriptures of the Sky," "The Reply of the Microscope to the Telescope," "Cells, Brain Cells and Human Nature," and "The Mind and the Soul in the Universe of God." Ruth had become obsessed with these scientific issues and their relationship to religion as evidenced by several articles in the *Sun* during 1929–30.

His engagements during 1929 revealed the extent to which his identity within his adopted denomination had been affirmed. He attended the Fifth International Congregational Council at Bournemouth in July 1930

---

71. *Brisbane Courier*, May 20, 1929, 14.

72. *Telegraph* May 23, 1929, 5; *Brisbane Courier*, May 24, 1929, 16.

73. The lectures were named after Dr. L. D. Bevan, the founding Principal of the College (1910–18).

74. George in Larsen, *Biographical Dictionary*, 194.

where he gave the "most eloquent of speeches" as a representative of Australia and other colonials.⁷⁵

On the Air

Religious broadcasting in Australia began in the 1920s and one of the earliest outside broadcasts was from the Pitt Street Church in 1924.⁷⁶ The church had been approached by Farmer Company, who owned 2FC, to broadcast services, "provided the rights of broadcasting be granted them for a period of 5 years," and the deacons approved as long as they had no expenses.⁷⁷ Ruth led regular broadcasts at Pitt Street in the following years. Many others joined in this opportunity, and by 1927 several *Wireless Weekly* correspondents were complaining that Sydney's airwaves on Sundays had become congested with religious services and were spoiling their day of leisure.⁷⁸

The restrictions of time and scheduling compared to a normal service were obvious, but Ruth entered into this new medium with enthusiasm and evident success. Reflecting on his first experience as a preacher on the wireless, he was reminded of John the Baptist who was described as "a voice crying in the wilderness" (Matt 3:3):

> The modern preacher is a voice crying in the wilderness of the wireless. He is nothing but a voice. And it is strangely unlike the old wonted wilderness. That is the wonder of the wireless, the wonder of the spoken word. But that is the bane of broadcasting from the preacher's point of view.⁷⁹

He had no objections to preaching to ten thousand people but he liked to see his hearers, to watch if they were looking at him and following his argument. "If they look dull it is probably because I am dull . . . There is no reason why I should be invisible all the week and incomprehensible on Sunday." But on the radio he had no idea how his hearers were responding. He understood that "sound can be communicated by aerial wires, but can soul?" The smile cannot be seen, nor the look of scorn, and the pointed finger has no impact. But the wireless gives his words wings: "It takes him out of his little garden walled around. It destroys his sectarianisms and his segregations—there are no sectarian wave-lengths. The wireless is weird

---

75. *Western Morning News*, July 9, 1930, 3.
76. Griffen-Foley, "Radio Ministries," 31–54; Kent, *Out of the Bakelite Box*, 195.
77. Pitt Street Deacons' Minutes, June 22, 1924.
78. Griffen-Foley, "Radio Ministries," 33.
79. *Sun*, November 30, 1924, 19.

and wonderful." In reality, preaching is "broadcasting" upon the open air, and not only within the church building. Not all can go to a building: "The church is more than a fellowship of the able-bodied."[80]

Many people wrote to Ruth in appreciation of his broadcast ministry. In 1925, Colonel Thomas Murdoch (1876–1961) had as his guest Sir Harry Lauder (1870–1950), the famous Scottish entertainer. They listened to the service, and Sir Harry, moved by hearing Ruth, said, "You's a good preacher." He then commented, "The finest thing about that service is that we missed the collection and I've kept my threepenny bit."[81]

Ruth and Brookes shared a deep commitment to radio. Brookes was one of the pioneers of the Australian Broadcasting Commission (ABC), appointed as its first vice-president when it was established in May 1932, and served enthusiastically for many years, retiring in 1940. His biographer suggests that outside his home, "The ABC was perhaps the last great love of Herbert Brookes's life."[82] Ruth wrote to congratulate Brookes on his appointment: "Radio has the latchkey to thousands of Australian homes and millions of Australian hearts. And I know you will invest your influence in the Commission as a sacred calling."[83] Moreover, the ABC established its New South Wales headquarters in the new building erected by the Pitt Street Church.

By its charter the ABC was required to provide "adequate and comprehensive" broadcasting, which meant a regular schedule of religious programs. Unlike the commercial stations, which relied totally on religious organizations to provide material, the ABC insisted on editorial authority over its programs although in fact it also needed churches and clergy for most of their religious programs. Groups such as Christian Scientists, Seventh Day Adventists, Mormons, Christadelphians, Plymouth Brethren and some others were excluded by the ABC because they were not part of the Christian mainstream and their ideas were "eccentric, confined to very small groups of people and unintelligible and annoying to the large body of listeners."[84]

The NSW Council of Churches had obtained a license for 2CH in 1931 with the mission "to educate, to evangelise, and to edify," with Sunday devoted to religious programs. The Theosophical Society had launched 2GB in August 1926 and established "resolutely highbrow" programming.[85]

80. *Sun*, February 13, 1925, 15.
81. Ruth to Brookes, 6 August 1925, Brookes Papers, NLA 1924/48/89.
82. Rivett, *Australian Citizen*, 191.
83. Ruth to Brookes, 24 May 1932, Brookes Papers, NLA 1924/48/140.
84. Healey, "A Critical Alliance," 15–28.
85. Griffen-Foley, "Radio Ministries," 32–33; Roe, *Beyond Belief*, 297–98.

Ruth drafted a confidential report in August 1932 for the ABC on religious broadcasting and declared:

> Frankly, 2FC is a poor copy of 2CH which is too poor to be copied, and not to be compared for spiritual lilt and vital interest with 2GB . . . I have been amazed at the pious platitudes which usually get put over on the air by 2FC with occasional interludes of fine thought out feeling. This seems inevitable with such a motley of ministry, with no continuity of thought, no consistency of appeal and sometimes no clear idea of the quality of the microphone, the use of the voice or the meaning of prayer in the home and into hospitals of the State.[86]

By the end of that year, Ruth was clearly upset by developments. He wrote to Brookes:

> Under the regime of the Commission there has been general deterioration in religious contact. The withdrawal of 2FC from Sunday evening church broadcasts has robbed me of little communities of listeners in every state (except in the West) in Australia, in Auckland, Dunedin, Gove [also NZ] and in American Samoa who have gathered together regularly on the 2nd Sunday in the month since 2FC belonged to Farmers. Now I have 2BL on alternate months only. But the distressing thing is that obscurantist stuff with no relation to life is now being passed off as the religion of Christ. Only some drastic action can stop the rot.[87]

Over the Garden Wall

This was the most unusual book that Ruth produced. The cover had a sketch of Ruth peering over a fence into the next-door garden and had the following dedication:

> With sincere apologies to any who have been unwittingly misrepresented in these pages and with sincere respect to all who conscientiously disagree with the convictions herein expressed.[88]

The ten chapters were an examination of various religions, along the lines of Ruth's analysis of different Christian denominations in "Letters to Church

---

86. Brookes Papers, 22 August 1932, Brookes Papers, NLA 1924/48/143.
87. Ruth to Brookes, 19 December 1932, Brookes Papers, NLA 1924/48/146.
88. Ruth, *Over the Garden Wall*.

Folk" when he was back in England. Many of his familiar ideas and emphases were included in his usual racy, humorous, epigrammatic, and alliterative style. Each chapter included suggestions for wider reading.

Cover, *Over the Garden Wall* (1928)

The first chapter outlined his ideas about the various gardens that people grow. His book is a "series of neighbourly peeps" to see what others are growing while recognizing that "we can all grow weeds." His aim was to engage in a ministry of mutual understanding, especially in modern "religious cults and movements." Ruth included his own experience of moving from one city to another and changing his denominational affiliation:

> There is not as much difference between some sects as there is between some cities in the same country. Ministers and members can pass from one denomination to another without suffering any loss of sunshine or quality of the soil . . . without suffering anything like the dislocation in the dark which the travelers from Melbourne to Sydney must suffer at Albury. Grace doesn't run different gauges in different denominations . . . And there is no reason . . . why you shouldn't actually have a share in the grace and glory of all the gardens of God.[89]

Ruth may have received the idea for his book from a quaint novel *Lovey Mary* from which he quotes. Miss Viny has what she calls "A Denominational Garden":

> "I got every congregation I ever heared of planted in it. These are the Baptists," said Miss Viny, waving her hand toward a bed of heliotrope and flags. "They want lots of water: like to be wet clean through."[90]

Ruth then commented on the impact of evolution, biblical criticism, and the new psychology on the churches and concluded the chapter on the dangers of exclusion:

> I make my definition. I draw my circle. But presently I find a man really and truly Christian in spirit. He isn't included in my definition, but my disposition cannot exclude him . . . Then I meet Gandhi, who isn't technically a Christian at all, or I open my mind and heart to Rabindrinath Tagore, and he brings me choicest flowers and fruits . . . And all I can do, to be true to myself and my God is to remember the words of Christ, "He who is not against us is for us" . . . The essential thing is Love . . . And who shall limit love?[91]

His next chapter dealt with "Gardens of Catholicity" where he made his oft-repeated distinction of spelling catholic with a small "c." Like Henry Ward Beecher he was "suspicious of people who think they are good Christians, mainly because they hate Roman Catholics." Extensive criticism of Roman

---

89. Ruth, *Over the Garden Wall*, 13–14.
90. Rice, *Lovey Mary*.
91. Ruth, *Over the Garden Wall*, 18–22. Ruth is quoting Mark 9:40.

dogma is offered but without the aggression that had characterized his apologetics in Melbourne days.[92]

His chapter "In Eastern Gardens" was, however, the most polemical of all. While he argued that "The East no less than the West, belongs to God" and employed simplistic contrasts between the two, he turned to Theosophy to find the most relevant exposition of what the East can offer the West.[93] However, his sharpest criticism was directed towards the Liberal Catholic movement and in particular Charles Leadbeater (1854–1934), the "regionary bishop" of the church, whose book *The Science of Sacraments* "reduces a non-sacramental religion to a system of clairvoyant vision and magic," which cannot be reconciled with all the essential ideas of Theosophy.[94]

Chapter four on "Reincarnation?" continued this broad theme by considering the "past lives" of Leadbeater, Annie Besant, and J. Krishnamurti.[95] Ruth conceded:

> I do not say that it is impossible or even improbable that some of us may be sent back here for our own education and development, though I do not think that the Great Architect of the Universe is so poor that among a million million stars He has only this little bit of stardust at His disposal for His plan and purpose of perfecting personality.

In the fifth chapter, Ruth discussed "In Gardens of Healing" as he examined "Human Nature and Mrs. Eddy," the founder of the Christian Science movement, which he conceded had a large space in the religious mind. He rejected Eddy's "science of metaphysical healing" since it "meets the problem of sin and evil by denying them altogether."[96]

"New Thought Gardens," the next chapter, asked whether "thinking made it so." He concluded, "New Thought, in countless ways, enriches us. It ought to emphasise, it must never be allowed to diminish, our sense of dependence on God."[97]

---

92. Ruth, *Over the Garden Wall*, 25–38.

93. Ruth, Over the Garden Wall, 44.

94. Ruth, *Over the Garden Wall*, 45. For Theosophy and Leadbeater, see Roe, *Beyond Belief*.

95. Ruth, *Over the Garden Wall*, 57–68. Annie Besant (1847–1933) was a British socialist, theosophist, women's rights activist, writer, orator, educationist, and philanthropist. Jiddu Krishnamurti (1895–1986) was an Indian philosopher, speaker, and writer. In his early life, he was groomed to be the new "World Teacher" but later rejected this mantle and withdrew from the Theosophy organization behind it.

96. Ruth, *Over the Garden Wall*, 78.

97. Ruth, *Over the Garden Wall*, 102.

BECOMING A SYDNEY IDENTITY (1923–30)

Ruth had often reflected on spiritualism in his sermons, and his next chapter considered the attractions of that "garden." Always the controversialist, Ruth declared:

> As far as its philosophy is concerned, I haven't the slightest hesitation in saying I am a Spiritualist... But as far as its phenomena are concerned, I could not call myself a Spiritualist. I confess that somewhat unwillingly, I find myself increasingly sceptical ... As far as its philosophy is concerned, I am as much a Spiritualist as Sir Oliver Lodge."[98]

Ruth had no sympathy with those who said spiritualism is of the devil and that mediums are possessed of demons. "There are imposters everywhere: let that be wholly acknowledged; yet still there are things that we cannot deny that point in spiritual directions that indicate the invisible and the eternal."[99]

The last three chapters all dealt with issues about which Ruth had often both preached and written: Rationalism, Freemasonry, and Adventism.

As for rationalism, Ruth's conclusion was simple: "Be rational and religious in your outlook on life. Be scientific. Be spiritual. Listen to God: 'Come now and let us reason together.' Find in Christ the Way, the Truth, the Life."[100] Ruth had often spoken publicly about Freemasonry. What he was concerned with in this chapter was the use of Freemasonry as a Church substitute: "A Mason has no more right to substitute his lodge for his church than he has to substitute his lodge for home, or a Masonic supper for a family meal."[101]

As to "the gardens of hope," in particular for the millennium, Ruth reiterated the arguments he had published in *The Advent Heresy*.[102]

Ruth's last page in the book was devoted to emphasizing the centrality of Christ:

> He comes into every garden. He only comes in your garden as He comes into every other garden. He is the Rose of Sharon and the Lily of the Valley. He comes not in the West only, but in the East. Not at the Antipodes only, but in all the world.[103]

---

98. Ruth, *Over the Garden Wall*, 106–7.
99. Ruth, Over the Garden Wall, 118.
100. Ruth, Over the Garden Wall, 133.
101. Ruth, *Over the Garden Wall*, 148–49.
102. Ruth, *Over the Garden Wall*, 163.
103. Ruth, *Over the Garden Wall*, 168.

Another Overseas Visit (1930)

Ruth was granted eight months' leave in recognition of his remarkable efforts for the church and headed overseas in May, visiting both America and Britain. He arranged for the distinguished Baptist essayist and preacher Dr. F. W. Boreham to occupy the pulpit for six months while he and his wife lived in Ruth's home at Manly. Boreham found this "a distinctive and notable experience" and thought the church "one of the richest and most prosperous that I have known."[104] Despite the popularity of Boreham's preaching, the year became a difficult time for the church, offerings dropping as the economic depression began to affect the life of the city.

His time overseas concluded the first half of Ruth's ministry at Pitt Street. That trip became significant preparation for Ruth as he returned to Sydney and shared in a strenuous and controversial confrontation between empire loyalists like himself and those who sought another way.

---

104. Boreham, *My Pilgrimage*, 241–42; Crago, *Story of F.W. Boreham*, 216–17.

10

A Political and Social Crisis (1930–32)

EVEN BEFORE RUTH LEFT for the USA and England in May 1930, the Australian political scene was troubled. Conservatives like Brookes and Ruth were alarmed that Labor under James Scullin (1876–1953) had come to power federally in October 1929, ominously in the same week as the Wall Street crash. Even worse, J. T. "Jack" Lang (1876–1975) had become Labor Premier in New South Wales in May 1925 although he was defeated at the October 1927 election. Lang had formed an alliance with Jock Garden (1882–1968), the former Baptist/Churches of Christ minister and communist leader.[1] The background to these developments was the Great Depression, an international crisis of unprecedented magnitude causing great hardship in Australia. Lang was returned to power in October 1930, while Ruth was still overseas.

---

1. For Garden's involvement in Baptist life, see Manley, *From Woolloomooloo*, 437–38.

J. T. Lang, Premier of NSW

In April 1929, Prime Minister S. M. Bruce (1883–1967), son of a leading Baptist in the Collins Street Church, appointed Brookes "Commissioner-General for Australia" to the USA, in succession to Sir Hugh Denison, based in New York. Ruth organized a farewell "dedication" service for Brookes at Pitt Street where a large and representative congregation gathered. He quoted Sir James Elder (1869–1946), who had served with Brookes on the Tariff Board, and who had said to him of Brookes, "There goes a man, a straight man, a white man."[2] This unconsciously racist sentiment was loudly applauded.

2. Rivett, *Australian Citizen*, 114.

Traveling Overseas

Brookes as commissioner was well placed to help Ruth prepare for his visit to the USA. Ruth had urged Brookes to "*meet* Dr. Fosdick and Dr. Parkes Cadman, not simply hear them preach."[3] Fosdick was minister at Riverside Baptist Church in New York where millionaire John D. Rockefeller Jr (1874–1960) was such an influential figure while Parkes Cadman (1864–1936) was at the large Central Congregational Church of Brooklyn.

Ruth later wrote to Rockefeller about his plans for the Pitt Street development, seeking financial support and advising that Brookes would vouch for him. He even had the audacity to suggest what Brookes might write: "If he should direct any enquiries to you, you could say that there is no one at the moment in Australia whose ministerial ideals more closely approximate to Dr. Fosdick's."[4] This is a revealing comment about how Ruth regarded himself: Australia's "Fosdick," no less. Brookes forwarded the letter from "our very dear friend the Rev. T. E. Ruth, formerly a Baptist minister but now incumbent of the freest pulpit in Australia":

> He is easily our greatest preacher and platform orator and exercises a splendid influence through a press which has the largest circulation. What he has said can be taken at its full value.
>
> Personally I can vouch for every statement. I do not exaggerate when I say he is the biggest British Australian in our Commonwealth and is the foremost amongst our spiritual uplifters.[5]

Rockefeller, however, does not seem to have given any money to Pitt Street.

Unsettled times made it difficult for Ruth to finalize his travel plans. As he reported to Brookes, the coal strike had brought New South Wales to "the verge of a civil war and Jock Garden who should have been deported is in his element." The Depression was so bad he thought he should cancel his trip, "thinking I might be of some use in preaching courage and good cheer in bad times," but his bank manager advised him that "things will be worse in 12 months' time."[6] So he sailed on May 6 for England.

Ruth spent the month of July preaching at the historic City Temple in London where Australian Dr. F. W. Norwood (1875–1958), also formerly a Baptist, was the minister and also Chairman of the Congregational Union of England and Wales. Norwood, who had been on leave, later commented

---

3. Ruth to Brookes, 15 August 1929, Brookes Papers, NLA 1924/48/115.
4. Ruth to Brookes, 1 November 1930, Brookes Papers, NLA 1924/48/126.
5. Brookes to Rockefeller, 6 December 1930, Brookes Papers, NLA 1924/48/128.
6. Ruth to Brookes, 7 May 1930, Brookes Papers, NLA 1924/48/118.

that he came back "to find my people facing life more gallantly because they had responded to the spell of his magnetic personality and his robust thinking."[7] The church's magazine reported: "Ruth certainly revealed himself to our people as a preacher of the first order—a preacher in the true apostolic succession."[8] Four of his sermons from that ministry were included in *Rendezvous with Life* and were devoted to "using the subconscious" and to the psychology of desire, success, and fear.[9]

Ruth and his wife left England on September 20 for New York where Brookes met the ship and insisted that they stay with him. It is not clear whether Ruth met Fosdick or not. After New York, Tom and Mabel traveled by train to Montreal where he had a preaching appointment. This was followed by a rail journey across Canada to Vancouver, and they both greatly enjoyed seeing the Rockies. They were disappointed that Victoria was shrouded in fog but enjoyed Seattle and Portland, then went by train to San Francisco where Ruth preached at the First Congregational Church. They sailed aboard the *Sierra* for Australia, calling in at Honolulu. They arrived in Sydney on December 23, 1933. Ruth discovered that the political scene in Australia had become even worse, and he was soon thrust into active defense of the "British" values that had shaped all his life.

Resuming a Ministry

Naturally, Ruth was keen to offer his congregation some account of his eight months away. On the first Sunday back, his sermon was "World Conditions and the Gospel Today."[10] Ruth reported that in every country he had visited he had found depression and that one of the chief tasks of the day was "to prevent politicians continuing their dirty game of party politics and to compel them to legislate with due regard for the good of all."[11] What Ruth did not say was just how politicians would be compelled to act in this way. This was a question that would dominate his thinking in the months that followed.

Ruth also used his newspaper articles to address these issues. In his first attempt to offer some guidance through his regular column, he wrote about "Weathering the Storm" of the Depression. He insisted: "The thing most to be desired in these trying times is the power to face adverse

7. Norwood, "Foreword," in Ruth, *Rendezvous with Life*, vii.
8. Ruth, *Rendezvous with Life*, viii.
9. Ruth, *Rendezvous with Life*, 21–80.
10. *Sun*, December 28, 1930, 5.
11. *SMH*, December 29, 1930, 6.

circumstances with pulses beating quietly and a heart that keeps its confidence, the power that will keep the soul steady, and sweet, and strong, lifting life clean above anxiety and worry."[12]

In his column on January 18, 1931, his topic was "What Australia Needs." He again emphasized the need for courage and without that spirit Australia could become the "mere puppets of capital on the one hand or of a class-conscious caucus on the other."

> Democracy may well become the greatest governmental agency of God, but an undisciplined democracy may easily degenerate into an organ of individual and class exploitation, destroy the very genius of government and play the very devil with every divine thing in human nature.
>
> Democracy must revert to the austere idealism of the prophets, the social teaching of the pilgrims, the social teaching of the gospels, the theocracy of the pilgrims if it would avoid the catastrophe of its own creation.[13]

This was provocative. Reverting to the pilgrims' theocracy in New England was scarcely a realistic ideal for Australia.

The *Sun* allowed Ruth an opportunity to state his views quite unambiguously. Headed "I Say Some Unpopular Things—Rev. T. E. Ruth Hits Out. A Tilt at Men and Affairs," he attacked Lang for extravagant gestures such as granting certain government employees extra pay that would run into £275,000 a year even though the State was on the verge of bankruptcy. Ruth ended with a rhetorical summary of his grievances: "To return as far as possible to payment by results; to wipe out our costly system of arbitration that does not arbitrate; to free labor from tyranny over genius and over average capacity and mediocrity; to remove the incubus of Government interference from industry."[14]

Meanwhile, Ruth continued to preach at Pitt Street, giving an address on "England Yesterday, Today and Tomorrow" as the first in what he called a series of "travel sermons." Ruth asked, "England Today! Is She on the Down-Grade?" According to the *Australian Christian World*, the congregation "as one man, held its breath as faithfully and frankly he sketched the industrial, political and ecclesiastical systems of England with all the marks of senile decay about them."[15]

---

12. *Sun*, January 11, 1931, 17.

13. *Sun*, January 18, 1931, 19.

14. *Sun*, January 25, 1931, 3–4. This article was chapter 1, "Anti-British Trend," in Ruth's *Australia at the Cross Roads*, 1–7.

15. *SMH*, January 12, 1931, 8; *ACW*, as cited by *BT*, March 12, 1931, 182.

On January 18, America was considered under the title "Uncle Sam in the family of Nations." In what must rank as a facile understatement, Ruth observed that "America is presented with the greatest racial opportunity of the ages."[16] Another sermon was devoted to prohibition, which President Hoover had called "a noble experiment" but which Ruth called "Half Farce and Half Tragedy."[17] While he believed that prohibition would eventually come, "public law cannot be far ahead of public sentiment" and therefore sentiment must be educated.[18]

His final travel sermon was devoted to Canada where he had been greatly impressed by "utmost devotion to the ideal of Imperial unity." Ruth had also admired the formation of the United Church of Canada, "which had succeeded beyond all anticipation."[19]

Ruth's overseas trip had confirmed him in his sense of an imminent crisis that threatened all that was important to him as an imperial Protestant in Australia.

Preaching in a Time of Crisis: A Theology for Fascism?

Ruth sensed that as a preacher and writer he had to face these serious challenges. How could he seek to lead his people and the wider community in those troubling days? He played his own part in the role of Australian Protestantism within the larger context of political conservatism in the time of the Great Depression.

Paul Nicholls has suggested that there were three reasons why Anglicans and Protestants shared the social and economic assumptions of the Nationalists and later of the United Australia Party. First, the attitudes and policies of non-labor were firmly underpinned by Protestant morality. Second, these denominations were largely unaware of the experiences and attitudes of the working classes. Third, they were firmly oriented towards Britain and empire.[20] Ruth demonstrates these characteristics, especially the empire orientation.

One of Ruth's foundational beliefs was that the gospel should relate to contemporary social and political life. That he should express his absolute

16. *SMH*, January 19, 1931, 10.
17. *The Age*, December 24, 1930, 7.
18. *SMH*, January 26, 1931, 6.
19. *SMH*, February 2, 1931, 8. The United Church of Canada had been formed in 1925 by the merger of Methodists, Congregationalists, some Presbyterians, and local Union churches.
20. Nicholls, "Australian Protestantism," 210–21.

belief in British Imperialism is no surprise, and he was well known as a critic of communism and all left-wing political movements. But he also preached in support of the right-wing New Guard. Was this arguing for a form of fascism? What had led to this situation?

A brief synopsis of recent political events is necessary. The labor movement had gained control in six states by 1925 amid serious tensions throughout the nation. The Communist Party had been formed in Sydney in October 1920, and the Nationalists under Bruce used the trade union links of the Labor Party to make the 1925 election an anti-communist crusade. Throughout the 1925 federal election, 100,000 copies of *Vigilant*, the Protestant Federation paper, were distributed each week, seeking "to maintain the authority of Government and the maintenance of law and order."[21] As the Depression increased, there was a series of long and often violent disputes with waterside workers, timber workers and, the bloodiest of all, the coal miners of New South Wales (1929–30). Conservatives insisted that "communists" were behind all these confrontations, and a great fear of civil disorder led to counter-revolutionary, military-style secret armies being formed. The "White Army," which was active in the Mallee, Wimmera, and Gippsland rural regions of Victoria, had reached fevered preparations for an "invasion" in March 1931.[22] Conservatives believed that communists were a substantial and well-armed faction that had already "white-anted" vital government departments and installations: "Many feared that their world was on the verge of being turned upside down."[23]

Andrew Moore has suggested that any right-wing group in Australia usually encompassed four main attributes. First, they take a more extreme position than that of a mainstream conservative group, such as the Liberal Party, especially in regard to anti-communism. Second, right-wing groups embrace a conspiracy theory as a central organizing concept, whether it is Jews in Nazi Germany or communists in Australia. Third, right-wing groups embrace nationalism and racism, even if the nationalism was an exaggerated "God, King and Country" imperial patriotism. Finally, right-wing politics involve a suspicion or rejection of the ideas and processes of liberal parliamentary democracy, placing an emphasis on the need for strong and authoritarian leadership.[24] These were all evident in the New Guard movement.

Definitions are clearly important. Fascism, while difficult to define, certainly "maintained an intense or ultra nationalism and stressed the

21. *Vigilant*, August 14, 1926, 2.
22. Cathcart, *Defending the National Tuckshop*.
23. Moore, *Secret Army*, 1.
24. Moore, "Writing about the Extreme Right in Australia," 1–2.

need for moral regeneration and held a mystic faith in the value of a strong leader."[25] Fascism became a form of government that is a type of one-party dictatorship and put nation (and often race) above the individual. Hence, Mussolini, and even Hitler in his early days, were at times strongly praised by some Protestants in Australia.[26]

This is why some have charged Ruth and other conservative Protestants with fascism since they supported the New Guard.[27] The fascist groups eventually had little electoral impact and the right-wing "revolution" never came, precisely because the electorate rejected strong left-wing politics. The story of how all this unfolded is important for any proper understanding of Ruth in his time.

When Lang returned to office in 1930, he proposed the suspension of interest payments to British bond-holders. Labor Prime Minister Scullin and Treasurer Theodore rejected this idea, but Lang refused to pay the interest, stating that it was more important to pay the dole. After Lang proposed this repudiation of debt obligations, opposition became even more intense. When the non-Labor government came to power federally in December 1931, they paid the interest on the New South Wales debt and used federal power to reclaim the amount from the state. But Lang instructed his public servants to pay all the money they collected to banks that were beyond the reach of the Commonwealth.

Between 1931 and 1932, Australia "came closer to civil war than at any other time in history."[28] Armed groups on the right and the left secretly prepared for battle. Richard Hall calculated that 130,000 males (or one in every fifteen men) were members of some kind of anti-Labor army during the Depression.[29] The NSW Old Guard had formed after the war although it is doubtful if Ruth had any involvement in this group, which drew heavily on the "upper-crust Protestant churches."[30] The New Guard, which had been formed in February 1931, was led by Eric Campbell (1893–1976), a fierce opponent of Lang.[31] This was most dramatically demonstrated at the opening of the Sydney Harbour Bridge on March 19, 1932, when one of their number, Captain Francis de Groot, rode up on his horse and slashed the ceremonial

---

25. Moore, *Right Road?*, 2–3.

26. Manley, *From Woolloomooloo*, 439; W Hudson, *Australian Religious Thought*, 126.

27. Moore, *Right Road?*, 96; Thompson, *Religion in Australia*, 70.

28. Knightley, *Australia*, 141.

29. Hall, *Secret State*, 22.

30. Moore, *Secret Army*, 75.

31. See Amos, *New Guard Movement*; Campbell, *Rallying Point*.

ribbon with his sword, so depriving Lang of that honor. Street fights and mass gatherings of rival sides added to the drama of the times.

Lang's eventual dismissal by Governor Game on May 13, 1932, was on the basis of his "illegal" instructions to his public servants. Lang stood again in the election in June. The possibility of his return alarmed many Protestants who were challenged to voice their opposition. On the eve of the election, the *Australian Baptist* attacked him in a hysterical leading article, "A National Moral Menace," insisting that Lang's party threatened to sweep across the whole nation, communists had infiltrated schools, and the public service was "swarming with Communists and disloyalists." This editorial provoked tension in the churches, as one minister reported: "Last Sunday in all the churches there was a sense of suppressed excitement, which somewhat interfered with the usual worshipful calm."[32] To the relief of so many distracted Protestants, Lang was definitively ousted at the election.

Ruth had been highly critical of Lang. As he wrote to Brookes in 1926: "Lang is worse than a party liar. He destroys the confidence of the people in public men and revels in making politics a dirty game."[33] When Lang was defeated in 1927, Ruth wrote, "Of course we are all in the seventh heaven over the defeat of our political Charlie Chaplin . . . It was thrilling."[34] Again, in 1931 he declared to Brookes, "Lang is a clever liar and had hypnotized the lowest elements, especially the anti-British, pro-Russian elements, in the community."[35] In May, he despaired, "What is there that one can do? Any response to his utter crookedness would help to rid NSW of the worst enemy of our political life."[36] Did "any response" include armed intervention and overthrow of an elected government? Ruth campaigned as energetically as anyone against Lang, not least in his support for another right-wing political movement.

Ruth and the "All for Australia League"

Social unrest was at a fever pitch when a large crowd gathered at the Sydney Town Hall on the evening of Monday February 16, 1931. A few days earlier at Killara on Sydney's Upper North Shore, the "All for Australia League," "a new non-party political organization," had been formed amid scenes of great enthusiasm. The objects of the League included "organising to meet the present

32. *AB,* May 31, 1932, 1; June 7, 1932, 9.
33. Ruth to Brookes, 21 December 1926, Brookes Papers, NLA 1924/48/97.
34. Ruth to Brookes, 10 October 1927, Brookes Papers, NLA 1924/48/102.
35. Ruth to Brookes, 3 March 1931, Brookes Papers, NLA 1924/48/130.
36. Ruth to Brookes, 5 May 1931, Brookes Papers, NLA 1924/48/131.

economic and social crises" and it was aimed at "cleaning up politics."[37] Employer-association office bearers, many of whom were Rotarians or linked to the Old Guard, dominated its interim board.[38]

Support for the League grew rapidly. There was seething anger over Lang's policies, and some regions of the state were seriously planning for secession. Daily updates in the *Sun* undoubtedly fanned the unrest. The paper gave a vivid report of the "wild scenes" at the Town Hall meeting that had been called to oppose the repudiation proposals: "Scenes verging on riot were witnessed ... when men fought, and women scuffled, while others gave vent to their feelings in tumultuous cheering, hooting and hand clapping." It was "probably the most disgraceful demonstration of hooliganism ever seen in the Town Hall." Small coteries of ardent communist supporters led by the placard-carrying Jock Garden had repeatedly cheered for Lang, another Labor candidate sought to grab the microphone, and serious scuffles involved some men who were dragged from the stage. The crowd, however, waved their handkerchiefs and cheered Thomas Bavin (1874–1941), the Leader of the Opposition, as he mounted the stage.

Ruth then rose to his feet and gave one of his more memorable platform speeches. He began: "I am not here as a politician but as a patriot, I have never been on a political platform." He seconded a motion from the Chamber of Commerce (which the Sydney Rotarians were also supporting) that protested against "the dishonourable proposals for the repudiation of our national obligations recently put forward by the Government of New South Wales," a policy which was "morally disgraceful and financially disastrous."

It was a characteristically aggressive speech. A man like Lang "is out of place in a British Parliament." "I could understand an emissary from Russia advocating repudiation. I could understand an inebriate muttering it in his cups. But I cannot understand a British Premier of a British State advocating so insane and immoral a policy." What was needed was not repudiation but retrenchment: "Not repudiation of debts but a drastic reduction of professional politicians."

He concluded: "It is time Australia put conscience into its citizenship. The road to recovery is the road of righteousness, the righteousness that exalteth a nation." Ruth sat down amidst thunderous applause. Other speakers followed, and when the motion was put, "thousands of hands—by far the great majority of those present—shot into the air."[39]

37. *SMH*, February 13, 1931, 11.
38. Robinson, "All for Australia League," 39.
39. *Sun*, February 17, 1931, 9. The full text is in *Australia at the Crossroads*, 8–12.

The meeting provoked responses in the New South Wales State Parliament. Mark Gosling (1874–1941), the Chief Secretary, reported that he had received a report from the commissioner of police and that there had been no bloodshed because most of the people there supported Lang! However, the remarks of some on the platform were "not conducive to good order," and he named Ruth. "When a vicar of Christ dares to get on a public platform and denounces the Premier of the State as a lunatic I say he should read the New Testament, which says, 'He who calls his brother a fool is in danger of hell fire.' (Uproar)." Labor members shouted "He is a hypocrite," and Gosling continued, "It is time this cleric stuck to his post and preached moral and ethical codes."[40] The time-honored tension between a ruler and a troublesome cleric was re-enacted.

The *Sun* asked in its leading editorial, "Has NSW a Premier or a Nightmare?"

> Throughout the country, generally, there have been declarations of sheer revolt . . . naturally, in times of financial difficulty, the people are more difficult to control, even by a good Government . . . As for the Lang Government, it will pass like a bad dream. All that the people must do is to determine that in no circumstances shall Socialism be given further shrift at the polls.[41]

Ruth later attacked Gosling for his views,[42] which provoked the Chief Secretary to renew his critique of Ruth: if Ruth had exhorted politicians to confine themselves to politics but had himself ventured into politics, then a politician may be permitted "a brief incursion into biblical teachings."[43]

Enthusiastic meetings were held in suburban halls, and by the end of March the League claimed 160,000 members. However, the members refused to be associated with the National Party or any political party; the League was a populist revolt against the conservative establishment. After the initial wave of enthusiasm, the membership faded away, and in November 1931 the League cooperated with the existing Nationalist organization at the federal election and helped form the United Australia Party (UAP) with Joseph Lyons (1879–1939), who had left the Labor Party over its policies during the Depression, becoming Prime Minister from 1932–39.

Meanwhile Ruth had continued to be attacked after his speech at the repudiation rally. Rev. C. W. Chandler (1994–78), an Anglican cleric,[44]

40. *Sun*, February 17, 1931, 9; *Barrier Miner* (Broken Hill), February 17, 1931, 1.
41. *Sun*, February 18, 1931, 6.
42. *Sun*, March 1, 1931, 5.
43. *Labor Daily*, March 3, 1931, 8.
44. Judd and Cable, *Sydney Anglicans*, 324.

wrote an "open letter" to Ruth in the *Labor Daily*. He wrote as "one-man-who-likes-shooting-the Manly-breakers-together" and claimed that his castigation of Lang "was of a nature ill-suited to one of your profession," and he wondered if he had unwittingly been chosen to fire other people's bullets.[45]

Ruth was unrepentant and in a sermon on March 8 said:

> If churchmen did not protest when politicians threatened to reduce the state to the level of a convict settlement by refusing to pay interest on the money borrowed from the English public to pay Australian wages, it was not easy to see what right the churches had to exist at all.[46]

Even more forcefully, Ruth devoted his column on March 15 to the assertion, "The Churches Must Interfere in Politics":

> People who think it is the sole function of the Church to coddle the saints for an hour and five minutes on Sunday morning and to give them short, simple, soothing sermons, have another thought coming to them . . . The Church isn't meant to be a cure for insomnia.[47]

This did not deter the labor press from maintaining its attack on Ruth. A vicious personal letter, headed "Left his Flock to Starve," criticized Ruth for living at Manly. "He is only a frail—a very frail—human after all . . . As the shepherd of his flock he proved a failure, for immediately he accepted his present billet at the Pitt Street Church . . . he promptly went to live at Manly." (Of course, his congregation did not live near the church in Pitt Street but was spread across the suburbs, some even living at Manly and further afield.)

> It is inconsistent for a loving shepherd to live so far from his sheep, but it saves such a lot of trouble, for one cannot study too well when the front door-knocker keeps banging, and, after all, even a shepherd does not want his sick sheep—his hungry sheep—his dying sheep—crying after him all day long.
>
> Not only that, but the well-advertised and no doubt lucrative article must be got ready for the sacred day's newspaper, so one must be away from the madding crowd, even though it be sick and hungry . . .

---

45. *Labor Daily*, February 27, 1931, 6.
46. *Barrier Miner*, March 9, 1931, 1.
47. *Sun*, March 15, 1931, 17.

> Is such a man fit to stand in judgment on J. T. Lang, who is the greatest Labor Premier and Leader this State has ever possessed.[48]

Again, another ALP branch secretary criticized Ruth:

> What hypocrisy! What cant! What humbug to say the church is not allied to capitalism... The Christianity that Jesus preached was: help the helpless, strengthen the weak, care for the sick and dying. Mr. Lang is trying to do this, and the Ruths are preventing him.[49]

During 1931 Ruth published *Australia at the Crossroads*, which was dedicated "To the newly awakened Members of the All for Australia League and to the brave men who 'carried the baby' what time the Crusaders slept." This was a booklet of 116 pages, with many of the eighteen chapters drawn from relevant columns published by Ruth. His book included his speech at the repudiation rally and other *Sun* articles that were relevant topics such as "The Anti-British Trend"; "The Churches Must Interfere"; "What Australia Needs"; "People and Party Politics" and "Weathering the Storm." Although his book had no official imprimatur, its dedication to the League and its emphasis on the crisis image of a crossroad means that it has often been taken to represent the hopes and policy of the League.

---

48. *Labor Daily*, March 19, 1931, 7.
49. *Labor Daily*, April 21, 1931, 3.

Cover, *Australia at the Crossroads* (1931)

In August 1931, Ruth wrote an extensive explanation for South Australian readers of "the political mess in Sydney" and suggested "a way out" with a biblical parable: "New South Wales is the prodigal State of the Commonwealth. It has wandered from the Councils of the Nation, from the common honesty and liberty of British people, and wasted its substance in extravagant, if not exactly riotous, living." Ruth's suggestion was not that the New Guard should be summoned into service, but rather what was equally alarming for many:

> There was only one governmental way out of the mess—that the State can be saved only as Sydney was saved from civic corruption in 1928, by government by commission. City aldermen were no worse then than our politicians are now. And the State is in a much dirtier mess. Democracy would be better served by a commission than by the present dictatorship.
>
> Representative government is dead. The mandate of the people is flouted. Democracy is defrauded.[50]

Ruth quoted Holman, the former premier of the state, suggesting to Prime Minister Scullin that in return for financial aid, the State Parliament should refer for a term of years the whole State administration to the Commonwealth to be executed by a federal commission. Ruth could see no other way out: "A term of years, say five, of freedom from the party political machine would at least stop the rot." The possibility of New South Wales, under any political party, agreeing to a federal commission was exceedingly remote. It is no wonder that Ruth was soon moving away from a "governmental way" to an alternate solution with possible action by the New Guard.

On the eve of the 1932 election, Ruth was hopeful:

> We are in for a big fight for righteousness. I hope our people will not be apathetic or underestimate the strength of Lang whose corrupt government has brought votes by the thousand . . . Stevens is proving a strong leader here. It's curious how closely the Labour people follow the papist plan. The *Labor Daily* declares all the other papers "black," puts them on the "Index" and forbids the faithful to read them.[51]

Ruth and the New Guard

Probably the most famous sermon ever preached by Ruth, certainly the most cited in histories of the period, is his address at Pitt Street on April 17, 1932, called "The Police and the New Guard—A Plea for Common Right." Full reports appeared in regional and interstate papers as well as in the Sydney press. The address was later printed as a pamphlet and widely distributed. This sermon is the main source for claims that Ruth articulated a theology for fascism in Australia.

---

50. *News* (Adelaide), August 17, 1931, 6.

51. Ruth to Brookes, 24 May 1932, Brookes Papers, NLA 1924/48/140. S. B. Stevens (1889–1973) was Premier of NSW for the United Australia Party from 1932–39.

There was a large crowd present giving frequent bouts of "noisy applause," and although Ruth rebuked them and asked them not to do so again, "there were frequent occasions when murmurs of acclaim resounded through the church."[52]

What exactly did Ruth say in this sermon? With his customary ingenuity, he found two texts that permitted him to make his salient points. "Remove scoundrels from a King and his throne will rest on justice" (Moffatt's translation of Prov 25:5) and "Honour all men. Love the brotherhood. Fear God. Honour the King" (1 Pet 2:17). Ruth claimed that these two texts "sufficiently indicated the duty of the police, the policy of the New Guard, and the common right." The key arguments were clear:

> The removal of scoundrels from a king was perhaps the primary duty of the police. It was necessary to the honouring of all men, which was the policy of the New Guard. The police had no doubt at all about the existence of scoundrels. Neither had the New Guard, which, like the Prophet of Israel found them in high places and like him, said so.
>
> The police were our permanent guardsmen and they had the appreciation of all decent people; but they were in duty bound to obey the orders of the Government, and many responsible citizens honestly believed that the Government was elected on false pretences, that it used its powers to thwart the will of the people, to degrade public life, to menace public morality, and to injure the Commonwealth and the common weal.
>
> Suppose the Government was corrupt and without honour? Then the citizens must adopt some other method to guard those things which were more precious in any British community than life and property. The Government had been guilty of the protection of Communists, animosity to loyalists, Soviet legislation, tin hare scandals, and a policy of default and repudiation, yet they were the political masters of the police. The policy of the Government was not the policy of the people.[53]

Clearly, Ruth was indeed proposing that "responsible citizens" had a right to remove "scoundrels," such as the Lang Labor government, "from the King," that is, from their duly elected position. This was an argument in favor of revolution, that an unelected conservative group had biblical authority to remove these "scoundrels." Ruth was "amazed at the supine surrender of the citizens to the decline of political morality."

---

52. *SMH*, April 18, 1932, 9. This report is reproduced in *Vigilant*, May 5, 1932, 17.
53. See Amos, *New Guard Movement*, 85.

So, here was the dilemma as Ruth saw it. The government was corrupt, but the police were obliged to obey this government. What to do? Rather than argue for a concerted political campaign to overthrow such a party at the next election—which was, after all, the traditional British way—Ruth dangled another possibility before his excited hearers and the many who would read the substance of his sermon in the press. He concluded:

> There was sufficient man-power in the New Guard, if consecrated to the cause of Christ and the cause of the State, to save New South Wales and re-establish the British tradition of honesty in government and to make contribution to Commonwealth and Empire worthy of being associated with the selfless courage of the supermen of the Southern Cross, the Anzacs who stormed the heights of Gallipoli.

Ruth did not propose any dominant political figure, a modern-day Oliver Cromwell, who might lead such a "revolution," but he clearly supported the New Guard as a possible answer to the state's dilemma. The use of physical force is at least suggested by the Anzac reference.

It should be recalled that in a less excitable period, in his "Mission to Democracy" in 1919, Ruth had argued: "I do not think Christ would hesitate to use force to secure the safety of the State, the sanctity of the home, the right to work, and the securing of daily bread."[54] Now, in this troubled situation of 1932 his theoretical argument found a concrete possibility, although just how "Christ" could "use force" remained the question. There is no evidence that Ruth shared in New Guard activities.

But was he a "fascist"? Andrew Moore rightly comments that the main question to ask about movements like the New Guard is:

> Whose interests did they serve? . . . Fascism is less a set of ideas and programs than a stage of capitalist development, though clearly there are beliefs and policies that can meaningfully be labelled "fascist" and "proto-fascist" . . . Potentially it existed wherever the ruling classes of embattled liberal democracies saw their economic and social order tumbling and socialist enthusiasms arising among the masses.[55]

This analysis suggests that Ruth's views, at least as shown in this sermon, were "proto-fascist."

In any case, the intervention by the State Governor to dismiss Lang on May 13, 1932, and his subsequent electoral defeat, quietened the hearts of

54. *AB*, July 29, 1919, 4.
55. Moore, *Secret Army*, 10–11.

Ruth and many others. Popular revolution had been averted; the "scoundrels" had been removed by constitutional, if controversial, means.

Meanwhile, there is no doubt that Ruth's "New Guard" sermon had sparked angry responses from the left. J. J. Graves, the Secretary of the ALP, condemned Ruth for taking a mean advantage of his congregation, who had no right of reply: "Is it any wonder that church attendances are dwindling?" Ruth had incited the police to revolt against the government. He was "an apologist for the capitalistic interests," declared O. Schreiber of the Trade Unions. "Though he claims to be a follower of the lowly Nazarene who threw the money changers out of the temple his aim evidently is to use his church as a voice of propaganda in the interest of the modern money changers." The congregation's applause was unmistakable evidence that a discussion on bonds, the New Guard, and such like contentious matter was more welcome and had a greater appeal than a sermon on faith, hope and charity."[56]

Jock Garden asked Ruth to allow him to preach at Pitt Street the following Sunday from the text, "Blessed are ye when men shall revile and persecute you," adding that when they read about churches being looted in times of revolution, as was the case in Spain, it is people like Ruth who are responsible. Ruth declined the request from a man "of the calibre of Mr. Jock Garden," and he did not intend to allow him to preach his propaganda from the pulpit.[57] The *Labor Daily* headlined this response as "Ruth is still Ruthless."[58]

On the eve of Anzac Day, George Howie in the Domain shouted that as Ruth wanted "to consecrate the New Guard" he would not be surprised if he next wanted "to consecrate the devil":

> Years ago the Churches turned their pulpits into recruiting offices, but today they are deaf to the cries and appeals of the men whom they induced to go overseas, and have come back maimed and diseased ... The parsons' pulpits today are dripping with the blood of victims of their war propaganda and the tears of widows.[59]

A mass meeting of railway workers adopted a motion condemning Ruth for "turning his pulpit into a political soap-box" and to leave government "to those who had been elected by a vast majority of the people."[60] The attack

56. *SMH,* April 19, 1932, 9.
57. *Daily Telegraph,* April 19, 1932, 6
58. *Labor Daily,* April 21, 1932, 4.
59. *Labor Daily,* April 25, 1932, 5.
60. *Labor Daily,* April 20, 1932, 6.

was unrelenting. Ruth naturally supported the Governor's action in dismissing Lang. "What was morally wrong could never be politically right," and the Governor was right. "The people waited with as much patience as they could for the Governor to declare the road open."[61]

A major scandal involving the granting of licenses for the use of tin hares (mechanical lures for greyhound racing), which the Lang government had introduced, had led to a Royal Commission, and Ruth proceeded to preach on this issue, advertising that he would declare "a house full of swindling gains." The *Labor Daily*, observing that Ruth "seems to be able to talk from the pulpit on almost every subject under the sun," headed its report "Ruth at It Again."[62]

Ruth must have been grateful to reach the end of a challenging couple of years. Even when he had tried some humor when speaking at a Congregational Conference in October 1931, he had been attacked by some women. He had suggested that "man's seven sacraments were the cheque-book, the motor car, the golf links, the chef, and three whiskies and sodas," but the next day unamused married women "attacked him in force," denying that their men were like this![63]

Preaching through 1931–32

While certain controversial sermons, notably the one dealing with the New Guard, have understandably attracted attention, a brief survey of his regular Sunday preaching and some reference to how other preachers faced the challenge of depression and political instability is helpful. Each Monday the *SMH* published a column called "From the Pulpit," which gave good summaries of several Sunday sermons across the denominations in both city and suburbs. Pitt Street was featured quite often, and these give a rich resource for tracing Ruth's pulpit themes. How many of these sermons had an overtly political thrust?

As a Baptist or a Congregationalist, Ruth was not bound by liturgical or lectionary disciplines, but there was a cycle of religious and secular milestones to be observed. Naturally he marked the major celebrations of Easter and Christmas, but Anzac Day, Empire Day, and Remembrance Day were also noted. At a harvest thanksgiving service on February 15, Ruth stressed the necessity of a spiritual vision, teaching that God was "entirely reliable and

---

61. *SMH*, May 16, 1932, 10.
62. *Labor Daily*, November 17, 1932, 4; *SMH*, November 21, 1932, 9.
63. *Sun*, October 28, 1931, 9.

absolutely righteous."[64] On the same Sunday, Rev. L. M. Sutton at St. Andrew's Cathedral sought to offer guidance for the difficult days of the Depression by insisting that the church was not so much to undertake relief work on a large scale, "though much is being done privately to alleviate distress," but rather "to set an example of faith in God and to show the world that our strength lies in quietness and confidence in our Heavenly Father."[65]

Ruth entered directly into the contemporary political scene with his sermon on "Government and God" on February 22 when he asserted: "If democracy is a mere mechanical grouping of man on the basis of a trade, a creed, or a class, it is bound to injure personal character and society. This is the day of judgment. It is high time for a governmental return to God."[66]

At Ashfield Baptist Church Pastor Weller was tackling the subject of "Christianity and Communism" by rehearsing "The signs and evidences of the return of Jesus Christ." He referred to the New Guard, noting that the government had condemned it while an Australian Labor Army had been formed, "its badge being the red star of the Russian Revolution." All "these calamitous events" were prophesied in the Bible. "Communism is slowly, steadily but surely gaining ground everywhere."[67]

Ruth preached at St. Andrew's Cathedral on Sunday May 24 to mark Empire Day. The following week, back at Pitt Street, Ruth outlined "The Challenge of Communism." The Russian revolution, he observed, was "one of the most colossal the world has ever seen."

> Communism renounced all religious belief . . . Bolshevism has no God at all, and only a collectivised man without a soul. It is suicide to refuse to take into consideration the terrific challenge of an atheistic communism in this community and in this Commonwealth.[68]

In the peaceful quiet of the annual Katoomba Christian Convention in 1932, the devout New South Wales Baptist Principal G. H. Morling (1891–1974) told his hushed hearers that "Even Lang cannot do as he likes; there is a God above Mr. Lang."[69]

Sunday after Sunday in both city and suburban pulpit, the challenges were posed. Alex Campbell, a Congregational minister preaching

---

64. *SMH*, February 16, 1931, 8.
65. *SMH*, February 16, 1931, 8.
66. *SMH*, February 23, 1931, 8.
67. *SMH*, April 13, 1931, 8.
68. *SMH*, June 1, 1931, 8.
69. Morling, "Spiritual Millionaires," 51. (I owe this reference to Rev. R. Benson.)

at Killara, the home territory of the All for Australia League, appealed for unity if we were ever to be "on the road for true recovery." Had not they as a people been only concerned with their own welfare? "Had they not been regarding the Government as existing mainly, by a system of tariffs, bounties, arbitration, awards and the rest, to help the individual to advance his own material ends?"[70]

Returning to the political scene, Ruth spoke on "A Plea for a Free Australia" on November 15. On the same day, Archdeacon Davies at St. Andrew's Cathedral made some "scathing observations regarding the political life of the State." Ruth claimed that if he were "the power—the ecclesiastical power if you like"—behind Prime Minister Scullin, he would advise him "to proclaim that every man in Australia is free to work for anything he can get."[71] This was an attack on "the atheistic Communist" control of many unions. Two weeks later, he insisted that collectivism "could have no real value without individual freedom of thought."[72]

Early in December, Ruth again took up an overtly topical and political thrust when he referred to the Old Testament book of Nehemiah, "an intensely political and patriotic document," and spoke on "The Working Tools of a Political Faith." There was a need for those who sounded the alarm, "especially in a community like ours where elementary loyalties are threatened, where active disloyalty finds expression in the Press, on the platform, and in Parliament."

Looking back across 1931, it may be concluded that while Ruth sought to address the contemporary situation and to criticize in a general way Labor and communist policies, there are no further recorded references to the New Guard. Other clergy also attacked the government policies and while Ruth may have been more outspoken and more regular in doing this, he did not neglect other biblical and social themes.

His infamous support of the New Guard was preached on April 4, 1932. Not surprisingly, Ruth preached more sermons with a political emphasis as tensions mounted, but his preaching also featured broader development of Christian themes.

By the beginning of March, Ruth's anxiety about what was happening politically grew dramatically. His sermon titles were posted each week outside the church, and his title for March 6 was "Where may political wisdom be found?" He claimed that the government's corruption was "notorious"; politicians themselves defamed Parliament and made the House "a disgrace

70. *SMH*, June 15, 1931, 8.
71. *SMH*, November 16, 1931, 8.
72. *SMH*, November 30, 1931, 9.

to the community." In a revealing argument, significant for all his sermons of this type, he acknowledged that everyone was suspicious of "political sermons." As he had so often claimed, "the pulpit must be free":

> If a preacher was not permitted to speak the whole counsel of God, preaching had lost its place ... Critics of the Church could not consistently blame the Church when the world went wrong, and curse it for trying to lead the world aright ... the Church must deal with belligerent politicians who fostered class hatred and the spirit of war.[73]

All Sydney had been distracted by the opening of the spectacular Harbour Bridge on Saturday March 19, and even the incident with De Groot slashing the ribbon did not spoil the carnival atmosphere. After expenditure of some £10 million, "the greatest single-arch bridge in the world," with a span of 1,650 feet, had been completed, and the next day Sydney's preachers excelled in adapting the bridge image in their sermons. Methodist R. J. Williams at the Lyceum service was inspired to preach about Jesus as the supreme bridge-builder while at St. Andrew's Cathedral Canon Begbie also remembered that it was Holy Week and that a gulf between God and sinful man had been bridged: "There was no dispute as to who should open it." Ruth insisted that men had a passion for bridge-building, but unless the foundation was on the Rock of Ages people would find themselves out of harmony with the great Architect of the universe.[74]

However, on Sunday April 3 at the Methodist Church in Croydon, there was "great excitement" when Rev. N. C. Goss preached on "The Religious Significance of the New Guard." This was a couple of weeks before Ruth's oft-cited sermon and was accompanied by extensive disturbances as stones were thrown on the roof, and attempts were made to disable some motor vehicles. As Goss pronounced the benediction, another volley of stones hit the roof. It was all very exciting. Goss declared that "he would not be turned from his path."

> Members of the New Guard should endeavour to foster all that was best in life while they actively organised to resist the enemies of their liberty and ideals. A member of the New Guard who did not support the Church ... was only half a New Guardsman in the same way that a Christian who did not actively combat enemies of the faith was only half a Christian.[75]

---

73. *SMH*, March 7, 1932, 8.
74. *SMH*, March 21, 1932, 10.
75. *SMH*, April 5, 1932, 9.

Ruth, then, was not the first and only minister to mention the New Guard in his preaching. Indeed, back on January 24, Rev. W. J. Grant of Randwick Presbyterian had envisaged a time when "we might even be permitted to stand to attention while the New Guard marches past."[76]

Ruth's "New Guard" sermon was preached on April 17. On the day that Ruth urged the overthrow of scoundrels, Rev. H. Steele Craike at Summer Hill Congregational Church preached on "Clean up the State!" His conclusion was unambiguous:

> There was a call from the Christian Church for a moral crusade, and love would dissolve all class hatred and bitterness. It needed a moral crusade to put things right, and at the next election they should drive the trouble-monger and the moral-wrecker to his own place—that of outer darkness.[77]

Ruth followed up his "New Guard" sermon by developing a theme he had often used in preaching and writing, "Jesus as a Patriot": "The Sydney citizen found in Christ an example of glowing indignation against wrong; of fearless courage and constructive righteousness." When reading of Christ's expulsion of the money-changers from the temple, "you will have no doubt as to what your attitude should be when, in the name of spurious philanthropy, personal and public character is being undermined, and the poor and the needy are being exploited for the enrichment of corrupt politicians."[78]

On June 5, Ruth asked his hearers, "Is there any vital connection between spiritual communion and practical politics, or are the enemies of the Christian faith, the red wreckers of community welfare and constitutional progress right when they say religion is an opiate?" He warned, "What happened in Russia would happen here if the altar-fires of their faith were allowed to go out."[79]

After Lang had been rejected at the ballot box, Ruth declared, "The election is over, but not the political responsibility of the people, nor the social mission of the Church . . . All the resources of religion were available for the solution of social problems and the ordering of public life."[80]

Subsequent weeks found Ruth preaching on prayer, the relation of science to religion and even discussing George Bernard Shaw's play *Saint Joan* in

---

76. *Daily Telegraph* January 25, 1932, 4.
77. *SMH*, April 18, 1932, 8.
78. *SMH*, May 1, 1932, 8.
79. *SMH*, June 6, 1932, 6.
80. *SMH*, June 13, 1932, 10.

which he suggested that "history and religion made many reversals."[81] Other weeks found him turning to people's personal problems and guiding his hearers about the use of leisure and the value of beauty for the soul.

He returned to a topical political issue after the report of the Royal Commission into tin-hare racing was released in November. This had revealed that "money had been made through the passions of the people" and that churchmen should not close their eyes to corruption and social sin. He linked several paragraphs from the report with a text from Jeremiah, "For rogues are to be found among my folk." For the balance of 1932, Ruth returned to familiar themes, such as "Heaven and Hell."[82]

This admittedly incomplete review of Ruth's preaching and that of some of his contemporaries during 1931–32, as reported in the *SMH*, suggests that while he did feel obliged to address social and political issues as they arose, and markedly so in his "New Guard" sermon, he more consistently addressed biblical and religious themes that related to the daily living of his hearers. He discussed a wide range of topics, as he had done throughout his career in both England and Melbourne. There was only one sermon that might be interpreted as "fascist," and he was not the only minister to advance the hope that some group such as the New Guard might be raised up to deal with the political "lunacy" that Lang and his government were thought to embody.

Ruth continued with his preaching and writing as his church moved positively into a new year that would celebrate the historic milestone of the church's centenary.

---

81. *SMH*, September 5, 1932, 8.
82. *SMH*, December 12, 1932, 8.

11

"The Little Napoleon" of Pitt Street (1933–38)

SLOWLY BUT SURELY, AUSTRALIA recovered from the fearsome Depression. Unemployment had reached a peak in the winter of 1932 but began to recede, and by the end of 1933 recovery was well under way. Australians began to worry more about the Test cricket series of 1932–33 with the success of Harold Larwood and his "bodyline" bowling under the arrogant leadership of Douglas Jardine as English captain. Stuart Macintyre suggests that as the specter of an unemployed uprising receded in the conservative imagination, it was replaced by two equally urgent fears: disloyalty and immorality. While the political left shared in a growing awareness of the need to contain fascism and defend democracy, the right feared that such concerns could minimize national pride. Indeed, such a fear led to admiration for the dictators and their firm authority as well as their vigorous national pride.[1] As late as 1938 Robert Menzies visited Germany and felt there was "a really spiritual quality in the willingness of young Germans to devote themselves to the service and well-being of the State."[2]

Ruth condemned dictatorship: "Dictatorship means the end of democracy. The difference between dictatorship and democracy in Australia is the difference between Australia, with its freedom, and Australia, where hundreds are committing suicide because they are not allowed liberty."[3] He later claimed many fine young people had been attracted to fascism:

1. Macintyre, *Oxford History of Australia*, 308
2. Macintyre, *Oxford History of Australia*, 309.
3. *SMH*, March 28, 1938, 10.

> The keenest young people I know are asking, not for liberty, but for discipline. They would rather have a freedom that has become little more than a fetish. They would prefer a live dictator to a decaying democracy. They ask what defence can be made for a democracy that keeps millions unemployed, while dictators keep everybody busy. God is not a fascist. He is a Father concerned with a growing family, some of whom are foolish enough to think they have reached finality. Christianity is a Divine Crown, not a dunce's cap. It is a window in the mind, not a ring through the nose.[4]

But prior to the growth of dictatorships later in the decade, Ruth had himself been affectionately dubbed "the little Napoleon" in a denominational report of a remarkable event, which Ruth largely engineered, to mark the centenary of Pitt Street Congregational Church on May 2, 1933. That "Napoleon" ascription has been interpreted as a clue for assessing Ruth's personality and leadership style.[5] However, it was definitely not intended as a criticism but rather as an acknowledgement of his leadership role in the success of the event. Certainly, Ruth had confessed to his friend Brookes at this time, "In an Independent church or in any democratic community the only way to get anything done—as you well know—is to do it yourself."[6]

Pitt Street: Centenary Celebrations

Although the first Congregational church in Australia had been formed in Tasmania in 1829, Pitt Street and the denomination regarded May 2, 1933, as the centenary of Congregationalism in Australia. While the denomination established a committee to prepare for the centenary, it was Pitt Street, and more particularly Ruth, who planned the celebrations.

So began an exhausting program for Ruth and many of his people. A major civic service was held at the end of April with the Governor, the Chief Justice, the State Premier, and Sydney's Lord Mayor in attendance. The intention was not only to mark their church's ministry in the city but also to celebrate Congregationalism in Australia more generally. Ruth pleaded that the Sermon on the Mount should be the guide for commercial, political, national, and international life. At a "service of fraternity" on the evening

---

4. *SMH*, July 25, 1938, 10.
5. Curthoys, *Pride of Place*, 193–247.
6. Ruth to Brookes, 21 May 1933, Brookes Papers, NLA 1924/48/149.

of that day, he repeated an oft-cited insistence that the Commonwealth was "one big union" and was the only union "really big enough."[7]

But the highlight of the centenary was a procession through the streets of the city on the evening of Tuesday May 2, the actual day of the centenary, and this culminated in a public meeting at the church. It was an ambitious but highly successful event to which the local press gave detailed and positive coverage. The *Telegraph* also included an illustrated account of the pioneer Congregationalist missionary William Pascoe Crook (1775–1846), who had helped found the denomination in Australia.[8]

The plan was that Ruth would lead his people to the other Protestant churches of the city where representatives from those places of worship would join "a procession of fellowship" as a demonstration of unity or "burying the hatchet." As the official program suggested—again with Ruth's imprint clearly evident—"Church union tarries. But Christian unity is a fact."[9] Ruth took great pains to visit all the other clergy in preparation for this evidently unique procession in Sydney.

The denominational paper recorded something of the excitement of the day:

> What a unique event! Folks said it could not be a success. Churchmen did not care to march in public streets! Certainly, no ladies would join in! But when we left the School of Arts, Pitt Street, inside which is still the original chapel of 1833—now used as a library—there were several hundreds, who lined up four abreast—and half of them were women, young and old! . . . We marched . . . headed by the "little Napoleon" and his deacons.[10]

The procession began with about two hundred from Pitt Street Congregational and Bathurst Street Baptist churches gathering at the School of Arts. They then moved to the Methodist Mission where, amid cheers, the procession was enlarged. With a large watching crowd, the group marched to St. James' church in King Street where the assembly received a blessing from the rector, Dr. P. Micklem (1876–1965) and shared a prayer "amid impressive ritual."[11]

Six years later when preaching at St. James', a High Anglican church, Ruth recalled how he had gone to Micklem and asked him, "What is the

7. *Congregationalist*, May 18, 1933, 8.
8. *Daily Telegraph*, May 3, 1933, 6.
9. *SMH*, May 3, 1933, 13.
10. *Congregationalist*, May 18, 1933, 6.
11. *SMH*, May 3, 1933, 13.

best thing you could give us"? Micklem hesitated before he said, "The very best I have to give is my blessing from the altar." Ruth replied, "We will come and get it." Micklem again hesitated, "But would your people come?" Ruth quickly retorted, "They are not so enriched by my ministry that they can afford to go without any good man's blessing." So they came, crowding into the church where they were blessed "before placing on the Anglican monument in this parish a wreath of remembrance, 'from the sons of freedom to the fathers of our faith and the apostles of order.'"[12]

"Like a snowball the silent procession gathered forces as it went," reported the *Herald*.[13] They moved to St. Stephen's Presbyterian Church (then still in Phillip Street) where various Presbyterian dignitaries welcomed them. There was a halt at the monument in Hunter Street marking the site of the first service of worship held in Australia, led by chaplain Richard Johnson (1756–1827) on February 3, 1788. Bishop S. J. Kirkby (1879–1935) welcomed Ruth and his cohort. Ruth here presented a laurel wreath and declared:

> Near this spot at the corner of Hunter and Bligh Street in 1810, Wm. Pascoe Crook, then a not fully ordained minister, attempted to found a Congregational Church but was forbidden by the Anglican colonial chaplain to administer the Lord's Supper. This wreath, inscribed with friendly greetings from the Pitt Street Congregational Church, is a tribute paid by the sons of freedom to the apostles of order in the same evangelical faith.[14]

The assembly applauded and then spontaneously burst into the hymn, "Blest Be the Tie That Binds." Standing either side of the wreath, Ruth and Kirkby clasped hands.

The next stop was at the Cenotaph in Martin Place where the crowd, now over 1,200, observed two minutes' silence in honor of the "heroic dead." Proceeding to the eastern door of St. Andrew's Cathedral, Ruth ostentatiously knocked four times on the door which was opened by Dean A. E. Talbot (1877–1936). Ruth declared, "We the representatives and friends of the Mother Church of Congregationalism in Sydney, knock on the door of the Mother Church of the Evangelical faith of our native land. We pray you open in the name of the Lord." Talbot welcomed the visitors, and Bishop Kirkby suggested that the "assemblage would be regarded by them all as a

---

12. Ruth, typed sermon, "Religion and Democracy," in Brookes Papers, NLA 1924/48/219.

13. *SMH*, May 3, 1933, 13.

14. *SMH*, May 3, 1933, 13.

sacrament of a yet greater gathering in unity, and that with one heart, one soul, and one spirit they would join in common praise."[15]

They all then marched to the Pitt Street church where Bishop Kirkby placed a wreath on the memorial tablet to Pascoe Crook. Many greetings from various denominations (excluding the Roman Catholics) were presented while Rabbi Francis Cohen (1882–1934) of the Great Synagogue thanked Ruth for his expression of profound sympathy with the Jewish people "arising out of the German situation." He also commented on the great debt that British Jews owed to the fathers of Congregationalism, "those Independents in the time of Cromwell who welcomed the Jews' return to England in 1658."[16] The Greek Orthodox Archbishop spoke through an interpreter.

The following Sunday, Ruth was moved to sense that he was joined by "men and women and children of a hundred years . . . The limitations of time and space seem for a moment removed. That which is timeless and non-spatial claims us." Moreover, this extended to the church universal and the church eternal. The "Lord of the infinite past" was also "the Lord of the infinite future."[17]

The celebration was a great encouragement to Ruth personally as well as his congregation, although it left him completely exhausted. He wrote to Brookes: "I think I have never been so spent in my life." Still, the "overwhelming success" of the procession was "most gratifying to me because churchmen of every school—save the Roman—rallied to the call and I knew that I had not lost the uniting touch in the identification of my pulpit work with a liberal theology."[18]

Ruth continued to give himself to the celebrations in the months that followed. A year after the 1933 celebrations, at the 101st anniversary services, Ruth conducted a civic service attended by the Lieutenant Governor, the Premier, and the Lord Mayor. His theme was "Treasure in Trust," and in the evening he spoke on "The Grace of Stewardship," distinguishing between "nationalists in love with their native land and internationalists in love with the Kingdom of God."[19] On the actual anniversary day on the Wednesday, Ruth gave a lecture-recital on "Lord Tennyson—Poet, Patriot, and Philosopher," noting that 101 years prior to this Arthur Hallam had

---

15. *SMH*, May 3, 1933, 13.
16. *SMH*, May 3, 1933, 13.
17. *Congregationalist*, May 18, 1933, 5.
18. Ruth to Brookes, 21 May 1933, Brookes Papers, NLA 1924/48/149.
19. *SMH*, April 30, 1934, 8.

died and Tennyson began to write his "immortal elegy 'In Memoriam.'" He was "the first British poet to write imperially."[20]

The following years followed the same format, with Ruth's lecture in 1935 on Robert Browning, such an influential figure on an earlier generation of Nonconformists.[21] Later lectures, which were also fund-raising evenings, were devoted to the county of Devon in 1936, the West Country in 1937, and Dorset in 1938. A souvenir program, inscribed and autographed by Ruth, was given each year to all donors.[22]

Continuing at Pitt Street (1933–38)

Ruth's ministry during the years 1933-38 continued in the same general pattern that he had developed. He also continued writing for the Sunday Sun until March 1937, which meant that he had to respond to numerous correspondents. During these years he was often ill with neuritis, influenza, and other complaints.

T. E. Ruth and friend outside Pitt Street Church (1934)

Ruth always missed Melbourne. In 1934, he wrote to Brookes, "I have a curious feeling—I've had it on and off for years—that Melbourne is my

20. *SMH*, May 3, 1934, 5.
21. *SMH*, May 9, 1935, 16,
22. Curthoys, *Pride of Place*, 231–32.

mental home. In speaking to a Melbourne congregation I never feel that I am above their heads—an unhappy feeling that haunts a good deal of my preaching in Sydney." Perhaps he should have been prompted to think that it was his preaching that had changed. The anti-Mannix days had been invigorating and unambiguous in their emphases. He had been quite chuffed once in Brisbane to have been introduced as "Rev. Auditorium Ruth"—those had been exciting if demanding days for him in Melbourne.[23]

Ruth and the Angus Controversy

A cursory review of his sermons from these years, as in the *Herald* sermon reports, shows his sermons were inevitably topical in theme and he seems never to have adopted the expository approach so popular with evangelicals. While Ruth obviously sought to base his preaching on the Bible, a somewhat startling ingenuity marked his use of the Bible. He often selected a text, sometimes an obscure Old Testament verse, which he took out of context and related to some contemporary event. He was an excellent example of a modern liberal in his ministry and was proud to be known as such.

This was clearly evident in Ruth's vigorous support for the Presbyterian scholar Samuel Angus (1881-1943), Irish-born Professor at St. Andrew's, the Presbyterian College since 1915, who had been accused of heresy by the Sydney Presbytery and then by the General Assembly of his church in 1932. The affair became a *cause célèbre* within the denomination and in the wider ecclesial and general community. As Susan Emilsen remarked, "In the early weeks of 1933 representatives of all the major denominations and sects—Methodist, Congregational, Church of England, Baptist, Church of Christ, Unitarian as well as Presbyterian—surrendered to what appeared to be a compulsive desire to stand up and be counted." Angus became the subject for the "seasoned controversialist."[24]

Ruth was not the first minister to discuss the teaching of Angus from the pulpit. For example, the evangelical Presbyterian Hugh Paton at St. Stephen's had begun the year with an attack on Angus's teaching on the atonement and questioning his influence on ministerial students.[25] But on January 15, Ruth preached on the question, "Is Professor Angus a Heretic?" Some wag had scrawled across the poster advertising the sermon, "Yes, and so are you!"[26]

23. Ruth to Brookes, 16 August 1934, Brookes Papers, NLA 1924/48/157.
24. Emilsen, *Whiff of Heresy*, 200.
25. *SMH*, January 2, 1933, 4.
26. *Sun*, February 26, 1933, 17.

Ruth's basic position was that "no man was answerable for his faith to any other man." The whole controversy was "an offence against a decent-minded public." He argued that Professor Angus had sought "to rescue the Christian religion from a complicated theology and disputatious theologians, and to restore it to the sweet reasonableness of Jesus." If Angus was a heretic, so were Isaiah, Jeremiah, John the Baptist, and Jesus himself. The faith was not something "to be kept in an orthodox box under lock and key." He continued to attack professional theologians (of which, of course, Angus was one): "Dr. Angus rescued religion from theologians who quarrelled. That was heresy today . . . When theology lost Jesus men like Professor Angus found him again."[27]

This sermon prompted an interview with the Advance Australia News Service, which provided copy for the rural press. So the *Grenfell Record and Lachlan District Advertiser*, for example, later published an extensive account of Ruth's views on various topics such as the Virgin Birth, which he now doubted, and his understanding of the atonement: "I do not believe that the great God and the Eternal Christ can find room in the spiritual world only for people with certain views of the meaning of the Cross."[28]

Later that year on October 1, Ruth preached about "Dr. Angus on Jesus" at Pitt Street:

> It was Spurgeon who said that a lie runs half-way round the world while truth is putting on her boots. That is what Dr. Angus is finding. But truth is fairly fleet of foot. And in his little book "Jesus in the Lives of Men," the truth as Dr. Angus sees it, the truth as it is in Jesus is well-shod and sure of its stride. Time is always on the side of truth. Truth is always on God's side.[29]

Ruth was proud of his own "free pulpit" and reiterated a theme he had often stressed:

> Some substituted for the infallibility of the Pope a much more frail and fallible authority. If Dr. Angus had been a Roman Catholic he would have been tried by a select company of New Testament scholars with a first-hand knowledge of the facts. The price he paid for his liberty lay in the submission of his scholarly findings not to his intellectual peers but to an assembly which, like other assemblies with less claim to scholarship, was apt to

---

27. *SMH*, January 16, 1933, 8.
28. *Grenfell Record and Lachlan District Advertiser*, February 9, 1933, 4.
29. Angus, *Jesus in the Lives of Men*.

forget that freedom of thought and the right of private judgment, belonged to the very essence of Protestantism.[30]

Sensing that some would query what concern it was to those outside the Presbyterian denomination, Ruth claimed that the issue was of "common concern" because every church was a part of the household of God: "The faith of a public body could not be a private and privileged affair" because truth and liberty were involved.

His familiar critique of theological "orthodoxies" was asserted. History is Jesus emerging from tomb to tomb:

> Give them time and fundamentalists become quite modern. And modernists are sound on the fundamentals if they have the spirit of Jesus. If they haven't, it doesn't matter how fundamentalist they are in their controversy or how modern. The impression they make upon the community is best illustrated by the little girl in London who was asked where the wild beasts were kept and replied, "In the Theological Gardens."[31]

The next day a letter from Rev. Ronald G. Macintyre (1863–1954), a colleague of Angus's at the Theological Hall and later to be a key political power in the Angus disputes, replied to Ruth. He began by observing that "Rev. T. E. Ruth is at it again." Agreeing that the issues had a wider concern, nonetheless at the present time they had to be determined "by and for the Presbyterian Church." Yes, they appreciated private prayers, but they would appreciate it if he could "refrain from butting in."[32]

Always sensitive to criticism, Ruth retorted that "not even the most disputatious Scot can claim exclusive right to theological argument." Moreover, he had been reviewing Angus's book, "That was my universe of discourse." Presbyterians should "read it before it was placed on any Presbyterian index."[33]

Angus published *Truth and Tradition* in the midst of the controversy within his denomination.[34] Susan Emilsen observes that this was "a polemic, a work of controversy designed to shock rather than to persuade his opponents."[35] This was a line of argument that would naturally appeal to Ruth, and it is not surprising that he preached about the book on May 13,

30. *SMH*, October 2, 1933, 8.
31. *SMH*, October 2, 1933, 8.
32. *SMH*, October 4, 1933, 12.
33. *SMH*, October 5, 1933, 6.
34. Angus, *Truth and Tradition*.
35. Emilsen, *Whiff of Heresy*, 227.

1934. Claiming to have read the book several times "carefully and critically," Ruth declared that he had found "a rich and full-orbed Gospel." Mindful of earlier Presbyterian condemnation of his interference, Ruth simply observed that he did not want to comment on the relationship between Angus and his church but did add that with regard to Presbyterianism "it is possible to carry it too far." Indeed, the Angus controversy "owed its bitterness to the confusion of Christianity with Presbyterianism."[36]

Ruth returned to his theme later in the month when he argued that there was something "so essentially great and so eternally good at the back of the Angus case" and it would be a pity to miss it. What was needed was a "longer look and larger charity." Christianity had seldom been without such men as Angus:

> The Apostle Paul was a sort of Dr. Angus, more of a controversialist, oftener in the wars and more frequently condemned. To read the Acts of the Apostles and the Epistles of Paul was to find the Angus controversy comparatively colourless . . . There was nothing in our day like the deep divisions, the deadly enmity, the theological hatreds of the Apostolic age.[37]

The Angus controversy dragged on through the Presbyterian courts until 1942, and he was never officially condemned.

Rendezvous with Life (1934)

Ruth's last substantial book, as compared with the pamphlets he wrote well into his old age, was a book of fifteen sermons, *Rendezvous with Life: Everyday Problems*, published in 1934 in Sydney as a hardback by Angus and Robertson. Ruth always gave careful thought to the dedication in his books, and this was no exception:

> To the deacons and members of my church and congregation who, in an atmosphere instinct with worship, think for themselves, and by their freedom of faith and catholicity of disposition, make ministry a delight.

Taken as a whole, these sermons suggest the type of relevant, life-based preaching of Fosdick in America and which would later be popularized in Britain by the strong psychologically-based preaching of Dr. Leslie Weatherhead (1893–1976), a successor of Norwood at the City Temple from 1936

---

36. *SMH*, May 14, 1934, 9.
37. *SMH*, May 28, 1934, 6.

until 1960. Ruth's preaching as in this volume was not of the memorable character of a Fosdick or a Weatherhead, but it was free of the pugnacious criticisms that marred some of his preaching and was a genuine attempt to relate the Christian faith to life issues.

Ruth's first sermon was titled "What Is the World For?" and dealt with the ambitious theme of "the purpose of being." It was typical of Ruth's style, including its extensive use of poetry. He argued that "the universe is our university," a "ladder of life" where experience is our teacher.[38] The purpose of the world was fulfilled in Jesus, who faced evil and defeated it. "In the world we find our rendezvous with life. Here. And now."

The second chapter was "The Way of Becoming." One of the loveliest lines in our literature, Ruth suggested, tells of "the most colourless man in the Old Testament": "And Isaac went out to meditate in the field at eventide."[39] In personality, there is this "meditative quality," and a rendezvous with life involves learning: Jesus said, "Learn of me."[40]

The sermons from his ministry at the City Temple in London dealt with using the subconscious. One example he gave was from his days at Southampton, when an exhausted Dr. John Clifford was present at a rally. He asked Ruth to choose a long hymn before his speech, then sat and slept for four verses. At the close of the fifth verse "he rose like a giant refreshed and held his audience spell-bound for an hour. His subconscious mind was his servant."[41]

Subsequent chapters reviewed the psychology of desire, the psychology of fear, and the psychology of success. Taken as a whole, this book was constructive and helpful, rich with quotations and insights. The *Sun* claimed that it "tackles all the human problems in straight-forward words and his philosophy satisfies."[42]

Sermons and Controversies

Ruth's reputation as a liberal as well as his public persona led him into some unusual situations. For example, in June 1933 he was a witness for the defense when a medical doctor was charged with obscenity. Dr. Robert Storer (1900–1958) had published *A Survey of Sexual Life in Adolescence and in Marriage*, and Dr. Harvey Sutton (1882–1963), medical professor at Sydney

38. Ruth, *Rendezvous with Life*, 8.
39. Ruth, *Rendezvous with Life*, 12.
40. Ruth, *Rendezvous with Life*, 20.
41. Ruth, *Rendezvous with Life*, 39.
42. *Sun*, August 5, 1934, 2.

University, insisted the book was "a medical treatise for the information of adults."[43] Ruth stated that he thought the book "a valuable contribution to sex education especially in a country where there was a growing need for such education and where there was such an amount of poisonous publications exposed for sale." Ruth did criticize the section dealing with eugenics, and that relating to modern literature, but did not consider these obscene.[44] A Unitarian minister Rev. Wyndham Heathcote (1862–1955) agreed with Ruth's judgement, and in the final decision the Magistrate dismissed the charge and made reference to the helpful evidence of the two clergymen who were "prominent in social welfare work."[45]

A larger public controversy was the case of Mrs. Mabel Freer.[46] In October 1936, Australia's Minister for the Interior, Thomas Paterson (1882–1952), ordered customs officials to bar a married, white British woman traveling with an Australian married army officer returning from India, from entering Australia. This was done by application of the infamous dictation test whereby an applicant could be tested in any language, inevitably one unknown by the candidate. In Mrs. Freer's case, the language was Italian, and she naturally failed. This test had been introduced with the transparently racial motive of excluding non-whites. In Mrs. Freer's case, the issue had been a moral one, in that both she and the officer were already married to other people. The Minister justified his action as "a noble intervention to protect the institution of marriage and to safeguard Lieutenant Dewar's marriage from the depredations of an immoral adventuress." Many Australians protested against this action, and Mrs. Freer's case became a *cause célèbre*. She was deported to New Zealand, but many women's groups campaigned against her exclusion.

Ruth joined in this chorus of condemnation of the Minister's decision. The dictation test was a "stupid subterfuge" and showed how ridiculous so many Australian politicians were.[47] Mrs. Freer was eventually permitted to enter Australia when it became apparent that maintaining Paterson's ban had become a political liability. As Jeremy Martens has concluded, "While this successful mobilisation against government overreach challenges the sexual double standard and patriarchal assumptions about marriage and women's respectability, it did not in any way contest the racist logic

43. Storer, *Survey of Sexual Life*.
44. *SMH*, June 20, 1933, 5.
45. *SMH*, June 23, 1933, 8; June 29, 1933.
46. Martens, "Mrs. Freer Case," 437–58.
47. *SMH*, November 30, 1936, 11.

underpinning the White Australia policy and its instrument of exclusion, the Immigration Act."[48]

Ruth's preaching also continued to mark various ecclesiastical and national days. On Empire Day in 1934, he made a characteristic assertion: "England is the greatest Protestant country in the world, and, in some respects, the greatest Roman Catholic country. More Roman Catholics attend Mass in London than in Rome."[49] This puzzled one Catholic reader, who wrote to the *Freeman's Journal* and asked if that was true. Headed "Rhapsodies of Rev. T. E. Ruth," the paper replied, "No, it is a loose oratorical statement which could not be substantiated," and proceeded to note that in Rome there were 989,000 Catholics with, at the most, 500,000 in London. But in any case the number of Catholics attending Mass in England is no tribute to England, which officially repudiates Catholicism.[50]

A new feature was a sermon to mark "Foundation Day" (or Australia Day, as it was later known), celebrated annually on January 26 to mark the anniversary of the 1788 arrival of the First Fleet at Port Jackson. Ruth suggested that Foundation Day "offered a fine parable of the outstanding quality of the Christian religion." In the same way that the pioneering adventurers of Australia led the way for the modern nation, so Christianity was "always breaking new ground." This was seen in the way that "conservative theologians and comfortable churchmen were always being disturbed."

The death of King George V in January 1936 led to expansive tributes in most of the nation's leading churches. Ruth praised the King, who had "earned the title of father of his people . . . His reign was the family idea extended and developed."[51]

However, the abdication of Edward VIII at the end of the year was a shock to the nation. The pulpits of Sydney resounded with discussions of this phenomenon. The Archbishop of Sydney, Dr. Howard Mowll, said that it was incredible to think that King Edward had passed outside the empire: "It is not for us to question his choice, and although he has left us we shall always keep him in our hearts." Some others were less sympathetic. Wilfred Jarvis at the Baptist Church in Bathurst Street criticized the king for three quarters of an hour and declared that Edward would live to regret his decision.[52]

---

48. Martens, "Mrs. Freer Case," 457.
49. *Daily Telegraph*, May 21, 1934, 5.
50. *Freeman's Journal*, July 19, 1934, 7.
51. *SMH*, January 27, 1936, 6.
52. *SMH*, December 14, 1936, 17.

Ruth also deplored what had happened in a flurry of characteristic alliterations:

> Certain things God has joined together—majesty and grace, sovereignty and sacrifice, monarchy and morality, royalty and religion, duty and discipline, purity and power, democracy and decency, faith and freedom, righteousness and peace. Certain things were fundamental to England and the Empire—constitutional monarchy, family life, national religion.[53]

The abdication had in fact deeply distressed Ruth:

> The abdication dealt me a blow in the solar plexus making me physically sick. But the foundations of the earth standeth sure. And the Empire instead of being broken is bigger and better than ever. There is still room for men who want "to do a bit of work for England."[54]

No one could complain about the lack of variety in Ruth's preaching, even if he did constantly repeat certain theological emphases. Several literary themes were introduced as "book sermons." On March 12, 1933, he discussed George Bernard Shaw's "The Adventures of the Black Girl in Her Search for God." This was from a book of his short stories published in 1932.[55] Its title story is a satirical allegory about an African girl, newly converted to Christianity, who attempts to seek out and speak to God, having taken literally the biblical injunction to "Seek and you shall find me." The story outraged many readers for its "irreligious" tone. Ruth's basic argument was that if this story led people to read the Bible for themselves it would do good: "Men were encouraged to swing their knobkerrie at all its superstitions, but they did not find God with a knobkerrie, but with a humble and contrite heart."[56]

Another "book sermon" was devoted to *The Laughing Christ* by Pearson Choate.[57] Not surprisingly, this theme greatly appealed to Ruth, who criticized the tendency to paint Jesus with "a great melancholy in his eyes" whereas "the outstanding characteristic of Jesus, according to his enemies, was his joyousness."[58]

---

53. *SMH*, December 14, 1936, 17.
54. Ruth to Brookes, 17 December 1936, Brookes Papers, NLA 1924/48/180.
55. Shaw, *Adventures of the Black Girl*.
56. *SMH*, March 13, 1933, 8. A knobkerrie is "a short heavy stick or club with a knob on one end used by South African natives" (*Macquarie Dictionary*).
57. Choate, *Laughing Christ*.
58. *Daily Telegraph*, August 7, 1933, 3.

John Masefield's poem "The Everlasting Mercy" commanded Ruth's presentation on another occasion. This poem was "an adventure of the spirit, with a wonder which outran the amazing wealth of words and beauty."[59]

A different kind of book was by the popular film star Mary Pickford (1892–1979), "the world's sweetheart," called *Why Not Try God?*[60] Ruth noted that "very few think of Mary Pickford as a woman with a very strong religious purpose." She had once hated God but she found out the right way of thinking that God was not a threatening deity but a friendly presence. Ruth's conclusion was somewhat unexpected: "You can think your way into practical omnipotence. Like Mary Pickford you can think your way out of any kind of trouble."[61]

Another example of Ruth's book sermons was his sad but warm response to Lloyd C. Douglas's novel *Green Light* (1935). Douglas (1877–1951), author of *Magnificent Obsession* (1929) and *The Robe* (1942), was a Lutheran pastor and one of the most popular American novelists of the time. Ruth confessed that the novel had described "exactly the ministry of his dreams." "For 35 years he had been feeling after a bureau of advice, a genuine confessional, a cure of souls," a ministry where he could help people adjust themselves to life. However, he sadly admitted "so inadequately were such ministerial ideals realised that at times they seemed like castles in Spain."[62] This confession revealed Ruth's sad frustration with the actual realities of his ministry.

A final example of a book sermon was his vigorous discussion of former Prime Minister W. M. Hughes's book, *Australia and the War Today*.[63] Ruth charged Hughes with preaching "the politics of the parish pump" when he described economic sanctions as "either an empty gesture, or war." Vigorously opposed to Hughes's immigration ideas, Ruth was emphatic: "He was more like a miniature Mussolini or an unhappy Hitler than an Australian prophet–pioneer dealing with empty spaces in a world of densely populated countries."[64]

During the Advent season of 1933, Ruth took up another of his oft-repeated emphases when he rejected the popular approach to the return of Christ:

---

59. *SMH*, December 3, 1934, 8. Masefield (1878–1967) was Poet Laureate from 1930 to his death and wrote this poem in 1911.
60. Pickford, *Why Not Try God?*
61. *Daily Telegraph*, May 20, 1935, 7.
62. *SMH*, October 14, 1935, 10.
63. Hughes, *Australia and the war today*.
64. *SMH*, December 2, 1935, 10.

> The inner truth of the Second Coming is that it has taken place, it is taking place, it must take place. He is coming in the firmament of faith and in the work of the world in all the earth so completely that comparatively the old, little, localised advent for which men looked was at best a legend, or perhaps an allegory.[65]

Contemporary events usually found a response from Ruth. When a centenary air race was being planned, Ruth completely rejected the notion that such a deed was "tempting Providence," and it was time to rid our minds of the idea that God was "a universal 'bogey-man' or some malign spirit opposed to human enterprises."[66]

When a referendum in March 1937 seeking to increase federal control over marketing and aviation was defeated, Ruth commented that the result indicated a feeling of antagonism, not towards the Commonwealth, but towards men who had lost the confidence of the community and uncertainty about how they would use extra powers. "They are servants who became dictators, bureaucratic while we remain democratic."[67]

Shortly after this, Ruth once again accused Canberra of being "a handicap to democracy" and "social segregation": "by their incomes shall ye know them."[68] The Canberra Tourist Bureau promptly denied this and told Ruth that he would be assured of a hospitable welcome to the federal capital.[69]

He continued to answer questions submitted from the congregation. Many of these reflected current issues in the minds of Sydney people. Ruth justified this approach by the example of Jesus. He noted that Jesus "never preached a sermon on a text" but gave his teaching in response to questions.[70]

Some questions were predictable: "Is it wrong for a divorced person to marry again?" Ruth's response was that he saw "no reason in religion or morals why a person should not help God to rectify the mistake and marry again."[71]

In the same service, he was also asked, "Do you think it wrong for a Church to accept money won in the State lottery to help people in distress?" Ruth asked the questioner could he think of "a better agency or use for the money" but the questioner pressed, "Would you accept for church purposes

---

65. *SMH*, December 18, 1933, 8.
66. *SMH*, October 29, 1934, 8.
67. *SMH*, March 15, 1937, 10.
68. *SMH*, May 31, 1937, 8.
69. *Canberra Times*, June 3, 1937, 3.
70. *SMH*, December 17, 1934, 8.
71. *SMH*, January 28, 1935, 8.

money from brewers or Tattersalls Club?" Ruth confessed that many problems were involved, and he could only venture an interim reply. Had any church the right to curb the generous instincts of a brewer? Why just the Tattersalls Club? What about the Millions Club (of which Ruth was a member)? Suppose all the business men in Sydney sent along "conscience money" to the church, would it not be an excellent thing for them and would it not be a good thing to distribute waste money for good purposes?[72]

A radio listener to Ruth posed the familiar question, "Can a God of love permit pain?" His reply was clear:

> Pain belongs to the personality of God, and it is something he cannot prevent. It has a positive value in developing sensitiveness, resourcefulness, inventiveness. If we could not get hurt, we would never be able to find ourselves. Pain offers no reflection on God's love or wisdom. It makes for the glory of humanity, for by fighting and overcoming pain we become nearer to the image of God Himself.[73]

On one occasion Ruth was asked whether an English woman who had poisoned her imbecile son because she had to undergo an operation and thought she might not live to care for him had committed a sin against God or only the law. He suggested that she did not sin against God but fulfilled the "law of motherhood," and this evident justification of euthanasia was widely reported. He trusted that the time would surely come when mothers and fathers "would be trusted with lethal powers."[74]

Questions could be quite specific. "Would you condemn the one excitement in my drab life—A share in a five-and-threepenny thrill?" Ruth replied that he was not going to condemn the questioner for buying a lottery ticket, but he was going to condemn him for having such a drab life that that was the only thing which excited him.[75] Some sounded like the proverbial "Dorothy Dix" questions, such as "Is conversion out of date?"; "Has Christianity failed?"; "Is the Christian attitude towards enemies effeminate?"[76] Another example was: "Would you give equal rights to unequal men?" to which his rather provocative answer was, "You will not make democracy safe for the world until you give as much care to the breeding of humans as you do to horses." During an extensive discussion

---

72. *SMH*, January 28, 1935. 8.
73. *Daily Telegraph*, December 9, 1935, 7.
74. *SMH*, December 17, 1934, 8; *Gundagai Independent*, December 17, 1934, 3.
75. *SMH*, October 28, 1935, 10.
76. *SMH*, March 30, 1936, 8; June 8, 1936, 8.

on marriage and divorce, Ruth asserted that he knew of a better cure for incompatibility than divorce: family religion.[77]

On another occasion, Ruth asserted that he believed in angels, "as the poets believed in them—angels in Pitt Street, angels in Charing Cross . . . I do not think it is necessary to believe that humans are the only intelligent beings in God's universe, or that this chemical body is the only tool that can be used by an Infinite Mind."[78]

A heavily loaded question was posed in May 1937: "How do you account for the character of a girl being spoilt by conversion?" Surprised by this, Ruth sought further details and was told that "an intelligent girl of affectionate disposition, never thinking ill of anyone" was converted several times, twice under the same evangelist, and had become "narrow, warped and angular." Nobody is right but her own little clique. "They denounce everybody they don't agree with. They write to clergymen telling them they have not been converted."

Ruth took up this cause with great gusto. "I know the type. It is not so common as it was. It will die out with that kind of evangelism." It was a pity that it was called "conversion," "which is the greatest, most broadening, most emancipating experience in human life, opening the eyes of the mind and soul to the Fatherhood of God, the Brotherhood of man and the loveliness of life." What this girl had experienced was rather "perversion": she had "taken a big dose of bad theology, bitter, blinding," and he believed she would ultimately find "the goodwill of God, the inclusive Christ and the gospel of everlasting and unconditional love."[79]

International developments provoked serious questions. Mussolini's troops invaded Abyssinia on October 3, 1935, but on August 25 Ruth had been asked "Would Christian Italy, using poison gas in Abyssinia, challenge all coloured races to fight the whites?" Ruth replied that the use of the term "Christian" with the use of poison gas "was incongruous." He added that if the Pope did not use his enormous power to prevent Italy from using poison gas in Abyssinia, "he himself would be as un-Christian as Italy." However, he added, "There was no difference, when it came to blind brutality between the idea that 'flogging is the only treatment aborigines understand' and Mussolini's proposed use of poison gas in Abyssinia."[80] This emphasis on Aboriginal people was a theme to which Ruth frequently returned.

---

77. *SMH* July 26, 1937, 8.
78. *SMH*, February 1, 1937, 8.
79. *Australian Christian Commonwealth*, May 21, 1937, 13.
80. *SMH*, August 26, 1935, 8.

Another questioner was told that there were necessary limits to free speech such as the commandment "Thou shalt not bear false witness" required. However, he added, "As a simple British citizen, I resented the denial of the Sydney Town Hall to Judge Rutherford. Though I disagree with him and think his interpretation of the Scriptures is worse than an old wives' fable." Rutherford (1869–1942) was a founder of the Jehovah Witnesses.

On another occasion, late in 1938, when the Nazi atrocities against Jews were increasing, Ruth was asked, "Can Christians pray with Jews?" Ruth replied that on the previous Sunday he had attended the intercessory service at the Synagogue for Jews suffering persecution in Germany and there prayed earnestly. "We should not forget that every day Christians used prayers taught us by Jews."[81]

Ruth and the Oxford Group

The Oxford Group was an international movement of renewal that had extensive influence in Australia. The effective founder was Frank Buchman (1878–1961), an American Lutheran. Honest and deep confession of failure was a marked feature of the movement while the four absolutes of the Group were absolute honesty, purity, unselfishness, and love. In the light of the rise of Nazism (the movement was proscribed by the Nazis and condemned by Communists) and the world-wide talk of re-arming, the Group came to be known as Moral Re-Armament, calling for spiritual revolution, and in its later stages was inclusive of various religious traditions.[82]

Baptists were influenced by the movement in both Britain and Australia as were Protestants of other traditions.[83] In Melbourne, Methodist leader C. Irving Benson wrote a popular account of the movement in 1936 and had extensive influence among Methodists.[84] Benson was minister at Wesley Church and indeed compared Buchman with Wesley. Like Ruth, he was a regular newspaper columnist (in the Melbourne *Herald*).

Ruth observed that the Group was "not a theological society" but "an actual romance and adventure in a day when Christianity had become largely a ritual and a routine . . . it was an experience not an explanation, a life not a

---

81. *SMH*, November 28, 1938, 13.
82. For the Oxford Group see *Oxford Dictionary of the Church*, 1204–5.
83. Randall, "Arresting People for Christ": 3–18, and for Australia, see Manley, *From Woolloomooloo*, 472–74.
84. Benson, *Eight Points*; Howe and Swain, *Challenge of the City*, 109–11.

label." He welcomed the insistence that the incarnation was "not so much a perplexing doctrine but an experience and a method of service."[85]

The Group was also welcomed by Ruth in his column as "a call to a new adventure": "It is not so much a new sphere as a new spirit, a spirit of discovery, exploring the possibilities of personality in private and in public life." The group showed that the spiritual society known as the church "transcends the historic divisions of Christendom." Describing a group in Paris, Ruth noted how a Roman Catholic monk, a Protestant clergyman, and a Roman Catholic professor were united to describe the Group in a pamphlet as "The Spiritual Help-One-Another Group." Their unity came from lifting their quest on to so high a spiritual plane as to efface all difference. This seemed to Ruth "to have all the marks of a New Testament Church." It was not proselytizing but uniting.[86] Ruth affirmed, "The Oxford Group seeks to rediscover God, to restore reality to religion and joy to life."[87]

Another aspect of the Group's contribution that impressed Ruth was that it influenced public life. Several examples from Britain of prominent business leaders being profoundly influenced by the Group confirmed that it could be a powerful influence on the international scene. As Frank Buchman had claimed, "God-controlled supernationalism is the only enduring foundation for world peace."[88]

Ruth was impressed by the principles behind the Oxford Group, read widely about its impact, and commended it to his readers. Yet there is no evidence that he was personally ever involved in any of its meetings, and while he identified with many aspects of its teaching and practices, he was not a Group convert.

Indigenous Australians and the Celebration of Australia's 150th Anniversary (1938)

Ruth had often spoken out about the treatment of Aboriginal people in Australian society. On July 28, 1935 he declared that nobody could defend Australia's treatment of its original inhabitants: "It is un-Christian, un-British, and inhuman, a survival of the spirit of the penal settlement days, a moral and political reminder of our first convict state." He continued, "They are forced to labour under conditions scarcely distinguishable from slavery, with no sanctity for their women-folk." Punitive expeditions used

85. *SMH*, January 20, 1936, 10.
86. *Sun*, May 24, 1936, 19.
87. *Sun*, May 10, 1936, 17.
88. *Sun*, May 17, 1936, 19.

stock whips and chains. He advanced a suggestion: "The best way of celebrating the 150th anniversary would be to make adequate compensation and restitution to the real Australian natives. There were difficulties in the way, the chief of which had been hit off in the remark, 'How can you expect politicians to be interested in people who have no vote?'"[89]

On the following Sunday he continued his attack.

> There was nothing as fatuous in the Australian policy of "hush" and the whispered plea, "Don't tell England." The native ability, domestic qualities, and spiritual intuitions of Aboriginal people offered the richest and most suggestive reply to the question, "Why bother about aborigines?" The problem of what to do with the race was not difficult to solve if a solution was really desired ... During the last ten years there had been seven successive Commonwealth Ministers in charge of Aboriginal affairs, and none of them with any previous experience. There would be no lasting reforms until there was a permanent commission with a national policy and a progressive program of emancipation and culture.[90]

Ruth's attack drew a response from Darwin where the Acting Minister for the Interior (Mr. Hunter) commented that as far as the Territory was concerned there was "no stock-whipping of natives." He challenged Ruth to give a concrete case in the Northern Territory that would authenticate his allegations.[91]

As the nation prepared for the 150th anniversary of British settlement, Ruth preached about the significance of the event. He had his own perspective. "Australians could not believe in God without believing in Australia." He saw it as "the duty of the church to give the sesqui-centenary its proper spiritual setting":

> The sesqui-centenary calls us to a more vivid realisation of the spiritual as well as the political importance of our nation to the British Empire. The baby colony of 1788 is now a vast continent with potentialities that are a world problem. Imperially we are at the beginning, not the end of things.[92]

On the actual day, some Aboriginal people participated in a re-enactment of the British landing, but others shunned the revelry as a day of mourning,

89. *SMH*, July 29, 1935, 8.
90. *SMH*, August 5, 1935, 8.
91. *Northern Territory Times*, August 13, 1935, 10.
92. *SMH*, January 19, 1938.

marking the dispossession of their land.[93] Ruth was quite emphatic: "The Australian who does not bother about the aborigines is not quite human, is something less than British, and is a long way from being a Christian." The reason for their mourning was the indifference of Australia to a race whose origins went further back; they were the earliest Australians. Ruth cited the trenchant criticisms of Professor A. P. Elkin (1891–1979), Anglican minister and anthropologist, and added: "We may deplore the invasion of mourning aborigines into our joy 150 years after our invasion of their land but they would have had the sympathy of Captain Cook. Governor Phillip's heart was with his instructions to conciliate the affection of the natives." Ruth added that Aboriginal people had been good enough to fight as Anzacs, "Why should they not be treated as human beings and as citizens."[94]

Ruth had met L. V. Biggs (1873–1944), editor of the Melbourne *Age*, when he visited Pitt Street. As Ruth wrote to Brookes, even though Biggs was "still Anglo-Catholic," he had enjoyed "a feast of worship" and had "begged" him to write some articles "on the lines of his sesquicentenary sermon for *The Age*.[95] A series of three articles duly appeared in the literary section of *The Age*.

The first of these, published on January 15, 1938, was on the spiritual significance of the sesquicentenary, along the lines of his Sydney sermon on that theme.[96] His second was on "Imagination and Emancipation" in relation to the celebrations for "Australia's 150th birthday."[97] Effectively giving an extended meditation on the convict origins of the nation, he reflected on how adverse conditions were conquered. Redemption was costly and came through great tribulation. He suggested that the scenes could be "almost scriptural in their simplicity and in their significance." "Placarded across our very convict history is the words "Christ died for the ungodly."[98]

For his third article, accompanied by a photo of "Anula and Mara" Indigenous people groups, Ruth asked why Aboriginal people mourn while Australia rejoices. He concluded with a quotation from David Unaipon (1872–1967), Aboriginal preacher, author, and inventor and at the time the best-known Indigenous figure in Australia. Unaipon had disagreed with the Australian Aborigines' League over the Day of Mourning, but in his letter

93. *SMH*, January 27, 1938, 8.
94. *SMH*, January 24, 1938, 12.
95. Ruth to Brookes, 14 January 1938, Brookes Papers, NLA 1924/48/198.
96. *The Age*, January 15, 1938, 5 (literary section).
97. *The Age*, January 29, 1938, 2 (literary section).
98. *The Age*, January 29, 1938, 2 (literary section).

to the Minister for the Interior, as quoted by Ruth, he had written, "Let my people come more fully into the national family."[99]

Ruth is an excellent example of how some contemporary Protestants responded to complex Indigenous issues at the time of the national celebrations in 1938.

Final Days at Pitt Street

When Ruth unexpectedly announced his resignation at the end of June 1938, the deacons were so surprised that they simply adjourned their meeting for several days. He confirmed that he had reluctantly come to the conclusion "that the time has come for you to seek another minister." He continued, "Leaving Pitt Street will be like pulling up life by its roots in a sense perhaps none of you can quite appreciate."[100]

He gave a brief review of his years at the church. Only life deacon Cuthbertson remained of the deacons who had called him. He recited the conditions he had given to the church including the renewal of church membership, assistance for pastoral care and complete renovations of the property,

> We have been spared the fate of overtaking our ideals though much has been accomplished. Some monuments will remain when we have all gone. Some amazing triumphs are among our happiest memories. But nothing holds the affection like trial heroically shared or deepens the roots like depression and adversity.

Patricia Curthoys attributes an egotism to Ruth in his reflections at this time, suggesting that he omitted to stress the collective work of the congregation. But it is perhaps understandable that his own emotions looking back across a significant period should have dominated his statement.

> I came in 1923 for three months, I have stayed for 15 years, during which time all our neighbouring churches which we visited in our Centenary procession have had ministerial changes . . . And I only am left. You deserve a change. And we must take count of the spirit of Sydney . . . Because the Church is an agency of the kingdom of God, the ministry must be adapted to the times. The time has come for this change.[101]

---

99. *The Age*, February 5, 1938, 4 (literary section). For Unaipon, see *ADB*.
100. Typed statement with Pitt Street Deacons' Minutes, June 20, 1938.
101. Curthoys, *Pride of Place*, 235.

But, just as he had done at Collins Street, he was rather vague about when he would conclude his time with them.

> There need be no unseemly haste. But there must be no undue delay. I have no plans whatever for the future. Until there is some clear guidance as to likely men available at home or abroad I may therefore continue to be used for the convenience of the Church to which I have given the best years of my life, fulfilling at least the particular work to which I was set aside in my induction.

In speaking to the church members, Ruth had claimed a sense of divine calling: "I do not want to go but God rules by facts and guides by events." In an unfortunate reference, he applied to himself the words of Jesus to the disciples, "It is expedient for you that I go away" (John 16:7).[102] While this suggests a commendable insight, the unintended Messianic parallel certainly does suggest an unseemly egotism in Ruth.

In fact, Ruth continued for several months. He was given leave to preach for five Sundays at Scots' Church in Melbourne in October, but when he returned the deacons wisely proposed that he should end his ministry with them at the end of January 1939.

Unfortunately, at a quarterly fellowship meeting during January, Ruth accused the deacons of having "dismissed" him from the pastorate and countered by reading several complimentary letters he had received regarding his ministry. The women of the church gave a farewell party for Mabel Ruth, and warm tributes were paid for her leadership and comradeship.

Ruth had obviously experienced the common dilemma of many another Baptist or Congregational minister. He was not yet wishing to retire completely but had no other income now that his weekly newspaper commitments had ended. Ruth's sharing with Brookes at this time gives some insight into his dilemma. In July 1938, he had noted that "the impelling was not unlike that at Collins Street in 1922," and he would have loved to have been able to discuss his decision with Brookes. "The step seems improvident. But it isn't . . . The way will open. My work is not done. I shall find my place."[103] In November, he observed that "Adolf Hitler is apparently responsible for a slight slump in property here."[104]

In December 1937, he noted that he was sixty-two that day: "At times I feel 28, occasionally 80, mainly 42." Toyohiko Kagawa (1888–1960), the Japanese Christian social reformer, had preached at Pitt Street when he

---

102. Pitt Street Church Members' Minutes, June 29, 1938.
103. Ruth to Brookes, 19 July 1938, Brookes Papers, NLA 1924/48/204.
104. Ruth to Brookes, 15 November 1938, Brookes Papers, NLA 1924/48/205.

was in Sydney, and Ruth now claimed a share in Kagawa's "Prayer for the Overstrung": "O Thou who didst give the rhinoceros its hide, the cow its placidity, and the kitten its irresponsibility, grant to Thy servants some measure of these Thy gifts."[105]

A wonderful farewell service was held on January 29, 1939, with a congregation of about 1,000 of whom 650 stayed for communion. Most of these shook hands with Ruth as he had requested, "So that with your hand in mine I may say, 'Go with God.'" A letter of appreciation and good wishes to Ruth from the Lord Mayor was read to the congregation. Ruth preached from the same text he had used in his first sermon there, "But he giveth more grace" (Jas 4:6).

> From first to last in every phase of my ministry it has been the supreme concern, the text all other texts expound, the one glowing and growing truth I have tried to apply to every problem. It has never failed me. I find even forgetfulness of farewell in its abiding reality.[106]

In December 1939, Rev. C. Bernard Cockett (1888–1965) began a fine ministry at Pitt Street, and a new era for the city church began.[107]

Pitt Street faced significant challenges in succeeding years, becoming Pitt Street Uniting Church in 1977. The church's current website describes Pitt Street as a "progressive faith community of justice-seeking friends in the heart of Sydney."[108] That would have delighted Ruth, who as early as 1922 was described in *Who's Who* as "a leader in the Australian Protestant forces and stands for a progressive theology and a comprehensive churchmanship."[109]

Ruth moved to Adelaide during 1939 but was still battling to find the way ahead. What ministry could this sixty-three-year-old preacher–writer find in "the city of churches"?

---

105. Ruth to Brookes, 17 December 1937, Brookes Papers, NLA 1924/48/195.
106. *SMH*, January 30, 1939, 8.
107. Emilsen *Pride of Place*, 249–86. For Cockett, see *ADB*.
108. <pittstreetunitingchurch.com.au> (accessed 11 July 2020).
109. *Who's Who Australia*, 1922, 239–40.

12

"A Good Secular Pulpit"

RUTH GRADUALLY BECAME SO well known in the community that he was invited to write weekly columns for daily newspapers, first in Melbourne with the *Herald* in 1922 (ten issues) and then when he moved to Sydney for the *Sunday Sun* from 1923 until 1937 (721 issues). The *Mail* in Adelaide also often used Ruth's columns, published the day before on a Saturday, although each paper claimed that the contribution was "exclusive" to it. After his final move to Adelaide, Ruth wrote for both the *Mail* (forty-five issues) during 1939 and 1940 as well as for the afternoon tabloid the *News*, for which during 1939 he contributed a brief daily comment of about two hundred words titled "Everyday Living." He also wrote occasional pieces for *The Age* in Melbourne.

THE REV. T. E. RUTH

T. E. Ruth, *Herald* (Melbourne), 5 August 1922

This was a remarkable achievement, about eight hundred columns. Ruth's basic approach was revealed in a comment to Brookes: "I hope to make the *Herald* a good secular pulpit for a while."[1] He felt a strong call to this ministry, and his "pulpit" reached many thousands of readers. The *Sun* was an afternoon tabloid paper first published in 1910, while the Sunday edition claimed every week on its masthead that it had "a circulation larger than that of any other Sunday paper in Australia." From time to time, it published circulation figures to substantiate this claim. For example, in April 1931 it reported that its average daily sales were 214,255 while for the Sunday edition it was 249,765.[2]

Ruth's newspaper writings add to our appreciation of him as a public theologian since he regularly connected questions of faith with everyday life. His involvement also demonstrates the welcome given to a select number

---

1. Ruth to Brookes, 10 July 1922, Brookes Papers, NLA 1924/48/71.
2. *Sun*, April 26, 1931, 2.

of gifted clergy within a secular context. Selected sermons from a variety of churches were faithfully reported each Monday in broadsheets such as *The Age* and the *SMH*. Tabloid readers clearly responded to Ruth.

Australian newspapers had played an increasingly important role in Australian society, so much so that by the end of the nineteenth century some Christians were anxious about the way in which the press was rivalling the pulpit as a shaper of opinion.[3] The press exercised a dominant role in providing information, educating readers, and influencing political and social thought in the community.

Editorials were a major source of public opinion, and some clergy wrote many of these. Ruth's Baptist contemporary F. W. Boreham wrote over 3,000 editorials in the Hobart *Mercury* and the Melbourne *Age* between 1912 and 1959.[4] Presbyterian Rev. Thomas Jollie Smith (1858–1927) wrote editorials for the Melbourne *Argus* from 1907 to 1927,[5] and Congregationalist Rev. E. S. Kiek (1883–1959) wrote for the Adelaide *Advertiser* from 1937 until 1959.[6] Fewer wrote for the tabloid papers, but these reached a wider audience. C. W. Benson in Melbourne was one, although his columns were generally a mix of news and short notices. But the religious doyen of the tabloid press was T. E. Ruth, who was unrivalled in the number of years he wrote in three states and the extraordinary range of topics he covered. This popular appeal meant that he was one of the best-known and most influential Protestants during a period of political and social upheaval.

A few months after he had commenced writing for the *Sun*, Ruth wrote "a parable of the newspaper," showing how it helped give a perspective on life.

> Take this particular issue of this newspaper. What is it? It is a piece of paper in several sheets. Well, explain it. You find it related to time and space; to cause and effect; to chemical, biological, and psychological affinities ...
>
> Glance through the paper. Begin at the first page. Can you take your place with the horses in the sun? [A reference to the distinctive logo of the paper.] Do you see the significance of "Sydney: Sunday, June 24, 1923"? Can you place Sydney in its proper State, Commonwealth and Imperial perspective?
>
> What is the relation of Sunday to the Pagan era? And to Christian civilisation? ...

---

3. Breward, *Australia*, 31.
4. Pound, "F. W. Boreham the Public Theologian," 2.
5. For Smith, see *ADB*.
6. For Kiek, see *ADB*, and Phillips, *Edward Sidney Kiek*.

You are reading the paper in an odd hour. But the hour, odd as it is, has its place in the day, in the week, in the month, in the year, in the century, in the millennium, in the age . . .

In the paper you have news from everywhere. What does that world neighbourhood, the creation of the modern newspaper, convey to you? . . . You are reading this article—some perhaps hardly ever get to the Sunday magazine section at all. And you belong to this curiously complex community of newspaper readers. We are bound up together in the bundle of life. And somebody must think of all of us. The State, after all, is simply all of us.

You see, what vast interests are involved in the name, date, news, and articles in the paper. Every man and event is spiritually significant. Think of the spiritual wonder of taking the twenty-six letters of the alphabet and making literature and music and worship of them. Think of that invisible dominating personality that creates environment.[7]

The editor gave freedom to Ruth to select his themes although they also encouraged him to comment on special community days such as Health Week and Music Week. They gave considerable care to the presentation of Ruth's column, especially in his early years. A short editorial précis of the column appeared together with artwork and small photos of people cited in the article together with photos of Ruth himself. Reproductions of his distinctive signature were featured in later columns.

Ruth's Style and Subjects

Ruth's pulpit style was substantially the same as his writing in his columns. That he was always listed as "Rev. T. E. Ruth" in the byline of his columns suggests that a religious perspective was expected. He did not shrink from this responsibility and constantly sought to emphasize the reality of religion and to help with the problems that many found in traditional religious language and ideas. His readers included those who were believers and church members of all denominational and theological persuasions as well as an undoubted majority who were either of a remote and vague faith or no faith at all. While this was a great opportunity, it also provided considerable challenge for Ruth to engage with as many of the readers as possible. Even so, some of his columns were clearly based on sermons, which suggests more about his pulpit style

---

7. *Sun*, June 24, 1923, 13.

than an ability to adapt sermons for the press. Of course, in the paper he had only about 1,000 or 1,200 words available.

It is worth stressing that, at least for the *Sun*, he was writing for a Sunday paper when people had more leisure for reading and many of the week's sporting and political events were reviewed. A typical issue could contain as many as fifty pages with special supplements in addition to the main news section. Ruth wrote alongside such well-known figures as Arthur Mailey (1886–1967), the famous slow bowler who had taken ninety-nine Test wickets before becoming a popular cartoonist and journalist. Mailey had joined the *Sun* in 1921.[8] On one occasion, Ruth was quietly having lunch in a city café when he heard a voice behind him saying, *sotto voce*, "Now we shall expect an article on the art of eating." Ruth duly obliged, insisting that he "would not be bowled out by Mailey."[9] He clearly enjoyed a measure of camaraderie with *Sun* employees and as early as May 1924 wrote to Brookes claiming that "my footing on the paper seems secure and the articles win appreciation in the most unsuspected quarters."[10] He later observed, "The Sun staff offers opportunity for team-work which is good for me, even when I don't exactly enjoy it."[11]

T. E. Ruth at work

8. For Mailey, see *ADB*.
9. *Sun*, May 15, 1927, 23.
10. Ruth to Brookes, 28 May 1924, Brookes Papers, NLA 1924/48/79.
11. Ruth to Brookes, 1 April 1929, Brookes Papers, NLA 1924/48/114.

In both preaching and writing, Ruth usually began with a striking question, quotation or incident to involve the hearer or reader in his theme. His characteristic and exaggerated use of alliteration was featured along with his provocative habit of using of some religious terms in an unusual way. Usually conversational in approach, Ruth also used memorable phrases relating to ordinary life with its problems and ideals. He was a gifted raconteur, and the skill with which he had entertained numerous church social gatherings was transferred to his columns, which contained many amusing tales.

In his political declarations, he spoke his mind with clarity and a force that often provoked negative responses from his readers. There was also evidence of considerable courage in Ruth's writing as he espoused a form of liberal or "modernist" theology, knowing that many readers would be looking for data with which to condemn him. How many conservative church people would actually read a secular paper on Sunday is uncertain. Evidently, some did criticize him for writing in a Sunday paper. At his welcome to Pitt Street, he declared that he was no advocate for Sunday papers but added:

> The Sunday paper was not secularizing Sunday as much as the motor car, or the ferry which the preacher used on his way to preach the Gospel. If he had to choose between the pulpit and the press, he would unhesitatingly decide for the press. It yielded an intensive opportunity that was very widespread. The heart of the natural man was really hungry for God. Men who were suspicious of the Churches realized that in the Gospel was the solution of all the problems, social, political and international of mankind.[12]

While Ruth did not hesitate to discuss overtly religious topics in his columns, he made no attempt to proselytize. He did not attack Roman Catholics, although on one occasion he did offer "A Protestant's Impression" of the Eucharistic Congress held in Sydney in 1928.[13] His main point was that Sydney "will stand where it stood before—a little more sympathetic perhaps to spiritual appeal." Insisting that "intolerance has no place in Protestant faith," he argued that "Providence" had largely made both Catholics and Protestants. He did not refer to his feud with Dr. Mannix but made a few general comments about prejudices found in both Catholics and Protestants. "I honestly believe Roman Catholics to be as wrong as Roman

---

12. *Australian Christian Commonwealth*, July 3, 1925, 9.
13. *Sun*, September 9, 1928, 25.

Catholics honestly believe Protestants to be." But when he saw Catholics "honouring Christ and Him crucified," he recalled Browning's words:

> Do these men praise Him? I will raise
>
> My voice up to their point of praise!
>
> I see the error; but above
>
> The scope of error, see the love.[14]

He concluded, "The love! That is what this Protestant appreciates. We can argue about the error any time." Ruth had clearly affirmed his Protestantism but tried not to unduly offend Catholic readers.

Ruth generated considerable correspondence from his readers, and their responses and questions sparked several columns. As he wrote in his 1924 column, "Letters from the Lonely":

> These weekly articles have in a most surprising fashion, brought me into somewhat remote touch with innumerable friends with whom it would be great joy to have something like personal fellowship. Every day I receive invitations to a more intimate comparison of rival views and visions.
>
> Someday it might be possible for me to enter upon a sort of ministry of correspondence. The mail certainly reveals the enormous possibilities before a bureau of friendly advice, a common confessional, a kind of moral and spiritual exchange and mart. As things are, it is not practicable even to acknowledge a very small proportion of the illuminating letters from regular readers.
>
> Some of my kindliest critics are clergymen. And lay preachers are expert in stating theological conundrums. But if my correspondence is typical, and my ministerial experience normal, there are more people outside the churches keenly interested in moral and religious problems than there are within.[15]

His hope of speaking from "a secular pulpit" was clearly fulfilled. He reflected on the fact that so many letters had come from lonely people. Many have found Australia to be "a Great Lost Land" and while some letters came from readers living in isolated centers, the "most pathetic" came from the most densely crowded places. Many rural folk appreciated his work: "We only have

---

14. These lines are from Browning's poem "Christmas-Eve and Easter-Day, a Poem" (1850).

15. *Sun*, March 30, 1924, 15.

church once a month out here. And we must have something worthwhile to think about. You can help break up the mental monotony."[16]

Not that all were positive: "Your articles have confirmed my wife in her unbelief." After reading the man's version of "belief," Ruth thought his wife was to be congratulated. Yet another asked if Ruth could help: "I live in a religious home where the creed is traditional and the disposition unlovely. What can I do to prevent the poison getting into my blood? Is it really true, as you seem to teach, that religion is natural and sweetly reasonable?"[17] Ruth answered that religion is relationship, and Christianity offers a friendly God.

This form of introduction—referring to a correspondent—was often used by Ruth. One wrote "to represent a crowd of readers" who "find it difficult to believe in the God of the Bible, and in the God of the churches."[18] This in many ways was exactly the audience for whom Ruth felt called to write.

On another occasion, he wrote that it was quite impossible for him to respond personally to correspondents: "I wish it were otherwise, if I had nothing else to do I could be kept engaged, happily engaged too, in a ministry of correspondence. But it cannot be." He explained that "all except anonymous letters I read carefully, and I honestly try to put myself in my correspondent's place" and that he often incorporated suggestions from readers in his articles. With very few exceptions, he declared, those who write anonymous letters are "cowards and fools, and when they happen to be conversant with pious phrases they prove themselves hypocrites." He gave one example: "Dear Sir, I think I have read every one of your sermons or whatever you call them, and there is not a grain of gospel in any of them. I shall hope on, and expect to find something which will build us up in our most holy faith."

Ruth replied, noting that his articles were not sermons. "Far from it. They have never pretended to be Gospel preachments. This column is not a pulpit."[19] (However, as we have noted, he did in fact regard his column as "a secular pulpit.")

A quite different type of letter—"a cry of distress"—was discussed by Ruth. "I have gone wrong and made shipwreck of everything. If anybody can help me, you can." Ruth wrote kindly, offering to pray for him and assured his reader that Christ would indeed help him even though he must

16. *Sun*, March 30, 1924, 15.
17. *Sun*, March 30, 1924, 15.
18. *Sun*, April 13, 1924, 17.
19. *Sun*, June 19, 1927, 27.

expect to face the consequences of the errors he had made.[20] One final example is the question asked by a chemist whose handwriting Ruth found difficult to read, "who seems to be taking revenge on me for all the doctors' prescriptions he has ever dispensed." Taking it with him on the ferry and in the train, he managed to decipher enough to discuss science and faith for several columns.[21]

Through the Calendar Year

Ruth faithfully observed a kind of editorial lectionary. These normally included: New Year; Foundation (or Australia) Day; Easter; Anzac Day; Mother's Day; Empire Day; Health Week (October); Armistice Day; Christmas Day; and Holiday season.

Marking these days gave him a predictability of theme as well as the necessity to vary his approach for each successive year. While there was some inevitable repetition, even recycling some columns across the years, Ruth generally achieved a freshness and relevance. The calendar gave him ample opportunity to highlight his imperial and national ideals as well as justifying an overtly religious approach at Easter and Christmas. He also often proclaimed his belief that the Bible is "an-out-of-doors book" and that Christianity is "an open-air religion." This was a theme to which Ruth would often return: "I have worshipped in the Blue Mountains, at the Buffalo Mountains, at Macedon in the autumn. My prayer went to God who gave colour and that balmy air and who gave me perception."[22]

Christmas and Easter

Ruth obviously had many sermons from across his years of ministry to adapt for these principal days in the Christian year.

Christmas was inevitably a commercial day as much as a religious observation. In 1925, Ruth wrote that Christmas time is "the time of the child," the season in which "the spiritual primacy of childhood is most clearly seen ... Peter Pan and all who are wise enough not to grow up are in their proper element." The challenge is that we do grow old, and "the torpor of custom creeps over us." He describes how as adults even the best of activities can

---

20. *Sun*, June 19, 1927, 27.
21. *Sun*, July 22, 1928, 27.
22. *Sun*, December 2, 1923, 13.

become routine and humdrum, even prayer. His description of church attendance is striking:

> Once a week, perhaps we go to church, lounge in the same pew, drowse through the same service, duck our heads in the same attitude of prayer, pass through the same routine of religious and social duties, read the same papers, repeat the same ideas to the people we meet, until by a process of decay the savour, the vital juice, the animation has gone out of life. We should pray not to be saved from sudden death but from gradual decline.[23]

Scarcely a theological exposition of the meaning of the incarnation, Ruth's column did provoke an examination of life, insisting that "within the gift of God nothing is greater than childlikeness." On this basis, he wished all his readers "the best Christmas within the gift of God."

Ruth also described how Christmas was celebrated around the world.[24] After the bitter federal election debates of 1931, he wrote about "Peace after the Battle," imagining that he needed to take a megaphone and declare to distracted hearers, "I am calling you to the calm that follows the conflict, to the benediction after the battle, asking you to recall the magic of the Christmas glory."[25]

For another Christmas Day, Ruth wrote on "The Story of the Stars" and reflected:

> An Englishman isn't likely to forget his first Christmas in Australia. The distance makes all the difference between winter and summer; between hissing logs and brilliant sunshine; between indoor festivities and out-of-door picnics, between fur-lined coats and flannels; between snow-balling and surf-bathing.[26]

A single star may have led the wise men to the manger, but modern science had revealed "a swarm of universes" so that "the Christmas Christ is the cosmic Christ."

Easter naturally necessitated a more obvious theological emphasis, in particular that Christ had overcome death. Ruth never failed to invite his readers to embrace the truth and power of that belief. As he bluntly declared in 1924, "There are no dead"—this was his summary of the difference that

---

23. *Sun*, December 20, 1925, 19.
24. *Sun*, December 23, 1928, 21.
25. *Sun*, December 20, 1931, 37.
26. *Sun*, December 25, 1927, 17.

Easter had made.[27] In 1926, he wrote on "The Triumph of Life," and in 1933 he explored what he called "The Radiant Faith of Easter":

> All the progress of personality, all the progress of the race we owe to the fact that death is involved in life . . . It never occurred to Jesus that death was final. He never thought of going to the grave to stay there. It was not the hole in the ground that He saw. It was a door through which angels could come.[28]

Anzac Day

Ruth clearly welcomed Anzac Day and Armistice Day, always writing detailed columns, sometimes over more than one week. The emphasis that he laid on both these days of memory was prominent in his preaching and was also in these newspaper columns. Ruth helped develop a form of civic religion by insisting that Anzac Day was a community sacrament.

One approach that Ruth developed was to raise the whole question of death and immortality in the light of Anzac Day. In 1924, for example, he wrote about these topics over two weeks. On April 20, he asserted, "There Are No Dead."[29] The kind of comfort that he had offered to those who lost loved ones during his ministry at Collins Street was encapsulated in this column. The following week, he wrote about "Anzacs and Immortality," reviewing its significance for the young nation:

> Anzac Day commemorates more than the emergence of Australia from adolescence into nationhood nine years ago. Only incidentally and not of set design did that transition take place, in self-sacrifice the nation found self-fulfilment without seeking it . . . It is a story that can never die. It will be re-told whenever Anzac Day recurs . . . The Anzac anniversary is an Australasian sacrament.[30]

Ruth also pursued the question, "What Are the Anzacs Doing Now?" He explored the idea that they were not dead and that indeed they had happy work to do.[31] Another year he sought to invoke the Anzac spirit for

27. *Sun*, April 20, 1924, 13.
28. *Sun*, April 16, 1933, 13.
29. *Sun*, April 20, 1924, 13.
30. *Sun*, April 27, 1924, 15.
31. *Sun*, April 24, 1927, 19.

peace.³² Not surprisingly, Ruth also commended the practice of prayers for the dead.³³

In later years, Ruth argued that the Anzacs had distinct civic implications, saying, "We must not substitute the glory of the Anzacs in April 1915 for the duty of their fellows in 1925," and he then quoted his Australian version of the Ten Commandments as offering "an Anzac decalogue."³⁴ He also suggested that what Thermopylae was to the Spartans, what Trafalgar was to the Englishman, Gallipoli is to the citizens of the Southern Cross.

> Ye of bush and open highway,
>
> Ye of crowded street and byway,
>
> Lo for you along the skyway
>
> March the Anzac men.³⁵

These lines are from an Anzac hymn that had been written by Ruth's predecessor at Pitt Street, poet and greatly loved friend Rev. N. J. Cocks, after Ruth had asked him to compose a "glad Anzac hymn . . . a martial song with some sense of victory in it." Cocks wrote the hymn to be sung to the tune of "The Men of Harlech" and, according to Ruth, "March of the Anzac Men" was now sung "all over Australia" on Anzac Day.³⁶

This was how preachers and writers like Ruth helped develop the Anzac myth, the collective national remembering that has enjoyed a revival in the present age. As James Brown has observed, "Anzac has become our longest eulogy, our secular sacred rite, our national story."³⁷ But for Ruth and his contemporaries, the myth was still evolving, and for that first generation of those who had lost so many young lives, the annual celebration was truly sacred. The way in which Christian motifs were incorporated into Anzac ceremonies is well demonstrated by clergy like Ruth.³⁸

---

32. *Sun*, April 23, 1933, 19.
33. *Sun*, July 17, 1927, 23.
34. *Sun*, April 26, 1925, 15.
35. *Sun*, April 25, 1926, 19.
36. Ruth, "March of the Anzac Men: How it was written," *SMH*, April 23, 1938, 21.
37. Brown, *Anzac's Long Shadow*, 3.
38. See also Frame, *Anzac Day*.

Empire Day

For an imperialist like Ruth, Empire Day was always special. In his first year as a regular columnist on Empire Day, Ruth affirmed that Australia was "British by the will of God" and published what he named "Australia's Creed."[39]

Ruth exegeted this version of "Christian Imperialism" in his column. The political implications for the 1920s were transparent, especially when the affirmation referred to Australia's own "industrial and political salvation without the interference of alien agitators." As he commented:

> I do not know that there is anything more important from the point of view of Empire than the relation of Australia and the other Dominions to the Mother Country in the colossal constitutional changes incident to the waging of the world war, the terms of the Peace treaty, and the inception of the League of Nations. But that relationship is more than political. In the best sense it is religious . . . There is clamant need that the citizens of this Commonwealth should put more conscience into their citizenship.[40]

Year by year Ruth sounded the same note, sometimes becoming even more jingoistic such as in his 1926 version, "This England!"[41] In 1927, he commented on the golden key with which the Duke of York had opened the massive new doors of Parliament House on May 9. A crowd of some 30,000 had gathered in Canberra to hear Dame Nellie Melba sing the National Anthem on the steps of the shiny new building. The Duke had linked the event with "the noble army of the dead" and insisted, "They are still speaking." This, of course, was precisely the sentiment so loved by Ruth, who proceeded to explore the question of in what sense the dead were still speaking to us.[42]

Successive years always found similar sentiments expressed.

Remembrance Day

Closely linked with Empire Day was Armistice or Remembrance Day, held on November 11 each year. Again, Ruth did not miss any opportunity to highlight what Australia owed to those who had died in the cause of empire and nation. He had already drafted a creed for Australians; now

---

39. *Sun*, May 20, 1923, 13. This creed was published in *Playing the Game*, 256.
40. Ruth, *Playing the Game*, 260–61.
41. *Sun*, May 23, 1926, 19.
42. *Sun*, May 22, 1927, 23.

in 1923 he offered them an Armistice Day *Te Deum*, which extended for several stanzas but began:

> Thanks be unto God for securing for the world the existence of a free civilization, free from the military domination of the well-laid and far-reaching schemes and ideals of Germany, free from the crushing by brute force of the institutions of democracy, free for the development of democratic ideals and social sympathies unhindered by the military dictatorship of Prussianism . . .

His love for the Royal Family was unbounded, and the prayer of thanksgiving passed into offering further information for a listening deity:

> Thanks be unto God for the sacrificial service of our King and Queen, the Prince of Wales and all the Royal household. It is impossible to see how the Royal family could have identified themselves more completely with their people's cause and their people's sorrow. They gave an example which will live in the annals of the British Throne, an example of noble sacrifice, high courage and devout faith . . .

The note of thanksgiving was resumed with more information for God:

> Thanks be unto God for the seven million seven hundred thousand soldier and sailor saviours of the British Empire; for the old pre-war army, the "contemptible little army" of the one hundred and sixty thousand select men as well trained, as perfect in physique as any in the world—contemptible in its numbers but of such consummate tenacity, of such British bulldog grip, that it held vastly superior forces for weeks, held them, and held them finally, and saved France, and saved Europe.[43]

Succeeding sections thanked God for "the commanding genius" of Lord Kitchener, for the "thousand sons of Greater Britain," for "the super-men of the Southern Cross," the British navy, and the mercantile marine, for "the infantry of the air, the artillery of the air, the cavalry of the clouds," the munition workers, and "all civilian servants of the Empire," for nurses, the Red Cross, and "the religious ministrations of chaplains of all the churches"— and yet much more. The prayer finally came to a climax with thanks for "our heroic living dead, whose memory we crown with red roses of sacrifice and white lilies of triumph," concluding with an exhausted, "Thanks be unto God Who giveth us the victory."

Every year, something similar was published by Ruth. In 1924, he suggested that the Armistice Anniversary was different from Empire Day and Anzac Day, which were "occasions for oratory," but Armistice Day was

43. *Sun*, November 11, 1923, 13; Ruth, *Playing the Game*, 297–300.

"distinguished by its recognition of the significance of silence" (although Anzac Day has also become similarly noted for its time of silence). In silence, "memory exercises its ministry," and we must never forget "the tremendously religious significance of Empire."[44] Other Armistice Day articles included "Through Purgatory to Paradise" (1928); "War God Is Dead" (1931); "Memory Must Aid Peace" (1932); "Can Youth Abolish War? (1933), and "Peace—Is It Possible?" (1934). An outburst of imperial fervor prompted two columns in 1935: "Why Men Die for England" and "Something about Blighty."

After the outbreak of World War II on September 3, 1939, Ruth wrote "On Keeping Calm: The Scare-Monger Is Doing the Devil's Work." He supported Sir Henry Gullett (1878-1940), the Minister of External Affairs, in his deploring of ill-founded rumors. He asserted that there was no honorable way out of the European situation, "which leaves Hitler with power to do to France and Britain what he said he would not do, but has done to Austria, Czecho-Slovakia and Poland—these are the things that sometimes scare us." His response was, "We are personal spiritual beings. And if we know Christ, we cannot be scared."[45]

All that week, he wrote a short daily column in the *News*, and the following week in the *Mail* he wrote "Why Victory Is Sure." He claimed: "Victory is sure, because in the long run, truth is bound to triumph over lies. Time is on the side of truth."

> Religion is familiar with anti-Christ talking like Christ, with Satan rebuking sin, with the devil appearing as an angel of light. But Hitler has so overdone it now that there is not the slightest risk of "deceiving the very elect." Hitler, like Judas, will go to his own place.[46]

Ruth wrote two columns for Armistice Day in that fateful year: "Armistice: a Community Sacrament and Song" and a reissue of his *Te Deum* as an Armistice Epilogue.[47] In "An Aftermath of Armistice," he rejected any notion that the idea of "armistice" was now a misnomer, and he again stressed the place of silence in the observation of the day. "Hating war like hell—as no passive pacifist has ever hated it—the men of our race shouldered the cross and went through the flames. That is what the anniversary of the armistice will not let us forget."[48]

---

44. *Sun*, November 9, 1924, 13; *Playing the Game*, 292–96.
45. *Mail*, October 7, 1939, 8.
46. *Mail*, October 14, 1939, 9.
47. *Mail*, November 4, 1939, 7; November 11, 5.
48. *Mail*, November 18, 1939, 8.

Australia Day

The evolution of January 26 as Australia Day has been long and often controversial. Although the day marks the anniversary of the landing of the First Fleet at Sydney Cove in 1788, the significance for Sydney has gradually been extended to the whole nation. Ruth preached and wrote to mark the day, which invited patriotic affirmations.

In 1924, he noted the commemoration with an article on "Australia's High Calling" and suggested it revealed "the soul of the nation."[49] He had adopted the contemporary notion of a sleeping continent, "peopled for centuries by scattered tribes of backward beings strangely ignorant of the wonderful wealth of their home, a land lying as under a spell of enchantment, asleep within her borders of pearl and coral and her girdle of silver seas." Racist and offensive as this imagery is, it may be balanced in part by Ruth's later demonstration of sympathy and support for Indigenous people (as discussed in the previous chapter).

His basic perspective, as so often preached from his pulpits, was quite clear:

> Prior to January 26, 1788, other peoples thought of this new land as a desirable possession. And there is no reason why it should not be a holy land. Australians should believe in Australia as they believe in God. It was left to the British to possess it as a land of promise—why? Why British? ... To what great task has Australia been ordained in the providence of God?
>
> Australia, so far from being a mere antipodean appendage, is in the very center of the British Empire ... But let not our masters and teachers neglect the soul of the nation, the prophetic ministry of the Commonwealth, the spiritual significance of empire.
>
> Not less than ancient Israel, Australia has a divine calling.[50]

Ruth did not write about this day each year, but in 1930 he recycled something of his 1924 article with "Advance Australia Fair!" to warn that certain Australians were being "deceived by foreigners" and their revolutionary plans. Communism and Lang's regime as Premier in New South Wales were clearly dangers to his anxious mind, and this is an instance of Ruth's political views being expressed in this forum.[51] Anzac and Armistice days gave him ample opportunities to advance his political concerns. Indeed, nationalist and imperial concerns were a regular theme of his columns, quite apart from marking memorial anniversaries.

---

49. *Sun*, January 27, 1924, 13.
50. Ruth, *Playing the Game*, 264–66.
51. *Sun*, January 26, 1930, 17.

Health Week

Observed every October in Sydney, Health Week prompted a variety of approaches from Ruth. In 1924, he linked it with immigration and voiced his oft-cited opinion, "Australia is as under-populated as it is over-governed—almost." While acknowledging that most Australians grew into fine physical specimens, Ruth noted the shocking rate of children dying within a year of birth and that "it is among the illegitimate children that the death rate is alarmingly high." Every child has the right to a heritage of health.[52]

At a contemporary medical conference, Ruth noted, Sydney had been declared the healthiest city in the world, and the aim of health week was "to inspire civic pride and civic prayer and courage to help God to answer the prayer, 'God make thee healthier yet.'" Mental hygiene was also necessary, and Ruth strongly pleaded for adequate care of "the mentally-inflicted who are anti-social" as well as for child welfare. "The city has a right to expect more from us than it could get from our grandparents. We ought to labor and to pray for its complete health, physical, mental, moral and spiritual, to make it as healthy in spirit as it is beautiful for situation."[53]

The fashion for nominating certain weeks for some community emphasis was extended to "music week" each August in Sydney. Ruth linked it with health week: "It is with music as it is with health. Health does not begin and end with Health Week . . . Harmony like health, belongs to the wholeness of things." As he so often did, he quoted from a poem:

> Though with our dreams, the world we shape,
>   And with our love the world explain,
> For us there can be no escape,
>   From the sun's light, the lark's refrain,
> Music and colour, sound and shape,
>   Besiege the heart and flood the brain.[54]

Mother's Day, Women, Marriage, and Other Domestic Themes

Women and motherhood were topics on which Ruth frequently wrote from many different angles. The first column devoted to Mother's Day was in May

---

52. *Sun*, October 12, 1924, 15.
53. *Sun*, October 20, 1929, 21.
54. *Sun*, August 20, 1933, 43. I have not been able to identify the poet.

1924 when he asserted that motherhood was the highest thing in human life. He quoted Henry Drummond, who said that "the aim of evolution is the making of mothers."

In a concept Ruth often used, he insisted that "God must be mother as well as father. And He [sic] is." However, "the world owes its continuance and its consistency of progress to the mothers of men. Motherhood brought the Messiah into the world. Through the mothers of the world, the Christ will come again."[55]

In another year, he discussed "Women in the Pulpit." Australian Congregationalists led other denominations as to the place of women in the church with Winifred Kiek's ordination in 1926. Ruth's views were also strong and unequivocal about welcoming women into the pulpits.[56] Citing the familiar text that in Christ "there is neither male nor female," he wondered why there was still opposition to women preaching. Christ made no distinctions of gender in his ministry, and Ruth praised the Salvation Army for the role they gave to women: "The world will not forget Catherine Booth."

He specifically acknowledged the work of Miss Maude Royden (1876–1956), the remarkable English suffragette, lecturer, and preacher. An Anglican, Royden was denied ordination in her church but was appointed as assistant pastor to the City Temple in 1917. Ruth argued positively for women in the pulpit:

> I believe that women have something vital to contribute to the Christian ministry, something which will not detract from the necessary virility of the pulpit, but which will add maternal sympathy to masculine strength . . .
> If women in the pulpit would make our faith more human, and our love more divine, Fling wide the Doors![57]

Ruth noted that some of the songs that men sing about their mother are "dreadfully mawkish . . . too saccharine, too insipid, too suggestive of second childhood, too lachrymose" although he himself did not avoid this danger. He suggested that "mother" songs should be modeled on Mary's song, the Magnificat: "the ringing song of the Madonna is the Marseillaise of Reform."[58]

The place of the home, marriage, and family life was a theme of great interest to Ruth. His selection of essays for *Playing the Game* in 1925 was

55. *Sun*, May 11, 1924, 15; Ruth, *Playing the Game*, 69–72.
56. Lockley, *Congregationalism in Australia*, 300–302.
57. *Sun*, May 17, 1925, 15.
58. *Sun*, May 10, 1931, 18.

organized into six sections and included nine articles on "Playing the Game at Home," ranging from "Falling in Love" to "Mateship and Marriage" and "Kith and Kin." His sources were as diverse as the biblical Song of Solomon ("rather a sensuous song"), the apocryphal book of Enoch, poets like Browning and Tennyson, and writers like Shakespeare and Emerson. More controversially, he asked the question, "Should the Woman Obey?" in the marriage ceremony. He noted the unsuccessful efforts of Maude Royden and others to bring the marriage vows in the Anglican Prayer Book into "harmony with the social status of the modern woman." The notion of "giving away" the woman to the man was also rejected while Ruth insisted that "marriage without love was as bad as love without marriage."[59]

In an earlier column, Ruth had argued for equality of opportunity for both genders.

> In the beginning woman was a distinctive revelation of God. In His own image, "Male and female created He them."
>
> And through the centuries woman has been struggling into emancipation, and during the crimson years of war she revealed how completely she has arrived.
>
> And now that the old dominations of sex are destroyed, men and women must unite in equality of rights and equality of opportunity to build the new world. When the lecturer on women's work said, "Take women out of society, and what would follow?" A man in the audience cried, "I would." We all would![60]

Personal Character

Alongside his section on home life, the other five sections in *Playing the Game* reveal how Ruth analyzed his themes—playing the game in personal character; in religion; in the churches; in industrial relationships; and in the Commonwealth. These also offer a framework to examine his emphases across the following years.

Personal character became an increasingly popular theme for Ruth. His titles convey his essential ideas: "Having a Closed Mind"; "Can a Man Master His Moods?," and "How to Get On." Later topics included "Growing Old Gracefully," "Making the Best of Ourselves," "Cycles of Change," "The Art of Being Kind," "The Poison of Prejudice," "Outgrowing Our Problems" And "The Art of Cheerfulness."

59. Ruth, *Playing the Game*, 63–68.
60. *Sun*, June 3, 1923, 13.

Religion

Inevitably, many columns dealt with diverse aspects of "religion" as well as more general philosophical subjects. What annoyed Ruth was the confusion of traditional orthodoxies with "religion," and he regularly condemned all that was not strictly fundamental:

> A Christian is simply a man who has the spirit of Christ. If any man hath not the spirit of Christ he is none of His. Neither is churchmanship anything, nor anti-churchmanship; neither orthodoxy nor heterodoxy—my doxy or your doxy—but the spirit of Christ.[61]

Inevitably, this emphasis on what was fundamental prompted him to disassociate himself from "fundamentalists" in America. To his dismay, he observed that "this fighting disease" had spread to Australia, "which is by way of becoming a happy hunting ground for ignorant American Evangelists." Fundamentalism was "such a high-sounding, grandly-rolling word that it naturally allures some primitive souls, and is obviously fore-ordained to be a slogan." He contrasted fundamentalism with modernism although the latter could become just as spiritually unsatisfying. The absolutely vital reality is the validity of Christian experience: "Apart from the spirit of Christ, the system of Christianity, whether fundamentalist or modernist, is merely a corpse." He concluded that "every man is free to be his own theologian."[62]

Additional articles, somewhat more theological, included, in March 1925, "Ideas of God" and "Is Forgiveness Possible?" This was followed by "Is Religion Revolutionary?" in which he contrasted revolution with evolution but insisted that most doctrines did progress in the pattern of evolution:

> The Atonement is the crown of whatever truth there may be in the theory of evolution. The Atonement itself is evolutionary. In personal character, in the life of the church, in national politics, in international relationships, the Cross is necessary... Through the centuries of the Cross, Christianity has been capturing the world of thought and purpose and action, widening the horizon of life, making redemption real and regnant, so that now almost everybody knows that life is love, and love is life.[63]

The links between science and religion were regularly explored by Ruth, in particular the debates about evolution and creation. Ruth agreed with Sir

---

61. Ruth, *Playing the Game*, 121.
62. Ruth, *Playing the Game*, 126–30.
63. *Sun*, April 5, 1925, 17.

Oliver Lodge's claim that "evolution was a method of creation" and insisted that the Genesis account was not concerned with the process of creation but was wholly concerned with its divine origin: "Science deals with processes. Genesis reveals the primary cause." Ruth specifically rejected the notion that the theory of evolution disproves God.[64]

So, as he wrote in "Dust and Divinity," the story of Adam and Eve is "a pictorial parable of the most profound truth in human history." This story is "more than fact, it is truth. Its outward historicity isn't worth thinking about much less fighting for. But its inner, ethical spiritual reality, the soul of the old story is enshrined in our most modern experience." The story of the creation of woman from man was reviewed with humor:

> I can sympathise with the boy who for the first time heard the story graphically told by a kindergarten teacher and afterwards held his side and complained to his mother, "I'm afraid I've got a wife coming." When I was a boy I used to feel around for the missing rib. I found it at last. But a man doesn't find a wife as painlessly as Adam found Eve.
>
> The story stands for this sublime reality—man is a domestic animal. Apart from woman man is not made in the image of God. Sex is of divine origin. The idea that sex is unholy is one of the most mischievous ideas in human life.[65]

Ruth believed that the fall was real. "We are familiar with retrograde movements in morals, in our own morals . . . Life will be a garden only while God is in it. Companionship with God is not obsolete. It is far more general than at any time in history. And it is the story of human nature."[66]

"Science" was the theme of numerous columns. "Science and the Soul" and "Science and God" were published in 1926 (August and September) while special aspects of "science" were considered in "Science and Scripture" in 1927. A correspondent had criticized an earlier article on "Let the ape and tiger die" in which Ruth had claimed that "the evolutionary theory no less than the theory of traditional theology had emphasised man's need of Christ."[67] This in turn provoked another correspondent, who challenged him to reconcile Genesis with the theory of evolution. Of course, Ruth agreed that it could not be done but that the Bible was not a

---

64. *Sun*, March 6, 1926, 18.
65. *Sun*, March 14, 1926, 19.
66. *Sun*, March 14, 1926, 19.
67. *Sun*, September 25, 1927, 27.

scientific handbook: "The Bible is no more concerned with evolution than with bobbed and shingled hair."[68]

Ruth insisted that a change in mental gear was necessary for a modern person to read the Bible. "Why blame the Bible for not being what it doesn't pretend to be . . . It isn't a scientific text-book. It doesn't claim any scientific accuracy. It knows nothing whatever of modern science. And it is none the worse for that. It is concerned simply with God and the soul."[69]

Ruth often wrote about the nature of the Bible. His basic understanding was clearly enunciated: "The Bible is a record of religious experience. That is obvious. But it must be remembered that God is primarily in the experience. The record is secondary. The revelation is greater than the record." This record is of "a progressive religious experience."[70]

On the question of inspiration, Ruth was strongly of the view that inspiration had not ceased with the age of the Bible texts.

> Can it be that the political enterprises of a semi-civilized people many centuries ago were of tremendous concern to God, and that modern movements involving civilisation are of no concern at all? Has anything happened to Him that He has ceased to reveal Himself?[71]

That there was a strong apologetic thrust in much of Ruth's writing on "religion" was no surprise. For example, he asked, "Are Christians Better Than Other People?" He observed that they should be, but very often what was regarded as Christianity was really "churchianity," a mere caricature of authentic faith. "Some hypocrites profess to be much better than they are—and they are not all in the church. Others pretend to be much worse than they are."[72] Similar emphases appeared in columns such as "Is Religion Revolutionary?" (1925), "Is the Gospel a Guide?" (1925), "Faith and Feeling" (1926), "What Can We Get out of Prayer?" (1928), and "Faith Is a Friendly Affair" (1933).

Ruth evidenced the strong theodicy that he had previously shown in discussing tragedies (such as the sinking of the *Titanic*) in his reflection on the fearful earthquake in Tokyo on September 16, 1923, when some 300,000 were killed. He noted that "a fearful wave of atheism" was said to succeed such disasters, but he insisted that such catastrophes should rather strike a sense

68. *Sun*, October 16, 1927, 25.
69. *Sun*, October 30, 1927, 27.
70. *Sun*, September 1, 1929, 25.
71. *Sun*, September 8, 1929, 24.
72. Ruth, *Playing the Game*, 136.

of awe and impress a sense of "something approaching cosmic reverence."[73] The same arguments were repeated after the disastrous earthquake in Napier and Hastings, New Zealand, in February 1931.[74]

This theme was important for Ruth, and "the problem of pain," as the popular book by C. S. Lewis later described it, was often discussed.[75] In 1927, he gave three weeks to this important subject, dealing successively with "God and Accident," "Divine Share in Our Pain" and "The Purpose of Pain."[76]

Naturally, many of Ruth's favorite theological issues were regularly included. In "Converting the Devil," he showed that there are relatively few biblical texts by comparison with Dante, Milton, and Goethe although these latter have shaped most of the orthodox ideas about the devil. Ruth argued that "the devil has had his day" even in the most conservative theological circles.[77]

Similarly, Ruth regularly rejected traditional notions of hell and everlasting punishment. "Clear Hell out of the way" was his mantra, although he queried, "If we clear hell out of the way where shall we send people with whom we disagree?"[78] As he titled another discussion, "Heaven and Hell Are Now."[79]

Not surprisingly, Ruth rejected the popular understanding of the Second Advent of Christ. As he wrote in his column, "All Adventist programmes have one fatal lack—the Advent."[80] Inevitably this provoked an indignant response from "a believer in the Second Coming" who claimed that the visit of General Allenby to Jerusalem was fulfilling an ancient prophecy.[81]

"Creationist" was a term used to describe himself by a correspondent who foolishly invited Ruth to "deal a death-blow to Evolutionism." Ruth rather invited the reader to change his mind, insisting that "evolution is no more against the Bible than the Bible is against evolution. There is no antagonism whatever between science and religion."[82]

73. *Sun*, September 16, 1923, 13.
74. *Sun*, February 15, 1931, 17.
75. Lewis, *Problem of Pain*.
76. *Sun*, December 4, December 11, and December 18, 1927.
77. Ruth, *Playing the Game*, 149. The quotation is from "Ring and the Book."
78. *Sun*, October 24, 1926, 21.
79. *Sun*, August 18, 1929, 23.
80. *Sun*, January 24, 1926, 17.
81. *Sun*, January 26, 1926, 11. General Allenby (1861–1936) had entered Jerusalem on December 11, 1917.
82. *Sun*, February 22, 1925, 15.

The Churches

Inevitably, much of Ruth's writing on religion included discussion of the churches although some specifically discussed the values and responsibilities of churches. In successive weeks, he explored the questions of what was wrong and what was right with the churches. The clergy were often blamed for what was wrong, as Dickens had named them "right reverends and wrong reverends of every degree." Others rejected the churches, Ruth claimed, because of their doctrine of verbal inspiration, including an insistence on the historicity of "Jonah's strange sojourn within the hospitable whale, and the conversational powers of Balaam's ass."

> Some go to church—just for a walk.
> Some go to laugh and some to talk,
> Some go there for speculation,
> Some go there for observation.
> Some go there to meet a lover,
> Some the pulse go to discover;
> Some wander there to meet a friend,
> Some go, their tedious time to spend;
> Some go to learn a lady's name,
> And some go there to wound her fame,
> Many go there to doze and nod;
> But few go there to worship God.[83]

As for what was right with the churches, Ruth argued that churches stand for the social worship of God and the social well-being of man. Ruth insisted: "To the churches we owe the finest things in our life, intellectually, morally, socially, politically. All the saving, sweetening influences in city, in country, in Commonwealth and Empire, find their origin in the Christian community."[84]

Several other articles sought to demonstrate the value of the churches: "What Is a Church?," "Why Go To Church?," "If Jesus Came to Church," and "Why the Church Matters."

A few articles were devoted to the pulpit. His familiar argument that the pulpit should be "free" was stressed: "The freedom of the pulpit carries with it

---

83. *Sun*, June 10, 1923; Ruth, *Playing the Game*, 159–60. Various forms of this poem have been attributed to C. H. Spurgeon and Emily Dickinson.

84. Ruth, *Playing the Game*, 164.

the freedom of the pew."[85] "Is the Pulpit Passing?" was stimulated by reports from an Anglican Congress at which the Archbishop of Canterbury blamed the decline of the church on poor preaching. Ruth quoted the familiar story of a curate asking King Edward, "What shall I preach about?" to which the King was said to have replied, "About twenty minutes." Ruth insisted. "The pulpit will not pass. Preaching is not a mere profession. It is the expression of a sovereign power. And life is good, mainly because many a man hears and obeys the word—"Go, put your creed into your deed.""[86]

On another occasion, he admitted, "Preachers are a patient tribe. They must needs suffer constant criticism. It is good for their souls . . . Preaching isn't as good as it used to be—and it never was. Nothing is as good as it used to be—when you get to a certain age."[87]

Industrial and Political Issues

Ruth's idea that there was "only one union big enough," the Commonwealth of Australia, was repeated and the evils of strikes were rehearsed as evidence of communist influence. He argued that Christ had defended private property and insisted that communists were against the community.[88]

In the week leading up to the New South Wales elections in May 1925, Ruth wrote a series of five daily columns in the *Sun*, "A Plain Man's Letters," signed "John Sydney."[89] This was just as he was commencing at Pitt Street, which explains the use of a pseudonym, but the content and style, and the fact that they were preserved by Brookes, along with other Ruth columns, confirms that they were by Ruth. They were politically conservative, emphasizing Australia's imperial links and criticizing communism but avoided any specific naming of parties or individuals. They detailed the need for a sound defense policy and a sound immigration program. The final letter offered some clear advice:

> If we vote for a party, deciding not to split the vote, we are bound as Australians to vote for the party, least likely to lend itself to alien propaganda.
>
> If we vote for candidates independent of the party ticket, we must select those candidates who realize the relationship of the

85. Ruth, *Playing the Game*, 214.
86. *Sun*, January 17, 1926, 21.
87. *Sun*, February 16, 1930, 21.
88. *Sun*, August 12, 1923, 13; August 26, 1923.
89. *Sun*, May 25, 1925, 7; May 26, 1925, 9; May 27, 1925, 9; May 28, 1925, 11; May 29, 1925, 9.

Commonwealth to the Empire, and who are seized with the vital importance of maintaining Australia's hold on the Pacific . . .

Ignorance is one of our greatest enemies. Indifference is its twin.[90]

Despite the not too subtle advice of "John Sydney," Lang was elected at this election.

In his regular columns, a repeated question was "What is wrong with Australia?," and the companion piece, "What is right with Australia?"[91] In troubled political years, he wrote about the real meaning of democracy, claiming that its essential meaning was simply "all of us," that its dynamic was religious, and that "its real leader is Christ."[92] He explicitly asserted "that churches must interfere in politics," especially when there has been "a bad breakdown in public morality" and based his whole argument on the failures of the Lang government.[93]

As the Depression continued to take its toll, he asked, "Are We Politically Free?" He claimed that he was in sympathy with the ideals of the Labor Party as "they inspire and colour all my ministry" but defended the formation of the All for Australia League and all movements for political liberty.[94] The following week in "The Crisis Rediscovers Christ," he asserted that it was "impious to suggest that the Church is even remotely in league with capitalism," but you cannot have government without honest men. He condemned Lang for his policy of default.[95]

He was even more explicit in his cleverly phrased address: "To the Capitalists of the Trades Hall and the Workers of the Chamber of Commerce." He appealed to both sides to recognize the nature of property, quoting the famous Christian Socialist Washington Gladden that "Property is communion with God through the material world." Precisely how this would help solve fundamental political differences was not made clear although he did conclude by claiming that "we miss some divinest gifts because we do not sufficiently cultivate the art of distribution."[96]

In a more pastoral column, Ruth wrote about "The Other Side of the Depression." Admitting the hardship and uncertainty, he also asserted that

---

90. *Sun*, May 29, 1925, 9.
91. *Sun*, October 11, 1925, 17.
92. *Sun*, March 8, 1931, 17.
93. *Sun*, March 15, 1931, 17.
94. *Sun*, March 29, 1931, 21.
95. *Sun*. April 5, 1931, 15.
96. *Sun*, July 19, 1931, 17.

there is a divine purpose, "a Divine plan." "Events are charged with a power of development working out a universal plan."[97]

These are all examples of Ruth exercising a public theology. He explicitly wrote about "The Church and Politics: The Christian Charter of Public Duty." His justification for active involvement in the politics of the day is explained:

> When professional politicians cover the whole range of personal and public life with their crude and amateurish policies involving domestic integrity, devastating industry, demoralising society, polluting honesty at the spring, repudiating the very foundations of personal and public morality and then have the audacity to say that the Church should keep out of politics—What should the Churchmen do?[98]

His answer was unambiguous: "We must plunge into the public arena and to do battle for the common rights of man, the common sanctities of the soul, the ultimate decencies of life—or to lose our charter as a Christian Church."

> Churchmen cannot stand gazing up into Heaven anticipating for themselves the rapture of the saints and contemplating for others some post-mortem torture—while the earth is being captured by the enemies of human liberty . . . No Church worth its salt can acquiesce in the secularisation of society, in the divorce of politics from principle. No Church can be satisfied in being what Bishop Gore called "a singularly ineffective ambulance-cart."[99]

Week by Week

Writing almost eight hundred weekly columns posed a challenge for Ruth. He did not preach every Sunday, and even if he was away the column was provided. This remarkable effort required careful planning. Ruth covered a huge range of topics and while many were inevitably ephemeral and were perhaps dashed off in a hurry, most were the product of wide reading and thought over contemporary questions.

Ruth was fascinated by the invention of the wireless and its possibilities for religion: "Of a sudden the universe seems to have become an

---

97. *Sun*, August 2, 1931, 15.

98. *Sun*, December 6, 1931, 19.

99. *Sun*, December 13, 1931, 21. Charles Gore (1853–1932) was an Anglo-Catholic and Bishop of Oxford (1911–19).

auditorium."¹⁰⁰ After his first experience of "broadcast preaching," acknowledging that he was a novice and had never tuned in to a broadcast service, Ruth found it difficult to know if he was communicating. Ruth as a preacher was entirely committed to the new medium:

> The wireless gives his words wings. It enlarges his sanctuary. It annihilates space. It takes him out of his little garden walled around. It destroys his sectarianisms and his segregations—there are no sectarian wave-lengths . . . Words are flung out on the air and the world becomes an auditorium. All space becomes vocal.¹⁰¹

Ruth claimed that he and Canon Howard Lee had pioneered broadcasting of church services when 2FC was "a private station belonging to Farmer's, when church services held a much more important place in wireless programmes than they now enjoy." He noted that as he twisted the radio dial, earnest voices tried to sell him all manner of goods.

> I prick up my ears when the voice says earnestly, "Everything depends on the basis. The basis is what you hold. You must attend to what is fundamental." But almost in a split second I find the reference is not to my faith but to "foundation garments." Not mine.¹⁰²

Ruth did not fail to condemn gambling—"What's Wrong With a Bet?"—and argued that Sunday was "a day for tuning up."¹⁰³ In asking the question, "Is Swearing a Sin?" Ruth told a couple of golf stories, including that of a friend of his who after a missed shot used to say "Assuan!" On pressing his friend, he was told that "Assuan" was the biggest dam in the world."¹⁰⁴

Ruth inevitably commented on public events. The opening of the Sydney Harbour Bridge on 19 March 1932 led to a column, "Dream of Many Bridges." He began, "Suffering somewhat severely from a sort of Bridge-complex—in communion with most Sydney-siders—my virtuous couch has been haunted by bridges of many sizes."¹⁰⁵ The death of King George V prompted a column, "Victorious, Happy and Glorious."¹⁰⁶

---

100. *Sun*, July 15, 1923, 13.

101. *Sun*, November 30, 1924, 19. This theme was repeated with minor alterations in *Sun*, September 27, 1931, 19.

102. *Sun*, September 20, 1936, 13.

103. *Sun*, October 28, 1923, 13; October 21, 1923, 13.

104. *Sun*, August 24, 1924, 13. This was the earliest form of the later Aswan Dam.

105. *Sun*, March 20, 1932, 47.

106. *Sun*, January 26, 1936, 11.

Perhaps surprisingly for the times, Ruth was an advocate of animal rights.[107] But many more of his opinions led to surprises even on familiar topics. To be unconventional was, of course, part of his approach and appeal.

A suitable conclusion to this survey and his unusual style is perhaps well illustrated by his column, "Powdering the Nose."[108] He began:

> I saw a girl powdering her nose. It was not a pretty performance. And it was quite out of place. Not her nose—that was pretty enough. And the powder was probably quite the proper kind, though I did not like the whiff of it that reached me.

By this stage the earnest reader must have been wondering exactly what moral Ruth could draw from this everyday event. He continued:

> She was sitting opposite me at a luncheon table in town. She had finished her lunch. I was just beginning mine. Why should she fling her powder over my plate? She didn't know she did it. She used her little pink puff in just the usual way—she just dabbed her nose with it. And she forgot how nearly impalpable her precious powder is, and how unpleasant it may be—at the wrong time and in the wrong place. She meant it for her nose, not mine. She really ought not to make a toilet table of a luncheon table. It is an offence to taste—and to smell.

But this was more than a lecture on good manners. Ruth proceeded to reflect on the nose, claiming it has been sadly neglected. References to a "nose for news" or "a nose for investments" are not usually compliments. But the sense of smell is surely of great significance, and Helen Keller had suggested that "smell is a fallen angel." She had developed her sense of smell to be able to tell of a coming storm, to perceive the kind of home into which she had entered and to gauge the distance she found herself from others.

Ruth claimed that "the nose is a good evangelist, warning us of evil, wooing us to what is fair and fragrant." As so often, he was able to find a poem to confirm his point, this time from Rudyard Kipling:

> Smells are surer than sounds or sights
>   To make your heart-strings crack—
> They start those awful voices of nights
>   That whisper, "Old man, come back."

---

107. *Sun*, March 2, 1924, 15.
108. *Sun*, October 21, 1928, 25.

Ruth concluded his column, "I have got a long way from the girl powdering her nose at the luncheon table. I started out to do so. I like being a long way from her."[109]

Ruth's last column appeared in the *Sun* after 721 contributions. There was no explanation nor thanks for the writer. As Ruth wrote to Brookes, this came after fourteen years of writing for that paper, and he sadly commented, "I miss my *Sun* contributions."[110] Perhaps his readers did as well.

109. *Sun*, October 21, 1928, 25.
110. Ruth to Brookes, 21 March 1937, Brookes Papers, NLA 1924/48/185; and 20 June 1937, Brookes Papers, NLA 1924/48/188.

13

Adelaide and Retirement Years (1939–56)

ALTHOUGH RUTH CAME TO Adelaide in May 1939 with the expectation that this was only a temporary move, it proved to be the location for the last stage of his eventful life. In December 1937, he had written to a friend in London, "My program visions Pitt Street, then heaven, with possibly a little cottage of rest en route."[1] What he eventually found in Adelaide was a delightful seafront location at Seacliff, but scarcely a place of rest for his fevered dreams.

Ruth wrote to Brookes in January 1939:

> Nothing definite seems to be shaping as to the future. It will probably resolve itself presently into a choice between a suburban church somewhere—for which my city experiences do not especially fit me, and a freelance pen and pulpit existence which in Australia is not promising. A more intensive ministry in the capital cities—with Sydney or Melbourne as headquarters—along lines which we have so often considered—would be extremely useful—interchurch and international with emphasis on the actual contribution Church and country can make to civilisation and would be alluring, but I question whether I can, as Americans say "make" it without a backing which I could scarcely expect to get.[2]

His deep longing for this "more intensive ministry" and this renewed uncertainty account for his extended delay in concluding at Pitt Street. He tried

---

1. *SMH*, July 4, 1938, 12.
2. Ruth to Brookes, 15 January 1939, Brookes Papers, NLA 1924/48/206.

to find a way to commence this new task during 1939. He wanted to leave denominations behind and hoped to speak at a variety of places, including ministers' fraternals and various clubs.

On 2 April he had spoken at St. James' Church in Sydney on "Religion and Democracy" and later in other Anglican churches at Drummoyne and Manly.[3] This address he regarded as "a sort of manifesto," a statement outlining the campaign he hoped to conduct. His talk, however, is full of generalized statements about religion and democracy: "Religion is man's relationship to himself, his fellows and God . . . Democracy is the discovery of spiritual personality and its endowment for the service of the people." He expounded what he called "the freedom of the national soul" and pleaded for "a political equivalent for war."[4] Precisely what his hearers were invited to do by way of response is vague, as what Ruth called a "positive Protestantism" sounded suspiciously like the old anti-Catholic propaganda.

Ruth planned to adopt Adelaide as a "sort of temporary headquarters": "The Adelaide experience will, I think, be a test of my capacities for this new venture which must be considered tentative." He thought, however, that "the Anglican prejudice against non-Anglican clergymen was very strong."[5] If the St. James' address was typical, it is not surprising that clear-headed church leaders should be hesitant. Not all became "Ruthites," as Brookes once called himself when speaking to Archbishop Head in Melbourne.[6]

On his way to Adelaide aboard the *Duntroon*, he had stopped in Melbourne and warned Ivy Brookes, Herbert's wife, against the "Sane Democracy League," which was active in Sydney.[7] He told her that the movement was "violently anti-Communist and all those who unwittingly associated with any who are suspect are themselves suspected." He was himself convinced, however, that there was "abundant circumstantial evidence that the ramifications of Communism do not exclude movements such as the YMCA, the Youth Movement of the League of Nations, the International Bureau, the Victorian Refugee Council, Civil Liberties, the Student Christian Movement, the International or any other Peace movement."[8]

Once in Adelaide, Ruth judged that that city was "only just large enough to be a city, and quite small enough to be a friendly town. There is nothing cold, or even autumnal about the people." The Lord Mayor and

---

3. Ruth to Brookes, 30 May 1939, Brookes Papers, NLA 1924/48/218.
4. Typescript address in Brookes Papers, NLA 1924/48/219.
5. Ruth to Brookes, 13 April 1939, Brookes Papers, NLA 1924/48/230.
6. Ruth to Brookes, 20 March 1943, Brookes Papers, NLA 1924/48/308.
7. *SMH*, March 17, 1932, 8.
8. Ruth to Ivy Brookes, 2 May 1939, Brookes Papers, NLA 1924/48/231.

Premier gave him their blessing, but the clergy were not seized by the importance of a positive Protestant propaganda. Nonetheless, Ruth expressed to Brookes, "I cannot but believe that I may still be of some more public service to the Commonwealth and Empire in a way not possible in a pastorate. Experience will lead."[9]

By July 1939, Ruth decided to release Brookes from any responsibility for his work.

> My experience here confirms my fears (but brings no "jitters") that AD over which I have no genuine control, unfits me for the strenuous campaign for which I had hoped, and in which I must now play 2nd fiddle—but I shall play! I don't think I have as Americans say "gotten" soft but I couldn't stand constant travelling, uncertain lodgings and a homeless condition for us both.[10]

He planned to give at least twelve months to Adelaide, "which is certainly at the moment lending me its ears." He received £3/3/0 for a weekly Sunday article in the *Mail* and five "Everyday Living" articles in the *News*.[11]

So, the die was cast. "It is interesting at my age to be making experiments but I am thoroughly enjoying it, and perhaps my youth will be renewed like the eagles, and even unsettlement has something substantial to communicate to an eager soul."[12] Ruth's "eager soul" was to be tested even more by devastating news on September 3, 1939 after Prime Minister Robert Menzies's dramatic public announcement: "It is my melancholy duty to inform you officially that in consequence of a persistence by Germany in her invasion of Poland, Great Britain has declared war upon her and that, as a result, Australia is also at war."

Ruth was, once again, a Protestant minister in a time of war.

Preacher in Adelaide

Ruth had often visited Adelaide, preaching for both the Baptists and the Congregationalists. Now he had been invited to serve the Brougham Place Congregational Church in North Adelaide for three months. This was an important church, founded in 1860.[13] With its impressive tower looking

---

9. Ruth to Brookes, 17 April 1939, Brookes Papers, NLA 1924/48/230.
10. Ruth to Brookes, 12 July 1939, Brookes Papers, NLA 1924/48/236.
11. Ruth to Brookes, 12 July 1939, Brookes Papers, NLA 1924/48/236.
12. Ruth to Brookes, 12 July 1939, Brookes Papers, NLA 1924/48/236.
13. Lockley, *Congregationalism in Australia*, 175.

out over Brougham Gardens in the Adelaide Parklands, the church was still fashionable and Ruth enjoyed his time there.

He arrived in the city of churches with a burst of publicity. The local press gladly reported his advent and listed his forthcoming sermon titles on the theme "Questions Men are Asking."[14] Brougham Place printed an attractive card listing all his topics from May 7 until July 30 with the note: "Mr. Ruth reserves the right to substitute any question that seems more immediately important on any particular occasion." Ruth sent this card, with a photo of the church's manse where Mabel and he were living, to his friends back in Southampton when he had apologized for not being able to share in their planned centenary commemorations. He observed that Adelaide "is a lovely city, smaller than Southampton and as friendly as an English town." [15]

In June, Ruth addressed the Commonwealth Club, rehearsing familiar themes from his preaching and writing.

> Mr. Ruth is probably the best after-lunch speaker to be heard in Adelaide for a long time. A past-master of oratory, he sent his large audience into gales of laughter with the lighter touches of his opening passages and carried with him to a magnificent peroration on fairplay in politics and patriotism.
>
> We are not in Australia merely an antipodean appendage of Empire, he said, speaking for once with the care of a competitor attempting a tongue-twister at a radio intelligence and spelling bee.[16]

Ruth explained that in his question series, his aim "was not to expound text but to deal with what men are actually thinking and to attempt to find some contact with the Eternal Thinker."[17] His question–sermons sounded familiar notes. "What is God Doing in the World?" was timely as the European news was consistently alarming.

> Always, everywhere, and in everything God is doing the best He can with the material at His disposal. Creation is God's but the human world is a co-operative enterprise . . . It is vain to ask why God permits the manufacture of armaments, why He did not prevent Mussolini's Good Friday invasion of Albania and his bombing of Abyssinia into subjection, Hitler's crucifixion of the Jews, Japan's continued attempt to crucify China. Perhaps if Britain had not disarmed and if America had been in the League

14. *Advertiser*, May 5, 1939, 29.
15. Ruth to Bennett, 14 June 1939, Southampton City Archives.
16. *News*, June 13, 1939, 7.
17. *Advertiser*, May 5, 1939, 29.

of Nations these things would not have been ... God works only through human beings ... Men and nations may work together with God in creative energy, redemptive energy, and in the ministry of reconciliation.[18]

He also contributed a regular column, "Pulpit Replies," to the *Australian Christian World*. These were obviously drawn from his Pitt Street days and were generally well received.

While serving at North Adelaide, Ruth was also in demand for other ministries. Perhaps a good example of his proposed mission for empire was given in his address on "The Larger Catholicism—A Plea for a More Catholic Action" at Maughan (Methodist) Church under the auspices of the South Australian Protestant Federation on May 23, 1939. Many of his characteristic emphases were sounded. Canberra was a familiar target. State jealousies "had resulted in an exceedingly costly and premature, if not superfluous capital city." Another target was "an aggressive Catholic Action Movement," which had "created a militant Protestantism, dividing the Christian forces in a day when world conditions demanded a united front."

> As becomes the citizens of Adelaide, worthy to be considered a modern Athens, you refuse to be behind the times, and will not be stampeded into sectarian prejudice. You spell catholic with a small "c"...
>
> For us to preach world peace when we are so divided among ourselves is enough to make angels weep and dictators and devils laugh us to scorn...
>
> Praying together, working together, Catholics, Protestants and Jews are, I believe, in the providence of God capable of coping with the complex world situation.[19]

A few days later, Ruth was speaker at the annual meeting of the South Australia Council of Churches in Pirie Street Methodist when his topic was "Free Churchmen in the Modern World":

> Notwithstanding the claims of an alien ecclesiasticism, the forces of Fascism, and the menace of Communism we remain Free Churchmen. We do not need any imposing priest, or his counterpart, the political dictator. We are a spiritual and a social democracy. Our churchmanship, like our citizenship, is catholic

---

18. *Advertiser*, May 8, 1939, 20.
19. *Advertiser*, May 24, 1939, 7.

with a small "c"... The moral, social, economic, political conditions of the world today cry out for Christ.[20]

Ruth's interim ministry at Brougham Place was well received. He concluded on July 30 and then began preaching at the evening services for Stow Memorial Church (Congregational) in Flinders Street during August, speaking at their 102nd anniversary services on September 3.[21] Ruth explained to Brookes in November that he could not continue at Stow because he found himself being used to alienate the affection of the people for their pastor, "which would be fatal to the work I am doing." He was not going to make any particular church a center.[22]

Special services also found Ruth in demand, such as at the Violet Memory Day on August 20, 1939. Before the poppy became the recognized flower for war memories, the violet in South Australia was "the symbol of perpetual remembrance." The first Violet Day was held in Adelaide in July 1915 to mark the sacrifices made at Gallipoli. Speaking at the Adelaide Town Hall on August 20, 1939, Ruth commented, "Their memory would be honoured so long as their country lasts, and we must carry on their work and be encouraged by their example."[23]

At the end of 1939, Ruth reported to Brookes, "I am working hard for rather less than the basic wage and really, and truly, finding it fun." Tom and Mabel had finally let their house in Manly, and he was writing a weekly column for the *Mail* as well as conducting a weekly radio evening broadcast, "Nocturne," on 5DN. His daily short pieces for the *News*, which he had written during 1939 and that had provided £1/1/0 per week, were ended, "killed by war news and shortage of newsprint."[24] Moreover, the radio programs were also ended early in 1940 (another guinea lost) after the Macquarie Network decreed that because of wartime restrictions "all unsponsored broadcasts must cease."[25] Thus he had lost half his "assumed working wage" and was extremely grateful for a £50 cheque from Brookes.[26] To Ruth's disappointment, the *Mail* also ended in March 1940: "war space in a provincial place like Adelaide precludes my pen work."[27]

20. *Advertiser*, June 6, 1939, 17.
21. *News*, August 31, 1939, 21.
22. Ruth to Brookes, 7 November 1939, Brookes Papers, NLA 1924/48/243.
23. *Advertiser*, August 21, 1939, 20,
24. Ruth to Brookes, 7 November 1939, Brookes Papers, NLA 1924/48/243.
25. Ruth to Brookes, 23 February 1940, Brookes Papers, NLA 1924/48/245.
26. Ruth to Brookes, 1 March 1940, Brookes Papers, NLA 1924/48/248.
27. Ruth to Brookes, 14 May 1940, Brookes Papers, NLA 1924/48/249.

Ruth continued to speak at every opportunity on his empire mission, at Rotary meetings and on one occasion at the Commercial Travellers' Club where he claimed that "today's true conscientious objectors were Australian soldiers who had gone overseas to fight."[28] His message from the first war was unchanged.

One specific instance of his "Mission of Empire" was held at the Congregational Church in the town of Gawler in July 1940: "Gawler is the only country town to have been given the privilege of this famous pulpit orator's presence."[29] The "crux" of the mission was Ruth's address on "The God Hitler Made and the Gods We Are Making." This dealt "with the war as a conflict of God-ideas and the challenge to Australians to be as loyal to the Divine Leader of democracy as devotedly as Germans are to their anti-Christ Dictator."[30]

A Plea for the Preacher Today

One feature of Ruth's time in Adelaide was that he was able to move freely between both Congregational and Baptist Churches. Old friendships and loyalties were resumed. Dr. A. C. Hill, Secretary of the Baptist Union, was very welcoming. At the beginning of 1940, Ruth spoke at the commencement service of the Baptist College in the Flinders Street Baptist Church.[31] His address on "A Plea for the Preacher To-day" was published. Ruth's mature reflections on the ministry to which he had given so many decades of his life are valuable. Knowing that his time as a preacher must soon end, Ruth encouraged a new generation of preachers and amplified their ministry to churches.

This sermon, drawing on a lifetime of experience, was Ruth at his best, clear and powerful with flashes of humor. Even though the church had become largely irrelevant to so many in the community, Ruth insisted that the times dictated that the church does actually have the solution of world problems. The "outstanding sacrament" of the church was still "the Sacrament of the Spoken Word," and the outstanding need of the church today was preachers. The pulpit is "the hottest place in the firing line in the war of right with wrong. . .The pulpit is our 'altar,' always demanding living sacrifice."[32]

28. *News*, July 13, 1940, 6.
29. *Bunyip* (Gawler), June 28, 1940, 4; July 5, 1940, 1.
30. *Bunyip*, July 19, 1940, 4.
31. The college had no residential facility at that time. See Hill, *Still Thy Church Extend*, 20–23.
32. Ruth, *Plea for the Preacher To-Day*, 1.

Three "commonplace things" needed to be said. Ruth restated his fundamental evangelical beliefs as he insisted that the preacher is first an agent of the evangel, which is "Christo-centric and cruci-centric"—the precise terms he had used when he had first arrived in Melbourne in 1914 and avowed his evangelical identity.

Secondly, the evangelist is also an educationist, "the preacher is a teacher," and he warned against a form of evangelism which was merely an emotional appeal: "It confuses the acceptance of a shibboleth and the singing of a chorus with a change of character."

Third, "the preacher is not only an evangelist and a teacher. He is a prophet." This had, of course, been a marked emphasis of Ruth's own career as a preacher. The prophet's task was "to enlighten the national mind, quicken the national conscience and to insist, in season and out of season, that only righteousness exalteth a nation and that disaster overtakes a people who do evil."

Ruth next commented on the role of the college, insisting that its primary role must always be to supply preachers to the churches, although preachers are born not manufactured. There is a divine coercion in the making of a preacher. The student spends his most formative years in college, acquiring studious habits in theology, ethics, and sociology so that he may preach with a view to a church. But a prospective preacher is "almost at once sadly disillusioned" since "preacher" is the very last thing that he is encouraged to be. Rather he is expected to become "an errand boy to an audience," a sort of bush lawyer to a denominational committee, and struggles with his leadership:

> Go tell my deacons when I'm dead
>
> That they for me should shed no tears,
>
> For I shall not deader be then
>
> Than some of them have been for years.

This is why some leave the church, and the defection of ordained men should demand careful reflection. Were these ones self-deceived as to their calling? Speaking directly to the churches, Ruth made three declarations. First, the preacher should be properly paid: "the preacher who has to fight poverty has no energy to fight anything else." Secondly, the preacher must have time for preparation, and he needs all the time there is: "a sermon is a live thing. It needs time to grow." He spoke at length about his own method of sermon preparation and the time it needed. Thirdly, a preacher must have liberty to preach. He is not a gramophone and must be free to explore the riches of Christ:

> So the preacher must declare the truth, the whole truth and nothing but the truth—or God will not help him . . . Preaching demands brain sweat and sweat of soul . . . Preaching is an affair of personality, complete personality, personality set on fire by God . . . Convictions give him courage. Men of conviction never lack courage.

Here was the secret of Ruth's courageous preaching, laid bare in the hope of stimulating a similar succession of preaching among the Baptists of South Australia.

Ruth sometimes felt that he had perhaps exhausted South Australia and wistfully began looking interstate.[33] However, by the end of 1940, he was determined to remain in Adelaide and in the task to which he had been called. On his sixty-fifth birthday, he affirmed:

> I solemnly renew my resolution to give all that remains of me to England and the Empire believing, with every fibre of my being, that the Christian Church and the British Empire without claiming any divine monopoly for either have the same origin, the same duty, the same destiny.[34]

Writing for the *Mail* and the *News*

This resolution shaped his writing as well as his preaching. He was well known to many *Mail* readers as his *Sun* columns had been syndicated with the *Mail*. Ruth tried to bring relevant insights and encouragement as the war threat hardened. His first column in Adelaide appeared on Saturday June 3, 1939, and the Editor welcomed him as "a distinguished preacher who needs little introduction to newspaper readers," adding, "in these troubled days when ordinary values are being upset," Ruth can "give a lead and solve the problems which beset most of us whether we are religious or not."[35]

A photo of him in his preaching robe accompanied Ruth's first column, which was topical: "What the Churches Could Do." He sounded a call to "all Catholics, Protestants and Jews" and concluded, "Catholics, Protestants,

---

33. Ruth to Brookes, 15 August 1940, Brookes Papers, NLA 1924/48/250.
34. Ruth to Brookes, 17 December 1940, Brookes Papers, NLA 1924/48/257.
35. *News*, June 1, 1939, 5.

and Jews praying together, working together, are in the providence of God, capable of coping with the complex world situation."[36]

An enthusiastic reader commented, "During a residence of several years in Sydney I discovered that Mr. Ruth's articles in 'The Sunday Sun' were read with much interest by adherents of all churches—and even by misguided people who mistakenly considered themselves atheists."[37]

These columns naturally continued with the style and on the themes he had developed across his years in Sydney. After war had been declared, he wrote about keeping calm as "the scare-monger is doing the devil's work." Having recently been in Sydney, "Australia's most vulnerable city," he had been shocked by the extent to which so many of his friends had been terrified by rumors that hundreds of mines had been laid outside the Heads and that enemy submarines were haunting Australian shores.

A reader proposed a provocative question:

> Is it not a sad commentary on present-day civilisation that—after teaching black, red, and yellow races that it is wrong to fight, and putting an end to the inter-tribal feuds and racial wars of the North American Indians, the South Sea Islanders, the Maoris, the Zulus, Basutos, Hindus, West Indians, and others—the European nations are still bent on denying their own gospel and disobeying their own precepts?[38]

Ruth insisted that Britain had maintained all along the line for the maintenance of international justice and peace, and even now had no quarrel with the German people and preferred a war of pamphlets to one of bombs.

Something of a similar theme was developed when Ruth agreed with the essayist and academic Professor Walter Murdoch (1870–1970)—a dear friend of Brookes—who had admitted to being perplexed by the fact that the Christian churches continued to quarrel among themselves instead of agreeing, in the face of common danger, to show a united front to a united foe. Murdoch argued that the real issue was the distinction between Christianity and "a collection of theological beliefs." Ruth continued: "The one essential reality is the spirit of Christ, without which everything else is vain."[39]

The bulk of his articles during 1940, however, recycled old ideas and issues. It was not really a surprise when a hard-pressed editor decided to end

36. *Mail*, June 3, 1939, 5.
37. E. McEllister in *Mail*, June 10, 1939, 9.
38. *Mail*, December 9, 1939, 9.
39. *Mail*, January 20, 1940, 9.

Ruth's features. Once again, however, there were neither thanks nor public acknowledgement of his significant contributions.

His "topical message" was published each weekday in the *News*, beginning on June 12: "If you want to learn some of the true things of life you cannot afford to miss these articles... Protestants and Catholics, politicians, bankers, revolutionaries, and even atheists—all cannot help but be stirred by Mr. Ruth's clever and piercing analysis of the current problems."[40] These daily columns, titled "Everyday Living," were immediate and fresh in style. The shorter format meant that in many ways his messages were more effective. He certainly strove for local references:

> Twenty-five years ago, in my first year in Australia, when I was fresh and impressionable, I said, in my haste, that, theologically speaking, Sydney was 150 years behind, Melbourne 50 years and Adelaide 24 hours.
> Yesterday I heard a lady say, "Adelaide is last year."
> I don't think she was theologically speaking...
> Some of us linger by the old milestones that mark the pilgrim path, instead of marching forward into the advancing light, never doubting clouds will break.[41]

In the week that war had been declared, he argued that "war is not only irreligious now, it is irrational and ridiculous."[42]

A distinctly local note was developed by Ruth. Reflecting on Psalm 121 with its familiar refrain, "I will lift up mine eyes unto the hills," he likened this to "a digger returned to Adelaide from 'blighty.'" At night, "in mystic moonlight, when Mount Lofty shines with something like celestial glory," we discover the presence of God.[43] Mount Lofty will remain: "It is the man who looks up who sees the hills and the heavens—the mountain ranges of reality against the sky-line of life." We are "living in a world of acid discontent, held in the vice of economic nationalism, where every lovely thing in human life is threatened by military megalomania." What can be done?

> The way out is the look out, the look up to the hills, to the unchanging ranges of truths and values and relationships which will always gladden our questing vision, and quiet our perturbed souls and communicate confidence in the day of our need.

---

40. *News*, June 10, 1939, 2.
41. *News*, June 27, 1939, 4.
42. *News*, September 6, 1939, 6.
43. *News*, October 18, 1939, 6.

And, after all, Mount Lofty will still be there when Hitler has gone the way of all flesh.[44]

Ruth's newspaper writings offered a local spiritual interpretation of society and life's issues.

Pulpits and Pamphlets

During February 1941, Ruth was at the Collins Street Independent Church so that once again he was preaching in Melbourne during a world war but without anti-Roman Catholic and anti-Irish topics. His sermon titles included "Why Hitler Can't Scare Britain" and "Hitler and the Everlasting Empire." After a brief interlude back at Seacliff he undertook a strenuous trip to Sydney for a "Mission to Sydney" and was away for three months. One highlight was "a great Anglican rally at the Sydney Town Hall" where he was a replacement for former Prime Minister "Billy" Hughes. This was a meeting to celebrate the 85th anniversary of the Home Mission Society of the Church of England. Ruth had claimed that it was time for the nation to "cut the cackle" and get on with winning the war.[45] He commented to Brookes, "I didn't think that Anglicans had it in them to be so wildly enthusiastic."[46]

His main program in Sydney, however, was to lead a "Mission of Empire," which was described as "A plea for a more vital sense of personal and political responsibility for things as they are and for the shaping of things to come." This involved evening services at St. James' in King Street on October 5 and 12 with the topics "Hitler's God and Ours" and "What Dictators Do to Men." This was followed by an evening service at St. Matthew's Manly and a morning service at St. Mark's Darling Point where he spoke on "The English Church and the British Empire." All November he was at Scots' Presbyterian Church, Sydney, preaching at both services as well as a Wednesday lunchtime service each week.[47]

Ruth maintained an exhausting program. Back in Adelaide he preached at Glenelg and at Maughan in the city while a visit to Scots' in Melbourne was cancelled "because of the Japs," a reference to the bombing of Pearl Harbour on December 7, 1941. He added that "ultimately they will be as sorry for their treachery in the Pacific as Hitler for his invasion of Russia."[48]

44. *News*, October 20, 1939, 4.
45. *SMH*, May 28, 1941, 7.
46. Ruth to Brookes, 28 May 1941, Brookes Papers, NLA 1924/48/268.
47. Details on an advertising card in Brookes Papers, NLA 1924/48/273.
48. Ruth to Brookes, 17 December 1941, Brookes Papers, NLA 1924/48/281.

Prime Minister Curtin declared, on December 27, 1941, "Without any inhibitions of any kind, I make it quite clear that Australia looks to America, free of any pangs as to our traditional links in kinship with the United Kingdom." Naturally, people like Ruth and Brookes did not warm to this new orientation as a supplement or even an alternative to British loyalties.

Indeed, discussion about the Pacific War prompted Ruth to write a long letter to the *Advertiser* in which he asked, "Why blame Britain?":

> While our little Mother Country was being crucified, nailed hands and feet in the cross, crowned with thorns, with great gaping wounds in the side of the body politic, our representatives in Canberra were casting lots for the garments of office, and Australian people wondered ... Now they ask, "Why are not all political parties partners in a common peril?" Old political opponents of overseas service and old advocates of the repudiation of war debts to Britain now find salvation and do good work as Ministers of the Crown ...
>
> We pray that Canberra our national capital may emulate Westminster and Washington and rise above party politics ...
>
> Why blame Britain? Why blame Winston Churchill with faint praise? Why not put our own house in order while there is yet time?[49]

In general, Australian society agreed with Curtin, and a new orientation of partnership with the USA was inaugurated.

Ruth maintained his preaching in 1942, going wherever he was invited, such as Brighton Baptist, and he was becoming a regular at Maughan. Traveling interstate meant leaving Mabel behind, although she was supportive of his mission: "she is a good soldier's wife (take it both ways) but I mean the good wife of a soldier."[50]

At the South Australian Baptist Union half-yearly assembly in March 1943, Ruth spoke on "Politics for Free Churchmen":

> Jesus was not a clergyman but a carpenter who said little or nothing about Church sacraments but a great deal about the natural sacraments of humanity—birth and burden-bearing, living and loving, marriage and parentage, and the art of living together we call politics.[51]

---

49. *Advertiser*, June 28, 1942, 9.
50. Ruth to Brookes, 2 September 1942, Brookes Papers, NLA 1924/48/303.
51. *Advertiser*, March 16, 1943, 2.

He also undertook a ministry back at Collins Street Baptist for April and May 1943. A friend knitted a jumper for Mabel, and the thoughtful deacons sent to her a "love gift" of £15 along with a kind letter:

> Your esteemed and beloved husband has endeared himself to us all to such a degree that it will be hard to see him go, but we must be ever so grateful to you for enabling him to come back to the church of his first love in Australia with his fire, his rich and clear understanding of human nature and Divine plan.[52]

On his return, however, Ruth realized that such long absences could not be repeated. He found Mabel increasingly unwell, and he was reluctant to leave her at all.

At the end of the year, Ruth preached on Sunday evenings at the Flinders Street Baptist Church in Adelaide. Indeed, he later commented that he had been "playing John the Baptist for J. Arthur Lewis at Collins Street and now for Sam Millar at Flinders Street."[53]

He felt, however, that his career as "a peripatetic pulpiteer," as Brookes called him, was nearing its end. Ruth did, however, undertake a trip to Sydney early in 1944, which was "disappointing." He had been unwell with gastric trouble and had a Barium meal and x-ray before he left. In Sydney for twenty-four days, he spent half the time on his back with a sprained ankle. He did have extended talks with several key figures about "the menace to our heritage and liberty and the insidious encroachments upon our Democracy and the grossly unfair advantage our ecclesiastical enemies are taking of the contingencies of war." He felt the trip had been worthwhile, "to keep loyalty alive, to freshen faith and fellowship and to sow seed for future harvests."[54] Brookes responded by congratulating Ruth for all he was doing to combat the "Virus Vaticanus."[55]

Ruth was supported by an annuity fund, which Brookes had set up, but was increasingly anxious about Mabel's health, and he began to wonder about what would happen to her if she were left alone after he died.

Meanwhile, he preached wherever he was asked as well as maintaining an eagle eye for any further signs of Roman Catholic perfidy. One local issue especially bothered him, and this introduced Ruth to the strange story of what happened to Radio 5KA during the anxious days of World War

---

52. Ruth to Brookes, 11 July 1943, Brookes Papers, NLA 1924/48/309.

53. Ruth to Brookes, 17 December 1944, Brookes Papers, NLA 1924/48/335. J. Arthur Lewis commenced at Collins Street in July 1943 and Sam Millar (1911–81) at Flinders Street in August 1944.

54. Ruth to Brookes, 5 February 1944, Brookes Papers, NLA 1924/48/312.

55. Brookes to Ruth, 18 February 1944, Brookes Papers, NLA 1924/48/313.

II. On January 8, 1941, radio stations 5KA Adelaide and 5AU Port Augusta were closed down by the Postmaster General's Department for alleged "subversive broadcasts." 5KA was owned by the Jehovah Witnesses, and as a pacifist group they came under special surveillance. It was rumored that they were sending secret messages on air to German spies. Eventually the station was reopened in December 1943 after the Methodists secured an 80 percent interest in it.[56]

Ruth's special interest in 5KA was in the Roman Catholic allocation of a free hour for a broadcast on Sundays from 9 to 10 p.m.. Moreover, the Labor Party had acquired a 20 percent interest in the station during negotiations about the license for the station and had insisted on time for the Catholic Church. This was all too much for Ruth, who had commenced publishing a series of pamphlets called *Questions Men Are Asking* and No. 5 (which sold in thousands) was titled, *5KA Politically Compelled to Broadcast Rome? A Warm Tribute and a Strong Protest*.

Ruth's argument was characteristically blunt: "A Protestant Church in a Protestant country politically compelled to broadcast Rome?"

> The broadcast of the teachings of Rome was one of the conditions on which the Postmaster General issued the broadcasting licence to the Methodist Central Mission, Adelaide, 5KA. It is a commercial station run for profit. It broadcasts Roman Catholicism without payment. Why?[57]

That the Labor Party should control one-fifth, with one member out of five on the board of the station, offended Ruth. "The generous catholic-minded Methodists have been politically compelled to play their part in ecclesiastical machinations alien to the genius of Methodism." The challenge, as Ruth perceived it, was immense: "Will existing conditions, the compact, the agreement with Political Party and totalitarian Church mean that the tail must wag the dog? The tail is more than one-fifth of the dog."[58] In fact, the Anglicans and Catholics eventually shared one free hour on 5KA.

Arnold Hunt, the historian of South Australian Methodism, noted that the Pleasant Sunday afternoons from Maughan had previously been broadcast by the ABC and that the purchase of 5KA indicates the extent to which the "wireless" was at that time being used for communicating the gospel.[59]

---

56. Strawhan, "The closure of radio 5KA," 550–64.
57. Ruth, *5KA Politically Compelled*, 2.
58. Ruth, *5KA Politically Compelled*, 20.
59. Hunt, *This Side of Heaven*, 354–55.

At the opening of the station Rev. Samuel Forsyth, leader of the Methodist mission, declared:

> We shall endeavour to the best of our ability to represent the Christian Church—all sections of it ... While we are a commercial station, we are not commercial only ... we shall not allow ourselves to be dominated by the profit motive to the detriment of higher things.[60]

The 5KA issue had led Ruth to print an extraordinary number of pamphlets. He not only wrote these but arranged printing and posting from home. It kept him as busy as ever but at least he did not have to leave Mabel alone. During 1944, a lump in her neck had been diagnosed as cancerous, and she underwent surgery and extended radiotherapy. Brookes wrote in support, commenting, "What a beautiful and blithe spirit Mabel possesses."[61] Ruth replied that Mabel was in no pain and regarded the deep ray treatment as "a series of adventures ... Perhaps the miracle for which the Doctor said I should pray has already taken place." Mabel kept the medical staff happy. Ruth reported this typical conversation: "Dr: 'And how are you this morning?' Mabel: 'What's more to the point. How are you? I'm all right, I should be, I've a great God, a fine doctor and a middling husband!'"[62] Mabel was often very tired "but never depressed."[63] Ruth accepted that he would have to give the rest of his days to look after Mabel, or as he called it "The Ministry of Home Affairs."

While Brookes thought that Ruth had "lost none of his old punch," they were both afraid that they were increasingly isolated voices raised in defense of Protestantism.[64] They remembered the glorious Auditorium days in Melbourne. In Adelaide, Ruth was "a marked man in a greater degree"; everyone seemed to know him, and "nuns stop and stare," but the Protestantism of Adelaide "being almost wholly of the appeasement order offers no sort of compensation to the kind of service I am rendering."[65]

Ruth made it clear that he had not involved the Flinders Street Baptist Church with the sermons he had preached there and were the basis of the pamphlets. He simply left his literature in the vestibule. And although the people remained loyal to him, he felt many of them were glad the series was

---

60. Hunt, *This Side of Heaven*, 356.
61. Brookes to Ruth, 31 October 1944, Brookes Papers, NLA 1924/48/229.
62. Ruth to Brookes, 28 October 1944, Brookes Papers, NLA 1924/48/228.
63. Brookes to Ruth, 5 December 1944, Brookes Papers, NLA 1924/48/332.
64. Brookes to Ruth, 31 October 1944, Brookes Papers, NLA 1924/48/229.
65. Ruth to Brookes, 5 December 1944, Brookes Papers, NLA 1924/48/334.

over. "They would willingly do without the larger congregation for the sake of peace." Yet he felt the witness was "more necessary than ever."[66]

A New Crusade: Preparing, Packaging, and Posting

At the end of the war, Ruth had been greatly inspired by a "victory tribute" broadcast by Brookes, but his own battles continued.[67] He wrote pamphlet after pamphlet against Roman Catholicism although as he noted to Brookes this was much harder "without the advantage of platform preparation." Brookes maintained his general oversight of *Vigilant* with encouragement from Ruth.

While Ruth was greatly encouraged by Brookes and friends like "Comrade" W. A. Albiston in Queensland, who ordered significant numbers of his pamphlets, he realized that the majority of anti-Catholics now had a different perspective. As he remarked to Brookes, their own work was free from "the kind of fundamentalism, second Adventism, British Israelism that is the stock in trade of almost all Protestant propaganda."[68] What he perhaps failed to perceive was that one could be a fundamentalist propagandist or a modernist propagandist, but for most neutral observers the product was still largely irrelevant and unpleasantly bitter. What he himself called his "postal bombardment of parsons" was not always welcomed.[69]

Late in 1945, Ruth was forced to admit that "preaching is now beyond me," and in another sign of changed priorities he sold some of his Masonry regalia to pay for printing costs. Mabel had given his preaching gown to a local Red Cross so that they could do something useful with the material. He was also reconciled to never seeing England again.[70] Mabel "seemed to be fading away before my eyes." His only form of activity was his crusade of writing, "which shall have all there is of me."[71]

Friends encouraged him. F. W. Boreham, who was then seventy-four, wrote to him, "You Gallant Old Warrior, I marvel at the survival of the fighting spirit in that knightly soul of yours."[72] Another friend, Presbyterian

---

66. Ruth to Brookes, 5 December 1944, Brookes Papers, NLA 1924/48/334.
67. Ruth to Brookes, 22 August 1945, Brookes Papers, NLA 1924/48/343.
68. Ruth to Brookes, 17 August 1945, Brookes Papers, NLA 1924/48/341.
69. Ruth to Brookes, 29 July 1945, Brookes Papers, NLA 1924/48/342.
70. Ruth to Brookes, 2 April 1947, Brookes Papers, NLA 1924/48/357.
71. Ruth to Brookes, 16 February 1946, Brookes Papers, NLA 1924/48/346.
72. Ruth to Brookes, 17 December 1945, Brookes Papers, NLA 1924/48/345.

Rev. James Gillespie of Brisbane, hoped Ruth was not using up his old-age savings in his attempt to rouse Protestants.[73]

Even though he was resigned to his situation, Ruth greatly missed the pulpit and the platform:

> It is a great experience to serve at the altar of the spoken word, when it is an altar. And the thrill of holding an audience so that, as Mark Twain said, you could not only hear a pin drop, you could hear a ton, is something I should grieve for if I let my mind dwell on it.[74]

His "crusade" was now consciously directed towards the citizen rather than the church. The promotion leaflet defined this crusade:

1. Calling Patriots out of "Civil Death."

2. Providing inexpensive literature on R. C. Demands —uncatholic, unequal, alien to the Commonwealth.

3. Facing the sectarian dictatorship the Papacy imposes in Australian homes, Parliaments and Public Services.

4. Pleading for equal laws and equal liberty on equal terms for everybody.[75]

He once confessed to Brookes that "the fight so often seems like tilting at a windmill" and felt that he was condemned in his old age to several hours a day, writing, packing, posting. "The Crusade claims me—even Paul had his 'bonds.'"[76] He regretted that "the ready power to strike things down red (or white) hot at a moment's notice is now but a memory."[77]

His good Sydney friends Andrew and Florence Derrin regularly offered him a welcome respite. Andrew was a deacon at Pitt Street and one of the Derrin Brothers, who owned a successful chain of grocery stores. They lived in Killara but had a magnificent holiday home at Palm Beach. When they built this, they had installed a special "Prophet's Chamber" reserved for Ruth. They paid all expenses for him to fly to Sydney on January 9, 1947, so that he could enjoy a good holiday, leaving on February 3 for Melbourne where he stayed with the Brookes family and was back in Adelaide on February 5. Mabel, who could not possibly travel, was comfortably cared for in Adelaide: "Mabel and

---

73. Ruth to Brookes, 17 December 1945, Brookes Papers, NLA 1924/48/345.

74. Ruth to Brookes, 28 February 1946, Brookes Papers, NLA 1924/48/347.

75. Ruth to Brookes, 8 April 1946, Brookes Papers, NLA 1924/48/349. Copy of leaflet in Brookes Papers.

76. Ruth to Brookes, 28 August 1946, Brookes Papers, NLA 1924/48/353.

77. Ruth to Brookes, 28 August 1946, Brookes Papers, NLA 1924/48/353.

I continue our race to the happy land with varying handicaps, not knowing which will win. A dead heat would suit us both."[78]

Ruth gratefully took this opportunity. Despite suffering from vertigo, he managed to meet the management of the virulently anti-Catholic paper the *Rock* in Sydney and, vainly as it eventuated, hoped he had "saved their paper from a too iconoclastic type of journalism." He had declined to write a book for them on "Why Didn't They Hang the Pope?"[79]

There were so many pamphlets and letters published by Ruth in this last crusade that details are not always clear. The main ones were sold as packages ("at cost"). One series of ten booklets of "Questions Men are Asking" sold for 1/–, with an additional charge for posting. Then there were "Three Letters Sent to Mr. Menzies," which with the booklets cost 1/6. Other letters were added: to Dr. Beovich, Catholic Archbishop of Adelaide; to Archbishop Booth; and another one to his old foe, Dr. Mannix. Another later offering was an illustrated lecture on "The Bank Monopoly Parable."

The ten leaflets in the package had self-explanatory titles:

> 5KA Methodists politically compelled to broadcast Roman Catholicism? how? why? (1944)
>
> *The Irish–Australian complex: "Spare Rome and Support de Valera": A Protestant Patriot's Reply* [1944?]
>
> *The Irish–Australian Complex? Question Asked by Sir Keith Murdoch: "Do Those Who Carry On The Old Sinn Fein Feeling, Permit It to Dominate Them in Matters Purely . . ."* (1944)
>
> Can We Trust the Papers? Dr. Mannix Claims; Catholic Journalists Are in a Very Great Degree, Responsible for the Adult Education of the People: Stockwhip and Boycott (1944)
>
> Did Rome Prepare the Way for the World War: The Presbyterian Messenger Says So, Why? Australian "Appeasement" (1944)
>
> Why Bother about Catholic Action? (1944)
>
> Is the Papacy Anti-British? Does the Pope Represent Peter? What is the Power of the Priest? (1944)
>
> Rome and Russia: Is the Papacy Preparing for a Third World War? In Australia the Fight Is On! (1947)

78. Ruth to Brookes, 8 April 1946, Brookes Papers, NLA 1924/48/349.

79. The *Rock* had been founded by John William Wallace (1906–79.) The weekly publication mixed traditional anti-Catholic polemics with sensationalist stories of corruption, convent sex-scandals, and political intrigue in the Catholic hierarchy. Wallace lifted circulation to some 30,000 in the 1950s. For Wallace, see *ADB*.

The Money Motive: Cardinals on Parade—Why? An Exposure: My Reaction to the Charge that Decent Australian Citizens Are "Living in Sin" (1947)

"World Arbiter?": Imposing Claim or Colossal Imposition? (1947)

Ruth wrote three letters to Robert Menzies (1894–1978), Prime Minister from 1939 to 1941 and then from 1949 to 1966. These were written while Menzies was seeking to construct the new Liberal Party and uniting conservative forces against communism in an attempt to defeat the Labor Party. Ruth supported Menzies's anti-communist agenda, but was provoked into action by his statement on May 5, 1947:

> The Roman Catholic Church has fought Communism from the outset and—I say this as a Presbyterian—I give it full marks for the fight. Now in the world of industrialism Communism is based on a rampant sectarian brawl. This kind of nonsense illustrates the cunning of the Communist machine which is aiming to split the people by sectarianism.[80]

He advised Menzies that it was the Roman Catholics who were extremely sectarian, and they had a majority in the (Labor) Cabinet, and there were no communists in the House. "You couldn't even have a United Religious Service at Canberra on Anzac Day because Roman Catholics object!" He suggested that Catholic Actionists might be "cunning enough to exploit your fear of Communists."

Ruth picked up on Menzies's aside, "I say this as a Presbyterian," and proceeded to give him a lecture on Catholic–Presbyterian confrontations in Australia. He suggested that as a party politician Menzies was "nursing the Catholic vote—a party political necessity . . . Roman Catholics will use your Presbyterian opinion for all it is worth, and use you too, for their own political purpose and then throw you out like a sucked orange."

Menzies's spirited response was dated June 30, 1947:

> Quite frankly, I am horrified. In your personal letter you say that I hold a high place in your regard. Yet in your printed letter you do not hesitate in the most defamatory terms to accuse me of subordinating my principles in order to secure what you term "a Catholic vote." You then permit yourself to describe me (and it will amuse my friends immeasurably) as "a Scottish Presbyterian with an Irish–Australian complex." Realizing the absurdity of this, you go on to add the outrageous remark: "It is only a pose." . . .

80. Ruth, *Letter to Mr. Menzies*.

> What I object to, and will continue to denounce, is a form of sectarian controversy—from whatever source it may come—which turns away from the teachings of Christ as expounded in the New Testament and falls into hatred, malice, and uncharitableness.[81]

In his second letter, Ruth went through this reply with forensic detail, defending his understanding of the Catholic vote, but it was undoubtedly a case of "protesting too much." Menzies wisely did not deign to respond, having obviously dismissed him as an eccentric bigot.

Ruth supported Menzies in his opposition to Labor's attempt to nationalize banks and tried to develop what he called "the Bank-Monopoly parable." After Menzies had condemned the move as penetrating "the whole structure of life and liberty in Australia," Ruth argued:

> Much more disastrous to democracy than the monopoly of banking—the menace of which I am not minimizing—striking indeed at the very essence of democratic life and liberty is the monopoly of God—"God has given our Church the monopoly of God," to quote the Roman Catholic Press.[82]

After Menzies as Leader of the Opposition made an inspired speech against the nationalization of banks, Ruth sent a one-word telegram to him: "Magnificent!"[83]

Mercifully, the other public letters were briefer and to the point. One was to the Catholic Archbishop of Adelaide, Matthew Beovich (1898–1981), attaching a report that Ruth had sought to have placed in the *Advertiser* but was made to pay for as an advertisement. The issue was the alleged behavior of certain Catholic Action men, who had disrupted a Protestant Town Hall meeting, and the Archbishop's failure to disassociate himself from these tactics.[84]

Ruth wrote each of the last two letters on a single page in his neat distinctive script and had them photographed and made into a block that could be printed. One was to the Melbourne Anglican Archbishop Joseph Booth (1886–1965), who had succeeded Head in 1942. He alerted Booth to the fact that the Catholics were planning to perform "a worse than pagan"

---

81. Ruth, *Second Letter to Mr. Menzies*, 2.
82. Ruth. *Third Letter to Mr. Menzies*, 12.
83. Ruth to Brookes, 24 October 1947, Brookes Papers, NLA 1924/48/369. For a full report of the speech, see (for example), *SMH*, October 24, 1947, 1.
84. Undated clipping from *Advertiser* in Brookes Papers, NLA 1924/48/370.

ceremony of "Consecrating Australia to the Immaculate Heart of Mary." Ruth's question was: "What are you going to do about it?"

His last letter, published late in 1948, was a rather remarkable note addressed to his old foe, Dr. Mannix. "You are a wonderful old man of 84 . . . and I may not be here when you pass." So, he had written this letter, "kind as a funeral oration: and candid." He continued:

> You see, I know you mainly, as alien to the Commonwealth of Australia: associated a generation ago, with blotting the Union Jack out of the Australian flag. And now, I suppose your Ireland's final break with Britain, repudiating the King, which seems to me like flinging another spanner into the international workings—is like a divine benediction on your life and labours.
>
> You are a dominating personality, with dynamic ideas: ideas having consequences with which I am greatly concerned. You promised—threatened—to be the most influential man in my Australian life.
>
> Your priestly opposition fanned my prophetic fire. Your political enmity quickened my loyalty. Your clerical claims rediscovered for me the unclerical Christ. And through you, I met one who did become the most influential man in my Australian life. I owe you that, Dr. Mannix.

Precisely what prompted this note is uncertain. What was Ruth hoping to achieve by having what was cast as a personal letter distributed so widely? Did he really expect a reply from Mannix? Was it an acknowledgment of defeat after a long and weary battle? Surely it was not intended as such.

There is no evidence that Mannix made any response. What is obvious is the extent to which Ruth's encounter with Mannix and all he represented had determined the course of his life. Mannix and Roman Catholicism were still an obsession that denied him the kind of more leisurely retirement he might otherwise have enjoyed.

Brookes once asked Ruth, "Will there be anyone besides Satan and Mannix to worry us over there?" This "did not add any new terror to dying," replied Ruth. "I'm rather inclined to think that, together, we might find Mannix amazingly entertaining."[85]

Ruth wrote to Brookes: "The war horse must be turned out to grass, denied any whiff of battle, forbidden even to neigh—allowed only to get fat!" This appeared to be medical advice, but he added, "Not on your life! I'd rather die forthwith." But he did agree to take care and go slow.[86]

---

85. Ruth to Brookes, 1 July 1949, Brookes Papers, NLA 1924/48/390.
86. Ruth to Brookes, 17 December 1948, Brookes Papers, NLA 1924/48/399.

Ruth was very tired and constantly anxious about Mabel. They had celebrated their forty-sixth wedding anniversary on April 2, 1948. It may be wondered whether Ruth ever recalled his youthful advice on how to deal with retired ministers, including leading them over a cliff!

During 1951, Ruth was able to arrange care for Mabel, and with medical advice accepted the generous offer of the Derrins to fly to Sydney and once again stay with them for three weeks so that he could farewell one of their daughters who was going to England as well as enjoy a restful break. Mabel developed a form of dementia, and her memory faded. By the end of 1951, Ruth commented that her "memory was more erratic—and selective." He added, "I sometimes wonder, rather wistfully, what the future holds for Mabel and me, other than our departing... She does not worry. She is, almost always, happy."[87]

Ruth shared with Brookes intimate details about praying with Mabel:

> Every morning at our little service in Mabel's sleepout, her hand in mine, after answering such questions as "Who called yesterday," "Did I like them?," we read and pray.
>
> When I mention "Winwick" [the Brookeses' home] Mabel tightens her grip of my hand. She knows and understands, she is saying Amen and gives an extra squeeze for each petition for Herbert... for Ivy... and for the family...
>
> If only her mental faculties matched her physical power I should be looking after the dear old Mabel of other years. There is no cure for Anno Domini.[88]

Eventually the struggle ended, and Mabel died suddenly on January 18, 1954. She was privately cremated, and her ashes were interred at Centennial Park Cemetery. Ruth's friend Dr. A. C. Hill (1883–1979), of the South Australian Baptist Union, officiated at the service.[89]

Now, more than ever, Ruth needed friends such as the Brookeses and the Derrins. They did not fail him.

---

87. Ruth to Brookes, undated [November 1951?], Brookes Papers, NLA 1924/48/34.

88. Ruth to Brookes, 1 December 1953, Brookes Papers, NLA 1924/48/425.

89. *Advertiser*, January 21, 1954, 20.

14

Tom and Herbert: "A Religion of Loyalty"

ON DECEMBER 17, 1945, a few months after the war had ended, Tom Ruth sat down to write his annual birthday letter to his closest friend Herbert Brookes. Herbert's birthday was on December 20 while Tom's was on December 17. Each wrote to the other, and there was always gentle ribbing about who had written first as their letters often crossed in the mail. Brookes was older by eight years, and Ruth often joked about who would die first, once insisting that whoever died first should make every effort to contact the survivor from the other side.[1]

---

1. Ruth to Brookes, 20 January 1952, Brookes Papers, NLA 1924/48/420.

Herbert Brookes

In that year, as most years, Ruth reminisced about their friendship:

> Usually I make my birthday an occasion for recalling what we have in common—the same wave-length, a consuming love of liberty, a philosophy, a religion of loyalty and an overarching sense of responsibility for the preservation at the Antipodes of the spiritual reality enshrined in the catholic British Empire.
>
> Always I am proud of your friendship—it is my most cherished possession in my relations with my fellows, possessive as life, light, love are possessive. It belongs to the riches of your memory to be loved by a great multitude as I love you. More than you know bless you on your birthday even as I do in the name of the Father of us all. Recalling what we have in common makes me realize that you excel in things that are more excellent.

Ruth's memory reached back across the many happy days they had enjoyed in earlier years at "Winwick" (the Brookes family home in South Yarra, Melbourne), or at "Penola," their large holiday home high up in the Macedon ranges, or at "Arilpa," the beachside retreat at Point Lonsdale, and in the USA when Brookes was commissioner-general to the USA (1929–30):

This morning I am thinking of the Holy Communion I and mine have had with you and yours at Winwick—your study, Alfred Deakin's Library, the blue room; Arilpa and the altar; Kingboy and Demon; Penola, the Garden of Eden; the Hotel Gotham, Carnegie Hall, Broadway Church, Riverside; on the Comradeship belonging to the breaking of bread—many kinds of bread, being brothers of bread and salt and light. Christ finds His climax in the commonplace.

And what happens to you on the lawn as you salute God and the universe, adapt your liturgy to growing experience, harness the energy of the sun to the expansion of your life and the elevation of your interests into the heavenly places is happening to me now as I think of you, your lovely wife, your family far and near, all the generations of you and of your base in God's world, now and evermore.[2]

The friendship of Brookes has been a repeated thread throughout this account of Ruth's life in Australia. The main source has been the large collection of letters, mainly from Ruth, with a few by his wife Mabel and even fewer by Brookes himself, often in a draft form. That Brookes kept these letters, together with pamphlets and newspaper clippings written by Ruth, is of course suggestive of how significant the friendship with Ruth was to him.

Herbert Brookes: "A Good Man Through and Through"

A brief summary of Brookes's life will clarify the privileged place that Ruth enjoyed through this friendship.[3] When his friend for more than fifty years, Walter Murdoch, was asked to submit a foreword to the biography of Brookes by his nephew Rohan Rivett, he wrote, "He was a good man through and through; I have never known a better."[4] Murdoch identified Brookes's modesty, honesty, and kindliness as key traits.

The contrast between the son of a stonemason from a remote Devon village and the son of a wealthy pastoralist and businessman in Australia is dramatic. Herbert Brookes was the second son of William Brookes (1834–1910), who had made his money in speculative mining ventures in

---

2. Ruth to Brookes, 17 December 1945, Brookes Papers, NLA 1924/48/345.

3. See Rivett, *Australian Citizen*; Patrick in *ADB* (1979); Cochrane, "'Australian Citizens"; Cochrane, "How are the Egyptians behaving?"

4. Rivett, *Australian Citizen*, vii–viii.

country Victoria, founded the Australian Paper Mills in 1882, and left an estate valued for probate at £172,000.[5]

Herbert Brookes attended Wesley College where his sporting prowess was admired—his brother Sir Norman (1877–1968) was the Wimbledon tennis champion in 1907 and 1914. Herbert studied at the University of Melbourne where he was a member of Trinity College and graduated with honors in civil engineering. He at first worked on his father's properties in northern Queensland and then in management of a series of small Victorian mines. In later years, Brookes regularly visited his property, "Brookwood," at Muttaburra in Queensland.

Brookes, however, endured a major tragedy. For some years he attended Dr. Charles Strong's Australian Church, a theologically liberal center where he met and married Strong's daughter Jessie in 1897.[6] Less than two years later his wife died, and Brookes was devastated. For the next three years he was in a terrible state. Alfred Deakin, in the midst of his demanding political life, and also at Strong's church, became his mentor and welcomed him into his family circle.[7] Eventually, Brookes married Ivy Deakin in 1905 when she was twenty-two and he was some fifteen years older. They were devoted to each other and became an extremely formidable couple in the social and cultural life of Melbourne. Their home in South Yarra was next door to the Deakins' home, and Brookes remained under Deakin's influence as his own career developed.

Brookes was serious in temperament, reliable, and well-liked in his business life in which he was extremely successful. He became a director of Austral Otis engineering and developed an interest in the Australian secondary industry. Indeed, he was president of the Victorian Chamber of Manufactures from 1913 to 1917 and also maintained an active interest in the family's pastoral holdings. He was chairman of the Australian Paper Mills and during the war served on several committees such as the Munitions Committee. After the war, he was a valued member of the Commonwealth Board of Trade (1918–28) and the Tariff Board (1922–28). Prime Minister Bruce appointed him commissioner-general to the United States of America (1929–30) where he gave a strong lead to the promotion of Australian interests. His distinguished career in public service continued. He was a foundation member and vice-chairman of the Australian Broadcasting Commission (1932–39) and was also a valued member of

---

5. Patrick, *ADB*.

6. See Badger, *Reverend Charles Strong*.

7. Deakin (1859–1919) was the second Prime Minister of Australia: see Brett, *Enigmatic Mr. Deakin*.

the Council of the University of Melbourne (1933–47). Undoubtedly a rich man, Brookes was, however, unobtrusively generous to friends and employees and supported numerous good causes.

Brookes refused the offer of a knighthood on two occasions. Their family home, "Winwick," became "a sort of international house for imperial dignitaries, society ventures for high art and charity, poetry evenings and musical soirees."[8] Widely honored for both her musical gifts and her charitable work, Ivy contributed to many charitable and cultural groups such as the Women's Hospital, and she founded the International Club of Victoria. Tom and Mabel Ruth were warmly welcomed into their world. For the Baptist minister and his wife, this must have seemed an extraordinary experience, and they constantly reiterated their gratitude.

Politically, Brookes was naturally a strong supporter of Deakin, and although in his early days somewhat sympathetic to socialism, he was associated with the formation of the Commonwealth Liberal Party (1908) and the People's Liberal Party (1911). He regarded Billy Hughes, Sir George Pearce, Deakin, and Bruce as the outstanding political statesmen of the 1900–1940 period and later supported Robert Menzies. He had a strong antipathy to the Australian Labor Party.

While historians have uniformly honored Brookes for his public career and personal integrity, many have been somewhat uncertain when describing his religious beliefs and generally critical of his political activities. Ruth was, of course, closely linked with Brookes in both these areas. They influenced each other, reinforcing some basic convictions even when these were unpopular and created tensions. They shared "a religion of loyalty."

To understand the spirituality of Brookes requires a deeper look at Deakin. Deakin's religious beliefs were an integral feature of his character, and his influence on Brookes was profound. He was greatly attracted to spiritualism, as so many were in Australia at this period.[9] This religion provided an experience-based alternative to conventional religious belief. Encounters with the dead were for spiritualists compatible with disbelief in popular religious claims. As Wayne Hudson has suggested, there was in Deakin "a mixture of disbelief and credulity." He doubted institutional religion but pursued "multiple quests for enchantment and spiritual experience."[10] Al Gabay has analyzed the mystic life of Deakin and confirmed that his eclectic personal religion was integral to his public life:

---

8. Cochrane, "How are the Egyptians," 312.
9. See Gabay, *Messages from Beyond*.
10. Hudson, *Australian Religious Thought*, 27.

> His spiritual belief could be called Unitarian, and it had affinities with the Quaker faith. While he regarded himself as a follower of Jesus Christ, his pantheon of "World Teachers" included also Buddha, Socrates, and Mohammed, and his conceptions had more in common with Judaism, Neo-Platonism and Gnosticism than the Anglican faith in which he was nominally reared. Yet while they testify to the breadth of his vision, these terms fall far short of an adequate description of Deakin's intense spiritual faith.[11]

Gabay concludes that Deakin was a mystic, "if that term be defined by a heterodox world view, an explicit belief in personal guidance, and the operation of spiritual influences on this world."[12] The spiritualism that Deakin embraced undoubtedly reinforced his growing liberalism:

> It was essentially a Protestant religion, but without the pessimism and misanthropy of Protestantism's more Calvinist strains and without the belief in Original Sin ... evil was the result of misdirection or adverse circumstances, and the task of reform was to tackle ignorance and provide the circumstances for individuals to flourish.[13]

Many liberal reforms were derived from this kind of belief, and Brookes drank deeply from this well.

Although he did not become a spiritualist, there was a strong mysticism in Brookes's beliefs. It is tempting to think that he influenced Ruth's theology, rather than the reverse as might have been expected, even though Brookes's beliefs are almost impossible to construct in any systematic way. He certainly had an authentic encounter with evangelical Christianity when he met Henry Drummond (1851–97), the Scottish evangelist whose attempts to link Christianity with science influenced many students. Brookes met Drummond while a student at Melbourne and Cochrane suggests that he became "a Drummond disciple." Brookes wrote, "To have seen him, I have felt ever since, was to have a vision of his Master Christ."

Yet he was by no means a conventional evangelical Christian. He did believe in a God that he called the Immanent Deity or the Infinite Power of the Omnipresent Energy. He never forgot what Drummond had said to him:

> The most exciting situation in the universe is an unsaved soul. Picture it on the brink of Eternity. Tomorrow you may stand

---

11. Gabay, *Mystic Life*, 197.
12. Gabay, *Mystic Life*, 200.
13. Brett, *Enigmatic Mr. Deakin*, 42.

there for the last time—then Eternity. That future hangs upon the present: do not refuse today's decision upon the chance of tomorrow's reformation.

Many years later, he recalled what happened when he had first met Drummond:

> He taught me to give the universe my best thoughts and feelings—only to attempt to interpret it aright when my mind was at its largest and most lustrous and my heart possessed of a wisdom touched with grace. He taught me not to *look* at faith but to live in it and by it.[14]

As Rivett observed, "Here was the essence of the code by which Brookes sought to abide throughout the remaining days of his life."[15]

Cochrane suggests that Brookes was "a creative evolutionist with a spiritual twist" and adopts the notion of his being "a Protestant steward."[16] He sought others to pick up this stewardship. He most certainly regarded Ruth as one such steward.

The key question about interpreting Brookes's political and religious life is how he became such an intense militant Protestant. This cannot be attributed to Ruth's influence although they certainly reinforced each other in this crusade. As Cochrane explains, "In Brookes's mind, the battle between the lower and higher instincts of mankind were now institutionalized or symbolized in the Labor party and the Liberal Party respectively." It was not simply that the anti-conscription cause was the turning point, but it did intensify his criticism of the Labor party and made it seemingly "an instrument of Rome; it heightened his paranoia and his conspiratorial inclinations." It launched him into a new phase of his public life—"a Protestant loyalist extremism in which he was responding to his sense of an Empire threatened from within."[17] He shared with Ruth a conviction that they had been destined for such a significant hour in the history of the nation and empire. It was their joint total commitment to this imperial cause, the "religion of loyalty," that led them to each other and a lifetime of friendship.

Historian Michael Cathcart has concluded, "Brookes was not a democrat but a paternalist. His dream was a generous dream, but he had vicious

---

14. Rivett, *Australian Citizen*, 18.
15. Rivett, *Australian Citizen*, 18.
16. Cochrane, "How are the Egyptians," 307.
17. Cochrane, "How are the Egyptians," 314.

antipathy for people who challenged his vision."[18] The combined forces of the labor movement and Catholicism were at the heart of this challenge.

Deakin would have been horrified by the extreme sectarianism in which his beloved son-in-law became involved. As Judith Brett has concluded, the polarizations of the war destroyed in Brookes, as it did more generally in Liberal politics, "the intellectual openness and commitment to the middle ground associated with Deakinite liberalism." Protestant preachers, with Ruth an outstanding example, reinforced this ideology, preaching "the Liberal virtues of independence, self-discipline, duty, responsibility, loyalty and social harmony."[19]

Brookes and Ruth created what at times must have seemed like their own relatively small fortress of righteousness from which they waged their unceasing war. Along the way, as it were, they became the closest of friends. Some have wondered whether Ruth assumed the role of "Master" that Brookes had earlier found in Deakin and then in Drummond.[20] But there can be little doubt that it was Ruth's dependence on Brookes, not only for practical support in money but for ideological reinforcements through the supply of published materials, that profoundly determined much of their relationship and enhanced his various ministries.

Brookes and Ruth: A Growing Friendship

The first extant letter from Ruth to "My dear Brookes" is dated December 23, 1917. He commented on their mutual dealings with key figures in the loyalist movement such as Dr. Leeper of Trinity College, "A great old warrior, the soul of honour." Significantly, Ruth thanked Brookes for a generous cheque for his church, and while he could not refuse he noted that "the church has no claim on you other than you had already satisfied liberally and I have an uncomfortable feeling that I am bleeding a friend. And I really do not think that blood-letting will do 'those innards' of yours any good." Brookes's generous, at times embarrassing, support of Ruth and his projects was a constant theme.

This relaxed and confident note is characteristic of their friendship as revealed in their correspondence. Ruth's address to his friend progressed to "My dear Heretic" in 1918, "My dear friend," "My Comrade in Arms" and "My Dear Greatheart" during 1920, and "My Dear HB" in 1921 until the standard greeting became "My Dear Herbert" from 1925. Tom and

---

18. Cathcart, *Defending the National Tuckshop*, 123.
19. Brett, *Australian Liberals*, 51–52.
20. Cochrane, "How are the Egyptians," 312.

Herbert wrote to each other regularly, despite the demanding programs they both undertook.

Having mainly only one side of a correspondence is inevitably frustrating. Ruth's script is easy to read, and he clearly took care with his style. The few brief handwritten letters from Brookes in this collection are by contrast more difficult to decipher. Still, it is possible to construct from Ruth's letters a deepening and intimate friendship that embraced their family circles.

What did they write about? Initially they swapped notes about the campaign against Mannix and the Catholics. Brookes helped finance Ruth's publications in this shared cause, although few details are given. On one occasion, Ruth mocked Brookes who was chairman of Australian Paper Mills, "You paper kings are making publication almost impossible. We cannot get enough 'antique' for the two books, and cheap paper (which isn't cheap) is nasty." Certainly, wartime restrictions with paper did make these books look rather cheap.[21]

Signs of their growing friendship are numerous. For example, at Christmas 1918 Brookes gave Ruth a pony. "There is a kindness that makes man dumb. Therefore a gratitude that is speechless. And I have no proper word for your Christmas present." He added,

> When I rode him home my wife called him "Demon" ringing the changes on "Devil" and "Diabolos"—he was so fiery. Now she cannot find a name endearing enough—he is so affectionate. He is splendidly mettlesome but as friendly as a human—there'll be ponies in heaven.[22]

The vision of Ruth happily riding a pony around suburban Canterbury suggests much earlier times. Brief quips such as "You're a brick!" hint at other generous gifts.[23]

Ruth always found Brookes's attendance at his Auditorium gatherings a boost, and he missed him when he was away.[24] When Ruth was farewelled before leaving for his overseas trip in 1920, Brookes organized a collection, sending circular letters to appropriate people, topping it up himself.[25]

Brookes made it possible for Leslie to accompany Tom and Mabel on that trip. He had also provided Ruth with various letters of introduction to key people in England. Aboard the RMS *Mantua*, Ruth wrote the kind of

---

21. Ruth to Brookes, 29 July 1918, Brookes Papers, NLA 1924/48/4. The books were *Wake up, Australia!* and *The Catholic*.

22. Ruth to Brookes, 26 December 1918, Brookes Papers, NLA 1924/48/5.

23. Ruth to Brookes, 1 July 1919, Brookes Papers, NLA 1924/48/8.

24. Ruth to Brookes, 5 September 1919, Brookes Papers, NLA 1924/48/9.

25. Letters and records in folder 1, Brookes Papers, NLA 1924/48.

letter he often had to write. This reveals not only the remarkable generosity of Brookes but also the depths of their mutual regard:

> Among the multitude of men who befriend me there is no man more valued than you. Indeed in the ingenuity that love prompts in service dictated by the sense of comradeship, in personal generosity utterly free from the slightest suggestion of patronage you tower above all. You are I suppose a rich man. You made it possible for me to bring Leslie on this trip thereby multiplying its pleasure a millionfold for his mother and for me. I am a poor man and shall never be anything else. I ought to think of you—I do think of you as a benefactor. But that does not stand for the attitude of my soul to you. More grateful than I can possibly say. Grateful to God for you and for your princely gift. But gratitude isn't the word for the emotion kindled in my soul by the mention of your name and the sound of your voice. You are my friend. I'd share my crust with you. You sign yourself †Herbert Winwick†. You are a lay priest, a proper father confessor. More! You are comrade. And that word partakes of the quality of Christ.[26]

Ruth and his family visited the USA on this trip, and Tom reported to Herbert on mutual interests in both Britain and the Americas. He met many influential figures but only managed to see the secretary of Lloyd George although he made sure to keep his secretary wise about Mannix who, as Ruth reported, "had done the devil's own work" in the USA.

The Ruth family rejoiced in the birth of Alfred Deakin Brookes in April 1920, and Ruth later conducted a dedication service for this last child of Herbert and Ivy. Alfred was regarded as a "godchild" to Tom. Tom and Mabel came to be regarded almost as members of the family at "Winwick" and enjoyed visits to both "Arilpa" at Point Lonsdale and "Penola"—or "The Garden of Eden," as Ruth termed it—at Macedon: "inspiring, healthgiving, joyperfecting." After they had moved to Sydney, they still spent most Februarys on the mountain at Macedon. Even when unable to visit these homes, Ruth imagined being there: "I found myself circling over Queenscliff" (the port near to Point Lonsdale).[27]

The deepest questions of life and ministry were shared. Ruth regularly discussed his sermons and sometimes expressed his frustrations: "Sermon writing takes so much time. I have not cultivated the art of dictation. And the typewriter is anathema to me."

---

26. Ruth to Brookes, 10 March 1920, Brookes Papers, NLA 1924/48/25.
27. Ruth to Brookes, 24 January 1921, Brookes Papers, NLA 1924/48/48.

They supported each other when criticisms were raised. Ruth reported to Brookes that in that week's *Table Talk* he (Ruth) was not a sectarian, nor a bigot, but "a broadminded Imperialist," so he wrote "as one Imperialist to another."[28] At the end of 1922, Brookes established what he called the "Herbert Brookes and T. E. Ruth Account," much to Ruth's delight: "I preach and you practise—a delightful division of labour."[29]

Their exchanges continued after Ruth had moved to Sydney. The tragedy of Leslie's death took place in October 1923 while Brookes was overseas, but Ruth wrote immediately to report their inexpressibly sad loss.

The letter that Herbert wrote to Tom on March 30, 1924, is most revealing of their relationship and does suggest the "Master" kind of perspective that characterized Brookes's relationships with Deakin and Henry Drummond. Ruth was addressed as, "Friend, Scholar-loved, God's Messenger, in Press, on Platform and in Pulpit."

> Even though I can claim to know, in part, "How to be abased," still your affectionate expression of my helpfulness sends me to my knees in gratitude to Him who has enabled me to accept spiritual inspiration from you, and to yield, even though it be for the most part unintentionally, something in return. You do not need assurances from me as to what I think of your message and your work. That I have assisted in your mission to Australia and the Empire is a source of continuing joy to my soul.[30]

This kind of extravagant tribute was a feature of much of their correspondence. Ruth wrote to Brookes in the same month assuring him, "You have influenced my thinking and confirmed my willing mind on following the gleam," and he offered "a hug to my godchild [Alfred] and a kiss for Jess" (Brookes's first child, born in 1914 and named after his first wife).[31] The letters hint at the extreme pleasure Tom and Mabel experienced whenever they were with the family at South Yarra or at one of their other homes. For some years when the Ruths could not travel to Melbourne, Brookes arranged for them to enjoy holidays at the Mount Buffalo chalet. Their family friendship was enhanced by mutual concern for each other's health. As Tom wrote to Herbert in order to thank Ivy for some snapshots, "My divinity is much better," and Mabel soon wrote directly and simply to Ivy expressing her heartfelt thanks for yet another instance of the Brookeses' kindness.

28. Ruth to Brookes, 12 May 1922, Brookes Papers, NLA 1924/48/70. *Table Talk* (Melbourne), May 11, 1922, 10.
29. Ruth to Brookes, 4 December 1922, Brookes Papers, NLA 1924/48/72.
30. Brookes to Ruth, 21 March 1924, Brookes Papers, NLA 1924/48/78.
31. Ruth to Brookes, 21 March 1924, Brookes Papers, NLA 1924/48/78.

Brookes congratulated Ruth as his books appeared. Ruth commonly sent the first copy he had received to Herbert. News of mutual friends, problems and challenges at his churches or other uncertainties were shared with Brookes. But their constant theme was the problem of developing a greater empire loyalty, against Archbishop Mannix, Premier Jack Lang, or any other "enemy," as they strengthened each other's commitment to the cause.

One constant feature of their exchanges was discussion of books. Brookes supplied Ruth with many books as gifts, and he responded with extended comments. Ruth was still doing the occasional review. He was scathing in his response to Xavier Herbert's novel *Capricornia* (1938), which the *British Weekly* had invited him to review. Later considered a literary masterpiece, the novel provided a fictional account of life in the north of Australia. It depicted inter-racial relationships and abuses of the period. Ruth thought it "a ghastly novel, brilliant and beastly, certainly not for Scottish Presbyterians, the brains and backbone of the *British Weekly*'s constituency." In the same letter, Ruth warmly commended Pearce Carey's *Jesus* to Brookes.[32]

They both admired the work of Kylie Tennant (Mrs. Rodd; 1912–88) who wrote *Tether a Dragon*, a play based on Deakin's life that included a character said to be based on Brookes.[33] Ruth wrote:

> At first I feared that a Prize play would prove too theatrical for so sublime and many-sided a subject, but then, I remembered the people who have not read Walter Murdoch's *Alfred Deakin* or *The Federal Story*, with your Introduction . . . and I found they are legion and I found Kylie Tennant with her artistry and dramatic sense had written a really telling tribute to her hero and yours and mine and theirs.

He read her "Explanation" with appreciation:

> This play is about a political problem. Its argument is that Democracy needs a special type of man to lead it, and that such a man is nearly always devoured by the Democracy he serves . . . The strain of harnessing the dragon is too much. There is something really wrong with our body politic when it kills off good men with scarce a pennyworth of thanks.
>
> So I hand myself over to the playwright not only to be entertained, but to be enlightened and challenged.[34]

---

32. Ruth to Brookes, 23 February 1940, Brookes Papers, NLA 1924/48/245. Herbert, *Capricornia*; Carey, *Jesus*.

33. Ruth to Brookes, 20 January 1952, Brookes Papers, NLA 1924/48/420. Rivett, *Australian Citizen*, 209. For Tennant, see *ADB*.

34. Ruth to Brookes, 20 January 1952, Brookes Papers, NLA 1924/48/420.

"On the Same Wave-Length"

Tom and Herbert regularly shared one phrase to express their friendship: they were "on the same wave-length." Their relationship, mystical as well as practical, meant that they felt able to unburden themselves, knowing that the other would understand and be supportive. There are numerous examples of friendship that Brookes enjoyed with many people, such as Walter Murdoch or Sir Bernard Heinze, but for Ruth this kind of friendship seems to have been unique. Perhaps it was also unique for Brookes in the distinctive spiritual relationship they shared.

In Ruth's birthday letter for 1926, he claimed that the kind of friendship they enjoyed was not killed by death:

> That's the sort of thing that death doesn't kill. It isn't dust and doesn't return to the dust. It's divinity that must find a dwelling-place but is never limited to any house a man may lease. It's an open-air thing, one of the ministering spirits of the God of the open air ... I am more than ever convinced that the most telling service on the earthplane finds its inspiration—and its destiny over there.[35]

On the eve of Brookes's sixtieth birthday, Ruth wrote: "If for three days I could monopolise all the airwaves between Manly and Macedon and let every moment be taken with messages of goodwill I could add nothing to my prayers for your welfare and the happiness of those you love." He continued, "The fact that you on the roof of the *Australia* prayed for me in my sick room, letting your faith outstrip your belief is another link in the chain of comradeship."[36] This illustrates that Ruth understood that while Brookes did not hold a conventional Christian belief, they still embraced a spiritual connection. After a "great month" staying with them, Ruth wrote,

> Yours is as nearly a perfect home as we expect to find on earth ... Never has our little home seemed so little as when we entered it, entertaining vivid memories of your mansion, with its magnificent hall, spacious rooms and lofty ceilings—But you haven't our view! And it never looked so wonderful and more blue than it does just now.[37]

Naturally, the Ruths stayed with Brookes in 1930 while he was commissioner-general in New York, enjoying introductions to many church and

---

35. Ruth to Brookes, 21 December 1926, Brookes Papers, NLA 1924/48/97.
36. Ruth to Brookes, 17 December 1927, Brookes Papers, NLA 1924/48/105.
37. Ruth to Brookes, 24 February 1928, Brookes Papers, NLA 1924/48/107.

political figures. All through the Depression years and other national crises, they kept in touch, offering ideas and analyses of current events including the failures of certain political figures, notably "that maniac" Lang. On his sixtieth birthday, Ruth wrote in what had become their customary style: "One of the greatest privileges of my life has been the sharing of your ideals. You little know how you have helped me." He was greatly moved that young Alfred had declared that Ruth was "one of the family."[38]

Ruth gave considerable time and effort to helping Brookes prepare for publication a memoir by Arthur Henry Shakespeare Lucas (1853–1936) who had been Brookes's science teacher and greatly loved mentor at Wesley College.[39] Brookes said of Lucas, "He was the greatest and sweetest teacher I have ever encountered, a great scientist, a truly great and gentle spirit . . . he was wholly unconscious of the influence he exercised."[40] Lucas had prepared his memoir at the insistence of Brookes. Ruth represented Brookes at the funeral for Lucas in Sydney and did much of the negotiating with printers, including suggestion of the title: *A. H. S. Lucas: His Own Story*.[41]

Brookes encouraged Ruth when he moved to Adelaide in 1939. Ruth later thanked Brookes at the beginning of 1942 for his signature on the "Annuity and Survival Policy." He commented:

> And I warn you, in spite of the propaganda of suggestions on your part that I should now ease off a bit, and even of your prayers for the prosperity of your Assurance Association, and the notes of your address at my funeral, cremation or otherwise, which you have nourished through the years, I am resolved that every penny of the purchase money plus interest shall be returned before I remind you, on the other side of the pearly gates that on earth we were on the same wave length![42]

Scandal in "Smith's Weekly"

On December 13, 1941, *Smith's Weekly* published a story on its front page headed: "An Exclusive Circle and Altar in the Ti-Tree." The article was a typical example of the kind of stories that *Smith's* often published. Its name derived from its founder and chief financier Sir James Joynton Smith

---

38. Ruth to Brookes, 17 December 1935, Brookes Papers, NLA 1924/48/177.
39. For Lucas, see *ADB*.
40. Rivett, *Australian Citizen*, 14.
41. Lucas, *A.H. S. Lucas. Scientist. His Own Story*.
42. Ruth to Brookes, 29 January 1942, Brookes Papers, NLA 1924/48/286.

(1858–1943).[43] Mainly directed at the male (especially ex-Servicemen) market, it mixed sensationalism with sporting and finance news. The tabloid was published in Sydney but read all over the nation. Many cartoons and caricatures were characteristic inclusions. It had a special investigation department staffed by journalists with a bent for exposing activities of the elite class.

The opening paragraphs of that December edition grabbed the reader's attention:

> Spectacle of some of Australia's most prominent socialites and clergymen burning a fire before the sacrificial altar of a virgin Roman goddess has amazed the villagers of Point Lonsdale, sleepy Victorian seaport resort.
>
> "Vestal" Socialites whose names are on Plaques.
>
> Hidden in ti-tree groves at Port Lonsdale is an altar to Vesta, Roman Goddess of the Earth.
>
> The altar is on the property of the Herbert Brookes, leaders of exclusive Melbourne society.
>
> Despite "No Trespassing" signs, villagers did not take long to find the altar—a rock cairn in the center of a mysterious circle, cleared in the scrub.
>
> At times dense smoke arising from around the altar, and visible at some distance, led to speculation in Point Lonsdale.
>
> What strange rites were proceeding?
>
> Villagers talked about the altar in whispers because it was found on the property of very important people.

After giving brief accounts of Herbert and Ivy, the writer snidely observed, "It is not necessary to add that the aura of intense respectability would submerge any suggestion of paganism were such to be associated with the altar in the ti-tree." On surrounding trees, the report added, were small plaques, each of which bore a name. The seventeen names were duly published, including five women titled "vestal," together with some familiar names including Rev. W. Albiston, Rev. T. E. Ruth, and A. H. S. Lucas. Details of each name were given such as: "Sydney knows the Rev. T. E. Ruth who was the leading Congregationalist Minister, and a prominent publicist."

Smith's naturally sought an explanation of these strange goings-on. Mrs. Brookes was quoted as commenting, "Really, it is nothing . . . We have many guests at our Point Lonsdale place, and we like to commemorate their visits." As to the altar and its surrounds, it is "a pleasant place to sit and read and talk." Asked about why some ladies were designated "Vestals," Ivy laughed,

---

43. For Smith, see *ADB*.

"Well, a sort of joke, more or less." As to the fire, "We burn the grass-tree clumps there sometimes. They smell so nice, you know."

The article then described Vesta, the Roman goddess, the sacred fire that burned in the sanctuary and the Vestal Virgins who were consecrated to the service of Vesta. Point Lonsdale was described as "the playground of the rich."[44]

Certainly, Brookes loved this kind of ceremony. Rivett has described another ceremony Brookes conducted:

> He took a boyish delight in the investiture of friends he admired at what he came to call the Ceremony of the Laurel at Macedon. At his ceremony, usually in front of an augmented house party of about twenty, he would give a short address on the work and services of the chosen individual and his wife. Then with quiet good humour and a twinkling eye, he would press down on their crowns and foreheads a circlet of laurel leaves prepared only that morning from the tree behind the house by his daughter Jessie, her great friend, later his daughter-in-law Peggy Sawrey and other womenfolk. The final stage of the ceremony came when the laurelled hero, like some Roman triumpher of old, rose to his feet and descanted upon his work and strivings.[45]

Sunday gatherings at "Penola" on Mount Macedon were held outdoors whenever possible. The service lasted no more than thirty minutes and could include Bible readings and prayers if a minister, such as Ruth, was present. "It was mainly memorable for the superb reading from his favourite thinkers, philosophers and poets by the host himself. Henry Van Dyke, Francis G. Peabody, Phillips Brooks, James Martineau and Henry Drummond were especially favoured."[46]

The Brookes family was doubtless annoyed by the scandalous "exposure" of their activities at Point Lansdale, but it caused further problems for Ruth, whose name adorned one plaque hanging from the trees. His old adversary, the fiery fundamentalist and Adventist Baptist minister William Lamb, in his paper the *Advent Herald*, expressed his objection to the idea that any minister of religion should be concerned with any apparent resuscitation of Roman goddesses. Albiston wrote a fiery response, demanding an apology and threatening legal action.[47]

---

44. *Smith's Weekly*, December 13, 1941, 1–2.
45. Rivett, *Australian Citizen*, 153.
46. Rivett, *Australian Citizen*, 151.
47. *Smith's Weekly*, March 7, 1942, 7.

Tom immediately wrote to Herbert with a draft letter of which he asked him to have two copies typed and posted. A friend had written to Ruth, urging him to "treat Brother Lamb gently. He is getting old but not mellow." Ruth commented, "Poor fellow. I was moved to write it. He may not be able to appreciate it but it cleanses my mind from any bitterness."[48]

Brookes responded, suggesting that Lamb had seized upon the story without checking on it in order to lambast Ruth for having differences over the Second Advent: "poor devil, what an unconscious mind he must have."

Brookes understood that Ruth as a minister "could not permit the libel to go unnoticed and the libeller to go scot free." He reflected on how Henry Van Dyke, whose poem "God of the Open Air" had influenced them both so much, "would cheer you and deplore this misguided attack on the attempt to deny spots outside the churches where the 'God of the Open Air' can be worshipped."

> If they had heard of the Penola services they would have said something equally scathing about that elevated garden paths where we foregathered for the same purpose. And all this at a time when the very existence of the Christian religion and the Christian ethic is being challenged by the powers of darkness and barbarians.
>
> Dear old Tom we are up against it now in deadly earnest, and your expression of your faith in the ultimate triumph of goodness from your pulpits will be a comfort and a strength to your congregations.[49]

Ruth's response to Lamb, headed "Ecclesiastical War," duly appeared in *Smith's Weekly*:

> I know nothing of "the smoking Roman altar, with its vestal ladies." I never heard of it until recently, though apparently the experience is over twenty years ago. You have been misled by a fantastic newspaper article, which carries its falsehood on its face, as you will see plainly if you read it again.
>
> I find it rather difficult to be solemn about it or to regard it seriously. But to remove misunderstanding I do solemnly and sincerely declare:
>
> First. There never has been any "spectacle" of some of Australia's most prominent socialites and clergymen burning a fire before the sacrificial altar of a virgin Roman goddess.
>
> Second. There is no such sacrificial altar.

---

48. Ruth to Brookes, 17 February 1942, Brookes Papers, NLA 1924/48/287.
49. Brookes to Ruth, 20 February 1942, Brookes Papers, NLA 1924/48/288.

Third. There are no altar plaques.

Fourth. The mythical association of a virgin Roman goddess is merely the creation of a wandering journalist's perverted imagination.

Fifth. No more mystery attaches to that clearing in the scrub or to that cairn of stones, than to any flower-bed in your garden, any rockery in your suburban street, or any memorial in your cemetery.

There is a cairn of rough stones, as in other gardens at Point Lonsdale, on which clumps of grass-tree roots are sometimes burned.

The kindly host, who is a poet and philosopher as well as a man of affairs, has a whimsical mind and keeps a record of some of the scores of visitors by writing their names on such labels as gardeners use and tying them to the tea-trees.

It was over twenty years ago, when I was last a guest in that Point Lonsdale home, that my name was labelled.

That is all the truth that there is in the story . . . I know that when you wrote you were misled by a false report, and I have, at least, removed that misunderstanding.[50]

The paper interspersed reactions to Ruth's claims in its publication of his letter to Lamb. Ruth told Brookes that he was prepared for *Smith's* "to carry on after their publication of my personal letter to Mr. Lamb. Now I think it better to ignore them."[51]

He did, however, draft a letter to the editor, which he did not post but sent the draft to Brookes. Ruth began by claiming that this was "a simple appeal from one British Australian to another." He even suggested that their article was an example of "exact Nazi technique," such as invading private property, following the lines of *Mein Kampf*: "the bigger the lie the better," and accusing the victims of having started the war. But in fact, he suggested that *Smith's* "know the British way of playing the game." Criticizing the paper for printing what was a private letter without permission, he proceeded to make several rather pedantic observations. "You would know it to be false if you knew the people or the place."

He concluded: "You and I do not believe in the infallibility of print. We know newspaper men make mistakes. And I am asking you to do the decent thing, be British, acknowledge that you were mistaken . . . You would not lose caste. You would gain respect.[52]"

---

50. *Smith's Weekly*, March 7, 1942, 7.
51. Ruth to Brookes, 14 March 1942, Brookes Papers, NLA 1924/48/292.
52. Ruth to Brookes, 13 March 1942, Brookes Papers, NLA 1924/48/293.

Ruth was wise not to have actually sent this letter, which would have inevitably prolonged the issue and provoked mockery of his pleas. However, the crude criticisms of what happened at "Arilpa" seem to have influenced some historians. Edmund Campion, for example, describes Brookes building an altar at his home and conducting "Lawrentian sunrise services of his own devising."[53]

Another Crisis

A major crisis faced the Brookes family in 1949 when their son Alfred became seriously ill. Ruth sent a telegram to Ivy, "Am with you all the time, vainly yearning for some vicarious way of suffering reasoning with the Eternal that it would be so much better for me to take Alfred's place. God communicate strength and courage to you all." Tom wrote to Herbert:

> Somehow our dearest and deepest desires find their real expression when we really pray—and prayer is so much more than verbiage, that the spirit maketh intercession with groanings that cannot be uttered: your intercessions have been mainly of that kind lately, I expect. So have mine.

Ruth adopted something of a messianic role, observing that he had experienced something akin to Gethsemane,

> a wrestling with the Unseen, a vital "I will not let Thee go, unless"—strong determination, alternating with deep dark despair, praying that the cup might pass from you, earnestly offering to drink it myself instead, arguing with the Eternal that I was at the end of things here, that Alfred was at the beginning, his gifts full of promise of rare service to his day and generation.[54]

More days passed. Tom and Mabel inevitably recalled the loss of their beloved Leslie. On November 29, Ruth wrote,

> Literally day and night we are praying for Alfred and all of you, but all the other side seems to say is "Be still and know that I am God" ... And here I am, Herbert, writing to the man I love, with nothing to say. I've said it all in the soul of me these many weeks,

---

53. Campion, *Rockchoppers*, 86. This suggests the atmosphere of services Brookes conducted, but it may be noted that there is no evidence that Brookes was in any way influenced by D. H. Lawrence's writings.

54. Ruth to Brookes, 14 November 1949, Brookes Papers, NLA 1924/48/395.

> to God. And my soul is with your soul. And God is with you all. And God is all, <u>not minus man</u>!⁵⁵

Thankfully, to the relief of both families, Alfred recovered and went on to a distinguished public service career, becoming the first head of the Australian Secret Intelligence Service, living until 2005.

At the end of that stressful year, Tom wrote his usual birthday letter to Herbert. The intimacy of past years was maintained:

> I'm not dead yet. I'm still young enough to appreciate the kind things you say about my career. But "not half has ever been told." And <u>you</u> couldn't tell it, Herbert. That other half <u>is</u> you. You are the one who <u>did</u> become the most influential man in my Australian life, as I wrote Dr. Mannix without mentioning your name. In every place and in every phase of my ministry in all the main things you say about me you have been and are that "most influential man."
>
> I did a good deal of Auditorium work before we met. But you meant a world of difference to me and mine. We see Leslie on Kingboy! And, but for you, Leslie would not have gone to England and America in 1920. Memory associates "Whynbush" with Winwick, Arilpa, Penola and "View Point, Manly" with the Hotel Gotham in Fifth Avenue, and what Mabel still calls "the most wonderful eleven days of her life" . . .
>
> But it is of the bigger broader deeper higher associations that I'm really thinking—I see you saluting the Eternal and His Universe as you take all the regular and irregular steps in Freemasonry, rounding the Square as you pace the garden swinging your arms and legs and cane as though you were conducting the music of the sphere and putting every muscle in your body and every thought of your mind and every desire of your soul into the worship of the Lord your God . . .
>
> At Point Lonsdale you built an altar to the God of the open air, which ignorant men of evil intent derided and degraded . . .
>
> All the time, Herbert, in the vital New Testament sense, you are a priest, making an altar, anywhere—the Winwick garden, Arilpa stones, Mt. Macedon glades and cathedral trees, breathing awe and inspiring poetry of praise.⁵⁶

---

55. Ruth to Brookes, 29 November 1949, Brookes Papers, NLA 1924/48/396.

56. Ruth to Brookes, 17 December 1949, Brookes Papers, NLA 1924/48/399. "Whynbush" in Burke Road, Kew, was the home of Dr. H. Moore of the Collins Street Church.

Every year's birthday letters contained similar sentiments. The friendship of Tom and Herbert ran very deep, and they took care to rehearse just how much each owed the other. These intensely personal letters offer valuable insights into a relationship that was deeply significant for both men.

Last Days

Ruth's last years in Adelaide were a great strain, especially during Mabel's decline. He once commented, "In our loneliness of family life we have only each other in Australia."[57] Brookes arranged for a lady to help with domestic tasks two mornings a week. Mabel called these "Ivy and Herbert days."[58] The sad day came when Mabel died, and with no family in Australia Tom was then on his own.

Much older than Tom, Herbert was increasingly restricted as to what he could do for his friend by this point. However, he contributed greatly to support Menzies and the return of a Liberal government. He also gave countless hours to assist with the preparation of a fine biography of Deakin by J. A. La Nauze. Brookes continued to be greatly honored in the community and died at the age of ninety-five on December 1, 1963.[59] Ivy continued in public life and died on December 27, 1970. Both were buried in St Kilda cemetery.

After Mabel's death in 1954, it was apparent that Tom could not manage on his own. Details about his last years are found in letters that his Sydney friends wrote to Herbert. On one earlier occasion when Tom and Mabel were enjoying a holiday with the Derrin family at their Palm Beach holiday home, Mabel became unwell. She then told Tom that if anything should happen to her, he should go straight to the Derrins, and this became the family's understanding. When Mabel died, Florence Derrin sent him a telegram, "Come Home!" She traveled to Adelaide to see what he wanted to do and found he was a resident at "Illoura," the Baptist Home for the Aged in Norwood (opened in March 1949).[60] Florence commented that the home "for a place of that type was not too bad" but she felt that Tom was entirely "out of his element and I felt he could not possibly stay on there alone and be happy." After due consideration, Tom agreed to come to the Derrins, who lived in Killara on Sydney's North Shore.[61]

57. Ruth to Brookes, 17 December 1947, Brookes Papers, NLA 1924/48/371.
58. Ruth to Brookes, undated [1951?], Brookes Papers, NLA 1924/48/34.
59. La Nauze, *Alfred Deakin*.
60. Hill, *Still Thy Church Extend*, 93.
61. F. Derrin to Brookes, 1 June 1956, Brookes Papers, NLA 1924/48/438.

For the first six months, everything went well, but he "had no inclination to write." Florence then agreed to accompany her father on a last trip to England. While she was away, Tom wrote fairly regularly but there were signs that he was failing. Then he "must have had some mental decline quite suddenly," because he left the house without anyone knowing and as they later learned, "took the train to Lindfield where he was seen wandering about, and then to town where he was finally found at night and taken to the Clarence Street Police Station." Fortunately, he remembered who he was, and the police rang the Pitt Street Church where a meeting happened to be in progress, and the Rev. A. P. Campbell (a friend of Tom's), took charge.[62]

For the next three months he was in a private nursing home at Gordon. "Nellie," another mutual friend of Tom and Herbert, who lived in Gordon, reported that an old friend, Dr. Barling, helped get Tom into the home at Gordon, insisting that he must not be allowed to live in a private home again, nor to travel.[63] Tom was "very exhausted." He had a good big room, but "being with three other elderly men he does miss the privacy of his own room." He sent his love to Herbert. "Because he wandered so alarmingly the nurses could not cope with him in a single room. The Nursing Home is always wide open and there is no space between it and the road, so that anyone who wanders can easily disappear without being noticed."[64]

It is evident that various ministers and other Sydney friends did what they could for Ruth. He enjoyed talks but almost immediately forgot all about them, as Nellie reported. Reminiscences about Herbert and his family were a constant feature and he enjoyed letters that came to him. Ruth asked Nellie to tell Herbert, "I'm still keeping the flag flying and I'm emphasising more than ever the catholicity of the faith." He generally retained his sense of humor, "joking about his clothes and the restrictions of hospital."[65]

Knowing that Tom could not write, Herbert arranged for a lady to visit him and take a dictated letter from him.[66] Tom had been moved to another more satisfactory place at Killara where, when Florence returned from overseas, she found him "a shadow of his old self."

Florence very simply and movingly told Herbert about Tom's last days in April 1956:

---

62. F. Derrin to Brookes, 1 June 1956, Brookes Papers, NLA 1924/48/438.
63. "Nellie" was Eleanor Harriet Rivett (1883–1972), a former missionary with the LMS to India. See *ADB*.
64. "Nellie" to Brookes, 4 March 1955, Brookes Papers, NLA 1924/48/426.
65. "Nellie" to Brookes, 5 May 1955, Brookes Papers, NLA 1924/48/429.
66. A. Chortley to Brookes, 7 June 1955, Brookes Papers, NLA 1924/48/430.

The matron took great care of him and he slowly lost that dazed, vacant expression, and I took him for a drive every other day. But he was so thin and tottery, could hardly lift his foot and put it in front of the other until I took his arm and he suited his paces to mine for a few steps. His memory played tricks with him and he never knew what day it was. Even past events were hazy and at one stage he was very worried because he thought his mother was alive and he had sent her no money.

On the other hand your letter was received with great glee and he remembered all about you both and the ups and downs of your family affairs, and sympathized with you although he could not collect his thoughts sufficiently to convey them in writing.

Friends took him to church here most Sunday mornings, and he derived great pleasure from going. He was well enough to come home and spend Christmas with us, but got very tired. We are a large family when we are all together, so I took him back during the afternoon and put him to bed.

It was very pitiful and sad watching helplessly while a great mind slowly faded, cerebral anaemia. But the end came quickly. The last drive I took him was down to Church Point . . . and all the old haunts, and [he] said what a lovely run it had been and how he had enjoyed it.

He spent a week in bed, fretting to get up and out, and the second week collapsed into a coma from which he did not recover, dying at 6 o'clock on the Thursday evening . . .

Now after two months I cannot realize he has gone, so much of my time was spent with him and I feel a deep loneliness. He was a marvellous friend.[67]

Possibly the greatest tribute to Ruth is that he was able to develop such extraordinary friendships with people like the Brookes and Derrin families.

A private service was held in Killara led by Rev. C. D. Ryan, the minister at Killara Congregational Church, and Ruth's friend Rev. A. P. Campbell. Florence Derrin found this "a great help and comfort," while a memorial service was held at Pitt Street at which Campbell spoke: "T. E. Ruth with his voice and with his pen stood boldly as an advocate of civic and religious liberty."[68]

Rev. Gordon Powell (1911–2005) wrote a brief obituary for Ruth along with one for Rev. J. McLeod, formerly his predecessor at St. Stephen's in Macquarie Street. Headed "Two Great Preachers," Powell claimed that both

67. F. Derrin to Brookes, 1 June 1956, Brookes Papers, NLA 1924/48/438.
68. *SMH*, April 21, 1956, 9.

of them "had profoundly influenced the religious life of Australia." Powell suggested that Ruth "deliberately emulated Lloyd George and spoke as much with his limbs as with his voice."[69]

Both Baptists and Congregationalists noted Ruth's death but a new generation had emerged. There were, however, many who would have echoed the sentiment of Florence Derrin: "I am now trying to forget the frail old man and to remember him as he was, for he said to me only a month before he died, 'Don't remember me as I am now but remember me at my best.'"[70]

---

69. *SMH*, April 21, 1956, 9.
70. F. Derrin to Brookes, 1 June 1956, Brookes Papers, NLA 1924/48/438.

CONCLUSION

"Remember Me at My Best"

T. E. Ruth's understandable request to his kind friend Florence Derrin that she should remember him, not as a frail old man, but at his best, is not an option available to a responsible biographer. There were many events that showed Ruth at his best, but there were other times when, with the advantage of hindsight, it must be judged that he was not at his best.

Life contained numerous moments of high expectation for Ruth. Although he came from an obscure family situation in Devon, his rise to prominence in the English Baptist movement and the Free Churches more generally provoked a widespread optimism about his future. Certainly, he never lacked confidence, and his faith in Christ, so central to him for all his days, strengthened this natural temperament. During those early days, key mentors encouraged him. The Baptist church in Exeter recognized his preaching gifts and supported him for ministerial training at Bristol College where Principal W. Henderson became a lifelong mentor.

Denominational leaders like Dr. John Clifford, who invited the young Ruth to become his associate minister, and J. H. Shakespeare, denominational leader and respected advocate of unity among all the Free Churches, strongly encouraged him. They became Ruth's models for all that was good about Baptist life in England. Shakespeare also invited him to contribute to the denominational paper the *Baptist* Times which helped develop Ruth's career as a religious writer.

Ruth was almost immediately recognized as "a rising star" in the denomination. In the Baptist tradition, this first of all demands a successful ministry in a local church, and Ruth began with spectacular success at Portland where he also married his wife Mabel. At the same time, he was initiated into the political life of Nonconformity where he acquired a reputation, and his later career as a strident platform speaker began in those early days. He similarly rose to some fame, despite reservations about his ebullient speaking style, as a debater in both Baptist and Free Church circles. His career in the important civic center of Liverpool so enhanced his reputation that he attracted the attention of denominational figures, and this led to his appointment to Collins Street in Melbourne.

That church's two immediate predecessors, Samuel Pearce Carey and F. C. Spurr, had returned to Britain with widespread denominational recognition and influence. It must have seemed an appropriate move for the ambitious and prodigiously talented young minister. Ruth's physical appearance and speaking style, it was often noted, bore a striking resemblance to that renowned political speaker David Lloyd George.

Ruth's career in England as minister, preacher, platform debater, and religious writer undoubtedly would have been a part of the "best" for which he hoped to be remembered. Yet he received inevitable criticisms in these roles. Each of the three English churches he served felt that he had left somewhat prematurely. But the fact that he was called to this significant pastorate in Australia confirmed that he was highly regarded throughout the denomination. To move from England, where the relatively large denomination embraced a variety of theological views, to a smaller and more conservative denomination in another country, was a larger challenge than the young Ruth could have anticipated.

The new location, however, remained his home for the rest of his days. He announced himself as an evangelical preacher who was also an "apostle of reunion," an enthusiast for church union just like Shakespeare. But in Australia, this advocacy was met with suspicion and criticism. Collins Street Church, however, was soon crowded with hearers. Ruth's provocative and often aggressive response to some conservative critics, such as the Adventist preacher William Lamb, made him inevitably a figure of controversy. Through his days, he always reacted sharply to personal criticisms.

Ruth was scarcely established in his new pastorate when World War I erupted. The next few years changed his life. He immediately and consistently demonstrated his intense loyalty to the British Empire and, like many Protestant preachers, defended the righteousness of the war cause, calling on Australians to enlist in the armed forces. He was forever afterwards deeply moved by the sacrifices of the Anzacs. At the same time, he was called on to lead his own congregation through the challenges of wartime and the inevitable grief and loss that many endured. These experiences seem to have intensified his attitude to death. He insisted that death was not "a terminus" but a thoroughfare to a richer and fuller experience. Moreover, his encouragement to pray for the dead may have comforted many but aroused suspicion and even hostility from conservative Protestants.

However, Ruth's characterization by opponents and press as an "imported sectarian bigot" undoubtedly haunted him for the rest of his life. He had previously advocated church union, but this only included catholics "with a small c," and his exposure to the political ambitions of Catholics in Australia, especially when fused with Sinn Feinism, added the offence of disloyalty to Ruth's horror of Roman dogma. He studied Roman Catholic teachings and practices in a series of Auditorium addresses, which were also published. Those exciting and demanding days with huge numbers of supporters and vigorous opponents intensified his profile as a leader among political anti-Catholic figures. His call to *Wake up, Australia!* reflected the obsession that had captured him.

Ruth's work as a Protestant agitator extended beyond the fevered war years of Melbourne into his later life. He most probably imagined that this campaign occurred in the best years of his life, although few back in Britain could have anticipated this twist in his public life and theological interests. He had become a virulent Protestant, and it was the Australian scene that had changed him.

Ruth did try to move beyond his anti-Catholic rhetoric and agitations to advance some more generalized civic ideals as he published another series of lectures, *The Common Weal*, in 1918. He advanced a claim to be thought of as a "public theologian": his speeches and sermons attracted considerable public attention and provoked some helpful discussion of what it meant to live in a true democracy. He wrote an imaginative "creed" and a "decalogue" about being Australian.

The problem was that he had come to be primarily regarded as a Protestant extremist. Those who were Catholic or opposed to extremism of any kind were scarcely likely to turn to Ruth for leadership in civic matters even while many in the general public evidently welcomed his teaching.

At the same time, he gave considered attention to theological issues that were important to him. His lifelong quest to develop a satisfying theology about death led to his lengthy study, *The Progress of Personality after Death*. Doubtless this interest was intensified by the tragedies of the war years and the increasing popularity of spiritualism, which fascinated Ruth. This was the most theologically ambitious book that he wrote.

Another theological issue that Ruth tackled was the question of the second coming. In characteristically provocative fashion, he called this book *The Advent Heresy*. Ruth also reflected the gradual fading of belief in traditional eschatology, such as Hell and Eternal punishment, teachings which had terrified him as a young boy. His book showed wide reading in eschatology and argued against the dominant pre-millenarian views of many Baptists and other conservative evangelicals in Australia. Ruth ridiculed various attempts to nominate the date of Christ's return to earth, a preoccupation of many preachers during the war years.

Perhaps it was the demands of his extreme anti-Catholic work that prompted him to leave Melbourne and move to Sydney, even though his initial if somewhat vague hope was to embrace an empire loyalty mission with the support of Brookes and like-minded loyalists. In the "Americo–British" city of Sydney, Ruth was eventually offered a significant church placement at the historic Pitt Street Congregational Church. This necessitated him becoming a Congregationalist with its practice of infant baptism but otherwise familiar churchmanship. Just as he had cut most practical ties with England by his move to Melbourne, now he effectively severed links with his original denomination. His new denomination evidenced more of the breadth of theological perspectives that he had known in his English Free Church connections. However, he once again needed to establish additional friendships and new networks.

Ruth's time in Sydney was largely split between Pitt Street and his writing of a weekly column for the tabloid press, which he described as his "secular pulpit." These popular productions were free of sectarian anti-Catholic views and could be advanced as a claim for him to be judged a "public theologian." He wrote about all manner of public matters, discussing issues of national concern, promoting Anzac Day and Armistice Day to promote a civic religion. A wide range of contemporary events and views on the equality of women and his "advanced" theology were publicized. He attracted many thousands of readers with his humor and an attractive style. At this time, Ruth must have been one of the best-known Protestant ministers in the country.

However, it was from his Pitt Street pulpit that Ruth once again became the focus of heated controversy. This time it was not Roman Catholicism that was attacked but the politics of "that maniac" Premier Jack Lang, whose policy of debt repudiation so antagonized conservative politicians and their supporters. In particular, Ruth's support for the New Guard movement gave him a minor footnote in many histories of the period. He suggested that the New Guard might need to act militarily to save the state from the chaos of "Langdom" since even the police were under his direction. Ruth drew on an Old Testament text to justify the use of an unelected force to overthrow an elected government. Ruth was later said to have developed a "fascist theology" for the New Guard. It never came to anything as the State Governor dismissed Lang, and his government was defeated at the next election.

Was Ruth an incipient fascist? Scarcely. He strongly opposed all European forms of fascism. What he was passionate about, once again, was loyalty to nation and empire. In Melbourne, it had been the disloyalty of Irish Catholics, and in Sydney, it was the treachery of communists and their fellow-travelers, such as he judged Lang and many in the Labor party to be.

The Lang political crisis and the fearful challenges of the Depression era gradually gave way to a new and more optimistic period. Ruth led his church with care and strong leadership, guiding them through a massive rebuilding project in 1926 and the successful celebrations of the church's centenary in 1933. The "little Napoleon" of Pitt Street led a triumphant ecumenical procession, which included all the denominations except Roman Catholic. He led the church from 1923 until he resigned at the end of 1938. His preaching had been popular and topical, including defense of the controversial Presbyterian theologian Samuel Angus as well as commenting on industrial and political issues.

As far as can be gauged from his sermons and articles, Ruth had moved away from the evangelical position that he had gladly announced at his commencement in Melbourne to adopt a "modernist" position. He frequently criticized "orthodoxy" on such topics as the inspiration of the Bible and emphasized the positive impact of evolutionary theories and science more generally on Christianity.

The last stage of Ruth's working life was spent in Adelaide where he served in a variety of interim ministries in both Congregational and Baptist churches. He found the general theological atmosphere quite congenial and resumed some newspaper writing until the outbreak of World War II disrupted the calm of his life. With his beloved wife Mabel, a quiet and largely unsung strength, he continued to mourn the earlier loss of their adopted son Leslie and increasingly appreciated just how alone they were with no family in Australia.

There were, of course, strong and generous friends such as Herbert and Ivy Brookes with whom Ruth continued to share so much. There can be no doubt that Brookes recognized Ruth as a strong and public spokesman for the political conservatism that was the dynamic of Brookes's significant public and commercial life. They consistently affirmed to each other just how much they were "on the same wave-length" in their religious and political beliefs.

Ruth's last days were sad in various ways. He devoted himself once again, as in his Melbourne days, to attacking Roman Catholic dogma and leaders. Even Mannix, himself quietly ageing in the comfort of his home "Raheen" at Kew, received a rather lame public letter inviting some mild form of rapprochement. But the main occupation of Ruth's last years was the drafting and printing of numerous pamphlets, categorizing the latest evils of Catholics. He even took it upon himself to rebuke future Prime Minister Robert Menzies for embracing Catholics in his unyielding opposition to communism.

His last ministry of parceling up postal orders of his own small pamphlets was rather pathetic. He himself lamented that the only ones who now really seemed interested were religious cranks, fundamentalists with whom he shared nothing else apart from his anti-Catholic prejudices. The "proud son of Devon" had simply become a rather lonely Protestant; a frustrated and largely defeated man, sustained only by the memory of his glorious Auditorium days and a small circle of friends like the Brookeses.

Mabel slowly but surely declined into dementia and finally death. He himself gradually faded until kind and generous friends—who did remember his best moments—helped him slip away from life, and, as he had so often preached, he eventually entered the thoroughfare of death into what he had proclaimed to be a new and positive existence.

His is truly a life to be remembered, and not only for the best times, though these were significant and cast light on the life of the church in both England and Australia. Other times for which he is remembered by many still, such as leading criticism of Mannix and the Catholics as "disloyalists" during World War I as well as his condemnation of Premier Lang and advocacy for the New Guard in the 1930s, may not have been his very best moments. But these convictions, advanced fearlessly and honestly, were at the heart of his being.

Brenda Niall wrote an excellent biography of Daniel Mannix, the undoubted foe of Ruth in Melbourne. Perhaps it is appropriate that her sentiment on writing that biography may be echoed in this attempt to tell Ruth's story.

> Biographers begin with facts and opinions, find enlightenment along the way if we're lucky, and end with questions. We would delude ourselves if we thought the full truth could ever be found, or that any volume would be big enough to contain it. I keep in mind Henry James's warning, "Never say you know the truth about any human heart."[1]

Ruth was, as are we all, a man of his times, and certainly no one can know all the truth about his heart.

---

1. Niall, *Mannix*, 375.

Bibliography

Manuscript Sources

Brookes Papers. National Library of Australia, Canberra.
Church Records. Portland Baptist Church, Southampton City archives.
Church Records. Prince's Gate Baptist Church, Liverpool City Archives.
Church and Deacons' Minutes. Collins Street Baptist Church, Melbourne.
Church Records. Pitt Street Congregational Church, Sydney. State Library of NSW.
College Records. Bristol Baptist College, Bristol.
Parish Registers. St. Andrew's Church, Aveton Gifford.

T. E. Ruth Publications

Ruth published many articles in English and Australian religious and secular papers, but these are not listed here. Some of his Australian books included pamphlets that had been previously published. Where known, these more ephemeral materials are also listed.

The Advent Heresy and the Real Coming of Christ. Melbourne: Hutchinsons, n. d. [1922?].
"Anathema and Assassination." *[Memorial Service for Sir Henry Wilson.]* Melbourne: Loyalist League of Victoria, 1922.
Australia at the Crossroads. Sydney: Robert Dey & Sons, 1931.
"The Baptist Child and World Conquest." In *Our Baptist Sunday Schools*, by Ernest Price and Thomas Ruth. London: Kingsgate, 1910.
The Catholic. Nineteen Auditorium Addresses. Sydney: ABPH, 1918.
The Challenge of Papal Politics: An Auditorium Address. Address at Melbourne Auditorium, 26 October 1919. Melbourne: Loyalist League, 1919.
The Common Weal. Eighteen Studies in Social Subjects Sydney: ABPH, n. d.

Crusade 1947: Calling Patriots out of the Ways of Civil Death (Political Proscription.) Seacliff, SA: T. E. Ruth, 1947.
Did Rome Prepare the Way for the World War?: The Presbyterian Messenger Says So, Why? Australian "Appeasement." Adelaide: Hunkin, Ellis & King, 1944. [Preached at Flinders Street Baptist Church, 25 June 1944.]
Dr. Angus on Jesus: A Pulpit Review of "Jesus in the Lives of Men." Sydney: Christian World, 1933.
Dr. Mannix and the Press: Catholic Journalists Responsible for the Adult Education of the People: How Is It Done? Where Are the Others? Can We Trust the Papers? Adelaide: T. E. Ruth, 1944. [Preached at Flinders Street Baptist Church, 27 August 1944.]
Dr. Mannix as Political Commander-in-Chief of a "Sordid Trade War." Melbourne and Sydney: Australian Statesman and Mining Standard, 1917.
The Eucharistic Procession. Why? Why Not? Sydney: ABPH, 1928.
5KA Methodists Politically Compelled to Broadcast Roman Catholicism? How? Why? Adelaide: Hunkin, Ellis and King, 1944. [Preached at the Flinders St. Baptist Church, 29 October 1944.]
Flouting Australian Marriage Laws, "Ne Temere" at Work in Australia . . . an Address Delivered at the Melbourne Auditorium. Address, Melbourne Auditorium, 27 April 1919. Melbourne: Loyalist League of Victoria, 1919.
Four Personal Questions. London: Kingsgate, 1910.
"Getting the Perspective on Life." In *Youth and Life. Talks to Young People*, edited by C. Brown, 57–64. London: National Council of Evangelical Free Churches, 1908.
Industrial Sectarianism Versus Industrial Democracy. Melbourne: Loyalist League of Victoria, n. d. [1920?]
"Inspired Tasks." In *Easter Day in Pitt Street: Forsaken Tombs and Inspired Tasks*, N. J. Cocks and T. E. Ruth. Sydney: Christian World, n. d. [1923?]
The Irish-Australian Complex: "Spare Rome and support de Valera": a Protestant patriot's Reply. Adelaide: Baptist Book Depot,1944.
The Irish-Australian Complex?: Question Asked by Sir Keith Murdoch: "Do Those Who Carry on the Old Sinn Fein Feeling, Permit It to Dominate Them in Matters Purely Australian?" / Reply by T. E. Ruth. Sermon preached at Flinders Street Baptist Church, 23 April 1944. Adelaide: Baptist Book Depot, 1944.
The Irish-Australian Complex?: Questions Asked by Sir Keith Murdoch: "Do Those Who Carry on the Old Sinn Fein Feeling Permit It to Dominate Them in Matters Purely Australian?" / Reply by T. E. Ruth. Seacliff, SA: T. E. Ruth, 1947.
Is Dr. Angus a Heretic? Sydney: Christian World, 1933.
Is the Papacy Anti-British? Does the Pope Represent Peter? What is the Power of the Priest? / Replies by T.E. Ruth. Adelaide: Hunkin, Ellis & King, 1944. [Preached at Flinders Street Baptist Church, 26 November 1944.]
Letter to Archbishop Booth of Melbourne. Adelaide: T. E. Ruth, 1947.
Letter to Dr. Beovich. Archbishop of Adelaide. Adelaide: T. E. Ruth, 1947.
Letter to Dr. Mannix. Adelaide: T. E. Ruth, 1947.
Letter to Mr. Menzies. Adelaide: T. E. Ruth, 1947.
Letters to a Ministerial Son. Authored as "Geoffrey Palmer, A man of the world." London: James Clarke, 1911.

"Mannixisms." Address at Melbourne Auditorium, 29 April 1917. Melbourne and Sydney: Critchley Parker, 1917.
"Menin Gate at Midnight": Captain Will Longstaff's Picture / An Appreciation. Melbourne: Lee-Pratt, 1929. Reprint from *ACW*.
The Money Motive: Cardinals on Parade – Why? An Exposure: My Reaction to the Charge That Decent Australian Citizens Are "Living in Sin." From *Questions Men Are Asking* sermon series, no. 9. Seacliff, SA, T. E. Ruth, 1947.
The Open Secrets of Freemasonry. Melbourne: Loyalist League of Victoria, 1922.
Over the Garden Wall: Some Neighbourly Philosophy. Sydney: J. A. Packer, n. d. [1929].
The Parable of the Empire Broadcast. Sydney: T. E. Ruth, 1933.
The Picture in the Porch of the Pitt Street Congregational Church, Sydney, Painted by Herbert Beecroft after Axel Ende. Sydney: Book Room, 1926.
Playing the Game. Sydney: Cornstalk, 1925.
A Plea for the Preacher Today. Address at the Baptist College Commencement, Adelaide, 12 March 1940.
A Plea for the Prophet: Full Text of Lecture Delivered by the Rev. T. E. Ruth at the Annual Commencement of the Victorian Baptist College. March 9th, 1915. Sydney: ABPH, 1915.
The Priest in Politics: Ireland's Warning, Italy's Example, Britain's Danger. Melbourne: Australian Statesman and Mining Standard, 1917.
The Progress of Personality after Death. Melbourne: Hutchinson, 1919.
A Rendezvous with Life. Everyday Problems. Sydney: Angus & Robertson, 1934.
The Responsibility of Empire. Melbourne: Baptist Church, 1914.
Revolution or Evolution? Melbourne: Loyalist League of Victoria, 1919.
Rome and Russia: Is the Papacy preparing for a Third World War? In Australia the fight Is On! Seacliff, SA: T. E. Ruth, 1947.
Rome Rule in Australia. Address at Melbourne Auditorium, 27 May 1917. Melbourne: Critchley Parker, 1917.
Second Letter to Mr. Menzies. Adelaide: T. E. Ruth, 1947.
Sinn Fein (Ourselves Alone): Are Australians Sinn Feiners? Melbourne: Critchley Parker, 1917.
Sowing and Reaping: An Appeal to the Soul of Sydney. Sydney: ACW, 1934.
The Terms of Sectarian Peace? Melbourne: 1922.
Third Letter to Mr. Menzies: the Bank-Monopoly Parable. Seacliff, SA: T. E. Ruth, 1947.
Three Enemies of Democracy: The Priest, the Profiteer, the Agitator. Melbourne: Loyalist League, 1919.
Wake Up, Australia! Melbourne: Modern Printing, 1917.
Why Bother about Aborigines? Sydney: Robert Dey, n. d. [c. 1938]. Reprint from *ACW*.
Why Bother about Catholic Action? Adelaide: Hunkin, Ellis & King, 1944.
Will Jesus Come Again in the Flesh? With Some Reference to Mr. J. Krishnamurti: An Address Given in the Criterion Theatre. Sydney: Christian World, n. d. [1932].
"*World Arbiter?*": *Imposing Claim or Colossal Imposition?* From *Questions Men Are Asking* sermon series, no. 7. Seacliff, SA: T. E. Ruth, 1947.

Journals, Magazines, and Newspapers

Australia

Advertiser (Adelaide)
Advocate
The Age
Argus
Australian Baptist
Australian Christian Commonwealth
Australian Christian World
Australian Historical Studies
Australian Studies
Baptist Recorder
Barrier Miner (Broken Hill)
Brisbane Courier
Bunbury Herald and Blackwood Express
Bunyip (Gawler)
Canberra Times
Colloquium
Congregationalist
Daily Mail (Brisbane)
Daily Pictorial
Daily Telegraph
East Gippsland Gazette (Warragul)
Examiner (Launceston)
Freeman's Journal
Geelong Advertiser
Grenfell Record and Lachlan District Advertiser
Gundagai Independent
Herald (Melbourne)
Historical Studies
History Australia
Journal of Australian Studies
Journal of the Australian Catholic Historical Society
Journal of Religious History
Labor Daily
Labour History
Meanjin
Mail (Adelaide)

Maitland Daily Mercury
Mudgee Guardian
National Library of Australia News
News (Adelaide)
Our Yesterdays
Propagandist
Punch
Queensland Times (Ipswich)
Recorder (Port Pirie)
Smith's Weekly
Sporting Judge
Sun
Sunday Sun (Sydney)
Sunday Times
Sydney Morning Herald
Sydney Mail
Table Talk
Telegraph (Brisbane)
Truth
Vigilant
Watchman
West Gippsland Gazette
Western Morning News
West Wyalong Advocate
Worker's Weekly

United Kingdom and USA

Baptist Handbook (Baptist Union of Great Britain, 1861, published annually)
Baptist Quarterly
Baptist Times
Belfast News Letter
Birmingham Daily Gazette
Burnley News
Christian Herald
Christian World
Christian World Pulpit
Cornish and Devon Post
Daily Telegraph

Dublin Daily Express
Evening Standard
Express and Echo
Fifeshire Advertiser
Hampshire Advertiser
Hampshire Chronicle
Islington Gazette
Journal of the Southampton Local Forum
Lancashire Evening Post
Leicester Chronicle
Liverpool Courier
Liverpool Daily Post
London Daily News
Practical Theology
Salisbury and Winchester Journal
Salisbury Times
Southampton Times
Southern Echo
Sunderland Daily Echo
The Times
Western Morning News
Young Man

Books, Articles, and Dissertations

Abbott, Lyman. *Christianity and Social Problems*. Boston: Houghton Mifflin, 1896.
Amos, Keith. *The New Guard Movement*. Melbourne: Melbourne University Press, 1976.
Angus, Samuel. *Jesus in the Lives of Men*. Sydney: Angus and Robertson, 1933.
———. *Truth and Tradition: A Plea for Practical and Vital Religion and for a Reinterpretation of Ancient Theologies*. Sydney: Angus and Robertson, 1934.
Archer, Robyn, et al., eds. *The Conscription Conflict and the Great War*. Clayton: Monash University Publishing, 2016.
Badger, C. R. *The Reverend Charles Strong and the Australian Church*. Melbourne: Abacada, 1971.
The Baptist World Congress. *Authorised Record of Proceedings*. With introduction by Rev. J. H. Shakespeare, London, July 11–19, 1905. London: Baptist Union, 1901.
Bartie, Angela, et al. "Liverpool 700th Anniversary Pageant." *The Redress of the Past* (blog). http://www.historicalpageants.ac.uk/pageants/1123/.
Bashford, Alison, and Stuart Macintyre, eds. *Cambridge History of Australia*. 2 vols. Cambridge: Cambridge University Press, 2015.

Beaumont, Joan. *Broken Nation Australians in the Great War*. Sydney: Allen and Unwin, 2014.
Bebbington, David W. *Evangelicalism in Modern Britain. A History from the 1730s to the 1980s*. London: Unwin Hyman, 1989.
———. *The Nonconformist Conscience. Chapel and Politics 1870–1914*. London; Allen & Unwin, 1982.
Benson, C. Irving. *The Eight Points of the Oxford Group*. Melbourne: Oxford University Press, 1936.
Benson, Rod. "T. E. Ruth and *The Common Weal*." *I Digress* (blog). https://rodbenson.com/2012/04/23/t-e-ruth-and-the-common-weal/.
Black, A. *The Golden Jubilee of the World's Sunday School Association*. Glasgow, 1939.
Blainey, Geoffrey. *A Land Half Won*. Melbourne: Macmillan, 1980.
Boreham, Frank W. *My Pilgrimage*. London: Epworth, 1940.
Brett, Judith. *Australian Liberals and the Moral Middle Class: From Alfred Deakin to John Howard*. Cambridge: Cambridge University Press, 2003.
———. *The Enigmatic Mr. Deakin*. Melbourne: Text, 2017.
Breward, Ian. *Australia: "The Most Godless Place Under Heaven"?* Melbourne; Beacon Hill, 1988.
———. *A History of the Churches in Australasia*. Oxford: Oxford University Press, 2001.
Brown, Charles, ed. *Youth and Life. Talks to Young People*. London: National Council of Evangelical Free Churches, 1908.
Brown, James. *Anzac's Long Shadow: The Cost of our National Obsession*. Collingwood: Redback, 2014.
Bunyan, John. *Differences in Judgment about Water Baptism, No Bar to Communion*. London: John Wilkins, 1673.
Campbell, Eric. *The Rallying Point: My Story of the New Guard*. Melbourne: Melbourne University Press, 1965.
Campion, Edmund. *Australian Catholics*. Ringwood: Penguin, 1988.
———. *Rockchoppers. Growing up Catholic in Australia*. Ringwood: Penguin, 1982.
Carey, Samuel Pearce. *Jesus*. London: Hodder and Stoughton, 1939.
Cathcart, Michael. *Defending the National Tuckshop: Australia's Secret Army Intrigue of 1931*. Melbourne: McPhee-Gribble, 1988.
Chambers, A. *Our Life after Death, or The Teaching of the Bible Concerning the Unseen World*. London: n. p., 1894.
———. *Our Self After Death*. London: n. p., 1900.
Choate, P. *The Laughing Christ*. London: Ivor Nicholson & Watson, 1933.
Clements, Keith. "Baptists and the Outbreak of the First World War," *BQ* 26.2 (1975–76) 79–92.
Clements, Keith. *Lovers of Discord. Twentieth Century Theological Controversies in England*. London: SPCK, 1988.
Cochrane, Peter. "'Australian Citizens': Herbert and Ivy Brookes." *National Library of Australia: News* (March 1999) 19–21.
———. "'How are the Egyptians Behaving?': Herbert Brookes, British–Australian," *Australian Historical Studies* 29.113 (1999) 303–18.
Crago, T. Howard. *The Story of F. W. Boreham*. London: Marshall, Morgan & Scott, 1961.
Cross, F. L. and Livingstone, E. A., eds. *The Oxford Dictionary of the Christian Church*. Oxford: Oxford University Press, 3 ed, 1997.

Davison, Graeme, John Hirst, and Stuart Macintyre, eds. *The Oxford Companion to Australian History*. Melbourne: Oxford University Press, 2001.

Davison, Graeme. *Narrating the Nation in Australia*. 2009 Menzies Lecture. London: Menzies Centre for Australian Studies, 2009.

———. *The Rise and Fall of Marvellous Melbourne*. 2nd edition. Melbourne: Melbourne University Press, 2004.

Doughty, Kenneth. *Aveton Gifford: A Heritage*. Aveton Gifford: Aveton Gifford Parish Project Group, 2002.

Doyle, Mark. *Fighting Like the Devil for the Sake of God: Protestants, Catholics and the Origins of Violence in Victorian Belfast*. Manchester: Manchester University Press, 2009.

Ely, Richard. "The Forgotten Nationalism: Australian Civic Protestantism in the Second World War." *Journal of Australian Studies* 11.20 (1987) 59–67.

———. "Now You See It: Now You Don't! Issues of Secularity and Secularisation in Publicly Funded Elementary Schools in the Australian Colonies during the Middle Third of the Nineteenth Century." *Journal of Religious History* 38.3 (2014) 377–97.

Emilsen, Susan. *A Whiff of Heresy. Samuel Angus and the Presbyterian Church in New South Wales*. Kensington: University of NSW Press, 1991.

Emilsen, Susan et al. *Pride of Place. A History of the Pitt Street Congregational Church*. Beaconsfield, 2008.

Engel, Frank. *Australian Christians in Conflict and Unity*. Melbourne: Joint Board of Christian Education, 1984.

Featherstone, Guy. "The Millennial Voice in Victoria to 1914." *Journal of Religious History* 35.2 (2011) 233–63.

Ferguson, Sinclair B., David F. Wright, and J. I. Packer, eds. *New Dictionary of Theology*. Leicester, Inter-Varsity, 1988.

Fischer, G. *Enemy Aliens: Internment and the Destruction of the German Australian Community, 1914–1920*. St Lucia: University of Queensland Press, 1989.

Fosdick, Harry Emerson. *The Living of These Days. An Autobiography*. London: SCM, 1957.

Frame, Tom. ed. *Anzac Day: Then and Now*. Sydney: NewSouth, 2016.

Franklin, James. "Catholics Versus Masons." *Journal of the Australian Catholic Historical Society* 20 (1999) 1–15.

Gabay, Al. *Messages from Beyond. Spiritualism and Spiritualists in Melbourne's Golden Age*. Melbourne: Melbourne University Press, 2001.

———. *The Mystic Life of Alfred Deakin*. Cambridge: Cambridge University Press, 1992.

Gilbert, Alan. "The Conscription Referenda, 1916–1917: The Impact of the Irish Crisis." *Historical Studies* 14 (1969) 54–72.

Gladden, Washington. *Social Salvation*. Boston: Houghton Mifflin, 1902.

Green, V. "Preaching Places and Meeting Houses." *Journal of the Southampton Local Forum* 8 (Autumn 1999).

Griffen-Foley, Bridget. "Radio Ministries: Religion on Australian Commercial Radio from the 1920s to the 1960s." *Journal of Religious History* 32.1 (2008) 31–54.

Hall, Richard. *The Secret State: Australia's Spy Industry*. Stanmore: Cassell, 1978.

Hansen, David. "The Churches and Society in New South Wales: 1919–1939." PhD diss., Macquarie University, 1978.

Healey, Alison. "A Critical Alliance. ABC Religious Broadcasting and the Christian Churches." *Journal of the Catholic Historical Society* 26 (2005) 15–28.
Herbert, Xavier. *Capricornia*. Sydney: Angus & Robertson, 1938.
Hilton, Boyd. *The Age of the Atonement. The Influence of Evangelicalism on Social and Economic Thought, 1785–1865*. Oxford: Clarendon Press, 1988.
Himbury, D. Mervyn. *The Theatre of the Word. Traditions, Ministry, Future of the Collins Street Baptist Church Melbourne 1843–1993*. Melbourne: Collins Street Baptist Church, 1993.
Hogan, Michael. *The Sectarian Strand. Religion in Australian History*. Ringwood: Penguin, 1987.
Hovey, Craig, and Elizabeth Phillips, eds. *The Cambridge Companion to Political Theology*. Cambridge: Cambridge University Press, 2015.
Howe, Renate, and Shirley Swain. *The Challenge of the City. The Centenary History of Wesley Central Mission 1893–1993*. South Melbourne: Hyland House, 1993.
Hudson, Wayne S. *Australian Religious Thought*. Clayton: Monash University Publishing, 2016.
Hughes, William M. *Australia and the War Today: The Price of Peace*. Sydney: Angus & Robertson, 1935.
Hunt, Arnold D. *This Side of Heaven: A History of Methodism in South Australia*. Adelaide: Lutheran Publishing, 1985.
Hunt, Jane. "Cultivating the Arts: Sydney Women Culturalists 1900–50." PhD diss., Macquarie University, 2001.
Inglis, Ken S. "Conscription in Peace and War, 1911–1945." In *Conscription in Australia*, edited by Roy Forward and Bob Reece, 22–65. St Lucia: University of Queensland Press, 1968.
———. *Sacred Places: War Memorials in the Australian Landscape*. Melbourne: Melbourne University Press, 1998.
Jackson, F. *By-ways of Romance, Being Essays on Places and People*. Melbourne: E. A. Vidler, 1927.
Jordan, E. K. H. *Free Church Unity History of the Free Church Council Movement 1896–1941*. London: Lutterworth, 1956.
Keeble, S. E. *Industrial Day-Dreams: Studies in Industrial Ethics and Economics*. London: C. H. Kelly, 1896.
Kent, Jacqueline. *Out of the Bakelite Box*. Sydney: ABC Books, 1983.
Kildea, Jeff. "Australian Catholics and Conscription in the Great War." *Journal of Religious History* 26.3 (October 2002) 298–313.
———. *Tearing the Fabric: Sectarianism in Australia 1910–1925*. Citadel, Sydney, 2002.
Kingston, Charles. *It Don't Seem a Day Too Much*. Melbourne: Rigby, 1971.
Knightley, Phillip. *Australia. A Biography of a Nation*. London: Jonathan Cape, 2000.
La Nauze, John A. *Alfred Deakin: A Biography*. Melbourne: Melbourne University Press, 1965.
Lamb, William. *Purgatory and Prayers for the Dead: An Examination of the Teaching of Rev. T.E. Ruth's Book Wake Up, Australia!* Sydney: Australian Baptist Publishing House, 1918.
Larsen, Timothy T., ed. *Biographical Dictionary of Evangelicals*. Leicester: Inter-Varsity, 2003.
Lewis, C. S. *The Problem of Pain*. London: Centenary, 1949.

Linder, Robert D. *The Long Tragedy. Australian Evangelical Christians and the Great War*. Adelaide: Open Book, 2000.

Lockley, G. Lindsay. *Congregationalism in Australia*. Edited by Bruce Upham. Melbourne: Uniting Church Press, 2001.

Lucas, A. H. S. *A. H. S. Lucas. Scientist. His Own Story*. Sydney: Angus & Robertson, 1937.

Lucas, William, ed. *The Life and Letters of Norman Carey Lucas MA BSc (Edin), Second-Lieutenant Royal Irish Rifles*. Melbourne: n. p., 1920.

Lyons, Moreen. "Sectarian Catholics and Politics," *Meanjin Quarterly* (1973) 106–111.

Macintyre, Stuart. *A Concise History of Australia*. Cambridge: Cambridge University Press, 1999.

———. *Oxford History of Australia Volume 4:1901–1942 The Succeeding Age*. Melbourne: Oxford University Press, 1986.

MacRaild, Donald M. *Faith, Fraternity and Fighting: The Orange Order and Irish Migrants in Northern England, c.1880–1920*. Liverpool: Liverpool University Press, 2005.

Manley, Ken R. "Boreham, Frank William." In *Biographical Dictionary of Evangelicals*, edited by Timothy Larsen, 66–68. Leicester: Inter-Varsity, 2003.

———. "Defending 'the Freest Land in the World': Australian Baptists and Political Protestantism." In *Making History for God: Essays on Evangelicalism, Revival and Mission in Honour of Stuart Piggin*, edited by Geoffrey R. Treloar and Robert D. Linder, 133–50. Sydney: Robert Menzies College, 2004.

———. "From Assurance through Depression to Optimism: Baptists in Victoria 1880–1914." *Our Yesterdays* 10 (2002) 27–51.

———. *"An Honoured Name": Samuel Pearce Carey (1862–1953)*. Oxford: Regent's Park College, 2016.

———. "Insider Perspectives on Contemporary Nonconformity: T. E. Ruth in *The Christian World* 1910–1913." *BQ*, 51.3 (2020) 88–102.

———. "A Savonarola in Melbourne?": Preaching on Social and Political Issues at Collins Street Baptist Church 1900–1923." *Our Yesterdays* 23 (2015) 4–37.

———. *From Woolloomooloo to "Eternity": A History of Australian Baptists*. 2 vols. Milton Keynes: Paternoster, 2006.

Marsden, George M. *Fundamentalism and American Culture*. New York: Oxford University Press, 1980.

Martens, Jeremy. "The Mrs. Freer Case Revisited: Marriage, Morality and the State in Interwar Australia." *History Australia* 16.3 (2019) 437–58.

McKernan, Michael. *Australian Churches at War: Attitudes and Activities of the Major Churches, 1914–1918*. Manly: Catholic Theological Faculty, 1980.

———. *The Australian People and the Great War*. Sydney: Collins, 1980.

———. "Catholics, Conscription and Archbishop Mannix." *Australian Studies* 17 (1976) 299–314.

Meyer, F. B. *Our Sister Death*. London: National Council of the Evangelical Free Churches, 1915.

Meyers, Frederick W. H. *Human Personality and its Survival of Bodily Death*. London: Longmans, Green and Co., 1903.

Moon, Norman S. *Education for Ministry. Bristol Baptist College 1679–1979*. Bristol: Bristol Baptist College, 1979.

Moore, Andrew. *The Right Road? A History of Right-Wing Politics in Australia.* Melbourne: Oxford University Press, 1995.

———. *The Secret Army and the Premier: Conservative Paramilitary Organisations in New South Wales 1930–31.* Kensington: University of NSW Press, 1989.

———. "Writing about the Extreme Right in Australia." *Labour History* 89 (2005) 1–15.

Morling, George H. "Spiritual Millionaires." In *The Katoomba Convention 1932: Notes of Some of the Addresses Revised by the Speakers*, by H. S. Begbie et al., 51. Sydney: Katoomba Convention Council, 1932, 51.

Moses, John. "Anzac Day as Religious Revivalism: The politics of Faith in Brisbane 1916–1939." In *Reviving Australia: Essays on the History and Experience of Revival and Revivalism in Australian Christianity*, edited by Mark Hutchinson and Stuart Piggin, 170–84. Sydney: Centre for the Study of Australian Christianity, 1994,

———. "The First World War as Holy War in German and Australian Perspective." *Colloquium* 26.1 (1994) 44–55.

Moule, H. C. G. *Outlines of Christian Doctrine.* London: Hodder and Stoughton, 1889.

Mullins, Edgar Young. *The Axioms of Religion: A New Interpretation of the Baptist Faith.* Philadelphia: Judson, 1908.

Murphy, Denis J. *T. J. Ryan: A Political Biography.* Brisbane: University of Queensland Press 1975.

Neal, Frank. *Sectarian Violence. The Liverpool Experience 1819–1914.* Liverpool: Newsham, 1988.

Niall, Brenda. *Mannix.* Melbourne: Text, 2015.

Nicholls, Paul. "Australian Protestantism and the Politics of the Great Depression, 1929–31." *Journal of Religious History* 17.2 (1992) 210–21.

O'Farrell, Patrick. *The Catholic Church and Community: An Australian History.* Kensington: University of NSW Press, 1985.

———. *The Irish in Australia.* Kensington: University of NSW Press, 1987.

Parliamentary Debates. Senate and House of Representatives. Commonwealth of Australia. Volume 1, 1901/02.

Peabody, Francis Greenwood. *Jesus Christ and the Social Question: An Examination of the Teaching of Jesus in Its Relation to Some of the Problems of Modern Social Life.* New York: Macmillan, 1900.

Pearce, Stefanie. "'A Humble Effort to do Good': Melbourne's Gospel Hall 1866–2016," *Our Yesterdays* 28 (2020) 28–95.

Petras, Michael. *Australian Baptists and World War I.* Macquarie Park: Baptist Historical Society of NSW, 2009.

———. "The Life and Times of the Reverend William Lamb (1868–1944). *Baptist Recorder* 101 (May 2008) 1–11.

Phillips, Walter. *Edward Sidney Kiek: His Life and Thought.* Adelaide: Uniting Church Historical Society, 1981.

Pickford, Mary. *Why Not Try God?* New York: H. C. Kinsey, 1934.

Pierard, Richard V. "The Anzac Day Phenomenon: A Study in Civil Religion." In *Making History for God: Essays on Evangelicalism, Revival and Mission in Honour of Stuart Piggin*, edited by Geoffrey R. Treloar and Robert D. Linder, 239–54. Sydney: Robert Menzies College, 2004.

Pierard, Richard V., and Robert D. Linder. *Civil Religion and the Presidency.* Grand Rapids: Zondervan, 1988.

Pierard, Richard V., ed. *Baptists Together in Christ 1905–2000: A Hundred-Year History of the Baptist World Alliance.* Falls Church, VA: BWA, 2005.

Piggin, Stuart. *Evangelical Christianity in Australia. Spirit, Word and World.* Melbourne: Oxford University Press, 1996.

Piggin, Stuart, and Robert D. Linder. *Attending to the National Soul.* Clayton: Monash University Publishing, 2020.

———. *The Fountain of Public Prosperity, Evangelical Christians in Australian History.* Clayton: Monash University Publishing, 2018.

Pound, Geoffrey. "F. W. Boreham the Public Theologian: The Interplay of Faith and Life in the Newspaper Editorials of F. W. Boreham 1912–1959." DTheol diss., Melbourne College of Divinity, 2003.

Randall, Ian M. "'Arresting People for Christ': Baptists and the Oxford Group in the 1930s." *BQ* 38.1 (1990) 3–18.

———. *The English Baptists of the Twentieth Century.* Didcot: Baptist Historical Society, 2005.

———. *Spirituality and Social Change. The Contribution of F. B. Meyer (1847–1929).* Carlisle: Paternoster, 2003.

Rauschenbusch, Walter. *Christianity and the Social Crisis.* New York: Macmillan, 1907.

Reardon, Bernard M. G. *Religion in the Age of Romanticism.* Cambridge: Cambridge University Press, 1985.

The Report of the International Conversations between the Anglican Communion and the Baptist World Alliance. London: Anglican Communion Office, 2005.

Rice, Alice Hegan. *Lovey Mary.* N. p.: n. p. 1903.

Richardson, D. *Creating Remembrance. The Art and Design of Australian War Memorials.* Champaign, IL: Common Ground, 2015.

Ridley, John G. *William Lamb Preacher and Prophet: A Memoir.* Sydney: ABPH, n. d.

Rivett, Rohan. *Australian Citizen. Herbert Brookes 1867–1963.* Melbourne: Melbourne University Press, 1965.

Roberts, Keith D. *Liverpool Sectarianism: The Rise and Demise.* Oxford: Oxford University Press, 2017.

Robinson, Geoffrey. "The All for Australia League in New South Wales: A Study in Political Entrepreneurship and Hegemony." *Australian Historical Studies* 39.1 (2008) 36–52.

Roe, Jill. *Beyond Belief: Theosophy in Australia 1879–1939.* Kensington: University of NSW Press, 1986.

Santamaria, B. A. *Daniel Mannix.* Melbourne: Melbourne University Press, 1984.

Schreuder Deryck M., and Stuart Ward, eds. *Australia's Empire.* Oxford: Oxford University Press, 2008.

Sellers, Ian. "Baptists in Liverpool in the Seventeenth Century." *BQ* 20 (1964) 195–200, 277–81.

———, ed. *Our Heritage. The Baptists of Yorkshire Lancashire and Cheshire 1647–1987.* Leeds: 1987.

———. "Liverpool Nonconformity 1786–1914." PhD diss., Keele University, 1969.

Shakespeare, John Howard. *The Free Churches at the Cross Roads.* London: National Council of Evangelical Free Churches, 1916.

Shaw, C. C. *History of the Parish of Aveton Gifford.* Averton Gifford: published privately, 1966.

Shaw, George Bernard. *The Adventures of the Black Girl in Her Search for God.* London: Constable, 1932.
Shepherd, Peter. *The Making of a Modern Denomination. John Howard Shakespeare and the English Baptists 1898–1924.* Carlisle: Paternoster, 2001.
Smith, Karen E. "Charles Frederic Aked (1864–1941): 'A Fighting Parson' for Social Reform." *BQ* 50.1 (2019) 3–18.
Souter, Gavin. *Lion and Kangaroo. The Initiation of Australia.* Melbourne: Text, 2000 [1976].
Spurr, Frederic Chambers. *Five Years Under the Southern Cross: Experiences and Impressions.* London: Hodder, 1915.
Stackhouse, Max. "Civil Religion, Political Theology and Public Theology: What's the Difference?" *Political Theology* 5.3 (2004) 275–93.
Storer, Robert V. *A Survey of Sexual Life in Adolescence and in Marriage.* Melbourne: Science Publishing, 1932.
Strawhan, Peter. "The Closure of Radio 5KA, January 1941." *Historical Studies* 21 (1985) 550–64.
Streeter, Burnett Hillman et al. *Immortality: An Essay in Discovery.* New York: Macmillan, 1917.
Sweetnam, Mark S. "Defining Dispensationalism: A Cultural Studies Perspective." *Journal of Religious History* 34.2 (2010) 191–212.
Tampke, Jurgen, and Colin Doxford. *Australia, Willkommen: A History of the Germans in Australia.* Kensington: University of NSW Press, 1990.
Thompson, Roger C. *Religion in Australia. A History.* Melbourne: Oxford University Press, 1994.
Thwaites, Sandra. "Rev. T. E. Ruth, A City Preacher in a Time of War and After." *Our Yesterdays* 3 (1996) 19–46.
Tibbles, A. "Liverpool and the Slave Trade." Transcript, Gresham College Lecture 2007. https://www.gresham.ac.uk/lectures-and-events/liverpool-and-the-slave-trade.
Treloar, Geoffrey R., and Robert D. Linder, eds. *Making History for God. Essays on Evangelicalism, Revival and Mission.* Sydney: Robert Menzies College, 2004.
Turner, Ian. *Industrial Labour and Politics: The Dynamics of the Labour Movement in Eastern Australia 1900–1921.* Sydney: Hale and Iremonger, 1979.
Vamplew, Wray, ed, *Australian Statistics: Historical Statistics.* Broadway: Fairfax, Syme & Weldon, 1987.
Wallace, Alfred Russel. *The World of Life: A Manifestation of Creative Power, Directive Mind and Ultimate Purpose.* London: Bell, 1911.
Withers, Glenn. "The 1916–1917 Conscription Referenda: A Cliometric Re-appraisal." *Historical Studies* 20 (1982) 38–46.
Wolffe, John. "A Comparative Historical Categorisation of Anti-Catholicism." *Journal of Religious History* 39.2 (2015) 182–202.
Young, Robert J. C. *The Idea of English Ethnicity.* Oxford: Blackwell, 2008.

Index

Adamson, Lawrence, 150
Adelaide
    Ruth's retirement, 274–317
    visit from Ruth 1921, 123
    visit from Ruth 1929, 186
Adventism, 165–68, 193
Aked, Charles Frederic, 9
Albiston, Walter, 118, 290, 311–12
alcohol, 59–60, 141–42
All for Australia League, 203–7, 215, 269
Anglican Church, 24, 129
Anglican churches
    Darling Point, 285
    Drummoyne, 275
    Exeter, U.K., xvii
    Manly, 275, 285
    Sydney, King Street, 221, 275, 285
Anglo–American Conference on Christian unity, 17
Anglo–Catholics, 103
Angus, Samuel, 225–28
animal rights, 272
Anzac Day, 61, 134, 212–13, 254–55, 257–59, 293
Aquinas, Thomas, 101
Armistice Day. *See* Remembrance Day
Atkinson, Meredith, 138

Australasian Baptist Congress, Melbourne, 130
Australia Day, 231, 259
Australian Aborigines' League, 240
Australian Broadcasting Commission (ABC), 188
Australian Creed, 122, 129, 134

baptism, 25, 28, 37, 45, 47, 50, 60, 81, 90, 103–4, 175
Baptist Assemblies
    New South Wales, 46
    Queensland, 49
    South Australia, 49, 60, 286
    Victoria, 44, 60
Baptist Association, Southern, Great Britain, 7
Baptist churches
    Adelaide, Flinders Street, 78, 123, 280, 287
    Baptist church, London, Westbourne Park, U.K., 15
    Brighton, S.A., 286
    Exeter, South Street, U.K., 5
    Liverpool, Prince's Gate, U.K., 5, 8–18, 42, 120
    London, Ferme Park, U.K., 13
    London, Westbourne Park, U.K., 15–16, 120

Baptist churches (continued)
    Melbourne, Carlton, Sunday School, 32, 113
    Melbourne, Collins Street, ix, xvii, 1, 15n73, 17, 27, 30–168, 287
    Melbourne, Little Bourke Street Mission Hall, 113
    Southampton, Portland, U.K., 5–8, 121
    Southport, Hoghton Street, U.K., 5, 17–18
    Sydney, Bathurst Street (later Central), 170, 184, 221, 231
Baptist Colleges
    Bristol, U.K., xvii, 5–6
    Queensland, 108
    South Australia, 280
    Spurgeon's, U.K., 118
    Victoria, 32, 48
Baptist Men's Association, Melbourne, 45
Baptist Ministers' Fraternal School of Theology, Victoria, 47
Baptist Union, Great Britain, 8, 12–13
Baptist World Alliance Conference, London 1920, 121
Barrie, James Matthew, 156
Bavin, Thomas Rainsford, 204
Baxter, Richard, 161
Bean, Albert William, 108, 118–19, 123
Beaumont, Joan, 75
Bebbington, David, xiv, 36
Beecher, Henry Ward, 191
Beecroft, Herbert, 177
Begbie, Harold, 155
Begbie, Herbert Smirnoff, 216
Benson, Clarence Irving, 237
Beovich, Matthew, Archbishop, 292, 294
Besant, Annie, 192
Bhagavad-Gita, 159
Biggs, Leonard Vivian, 240
Black, Arthur, 16
Black, Willie Cleugh, 63
Blake, William (poet), 91
Blake, William Hunter Selby, 59, 111
Boer War, 31
Booth, Catherine, 261

Booth, Joseph John, Archbishop, 292, 294
Boreham, Frank William, 134, 194, 246, 290
Bournemouth, Fifth International Congregational Council, 186
Boylan, Eustace Joseph Ignatius, 104
Brahmanism, 42
Brett, Judith, 68, 304
Briggs, John, xiv
Brisbane, visit from Ruth 1929, 185–86
Brookes, Alfred Deakin, 306, 315–16
Brookes, Herbert Robinson, x, xviii, 67, 95–97, 109, 116, 118–21, 129, 148, 173–74, 188–89, 195–98, 203, 220, 223–24, 240, 242, 245, 248, 268, 273–76, 279, 283, 285–87, 289–91, 295–319, 324–26
Brookes, Ivy (m. H.R. Brookes). See Deakin, Ivy
Brookes, Norman Everard, 300
Brookes, William, 299
Brooks, Phillips, 104, 312
Brown, James, 255
Browning, Robert, 157, 224, 250
Bruce, Stanley Melbourne, 196, 201, 301
Buchman, Frank, 237–38
Buckingham, William, 167
Buddhism, 42
Bunyan, John, 60
Burgmann, Ernest Henry, Bishop, 137
Burgoyne, Emily, xiv
Butt, Clara, 184

Cadman, Parkes, 197
Cameron, Donald A., 60
Campbell, Alexander Petrie, 214, 318–19
Campbell, Eric, x, 202
Campbell, Reginald John, 12
Campion, Edmund, 56, 73–74, 315
Canada, England and U.S.A., visit from Ruth 1930, 194, 197–200, 309
Canberra, establishment of, 124, 150, 182, 234, 278, 286
Carey, Samuel Pearce, 15n73, 33, 36, 40, 44–45, 50–51, 120, 147n73, 308, 322

INDEX   343

Carlyle, Thomas, 43, 103
Carnegie, Andrew, 148
Carr, Thomas, Archbishop, 72, 81
Cathcart, Michael, 303
Cattaneo, Bartolomeo, Archbishop, 74
Chambers, Arthur, 154, 158, 160–61, 164
Chandler, Charles Walker, 205
Chatfield, Graeme, xiv
Choate, Pearson, 232
Christian Endeavour, 36
Christian Scientists, 192
Christian Socialism, 77, 138
church music, 23, 35
Church of Christ (denomination), 24, 26
Citizens' Loyalist Committee, 96
Civil Liberties, 275
Clarke, Henry Lowther, Archbishop, 103
Clements, Keith, 13
Clifford, John, xi, 14–15, 36, 120, 229, 321
Cochrane, Peter, 302–3
Cockett, Charles Bernard, 243
Cocks, Nicholas John, 172, 174, 255
Coe, Barbara, xiv
Cohen, Francis Lyon, Rabbi, 184, 223
Communism, 178, 186, 201, 214, 259, 268, 275, 278, 293
Complin, John, 184
confession, 79, 81, 88–89
Congregational Church, 24–25, 185–87, 213
Congregational churches
    Adelaide, Stow Memorial, 186, 279
    Birmingham, Carrs Lane, U.K., 120
    Brisbane, City, 186
    Gawler, S.A., 280
    London, City Temple, 12, 197
    Melbourne, Collins Street Independent, 285
    North Adelaide, 276–80
    Sydney, Pitt Street, x, xvii, 128–29, 169–273
Congregational College, Parkin College, Adelaide, 186
Congregational Unions
    Great Britain, 14
    South Australia, 186
conscription, xvii, 44–45, 66–70, 73–75, 79, 82, 85, 92–93, 110, 138, 143, 303
Conservative Licensing Bill, Great Britain, 8
Constitutional Club, Brisbane, 186
Cook, Joseph, 181
Costello, Tim, ix–xi, xiv
cricket, 219
Crook, William Pascoe, 221–23
Curthoys, Patricia, xiv, 241
Curtin, John, 286
Cuthbertson, William Neville, 241

Darcy, Les, 72
Davies, David John, 215
Davison, Graeme, 31, 124, 134
de Groot, Francis, 202, 216
de Valera, Eamon, 121, 123
Deakin, Alfred, x, 56, 136, 299–302, 304, 307–8, 317
Deakin, Ivy (m. H.R. Brookes), 275, 300–301, 307, 311–12, 317
Decalogue, xi, 129, 135–36, 255
Denholm, Gina, xiv
Denison, Hugh, 174, 196
depression, economic, 195–205, 214, 219, 269, 310
Derrin, Andrew and Florence, 291, 296, 317–21
Donaldson, St. Clair, Archbishop, 55
Dorcas Society, 59
Dorr, Julia, 161
Douglas, Lloyd Cassel, 233
Downing, John, 50–51
Doyle, Arthur Conan, 120, 164
Doyle, Mark, 79
Drummond, Henry, 186, 261, 302–4, 307, 312
Duffy, Frank Gaven, 74, 99
Dunn, Alfred, 80
Dwyer, Peter, 103

ecumenism, 25
Eddy, Mary Baker, 192
education, 182–83
Edward VIII, 231

Elder, James, 196
Elkin, Adolphus Peter, 137, 240
Emilsen, Susan, 227
Empire Day, 56, 182, 213–14, 231, 256–57
Empress of Ireland, 40
England and U.S.A., visit from Ruth 1919, 118–21
England, U.S.A. and Canada, visit from Ruth 1930, 194, 197–200, 309
eschatology, 152–68

Farquhar, John Carnegie, 118
fascism, x, xviii, 200–202, 209, 211, 219, 278
Fenians, 84
Fitchett, William Henry, 56
Fleming, Peter, 35
Fletcher, Lionel, 185
Forsyth, Samuel, 289
Fosdick, Harry Emerson, 53, 197–98, 228–29
Foundation Day. *See* Australia Day
Fraser, Morag, 73
Free Churches National Council, 13, 16
freemasonry, 8, 11, 98, 119, 124, 129, 193
Freer, Mabel, 230
Frost, Lillian, 176

Gabay, Al, 301–2
gambling, 59–61, 143
Game, Sir Philip Woolcott, x, 203
Gandhi, 16
Garden City movement, 140
Garden, John Smith (Jock), 197, 212
George V, King, 231, 271
Gilbert, Alan, 69
Gillespie, James, 291
Gladden, Washington, 269
Gladstone, William Ewart, 101
Goot, Murray, 118
Gordon, Alexander, 166
Gore, Charles, Bishop, 270n99
Gosling, Mark, 205
Goss, Norman Claridge, 216
Grant, William James, 217
Graves, James Joseph, 212

greyhound racing, 213
Griffith-Jones, Ebenezer, 155, 158
Gullett, Henry, 258

Hall, Richard, 202
Hallam, Arthur, 223
Harris, Rendle, 155
Harrison, Samuel, 167
Hartley University College (now University of Southampton), 6
Hatch, Edwin, 138
Health Week, 260
Heathcote, Wyndham, 230
Heber, Reginald, Bishop, 161
Heinze, Bernard, 309
Henderson, William J., 5, 321
Herbert, Xavier, 308
Heydon, Charles Gilbert, 74
Hickford, Frederick Thomas, 123, 129
Hill, Albert Charles, 280, 296
Hoare, Benjamin, 74, 84, 96
Hoban, Samuel John, 175
Hogan, Michael, 71
Holman, William Arthur, 60–61, 209
House of Commons, 44
House of Lords, 17
Howie, George, 212
Hudson, Wayne, 137, 301
Hughes, Thomas, 74
Hughes, William Morris, 68–69, 96, 233, 285, 301
Hunt, Arnold, 288
Hunter, James Aitchison Johnston, 239

I.W.W.ism (International Workers of the World), 79n57, 92–93, 101, 146
Imperialism, 17, 31, 57, 60, 67, 76, 117, 136, 201, 307
Indigenous Australians, 236, 238–41
industrial disputes, 145
Inglis, Ken, 68
International Bureau, 275
International Eucharistic Congress 1928, 183, 249
International Peace Movement, 275
Ireland, Home Rule, 44–45, 85, 98, 122
Islam, 42

Jackson, Francis, 182–83
Jardine, Douglas, 219
Jarvis, Wilfred, 231
Jehovah Witnesses, 237, 288
Jews and Judaism, 42, 223, 237
Johnson, Richard, 222
Jones, John Daniel, 155, 158, 160

Kagawa, Toyohiko, 242–43
Katoomba Christian Convention, 214
Keating, Paul John, x–xi
Keble, John, 161
Kelly, Michael, Archbishop, 72, 182–84
Kench, William Thomas, 176
Kerr, Sir John Robert, x–xi
Kiek, Edward Sidney, 246
Kiek, Winifred, 261
Kildea, Jeff, 71
Kingsley, Charles, 161
Kingston, Claude and Ella, 35, 76–77, 111
Kipling, Rudyard, 272
Kirkby, Sydney James, 222–23
Krishnamurti, Jiddu, 192

La Nauze, John Andrew, 317
Labor Party, 201, 205, 207, 288, 293, 301
Lady Mayoress's Patriotic League, 59
Lamb, William, 63–65, 153, 168, 312–14
Lang, John Thomas (Jack), x, xvii, 170, 195, 199, 202–18, 259, 269
Larwood, Harold, 219
Lauder, Harry, 188
Law, Mabel Edith (m. T.E. Ruth), 6, 16, 29, 242, 286–91, 296, 307, 316–17, 326
Leadbeater, Charles, 192
League of Nations, Youth Movement, 275
Lecky, William Edward Hartpole, 101
Lee, Howard, 271
Leeper, Alexander, 67n2, 95, 118–19, 129, 304
Lees, Harrington Clare, Bishop, 125
Leo XIII, Pope, 88, 101
Lewis, Clive Staples, 266
Lewis, Joseph Arthur, 287
Liberal Party, 293, 301, 303
Lloyd George, David, 306, 320, 322

Lockington, William Joseph, 80, 87–88, 103, 106, 183
Lodge, Oliver, 193, 264
lotteries, State, 234–35
Loyalist leagues, x, 117, 119, 123, 125
Lucas, Arthur Henry Shakespeare, 310–11
Lucas, Norman Carey, 111–12
Lucas, William, 111–12
Lusitania, 93
Luther, Martin, 90
Lutheran Church, 62
Lyons, Joseph, 205
Lyons, Mark, 71

Macintyre, Ronald George, 227
Macintyre, Stuart, 219
Maclaren, Alexander, 5, 47
Mailey, Arthur, 248
Malyon, Thomas John, 108
Manley, Margaret, xiv
Mannix, Daniel, Archbishop, ix–x, xvii, 56–57, 66–67, 72–80, 82–105, 110, 118, 121–25, 127, 145–46, 249, 292, 295
Marks, Walter, 165–66
marriage and divorce, 140, 150, 236, 260–62
Martens, Jeremy, 230
Martineau, James, 312
Masefield, John, 233
McCreary, John L., 157
McLeod, James, 319
McPhee, J., 183
McPherson, Duncan P., 5n13
Melba, Nellie, Dame, 184, 256
Melbourne
    Ruth's last years, 317
    visit from Ruth 1941, 285
    visit from Ruth 1943, 287
Melbourne Cup, 61, 143
Menzies, Robert Gordon, 219, 276, 292–94, 301, 317
Merner, Francis Albert, 105
Methodist Church, 24–25
Methodist churches
    Glenelg, S.A., 285
    Maughan, S.A., 278, 285–86

INDEX

Meyer, Frederick Brotherton, 7, 13, 47, 154, 160
Micklem, Philip Arthur, 221–22
Mill, John Stuart, 148
Millar, Samuel, 287
Millions Club, N.S.W., 174, 182, 235
Milton, John, 103
money, attitude to, 148
Moore, Andrew, 201, 211
Morling, George Henry, 63, 214
Mormonism, 103
Mother's Day, 260–62
Moule, Handley Carr Glyn, Bishop, 4
Mowll, Howard West Kilvinton, Archbishop, 231
Mullins, Edgar Young, 19
Murdoch, Thomas, 188
Murdoch, Walter, 283, 299, 309

National Council of the Evangelical Free Churches, 5
National Party, 165, 205
New Guard movement, x, xviii, 145, 201–2, 208–18, 326
new theology, the, 12
newspaper columns, 72–74, 270–73, 279, 282–85
Niall, Brenda, 326
Nicholls, Paul, 200
Norwood, Frederick William, 197

O'Farrell, Patrick, 68, 74
O'Leary, Patrick, 123
Orchard, William Edwin, 120
Oxford Club, 237–38

Packer, Jabez Alexander, 36, 44–45, 47, 65, 70, 107–8
Parker, Frank Critchley, 85
Paterson, Thomas, 230
Paton, Hugh, 184, 225
Peabody, Francis Greenwood, 312
Pearce, George Foster, 301
Pickford, Mary, 233
Piggin, Stuart, xiv, 53
Pius X, Pope, 37, 80
Plymouth Brethren, 24, 26
Portland Public Home, 6

Pound, Geoff, 134
Powell du Toit, Megan, xiv
Powell, Gordon, 319–20
Presbyterian Church, 24, 60
Presbyterian church, Sydney, Scots', 285
Price, Ernest, 19
prohibition, 108, 121, 141–42, 200
prostitution, 61
Protestant Federations, 91, 118, 129–30, 201, 278

Quakers, 24, 26
Queensland, 117

radio broadcasts, 187–89, 271, 287–89
Railways Union, Australian, 122
Rationalism, 193
Red Cross, 59
Remembrance Day, 213, 256–58
Rentoul, James Laurence, 89, 97, 118
Rice, Alice Hegan, 191n90
Rivett, Eleanor Harriet, 318
Rivett, Rohan, 299, 303
Roberts, Keith D., 71
Roberts-Thomson, Edward, 48n69
Rockefeller, John D. Jnr, 197
Roe, Jill, 165
Rogers, Ernest James., 182
Rollings, William Swift, 108–9
Roman Catholic Church, x, xiii, xvii, 7, 11, 24, 37, 66–105, 110, 125, 145, 158, 162, 173, 183–84, 192, 288, 290, 293, 295
Royal Colonial Institute, N.S.W., 182
Royden, Maude, 261–62
Ruth, Leslie James, 6, 29, 119, 170–71, 305–7, 315–16
Ruth, Mabel Edith (m. T.E. Ruth). See Law, Mabel Edith
Ruth, Thomas Elias
  Adelaide, retirement, 274–317
  Adventism, 165–68, 193
  alcohol, 59–60, 141–42
  All for Australia League, 203–7, 215, 269
  Anglican church, Darling Point, 285
  Anglican church, Drummoyne, 275
  Anglican church, Exeter, U.K., xvii

INDEX 347

Anglican church, Manly, 275, 285
Anglican church, Sydney, King Street, 275, 285
Anglican studies, 4
animal rights, 272
Anzac Day, 61, 134, 212–13, 254–55, 257–59
as Geoffrey Palmer, 18–21, 26
as preacher, 35–51, 114–17
as public theologian, xviii, 111, 133–51
Australia Day, 231, 259
Australian Creed, 122, 129, 134
baptism, 4, 25, 28, 37, 45, 47, 50, 60, 81, 90, 103–4, 175
Baptist Assembly, New South Wales, 46
Baptist Assembly, Queensland, 49
Baptist Assembly, South Australia, 49, 60, 286
Baptist Assembly, Victoria, 44, 60
Baptist church, Adelaide, Flinders Street, 78, 123, 280, 287
Baptist church, Brighton, S.A., 286
Baptist church, Exeter, South Street, U.K., 5
Baptist church, Liverpool, Prince's Gate, U.K., 5, 8–18, 42, 120
Baptist church, London, Ferme Park, U.K., 13
Baptist church, London, Westbourne Park, U.K., 15–16, 120
Baptist church, Melbourne, Collins Street, 30–168, 287
Baptist church, Southampton, Portland, U.K., 5–8, 121
Baptist church, Southport, Hoghton Street, U.K., 5, 17–18
Baptist church, Sydney, Bathurst Street (later Central), 170, 184, 221, 231
Baptist College, Bristol, xvii, 5–6
Baptist Congress, International, Melbourne, 130
Baptist Men's Association, Melbourne, 45

Baptist Ministers' Fraternal School of Theology, Victoria, 47
Baptist World Alliance Conference, London, 121
birth and family, xvii, 1–3
call to Australia, 27
Christian Socialism, 77, 138
Christmas and Easter (writings), 252–54
church music, 23, 35
churches (writings), 267–68
Citizens' Loyalist Committee, 96
Commercial Travellers' Club, Adelaide, 280
Communism, 178, 186, 201, 214, 259, 268, 275, 278, 293
confession, 79, 81, 88–89
Congregational church, Adelaide, Stow Memorial, 186, 279
Congregational church, Birmingham, Carrs Lane, U.K., 120
Congregational church, Gawler, S.A., 280
Congregational church, London, City Temple, 197
Congregational church, Melbourne, Collins Street Independent, 285
Congregational church, North Adelaide, 276–80
Congregational church, Sydney, Pitt Street, x, xvii, 128–29, 169–273
Congregational College, Adelaide, Parkin College, 186
conscription, xvii, 44–45, 66, 79, 82, 92–93, 143
conversion, 4
Decalogue, xi, 129, 135–36, 255
departure from Adelaide, 243
departure from Melbourne, 128–32
early years, 3–5
education, 182–83
Empire Day, 56, 182, 213–14, 231, 256–57
eschatology, 152–68
fascism, x, xviii, 200–202, 209, 211, 219, 278
Fenians, 84

Ruth, Thomas Elias *(continued)*
    financial appeal, 176–80
    freemasonry, 8, 98, 119, 124, 193
    gambling, 59–61, 143
    Garden City movement, 140
    greyhound racing, 213
    health, 123, 224, 287
    Health Week, 60
    House of Lords, 17
    I.W.W.ism (International Workers of the World), 79n57, 92–93, 101, 146
    Imperialism, 17, 57, 60, 67, 76, 201
    Indigenous Australians, 236, 238–41
    industrial and political issues (writings), 268–70
    industrial disputes, 145
    Ireland, Home Rule, 44–45
    Ireland, Sinn Fein, 45, 79, 84
    Jews, 223, 237
    Labor Party, 98, 288
    last years in Melbourne, 317
    lotteries, State, 234–35
    marriage and divorce, 140, 150, 236, 260–62
    meeting Gandhi, 16
    Melbourne Cup, 143
    Methodist church, Glenelg, S.A., 285
    Methodist church, Maughan, S.A., 278, 285–86
    Millions Club, N.S.W., 174, 182, 235
    money, attitude to, 148
    Mother's Day, 260–62
    New Guard movement, x, xviii, 145, 201–2, 208–18, 326
    new theology, the, 12
    newspaper columns, 72–74, 270–73, 279, 282–85
    Oxford Club, 237–38
    personal character (writings), 262
    Presbyterian church, Sydney, Scots', 285
    prohibition, 108, 121, 141–42, 200
    prostitution, 61
    radio broadcasts, 187–89, 271, 287–89
    Rationalism, 193
    religion (writings), 263–66
    Remembrance Day, 213, 256–58
    Roman Catholic Church, x, xiii, xvii, 7, 24, 37, 66–105, 110, 145, 173, 183–84, 192
    Royal Colonial Institute, N.S.W., 182
    Sabbath, 22, 143
    salary, 113
    segregation, 141
    sexuality, 140–41
    sexually-transmitted diseases, 61, 141
    Sinn Fein, 92–93, 96–101, 106, 121–22, 126–27, 148
    Smith's Weekly scandal, 310–15
    South Australia Council of Churches, 278
    spiritualism, 164–65, 193
    support for Samuel Angus, 225–28
    temperance, 142
    trades unions, 146–47
    Violet Memory Day, Adelaide, 279
    visit to Adelaide 1915, 60
    visit to Adelaide 1921, 123
    visit to Adelaide 1929, 186
    visit to Brisbane 1929, 185–86
    visit to England and U.S.A. 1919, 118–21
    visit to England, U.S.A. and Canada 1930, 194, 197–200, 309
    visit to South Africa 1909, 16
    visit to Sydney 1941, 285
    Winchester, U.K., District Free Church Council, 7
    women, 88, 150–51, 260–62
    World War I, 52–109
    writing style, 247–52
Rutherford, Joseph Franklin, 237
Ryan, Cyril Denis, 319
Ryan, Thomas Joseph, 117

Sabbath, 22, 143
Salvation Army, 24, 26, 261
Sampson, John, xiv
Sane Democracy League, 275
Schreiber, Oscar Ferdinand Gordon, 212
Scullin, James Henry, 195, 202, 215
Second Vatican Council, 125

sectarianism, 11, 24–25, 31, 42, 49, 51–53, 67, 70–72, 79–80, 83, 87, 91–92, 97–98, 110, 119, 124–25, 146–47, 174, 293, 304
segregation, 141
sexuality, 140–41
sexually-transmitted diseases, 61, 141
Shakespeare, John Howard, 5, 10, 46–48, 60, 321
Shaw, George Bernard, 217, 232
Sinn Fein, 45, 79, 84, 92–93, 96–101, 106, 121–22, 126–27, 146, 148
Smith, James Joynton, 310–11
Smith, Thomas Jollie, 246
Smith's Weekly scandal, 310–15
South Africa, visit from Ruth 1909, 16
South Australia Council of Churches, 278
Spanish flu, 115
spiritualism, 164–65, 193, 301–2
Spurr, Frederick Chambers, 15, 27–28, 30, 33–35, 40, 50–51, 120, 322
St. Patrick's Day march, 94, 121–22, 127
Steele Craike, Henry, 217
Stevens, Bertram Sydney Barnsdale, 209n51
Storer, Robert, 229
Streeter, Burnett Hillman, 154
Strong, Charles, 300
Strong, Jessie, 300
Student Christian Movement, 275
supralapsarianism, 22
Sutton, Harvey, 229
Sutton, Leonard, 214
Sydney, visit from Ruth 1941, 285

Talbot, Albert Edward, 222
Tasmania, 117
Taylor, Isaac, 43
temperance, 142
Tennant, Kylie, 308
Tennyson, Alfred, 158–59, 161, 223–24
Theodore, Edward Granville, 202
Thompson, Francis, 160

Tinsley, Charles James, 62
trades unions, 146–47, 201, 212
Turner, Ian, 70

U.S.A. and England, visit from Ruth 1919, 118–21
U.S.A., England and Canada, visit from Ruth 1930, 194, 197–200, 309
Unaipon, David, 240
Unitarians, 24, 26
United Australia Party (U.A.P.), 205

Van Dyke, Henry, 116, 312–13
Victorian Baptist Fund, 32
Victorian Refugee Council, 275

Wallace, Alfred Russel, 46
Wallace, John William, 292n79
Watt, William Alexander, 119
Weatherhead, Leslie, 228–29
Weller, James John, 214
Wender, Axel, 177
Wentworth, William Charles, 136
Wesley, John, 161
Wharton, Edith, 113
White Army, 201
White Australia policy, 124
Whitlam, Edward Gough, x
Whittier, John Greenleaf, 163
Williams, Charles, 20, 47, 153
Williams, Rupert James, 182, 216
Wilson, Henry Hughes, 125–26
Winchester, U.K., District Free Church Council, 7
women, 88, 150–51, 260–62
Woolfe, John, 78–79
Workers' Educational Association, 138
World War I, 37, 52–109
World War II, 276
wowserism, 31
Wren, John (Jack), 89, 96, 121

Y.M.C.A., 275